Word Processing Power with
MICROSOFT®
WORD

2nd Edition

Word Processing Power With

MICROSOFT®

WORD

2nd Edition

Peter Rinearson

PUBLISHED BY
Microsoft Press
A Division of Microsoft Corporation
16011 N.E. 36th Way, Box 97017
Redmond, Washington 98073-9717

Library of Congress Cataloging in Publication Data
Rinearson, Peter, 1954–
Word processing power with Microsoft Word.
Includes index.
1. Microsoft Word (Computer program)
2. IBM personal computer—Programming.
3. Authorship—Data processing.   I. Title.
Z52.5.M52R56   1986   652′.5   86-12788
ISBN 0-914845-89-6

Printed and bound in the United States of America.

4 5 6 7 8 9 FGFG 8 9 0 9 8 7

Distributed to the book trade in the United States
by Harper & Row.

Distributed to the book trade in Canada
by General Publishing Company, Ltd.

Distributed to the book trade outside the United States and Canada
by Penguin Books Ltd.

Penguin Books Ltd., Harmondsworth, Middlesex, England
Penguin Books Australia Ltd., Ringwood, Victoria, Australia
Penguin Books N.Z. Ltd., 182-190 Wairau Road, Auckland 10, New Zealand

British Cataloging in Publication Data available

To my mother

Contents

Acknowledgments

Many people at Microsoft provided insights into Word, so that I could pass them along to you. Richard Brodie, the main author of the original version of Word, contributed dozens of hours. So did Jonathan Prusky and Greg Slyngstad. For the book's second edition, Greg spoke almost daily with me for months.

A friend at Microsoft, Jeff Raikes, first introduced me to Word. Seeing my enthusiasm for it, he suggested to Tracy Smith that perhaps I'd write a book. I heard of the idea from Tracy, who at the time acquired manuscripts for Microsoft Press, and who gave me assurances of editorial freedom. A fine and demanding editor, JoAnne Woodcock, shared my vision. I hope she feels this book is at least a little bit hers, too, for it is.

Among those who helped create Word, and were repeatedly helpful to me, were Frank Liang, Rob Glaser, Charles Simonyi, and Charles Stevens. Frank, who devised many of Word's cleverest features, keeps office hours as odd as mine, and answered questions at midnight, or 1 a.m., or later. My thanks also to Jabe Blumenthal, Russ Borland, Michael Donat, Bill Gates, Jeff Harbers, Ross Hunter, Cynthia Kraiger, Dan Lipkie, Suchada MacDonald, Ford Martin, David Moore, Bill Roland, Jeff Sanderson, and Cliff Swiggett.

At Microsoft Press, countless hours were poured into this book by people whose contributions were invisible to those not able to watch firsthand. For the second edition, Marianne Moon coordinated, edited, and showed a passionate regard for detail that I respect very much. Salley Oberlin and Joyce Cox made important editorial contributions, and Chris Kinata, Steve Lambert, and Eileen O'Connor tested the examples and tutorials. Barry Preppernau, David Rygmyr, and Lia Matteson were eager to help. Lia's cheerfulness is a pleasure.

For this edition, Darcie Furlan adapted John Berry's original design. Debbie Kem used Word to incorporate editorial changes in the manuscript, and Carol Luke, Lisa Iversen, and Beth Huellemz got the book into type. Dale Callison proofread, and Gloria Sommer assembled the type into pages. Larry Levitsky named and marketed the book, with the assistance of Theresa Mannix, Karen Meredith, and Jim Brown.

Several people outside Microsoft made contributions of one kind or another. Among them were Amanda Urban, Jane Adams, Tari Eastman, Peter Norton, and my brother, Wistar.

Last, but never least, my special thanks to Trina Wherry, for enduring the creation of this book. She, more than anyone, knows what it took.

Introduction

It is astounding how much personality can be packed into a flimsy little disk of plastic. At first, a computer is like a newborn child, full of undeveloped potential. But feed it a floppy disk—a seemingly nondescript piece of black mylar—and suddenly the computer grows up. It assumes a function. It becomes a tool, or a game, or even a companion. Its keyboard and screen take on distinctive features. If the software hidden on the disk is powerful and elegant, it transforms the computer utterly, and gives a machine fashioned of switches and silicon a most pronounced and even pleasing personality.

Microsoft Word turns your computer into a dedicated, state-of-the-art word processor. It is a powerful tool for writing, editing, and printing documents of all kinds—from memos to book manuscripts, from outlines to form letters. It lets you work on several documents at once, and it takes much of the drudgery out of tasks such as footnoting and indexing. Because it checks spelling and can format and print documents following predetermined guidelines, Word handles troublesome details and frees you to concentrate on writing. Even when you graduate to complex tasks, Word's underlying consistency makes it relatively easy to use— although this book doesn't suggest that grand success is effortless.

Word offers a lot and lets you decide what to learn and what to ignore. With its many facets and potentials, it is an instrument as simple or demanding as you choose to make it. Whether you learn only its easy features or you explore the far reaches of its capabilities, Word is rewarding and worthwhile—not just for what it does, but for what it lets you do.

THIS BOOK

This book is a tool with personality, too. Like Word, it offers a lot and lets you choose from it what you want. This fully revised and expanded version of *Word Processing Power with Microsoft Word* is intended for users of any version of Word that runs on an IBM personal computer or compatible. The book is fully updated to reflect all the features of Word version 3.0 and Word version 3.1, which was first released in 1986.

Many books promise to make using computers simple, but often it's the books that end up being simple. By analogy, how well can you really learn a city, or even find your way through one, with an oversimplified tourist map that shows only some of the important roads and few of the interesting side streets? Many computer books simplify by being tour buses that follow set routes past main attractions. Others simplify by giving instructions only for particular tasks. This book contains tours and instructions, but its more important contribution is helping you become comfortable getting from one place to another on your own. Tours are valuable, but there comes a time to explore and really understand—a time to grab a good map and an entertaining guide and get off the bus.

This book is a map, a guide, and an invitation—your invitation to explore the simple side, or the many sides, of Microsoft Word.

A GAME PLAN

Word Processing Power with Microsoft Word is meant to be read and used in whatever order you like. Most people learn powerful software in their own way, exploring features and capabilities as they need them. It's a sensible approach, particularly when you can quickly find the information needed to accomplish a particular task or solve a problem. This book is organized and indexed to help you locate what you need. Even so, you'll advance faster if you can avoid wandering aimlessly among Word's many features.

Learn most of Word's simple features before tackling more specialized or complicated ones. When you're exploring a particular feature, try to develop a sense of what it's supposed to do for you. This way, you're not working blindly. When Word offers several ways to accomplish the same thing, learn one or two ways first, preferably the easiest ways. Later, you'll be pleased by the flexibility that alternatives give, but in the beginning they can muddle your thinking and learning by offering too much, too soon.

The stages of learning Word correspond roughly to the parts of this book—Learning, Using, and Mastering. There's nothing sacred about the book's organization, though; skip around as you wish.

If you're like many people, as you become adept with Word you'll find your productivity is rising, your creative impulses are freed of the burdens of retyping and awkward revising, and your printed work is more handsome. Tomorrow, everyone will have these advantages, as Word and other powerful computer programs redefine the ways we write and work. Today, this advanced tool is yours. Soon you won't think about Word much. You'll just use it.

I

Learning

To begin, this section is a hands-on
guide to setting up Word and learning its
easy features—features that may
be all you need at first.

Powers

In plain English, what does Microsoft Word let you do? What is it like to use? Truthfully, how easy is it? What are the names of Word's main features? Is the mouse— the palm-sized box you roll around a desktop—really useful for writing?

This chapter and the next answer these questions without getting into technicalities. Reading them is like preparing for a vacation trip by looking at a travel book. They'll help you sense what's ahead and may make you eager to start.

WHAT DOES WORD LET YOU DO?

The literature of centuries proves that people can write well without computers. Calligraphers and typing pools demonstrate that the written word can be made handsome without computers. And sharp eyes, dictionaries, and retyping can correct mistakes in documents of all kinds—again, without computers.

But word processing offers distinct advantages to people who work with words, so let's consider the virtues of Word in more depth. Most of Word's powers come from its commands; in this chapter, specific command names are shown in italics after the description of the work they do.

Standard features.

Like most word processors, Word:

- ◆ Frees you from retyping. It allows you to make corrections and changes efficiently, because you alter only the appropriate letters and words, without having to redo whole pages or sections.

- ◆ Helps you reorganize a document, or add or subtract material from the middle of it. As you make changes, paragraphs automatically adjust, and when there isn't enough room for a word on one line, the program moves it to the next for you. *The Copy, Delete, and Insert commands.*

- ◆ Assures a neat and uniform appearance for letters, manuscripts, reports, and other documents. You give Word formatting rules to follow, and then let it worry about the details. *The family of Format commands, and Word's built-in formats.*

- Finds a word or phrase anywhere in a document, substitutes a different word or phrase, or corrects a spelling. *The Search, Replace, and Library Spell commands.*
- Offers creative opportunities. For example, you can copy a passage onto the screen several times, edit or rewrite each differently, then compare results and erase all but the best version. *The Copy and Insert commands.*
- Lets you prepare messages and documents to be transmitted by telephone, either directly from one computer to another, or indirectly through an electronic-mail or message service. *The Print File command.*

Special features.

Unlike most word processors, Word:

- Has a feature called the *glossary* that lets you give names to words and passages. You can insert frequently used text into a document by typing the name or picking it from an on-screen list. You can reorganize complex documents easily by putting the names in any order you want. *The Copy, Delete, and Insert commands.*
- Gives you several methods for copying or moving text between different documents. You can display multiple documents or parts of the same document at once in different windows, and move text among them. *The family of Window commands and the Delete and Insert commands.*
- Has an Undo command that reverses the effect of any editing action. Some other word processors have an Undo that lets you retrieve a deleted passage, but Word's Undo also lets you recover from any other kind of editing action. For instance, if you underline a passage or change its indentation, you can undo your decision in a flash. *The Undo command.*
- Permits you to quickly jump any number of pages—1, 10, or 100—forward or backward through a document. *The Jump Page command.*
- Makes even massive formatting changes almost instantly. For example, Word can justify the right margins of a 50-page document in a few seconds—from beginning to end. *The Format Paragraph command.*
- Shows on the screen a close approximation of what prints on a printer. The on-screen layout of lines and pages is identical to the printed version, and characters that print in bold, italic, or underlined show that way on the screen. This, however, depends somewhat on the capabilities of your computer and printer, and on what you want Word to display for you. *The Options command.*
- Can format and print with up to 64 different typefaces (fonts) at a time, and in many different sizes. The specific fonts depend on the printer you use. Word describes the available fonts by name and size for each printer. *The Print Options and Format Character commands.*
- Dramatically reduces the work involved in creating indexes, tables of contents, and such things as lists of illustrations. *The Library Index and Library Table commands.*

◆ Automatically adjusts text formatting to suit the characteristics of virtually every popular printer. For example, you can print the same document on a dot-matrix printer, a letter-quality printer, and a laser printer. Word knows what type fonts and sizes are available for each printer, by brand and model, and automatically makes adjustments and substitutions, as needed. With more than 100 choices, it takes only a moment to switch from one printer to another. *The Print Options command.*

◆ Gives you broad control over how a page will look. You can have one, two, three, or even more columns on a page. You can print odd-numbered pages with a wide left margin and even-numbered pages with a wide right margin to provide a "gutter" that facilitates binding. You can change type fonts and sizes in the middle of a line, even if the line is justified. You can print special text, such as page numbers and titles, at the top or bottom of every page. *The family of Format commands.*

◆ Permits columns of text or numbers to be easily moved, modified, or deleted. Word will sum a column of numbers, too. (For that matter, any numbers that appear on the screen can be added, subtracted, multiplied, divided, or computed as percentages.) *The Format Paragraph command, the Insert command, and the F2 and Shift-F6 keys.*

◆ Accepts very precise instructions about spacing and measurements, although it doesn't require precision. In fact, for many general types of documents you don't have to give measurements at all because Word's built-in settings are often what you need. But when you're creating something with exacting requirements, you can specify a margin or other measurement in inches, in pica or elite characters, in centimeters, or even in typographical points (there are 72 of these to an inch). For truly demanding circumstances, such as typesetting, Word is accurate to better than a thousandth of an inch. *The Options command and the family of Format commands.*

◆ Allows annotations (or other text) to be hidden in a document, so that particular comments (or passages) appear on the screen and print only when you want them to. *The Window Options command.*

◆ Gives you a new and fast way to organize ideas, words, and information. Word's outlining feature permits you to look at and rearrange a document in an abbreviated, outline form. Subsidiary thoughts and whole text passages are removed from the screen temporarily, permitting you to focus on—and rapidly reshape—the structure of what you are writing. *The Window Options command.*

◆ Has easy, powerful footnoting capabilities. Word formats your document so that footnote text either appears at the bottom of the proper page (or of several pages) or is collected at the end of each section. Depending on your computer system, Word also superscripts footnote reference marks, both on the screen and on the printed copy. At your option, Word automatically numbers footnote references. If you add, delete, or move footnote references, Word automatically renumbers and reorders the footnotes to match. Footnotes can be viewed in a special window. *The Format Division, Format Footnote, and Window Split Footnote commands.*

♦ Gives you the opportunity to format documents with style sheets. One style sheet can control the look of many documents, making them consistent in format, freeing you from worry about spacing, indentation, type sizes, underlining, and similar issues. This lets you concentrate on content when you write. A style sheet also lets you give an often-used format combination a name that you can use to quickly call it into effect. *The Gallery and four Format Style commands.*

♦ Permits you to run paragraphs side by side, either in comparison tables or to change the number of columns in the middle of a page. *The Format Paragraph Command.*

♦ Lets you change the whole appearance of a document in a second or two by switching from one style sheet to another. For example, if you frequently write a double-spaced draft and then type a single-spaced final copy, having a style sheet available for each format eliminates not just all retyping but all reformatting. *The Format Style Sheet command.*

♦ Lets you easily and automatically alphabetize or renumber lists, lines, columns, paragraphs, or outlines. *The Library Autosort and Library Number commands.*

♦ Lets you automatically put the correct date or time in a document. The date and time can, if you wish, update themselves each time you print the document. *The Insert command and Options Command.*

♦ Gives you an on-screen thesaurus with a dictionary of more than 220,000 words. Select a word in your document and press a key to see a list of alternates. *The Ctrl-F6 key combination.*

♦ Hyphenates words, using a sophisticated formula that is surprisingly accurate. *The Library Hyphenate command.*

♦ Helps you when you're unsure of what to do. Menus at the bottom of the screen show the commands that are available, extensive on-screen help information reminds you of what to do, and you can take lessons in Word while using the program. *The Help command.*

Some of the features in the preceding list can be found on one word processor or another. Word has them all.

EASY? CHALLENGING?

Word, like many other powerful tools, has great versatility. Learning every detail takes time, but its subtleties will delight people who prize performance and are challenged to tap its flexibility. At the same time, Word can be used in simple ways. You don't need to know every facet of Word to use it, any more than you have to master the piano fully before you can create music. Word lets you grow.

Consider Word your partner. You contribute intelligence and creativity, while the software lends its almost magical ability to quickly transform human ideas into polished form. You're a potent team.

Fundamentals

Writing and editing with Word is a conversation of sorts: You tell it what to do, and it tells you what's going on and what's possible. You give instructions with the keyboard or the mouse; Word talks back by showing symbols and messages, and it lets you watch your work take form on the screen.

THE KEYBOARD

Depending on the model of computer, a keyboard has one of several designs. The text and graphics in this book refer to the original IBM PC keyboard layout, which you can see in Figure 2-1.

The revised IBM keyboard, offered as an option beginning in 1986, moves several keys to make the keyboard more like that of a Selectric typewriter. Also, the function keys are increased in number from ten to twelve and placed across the top of the keyboard instead of in pairs to the left. The direction keys (also called cursor keys or arrow keys) are separate from the calculator-style numeric keypad on the new keyboard, as well.

A computer keyboard has similarities to a typewriter keyboard. Most keys are used individually. Some are used in combination with others: The Shift key, for example, is used to give another key a second, often "capitalized," meaning. But because you can give your computer many more kinds of instructions than you can give a typewriter, Word uses several keys on your keyboard as "shift" keys of different sorts: Each gives an alternate meaning to other keys. The main ones are Shift, Alt (for Alternate), and to a lesser extent Ctrl (for Control). The Esc (for Escape) key has a similar role, too.

The Shift key "capitalizes" printable characters and "turns on" the numbers (and "turns off" the direction keys) in the numeric keypad. The Alt key, in combination with others, enables you to give predefined formatting instructions to your computer. Some of these instructions are built into Word and give you easy access to many often-used text layouts; Alt-F, for example, indents the first line of a paragraph. You'll learn more about these built-in formats in Chapter 5, "The Simple Word." You can also define other Alt-key formats yourself, using style sheets, an advanced Word technique. The Ctrl key has only a few uses, and the Esc key is used mostly to gain access to commands.

Appendix B is a guide to the use of the keyboard with Word.

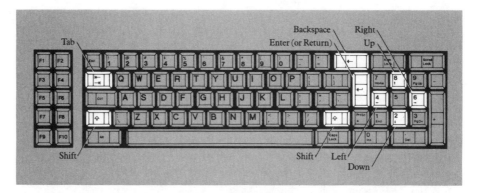

Figure 2-1. *The original IBM PC keyboard (Note: Left, Right, Up, and Down are the direction keys. On the newer IBM keyboard, the direction keys are separate from the numeric keypad.)*

THE MICROSOFT MOUSE

The Microsoft Mouse is an extension of the keyboard—another way to give instructions to your computer. The mouse rests on ball bearings or teflon skids, and you roll it on your desktop a few inches in one direction or another to move a special pointer around the screen. Generally, the mouse pointer appears as an arrow (if your computer is equipped with a graphics-display card) or as a blinking rectangle (if it is not, or if you choose not to use graphics capabilities).

Moving the mouse pointer around the screen does nothing by itself. To make something happen, you press either or both of the buttons on the mouse. Sometimes you hold down the left or right button as you move ("drag") the mouse pointer, but more often you quickly press and release ("click") one or both of the mouse buttons.

Which is the left button and which is the right? Put your palm over the mouse so that a finger rests on each of the buttons. Now the meanings of the instructions "click the right mouse button" and "click the left mouse button" are clear.

Generally, clicking the left mouse button accomplishes something more limited than clicking the right one. For example:

♦ Clicking the left button when the pointer is on a single character selects only that character. In other words, the selection (cursor) moves to and highlights the character.

♦ Clicking the right mouse button with the pointer on the same character causes the selection (cursor) to stretch to highlight the whole word, instead. Your next editing act (such as pressing the Del key) will apply to the entire word.

If you don't have a mouse, fear not. The keyboard can do 99 percent of what the mouse can, though often not as quickly or efficiently. For small jobs, such as moving the cursor just a character or two or picking a command from a menu, the mouse is easy to use but far from essential. The keys may be as fast or faster. Where the mouse really proves its worth is when you want to move text or the selection (cursor) an appreciable distance on the screen or do something graphic, such as make a text window larger or smaller. Keystrokes and mouse actions can be mixed and matched with good results. Before long, many Word users are no more conscious of using a mouse when writing than they are of steering when driving.

THE SCREEN

When you write or edit with Word, your text appears inside a double-lined box that takes up most of the screen. It typically looks like this:

```
┌─────────────────────────────────────────────────────────────┐
║                              MEMO                             ║
║                                                               ║
║  TO:    New users of Microsoft Word                           ║
║  FROM: Sarah Surefoot, manager                                ║
║                                                               ║
║  Welcome to word processing with Microsoft Word!  I'll boldly ║
║  predict that you'll find it rewarding and enjoyable.  Those  ║
║  of you who seek challenges will find them, and those of you  ║
║  who just want a dependable tool that saves time will be      ║
║  pleased, too.                                                ║
║                                                               ║
║        This memo was written with Word. The word "MEMO" at the║
║        top  of  the  page  was  centered  automatically.  This║
║        paragraph was indented at the touch  of  two  keys  and║
║        justified at the touch of two more.                    ║
║                                                               ║
║  █                                                            ║
║                                                               ║
║                                                               ║
└─────────────────────────────────────────────────────────────┘
COMMAND: Alpha Copy Delete Format Gallery Help Insert Jump Library
         Options Print Quit Replace Search Transfer Undo Window
Edit document or press Esc to use menu
Page 1   {}                         ?            Microsoft Word: MEMO.DOC
```

The screen is divided into two main parts:

♦ The *text area*, a large window with a double-lined border, covers the top and middle of the screen. This is where you write and edit.

♦ The *command area*, at the bottom of the screen, is where you choose, with the keyboard or mouse, from a list of available commands. It is also where you see messages from Word and keep track of things such as the name of your document and the page number you are on.

The text area

The text area can be divided into as many as eight windows, in which you can view and work on different parts of one or more documents. At first, you'll probably leave the text area undivided as a single window. By turning off the menu with the Options command (described in Chapter 11), you can expand the text area by three lines to gain working room. When the menu is off, only the last line of the command area is displayed. When you signal that you want to choose a command—by pressing the Esc key or by clicking either button while the mouse pointer is on this line—the entire command menu returns.

The text area includes two features of special interest if you use Word with a mouse. They are the *selection bar* and the *scroll bar.*

```
┌─────────────────────────────────────────────────────────┐
│ This is what the screen looks like with the command menu │
│ turned off. Word doesn't rely on you to remember the     │
│ commands. Pressing the Escape key or clicking the mouse  │
│ while the mouse pointer is on the bottom line brings the │
│ Edit menu to the screen.                                 │
│                                                          │
│                                                          │
│   ← In the selection bar the mouse pointer has special properties. │
│                                                          │
│     The thumb shows your relative position in the document. It is │
│   ← a horizontal line in the left window border which is called the │
│     scroll bar because it lets you scroll rapidly with the mouse. │
│                                                          │
└─────────────────────────────────────────────────────────┘
```

Page 1   {}   ?   Microsoft Word: MEMO.DOC

The selection bar

The selection bar is a blank vertical band that runs from the top to the bottom of the text window, just to the left of the text. Beginning with version 1.15 of Word, the selection bar is two characters wide; in previous versions, it is one. If you place the mouse pointer in the selection bar, you can select large amounts of text easily. Click the left button to select a whole line of text, click the right button to select a paragraph, or click both buttons to select the whole document. You can also drag the mouse pointer up or down inside the bar in order to select multiple lines or paragraphs.

The mouse pointer changes shape as it enters the selection bar. If your computer has graphics capabilities and you're using them, you see the mouse pointer tilt to the right. If you're not using graphics, you see the mouse cursor become a taller blinking rectangle.

The scroll bar and the thumb

The window borders are double lines. The one on the left is called the scroll bar because you can use it to scroll through a document with the mouse—that is, you can use it to roll the screen's contents to see passages either "above" or "below" the text displayed at a given time. There are many ways to scroll. In this case, position the mouse pointer in the scroll bar, as many lines from the top of the window as you want to scroll. Then, click the right button one time to move "down" that many lines (toward the end of the document), or click the left button once to move "up" that many lines (toward the beginning of the document).

The *thumb* is a small horizontal line that moves up and down in the scroll bar to show you your relative position in a document. It is a reference point for you: The closer the thumb is to the top of the bar, the closer the contents of the screen are to the beginning of the document.

The thumb moves regardless of whether you scroll with the keyboard or the mouse. With the mouse, however, you can also "thumb" quickly through your electronic document by placing the mouse pointer on the scroll bar at roughly the point in your document you want to move to. Click both mouse buttons at the same time. The thumb moves to the location of the mouse pointer, and Word almost instantly moves to the new location suggested by the thumb's relative position. This is a fine example of a job made much easier with the mouse: Just point at what you want and click—you've got it.

The command area

When you start Word for the first time, the command area occupies the bottom four lines of the screen. It looks like this:

```
COMMAND: Alpha Copy Delete Format Gallery Help Insert Jump Library
         Options Print Quit Replace Search Transfer Undo Window
Edit document or press Esc to use menu
Page 1  {}                              ?                  Microsoft Word:
```

The top two rows of words are a *menu* of available commands. Most often you'll see the Edit menu, the one shown in the preceding illustration. The Edit menu is your point of departure for reaching editing commands and other menus.

Below the menu area is the *message line*. Word gives you advice and explains problems here, with such comments as *Edit document or press Esc to use menu*, a message telling you to either write ("edit") or else press the Esc key so that you can use the menu to pick a command. This line displays any of more than 175 different messages in version 3.0 of Word. Appendix A explains and offers advice on important messages.

The last line, the *status line*, tells you the status of Word and your document. It is the only line of the command area that is always displayed, even when you have turned off the menu with the Options command. There is useful information in the status line:

```
Page 1   {Twinkle·twi...at·you·are} ? SAVE      EX Microsoft Word: RHYME.DOC
```

Page 1. Word updates the page number when you print (with the Print Printer command) or repaginate the document (with the Print Repaginate command). Until you use one of these commands on a document for the first time, the entire document will be labeled *Page 1*. If, instead of a page number, this corner shows the word *OUTLINE* or *text*, or the word *Level* followed by a number, it means Word is in Outline mode. This is an advanced feature. If necessary, turn off the Outline mode by holding down the Shift key and pressing the F2 key.

{Twinkle·twi...at·you·are}. The text between the scrap brackets, {}, shows whatever is in Word's special temporary memory, the *scrap*. In the preceding example, the rhyme "Twinkle, twinkle, little star" has been placed in the scrap. Note that the beginning and the end of the passage are shown, but the middle is indicated by an ellipsis (...). Beginning with Word version 1.15, the spaces between words are indicated by tiny dots, as shown. Uses of the scrap are explained in Chapter 10, "The Scrap and Glossary Commands."

? The *?* is the help mark, and appears only if you have installed a mouse. You can obtain help with a specific command by highlighting the command name in the command menu, positioning the mouse pointer on the *?*, and clicking either button.

SAVE or *% Free.* In Word versions with numbers lower than 2.0, there is a *% Free* indicator that tells you what percentage of random access memory (RAM) you have available for use. Beginning with version 2.0 of Word, a *SAVE* indicator replaces *% Free.* If your version of Word shows *% Free,* avoid frustration and lost documents by saving to disk (with the Transfer Save command) when the percentage drops to about 55. If you have a *SAVE* indicator, it comes on when the available memory drops to 60 percent. It begins to flash at 40 percent. Either save your document or risk losing your work. You can, of course, save more frequently.

CS, EX, NL, SL, CL, or *OT.* Right of the *SAVE* or *% Free* indicator is a two-character space that is usually blank. However, when any of six special conditions is turned on, letter pairs fill the space. A key (or combination of keys) for each condition functions as an on/off switch. Although you can turn on more than one condition at once, the space can show only a single pair of letters. The pairs are displayed in this priority:

- ♦ *CS — the Shift-F6 key combination.* When the Column Select mode is on, Word's selection (cursor) expands to cover rectangular regions of a document, presumably columns of numbers or columns of text.

- ♦ *EX — the F6 key.* Turning on EXtend causes the selection (cursor) to grow (extend), rather than to move. For instance, turning on extend and pressing the Right direction key causes the selection highlight to stretch to the right.

- ♦ *NL — the NumLock key.* When NL appears, the squarish numeric keypad is locked on, and its keys no longer move the selection (cursor).

- ♦ *SL — the Scroll Lock key.* When SL is on, the selection remains stationary and the screen scrolls when the direction keys are used.

- ♦ *CL — the Caps Lock key.* Turning on Caps Lock is like holding down a Shift key, except that only letters (not symbols) are affected.

- ♦ *OT — the F5 key.* When OverType is on, newly typed letters replace existing letters, instead of pushing them to the right and down, as is usual. Overtype can be turned on at any time, but the OT is displayed only when no other condition (CS, EX, NL, SL, or CL) is turned on.

Microsoft Word: RHYME.DOC. The name of the document on which you are working appears to the right of the colon. If the document has no name, you can give it one by saving it on disk with the Transfer Save command. Word normally adds the file name extension .DOC automatically.

COMMANDS

Commands are the main way you tell Word what you want. Command names usually suggest what they do, though sometimes (as in Alpha, the "type text" command) rather vaguely. Many of Word's commands are lumped into families; other choices from the Edit menu are commands in and of themselves. Delete, for example, is a command in itself, whereas Transfer represents a family of commands that all have something to do with transferring information from one location to another.

To see how commands are used, let's look briefly at Transfer Save. The first step in saving a document is to tell Word you are going to use a command, specifically a Transfer command. You either place the mouse pointer on *Transfer* in the Edit menu and click the left button, or you press the Esc key to tell Word that you want to use the Edit menu, and then press the letter T (for Transfer). In either case, Word responds by replacing the Edit menu with a submenu of the Transfer commands and a message telling you what to do next:

```
TRANSFER: Load Save Clear Delete Merge Options Rename Glossary

Select option or type command letter
Page 1   {}                          ?            Microsoft Word:
```

You pick Save from the Transfer menu just as you picked Transfer—with the mouse or by pressing the letter S (for Save). Word responds by replacing the Transfer menu with the two *fields* of the Transfer Save command:

```
TRANSFER SAVE filename: ■              formatted:(Yes)No
```

The first field is a fill-in blank. You type in the name you want the document to have once it is saved on disk.

The second field is a menu. (Yes) indicates that the document will be saved "formatted."

Fields let you increase the precision of your instructions. Some commands have many fields; others have none. In the second of the Transfer Save fields illustrated here, don't worry yet about what *formatted* means. That understanding will come. For now, it's enough to understand that you can change settings by adjusting the appropriate fields. The Tab key moves you between fields, and the Spacebar allows you to make choices from a menu field, such as switching between *Yes* and *No*.

It may help you understand the relationship of menus, commands, and fields to see the path from the Edit menu to the fields of the Transfer Save command illustrated this way:

```
COMMAND: Alpha Copy Delete Format Gallery Help Insert Jump Library
         Options Print Quit Replace Search Transfer Undo Window


TRANSFER: Load Save Clear Delete Merge Options Rename Glossary


TRANSFER SAVE filename: ■              formatted:(Yes)No
```

If the file doesn't have a name, you type one in (up to eight letters long). Then, only one task remains to complete the Transfer Save command and save your document: Press the Enter key.

That's it.

Thinking About Word

If you work with other Microsoft programs, such as Multiplan or Chart, you already understand some essentials of Word. Though the programs differ in detail, they share key characteristics. The obvious example is the menu of available commands at the bottom of the screen. Menus differ among the programs, but their general design doesn't. With all of them, you express your decisions in similar ways.

The rules of using menus are important enough that all of Chapter 6 is devoted to them. But not all information necessary to mastering Word is distilled so readily into step-by-step instructions. A good grasp of several concepts will help you to make better sense—and better use—of Word. Two are especially useful. One, the concept of *Select-Do,* governs most of your actions with Word; the other, *Content versus Format,* distinguishes between two types of editing.

This chapter is likely to be slower going than others, because it is somewhat abstract. It's probably best to read it quickly the first time and come back when you know Word a little better or if some aspect of the program's behavior puzzles you.

CONCEPT 1: FIVE PHASES

There are five phases to creating a document with Word. As taught on the Learning Microsoft Word disk, they are:

- ◆ Enter. You place a document on the screen, either by typing new text or by loading previously typed text from a file on disk.

- ◆ Revise. You edit the contents of the document, changing words and spellings or adding, subtracting, and moving passages.

- ◆ Format. You specify or change the appearance of all or part of the document— from individual characters . . . to lines and paragraphs . . . to whole pages.

- ◆ Print. You order one or more copies of the document to be printed.

- ◆ Store. You record the document on a disk, for reference or for later additional text entry, revision, formatting, and printing.

These five steps form a simplified model of using Word, but it's possible that you'll sometimes follow this pattern cleanly. For example, you might type (enter) a letter in a spurt of creativity, then revise its contents, format it to look like a letter instead of lines of type, print it, and finally store it on a disk for future use. Most often, however, the process probably won't be so orderly. You'll mix up the five phases at least a bit, possibly deciding on some of the formatting in advance, or revising as you write.

CONCEPT 2: SELECT-DO

Your instructions to Word are based on the concept of Select-Do. First, you tell Word where you want to do something in a document, such as enter text, revise, format—in some cases, even print or store. This is the Select part. Then, you tell Word what action you want to take, such as delete the selected text or format it in a particular way. This is the Do part.

Where many word processors require you to use different commands to delete a character, word, line, or block of text, Word simply says, "Tell me where and how much, then tell me what to do." With this Select-Do model, no matter what action you intend to do next, you use the mouse or keyboard to select text in the same way. It doesn't matter whether you will delete, copy, move, or format it.

CONCEPT 3: CURSOR VERSUS SELECTION

Most computer programs display a cursor, a little underline or rectangle of light, that shows where you are on the screen. As you type, the cursor moves along, leaving a trail of characters behind it. The cursor can also be moved without leaving a trail of characters— much as a pen can be lifted from paper and placed elsewhere without leaving a trail of ink. This is accomplished most often with the four direction (arrow) keys.

```
‖  In this sample sentence, the cursor is over the first                    ‖
‖  character.

‖  In this sample sentence, the cursor has been moved to the                ‖
‖  "M" in "moved."
```

Word has something called a *selection* that appears to be a cursor much of the time. It is a highlight that behaves just like a cursor whenever you type new characters into a document or press a direction key.

Word's cursor is called the selection because you also use it to select text for subsequent editing. The selection/cursor is the way you *select* before you *do,* so the selection is elastic; it is not limited to the size of a single character, like a conventional cursor is. You can extend it to cover two characters, three characters, a word, a phrase, a line, a sentence, a paragraph. In fact, you can expand the selection to cover any number of characters and words, including every word, space, and punctuation mark in a document.

There are many ways to expand the selection. With the mouse, you hold down the left button while dragging the mouse pointer up, down, or sideways to select contiguous lines or characters. With the keyboard, the function keys labeled F7 and F8 move and expand the selection from its current position to cover the preceding (F7) or following (F8) whole word. Other function keys or function-key/Shift-key combinations allow you to select anything from sentences to the entire document. The F6 key is particularly useful because once it is pressed, other keys that normally move the selection *extend* it. (For details, see Chapter 18, "Speed.")

```
In this sample paragraph the selection has been expanded to
cover the whole word "paragraph." We say that the word has
been "selected," or that the word is the "selection."
```

Word is clever. In the preceding sample, Word has included the space following the word *paragraph* as part of the selection. If you delete the selection, the space will be deleted along with the word. That's what you want, because the space isn't needed in the sentence if the word has been removed from it. But if, instead of deleting the selection, you format it — underline it, say — Word won't underline the space. Word will "know" you probably don't want to underline the space after a single underlined word.

Two general rules of selecting:

♦ Whenever you type a character or insert text into a document, it appears at the beginning of the selection. If the selection was larger than a single character before, it is reduced to a single character with the first new character or insertion, and moves one space to the right.

♦ You needn't select all of something when the action you wish to take can only be applied to the whole. For example, you needn't select all of a paragraph in order to exercise the command that formats paragraphs. Selecting a single character in it is enough. By the same token, you needn't select a whole document in order to print it or to save it on disk; just make sure that, if documents are in more than one window, the selection is in the window of the document you want to print or save.

CONCEPT 4: SPACES AS CHARACTERS

There is a crucial difference between the absence of characters and the existence of characters that create blank spaces. Cryptographers know that *e* is the most common letter in the English language. When you write something of any length, chances are it will contain more *e*'s than any other letter. But when you write on a computer, the most common character is the space. There's one between almost every pair of words.

Sometimes people don't understand why the selection won't move to certain blank parts of the screen. This situation is most apparent when Word is first started and the screen is almost empty. At this time, the selection is in the screen's upper left corner, highlighting a small diamond that marks the end of the document (which, in this case, happens to be the beginning of the document, too). If you have a mouse, the mouse pointer may be on the screen somewhere, but all in all the screen gives you a blank stare. And Word won't let you use the direction keys to move the selection anywhere, because only characters can be selected, and there aren't any on the screen yet.

Now, imagine that you press the Spacebar 75 times, moving the selection (and the end marker with it) across the top row of the screen. The top row doesn't look too different now, nor does it look different from the blank lines below it. In reality, however, the top row is much different: It is filled with the 75 spaces you created with the Spacebar. To Word and your computer, these spaces are characters as much as *a*, *b*, or *c* and *1*, *2*, or *3* are characters; they simply print, both on-screen and on paper, as spaces, instead of letters or numbers.

The Tab key is another key that creates a spacing character, rather than a printing character. The tab character appears as a bar of light when it is selected, because it is generally wider than a single character.

You can move the selection with the direction keys or the mouse to any spacing character, just as you can move the selection to any letter, number, or symbol in a sentence. Although the mouse pointer can be anywhere on the screen, if you click the mouse when its pointer is on a place absent of any characters, the selection will move to the nearest preceding character—whether visible or invisible.

You can see on-screen the difference between spacing characters and the absence of characters if your version of Word is numbered 2.0 or higher. Spacing characters show on the screen if you use the Options command to set a field called *visible* to *Complete*. Spaces made with the Spacebar show up as tiny dots, much smaller than periods:

```
‖ Spacebar·spaces·show·as·tiny·dots.                                          ‖
```

In most versions of Word, these dots also show between words inside the scrap brackets at the bottom left of the screen.

CONCEPT 5: MOVING VERSUS CHANGING

There is a difference between just moving your selection around in a document and actually changing the document.

Some beginners mistakenly try to use the Spacebar to move the selection across a line of text. It's an easy mistake to make. But while the computer's Spacebar moves the selection to the right, it also adds spacing characters to the document as it goes. (If you've turned on Overtype with the F5 key, the Spacebar overtypes existing characters, instead.)

To move the selection without changing the document, much as you would skim your eyes or pencil along a printed line without changing it, use either the mouse or the direction keys. To scroll through a long document, much as you'd page through a report or a book, use the PgUp or PgDn key. These actions don't change the document's content or format, and so they aren't editing acts.

Most writing and editing involves both moving and changing: You move the selection up a line to correct a misspelling, move it down a paragraph to tune up an idea, and so on.

CONCEPT 6: CONTENT VERSUS FORMAT

Editing falls into two broad categories: establishing or changing *content* and establishing or changing *format*.

You control content by entering and revising text, including spacing characters. Content changes alter the substance but not the appearance of the document. Format, on the other hand, has nothing to do with substance and everything to do with appearance. Underlining, justifying or centering paragraphs, and setting page margins are examples of formatting acts.

CONCEPT 7: THREE TYPES OF FORMATTING

Although the family of Format commands has many members, Word breaks formatting into three broad categories:

♦ Division formatting controls the overall appearance of pages, and is applicable to a whole document or a major division (section) of a document. The Format Division commands are used to specify such things as page length and width, location of page numbers, and the dimensions of margins.

♦ Paragraph formatting controls the way lines of text are laid out, and applies to one or more whole paragraphs at a time. You can set paragraph indentation, centering, justification, and line spacing with the Format Paragraph command, or you can choose from among built-in paragraph formats that offer you popular choices at the touch of two keys.

♦ Character formatting controls the appearance of your text characters. A particular format can apply to as little as a single character or to as much as a whole document. The Format Character command applies such features as underlines, italics, and different fonts and type sizes to whatever characters you have selected. As an alternative to the command, built-in character formats offer you popular choices at the touch of two keys. (For example, holding down the Alt key and pressing U will underline the selected text.)

CONCEPT 8: FORMAT AT ANY TIME

You can make formatting decisions before, during, or after typing a document.

♦ Before. You can make formatting decisions in advance by creating or choosing a Word style sheet. As you type, you need only tell Word which styles (formatting rules) you want attached from the style sheet to various parts of the document. Creating a style sheet is an advanced technique, but using one is easy.

♦ During. You can format while you create a document. If you specify a format as you type, it won't change—letter after letter and page after page will have the same format until you specify otherwise.

   — To apply one character format or another while typing, use the Format Character command or a built-in character format when the selection is a single character.

   — To apply a particular paragraph format, select any character in the paragraph where you want the formatting to begin.

   — To assign a division format, execute one of the Format Division commands while the selection is anywhere in the document. If the document has several divisions, place the selection anywhere in the division you want to format. (You divide a document into divisions by holding down the Control key and pressing the Enter key.)

♦ After. It is easy to format a document after writing and revising are done. Use the Select-Do model: First select the text to be formatted, and then apply the formatting with the appropriate Format commands or the built-in formats.

CONCEPT 9: FORMATTING CHEMICALS

You've already seen that Word divorces formatting from content. The benefit is efficiency and flexibility in formatting and reformatting what you write. The disadvantage, for people who already know other word processors, is that Word's approach is novel and contrary to what they expect. To understand how formatting is applied to content with Word, think of a format as a chemical you spread on selected parts of your document.

Many word processors supply you with what amounts to a cup of pens. You use one to write normal characters, another to write italics, and so on. Formatting is a property of the pen that's in use. To change the appearance of what you write, you pick up a different pen. Going back into your document later to alter the appearance of what's already been written can be a major chore.

Not so with Word. Instead, you use a single pen for everything. It only creates content. To give the document the appearance you want, you use a "formatting chemical." One chemical underlines, another italicizes, another changes the size of type, and so forth. You can use several at the same time to combine formats for just the look you want, and your chemicals can be dabbed on a single character or brushed over a passage, or even a whole document. The underlying content never changes, but different formatting can utterly change the look of the document.

The key to skillful formatting is spreading the "chemicals" in such a way that they touch only the characters and paragraphs you want to format. If you've already finished writing and revising, you just select the text and apply the chemical with a Format command, a built-in format, or a style from a style sheet.

Formatting while you write and edit is a little trickier, but not much. You dab some chemical on a selected spot and begin to write from that place. The formatting will stay with the selection as long as you type new content without moving away from the properly formatted area. To achieve multiple formats within a single document, treat different passages with different formatting chemicals. Any writing done in an area treated with a particular chemical will automatically be given that area's format.

Sounds easy, and it is, once you get the hang of it. But newcomers sometimes run into difficulties when different parts of a Word document have been treated with unlike formats. They become puzzled when they move the selection away from the text that is formatted in the way they want. It seems to them that the formatting is changing of its own volition. If you fall into this situation on your road to mastering Word, remember that formatting exists only where it's been placed, either because you selected the area and put it there, or because it was "carried" there when you typed. These pointers may help, too:

- ◆ All new text initially assumes the "look" of the position at which it is typed.
- ◆ If you use the mouse or direction keys to move around in a document, you might accidentally move away from the formatting you want. Return to an area that has the formatting and resume your work there, if you can, or apply the desired formatting to your new location.
- ◆ Every character in a document is formatted in one way or another. If you haven't given it a specific format, Word gives it the "normal" format. The definition of "normal" varies, depending on what printer you use and, when you use style sheets, on the character formatting used in paragraph styles.

CONCEPT 10: DIFFERENT VIEWS

There's more than one way to look at most things, and documents on your Microsoft Word screen are no exception. Though what you write may not change in any inherent sense, it can take on different appearances depending on your preferences and on what you are trying to accomplish.

The simplest example has to do with the way spacing characters are treated. These "invisible" characters, such as tab characters and the spaces between words, never print on a printer. As Concept 4 explained, whether or not such characters appear on your screen depends on how you set the Options command. If "invisible" characters are displayed, you merely get a second way to view your document.

Another example involves hidden text, a feature that first appeared in version 3.0 of Word. Just as you might underline or boldface certain parts of a document, you can instruct Word to make parts "hidden." This is useful when you want to add a private or temporary comment to a document, or when you are hiding the information Word uses to make an index or create a table of contents. How you view a document—that is, whether the "hidden" text is actually hidden—is up to you. Using Word's capability to have more than one window displayed at a time, you can even put the document on the screen twice, once with the comments showing and once with them hidden. The same document is in both windows, but you have different views of it.

Similarly, you can open two windows and load different parts of the same document into them. For instance, you might view the beginning of the document in one window and the end of the document in another.

Style sheets provide a means to rapidly alter the way a document looks. You can view (and print) a document in a double-spaced draft form, for example, and then within a few seconds completely change the way it looks by switching control of the document's appearance to a different style sheet — perhaps one that makes the document single-spaced and with narrower margins.

The most dramatic example of different ways to view the same document involves Word's outlining feature, which was introduced in version 3.0. Briefly, this feature lets you transform a document into an outline of itself, and then examine and manipulate the underlying structure of what you have written. When viewed in outline form, a document appears on the screen hierarchically, with subordinate ideas indented or "collapsed" (temporarily removed from the screen, so that only the most important ideas appear). Nothing inherent to a document changes when it is viewed as an outline. It's just a different view of the same thing.

Setting Up

You can snow ski with bent poles and misadjusted boot bindings. You can play basketball with a hoop that's too high and a slightly flat ball. But for the most satisfaction and the least frustration, you want to match your equipment to the job before you invest time in making it perform.

So it is with Word. This chapter tells you what you need to run Word and about the different versions that have been released: It explains how to prepare your software for best results, shows how to start Word in various ways, and gives step-by-step details on setting options that refine Word's performance.

WHAT YOU NEED

You need a computer, of course. It must be relatively powerful, with at least the computing power of the original IBM PC. Unlike many word processors, Word has features that require too much computing for the program to operate on an 8-bit computer. But Word is a good match for 16-bit computers, especially those such as the IBM PC AT, because the program takes advantage of the power of the machine.

You need an appropriate version of MS-DOS, and the computer must have 256K of random access memory (RAM). As a practical matter, Word operates noticeably faster with 320K than it does with 256K. (And with the increasing prominence of windowing, multi-tasking programs, and even Word's Library Run command, there's much to be said for the convenience of 512K or more of RAM.)

Display and adapter

Many computers come with built-in video-display adapters, and some come with displays (monitors) as part of the package. The Compaq portable and Data General/One are examples of computers that run Word and come standard with both a display and matching adapter.

But if you're using any of the nonportable IBM personal computers, you have a choice of many adapters and displays made by IBM and other manufacturers. The following list of the main combinations of displays and adapters will help you make a choice if you're considering a purchase, or understand what you've got and how Word uses it. You'll see references to "text" and "graphics." *Text* mode shows only certain predetermined characters (including the distinctive ones that make up the double-line Word border), while *graphics* mode shows such things as italics and enables the mouse pointer to assume many distinctive shapes.

♦ *IBM Monochrome Display and Printer Adapter* with *high-resolution monochrome display.* This combination is relatively inexpensive, gives high resolution (720 by 350 pixels on the screen), and is faster than any other at scrolling and displaying characters on the screen when you type or edit. The adapter has a parallel printer port, which is handy. The adapter cannot show graphics or color. Italics show as underlining, and the mouse pointer is always a flashing rectangle. The quality of the monitor itself (the monochrome display) is important. When comparing different brands of monitors, check the sharpness of characters at the center and edges of the screen.

♦ *Hercules Graphics Card* with *high-resolution monochrome display.* This combination gives you graphics capability with the high resolution of the monochrome card (720 by 348 pixels on the screen). The Hercules Graphics Card emulates the IBM Monochrome Display and Printer Adapter in text mode, and it also has a parallel printer port. However, the Hercules card (and its many imitators) can provide graphics only when the software has been modified for it, as Word has been; the card cannot run the graphics commands of IBM BASIC, for example. Using the Hercules card with Word, you can switch to a special, condensed-character mode that shows 42 lines of 90 characters, instead of the normal 25 lines of 80 characters. (See the word/h command later in this chapter.)

♦ *Hercules Graphics Card Plus* with *high-resolution monochrome display.* Through creative technology, this combination lets you run Word in monochrome mode—with all of its speed—and yet see such things as italics. The mouse pointer remains a rectangle, not an arrow, however.

♦ *IBM Color/Graphics Monitor Adapter* with *low-resolution color display.* This combination gives up to 16 colors and medium resolution or it gives non-color graphics and higher resolution (640 by 200 pixels). Many IBM PCs and essentially all PCjrs use the combination of a color/graphics card and a color monitor.

♦ *IBM Color/Graphics Monitor Adapter* with *low-resolution monochrome display.* This is the option built into the IBM Portable Computer, the Tandy 1000, and several other computers. It is also popular in many offices, because it is among the least expensive ways to put a monitor and adapter on a PC. IBM doesn't sell a monitor like this one separately, but a common choice is the Amdek 300. Resolution is not the best (640 by 200 pixels), but sharpness is better than with the same adapter and a color monitor, and it shows graphics.

♦ *IBM Enhanced Graphics Adapter (64K)* with *high-resolution monochrome display.* IBM's EGA card comes with 64K of dedicated display memory and gives high-resolution graphics on a monochrome display. With a high-resolution monochrome monitor, version 2.0 or later of Word shows high-resolution graphics, much as the

Hercules card does. The resolution (at 640 by 350 pixels) is slightly lower than for either the monochrome or the Hercules cards, but the apparent difference is almost negligible. Beginning with Word version 3.0, the EGA card permits using Word with a condensed 42-line by 80-character screen display. (See the word/h command later in this chapter.)

♦ *IBM Enhanced Graphics Adapter (64K)* with *low-resolution color display.* This combination gives the same resolution (640 by 200 pixels) as the traditional and much less expensive Color/Graphics Monitor Adapter. However, it gives both graphics and color at the same time.

♦ *IBM Enhanced Graphics Adapter (64K)* with *IBM Enhanced Color Display.* This gives the same performance as the immediately preceding choice, except that—beginning with Word version 3.0—it is possible to get high resolution (640 by 350 pixels) *black and white* from the color monitor. The resolution isn't as good as that of a quality monochrome monitor, however. (See the word/m command later in this chapter.)

♦ *IBM Enhanced Graphics Adapter (128K)* with *IBM Enhanced Color Display.* With this combination, word processing with a color monitor finally becomes acceptable, though the Enhanced Color Display's resolution still falls short of a high-quality monochrome monitor. Adding the piggyback-style IBM Graphics Memory Expansion Card to the Enhanced Graphics Adapter boosts the adapter's memory to 128K. This gives simultaneous high resolution (640 by 350 pixels), color, and graphics. It is possible to increase the EGA card's memory to 256K, but Word doesn't take advantage of more than 64K, when hooked to a monochrome monitor, or 128K, when hooked to an enhanced color monitor.

NOTE: Some companies manufacture display adapters compatible with the EGA that come standard with more than 64K of memory. For instance, Quadram offers the Quad EGA + with 256K as standard. The EGA + also emulates a Hercules Graphics Card. Some companies offer monitors compatible with the IBM Enhanced Color Display. The NEC JC-1401P3A Multisync may even provide more text clarity than the IBM monitor, although IBM's entry is regarded as superior in its ability to display graphics and rich colors.

In their quest to equal or exceed the performance of IBM's computers while maintaining essential compatibility, many manufacturers build adapter cards into their machines that mimic one or more of the IBM cards. Compaq's portable computers, for example, have a single card that emulates both the monochrome and color/graphics cards, displaying either mode on a built-in monochrome screen. The AT&T 6300 and 6300 + have similar adapters, although their resolution is better than that of the corresponding IBM and Compaq adapters. Word version 3.0 takes advantage of the high-resolution 640- by 400-pixel mode of certain computers by AT&T and Xerox. Finally, note that some supposedly PC-compatible computers aren't hardware compatible when it comes to display adapters. In my experience, a Tandy 1200HD would not work with either an IBM EGA card or an IBM monochrome display adapter, although it ran Word just fine with the display cards, including a Hercules-compatible card, sold by Radio Shack.

Printers, ports, and .PRD files

Chances are you need a printer. The main categories are *daisy wheel*, which gives true typewriter quality; *dot matrix*, a fast printer that doesn't equal a good daisy wheel in print quality, although some models come quite close; and *laser*, a fast, flexible type of printing that emulates a typesetter or typewriter with equal ease and produces originals that look like good photocopies (which, in a sense, they are).

Word works with any printer that works with your computer, but it makes the best use of your printer if it can use one of the *printer description files* (*.PRD files* for short) that have been written specifically for certain printers. Some printer manufacturers may supply .PRD files for Word, but you'll find more than 100 of them on the Printer and Utility disks of Word version 3.0. (Earlier releases of Word have fewer .PRD files, and they come on the Utilities disk.) A .PRD file contains the instructions that tailor Word to a particular printer, allowing superscripting, automatic changes of typefaces (on non-daisy-wheel printers), and so forth. If you're thinking of buying a printer, there's some logic in picking one for which there exists a Word .PRD file—although virtually all popular printers now have .PRD files, and for those that don't, the generic files TTY.PRD and TTYWHEEL.PRD allow the basic features of any printer to be used with Word. Shop carefully, and consider checking the cost of maintenance and parts before choosing a printer. They are mechanical and inclined to need repair occasionally. Sometimes printer prices are low, but parts extremely expensive. Replacing a print head on some dot-matrix printers can cost almost as much as the printer, for example.

NOTE: Be sure to use the .PRD files that came with your version of Word. It is impossible to use a .PRD file that came with version 2.0 of Word while using version 3.0 of Word.

Printers are classified as *parallel* or *serial*, depending on how they communicate with computers. A parallel printer must be connected to a *parallel port*, located on the back or side of the computer, while a serial printer must be connected to a *serial port*. All else being equal, you might consider a parallel printer before a serial one, because most computers have only two serial ports, and they are needed for hooking up modems, serial versions of the mouse, and that *next* printer that may be manufactured in a serial version only.

If you choose a serial printer, your computer and your printer must be matched to one another. This matching (configuring) takes many factors into account, among them the specification of certain settings, such as transmission rate, that are handled via the DOS Mode command. The instructions for doing this are extremely variable and beyond the scope of this book, but fortunately, you can usually rely on your dealer to help you take care of these details.

The Microsoft Mouse

The mouse is handy, but both the hardware and software must be installed before you can use it. Your mouse manual covers the installation of the hardware. (Also, see the tip on installing the bus mouse on page 228.) The SETUP program installs the mouse software, if you have a recent version of Word.

VERSIONS OF WORD

Since its introduction as version 1.0 in the fall of 1983, Word has been improved once or twice a year. This book discusses all versions, and is up-to-date through version 3.0. A small change in version number, such as from 3.0 to 3.1 or 3.15, usually indicates only a small change in the product. It is generally worthwhile, however, to update older versions (at moderate cost) through your dealer or directly with Microsoft. Word 3.0 and 3.1 are not copy protected, although earlier versions were.

Version 1

Version 1.0 is slow in operation compared with newer versions, and lacks some of their features. If you're still using it, I *strongly* recommend updating it. Version 1.1 is a big improvement over 1.0, and it has one advantage over later versions—it will run, though slowly, on a computer with as little as 128K of RAM. Version 1.15, an enhanced version of 1.1, was released in the fall of 1984 along with Microsoft Spell. It is compatible with the IBM PC AT and with the HP LaserJet printer.

These copy-protected versions of Word have a program called MWCOPY, which lets you copy Word onto a hard disk.

Version 2

Version 2.0, released early in 1985, added notable new features, including a family of Library commands that let you check spelling, hyphenate words, or run almost any other program without quitting Word. Version 2.0 let you use almost the entire screen for text, and offered high-resolution graphics with the new IBM Enhanced Graphics Adapter.

Version 2.0 came on five disks: two identical Program disks (one labeled as a backup copy); a Utilities disk; a Learning Word tutorial disk; and a Microsoft Spell disk. A program called SETUP on the Utilities disk lets you prepare floppy disks or copy each Program disk once onto a hard disk.

Version 3

Version 3.0, released in the spring of 1986, runs faster and adds a wealth of new tools and refines a number of the old ones. The added features have been incorporated in such a way that experienced users of Word will have to relearn little. Version 3.1, released in the fall of 1986, goes a small step further—adding a thesaurus, support for almost a dozen new laser printers, and enhancement to the Options command.

Beginning with 3.0, the family of Library commands has been expanded, letting you automatically create indexes and tables of contents (and other tables, such as of illustrations), as well as alphabetize lists and automatically renumber lists. Text can be "hidden," so that notations that won't print can be placed in a document. Several improvements also have been made in the way Word handles tables and other tabular material. Vertical columns can be moved, and a special arithmetic key (F2) allows numbers in a column (or elsewhere on the screen) to be added, substracted, multiplied, divided, or computed as a percentage. Perhaps most significantly for writers of long or complicated material, an outlining feature has been incorporated that permits words and information to be organized rapidly and flexibly.

Because Word 3.0 is not copy protected, it can be copied directly onto a hard disk using the DOS Copy command. However, the SETUP program will do this for you, and take care of other details. Importantly, the SETUP program will, at your option, completely remove old versions of Word from a hard disk (something you can't do otherwise, because of the cleverness of the copy-protection scheme that previous versions of Word used).

USING SETUP

If you are not sure which version of Word you have, look at the small type on your disk or execute the Options command—that is, press Esc, then the letter O, then the Enter key; the version number will appear on the message line. If you have Word version 2.0 or higher, your Utilities disk contains the SETUP program. Place the disk in drive A, type the word *SETUP*, press the Enter key, and follow the on-screen instructions. The program detects whether you have a hard disk, and accordingly sets up either the hard disk or your Program disk for use with Word. SETUP gives you a menu of different things you can do, but the menu choices vary depending on whether you have a hard disk or not.

On a floppy disk

The SETUP program makes a working disk by copying your Word Program disk onto a blank disk. It lets you copy an appropriate printer description file (.PRD file) onto your working disk. As you go through the SETUP instructions, you will see and choose from a list of printers, identified by their full names. For example, if you have a Diablo 620 printer, you simply pick the name *Diablo 620*, rather than the more cryptic name of the .PRD file, which is *D620.PRD*.

The SETUP program asks if you have a mouse. If you do, it copies the mouse software (MOUSE.SYS) onto the Word Program disk and creates a file on the same disk called CONFIG.SYS. The CONFIG.SYS file includes the instruction *DEVICE = MOUSE.SYS* and enables your computer to use the mouse software. Beginning in version 3.0, SETUP modifies an existing CONFIG.SYS file, if any, to add the *DEVICE = MOUSE.SYS* instruction to it.

As you go through the instructions, the SETUP program also asks if you want to format any floppy disks for use as document disks. Because disks must be formatted before they can be used with any DOS-based program, you'll want to format a generous supply. If you have already formatted disks with the DOS Format command, you needn't concern yourself with SETUP's ability to format.

On a hard disk

If you have a hard disk, the SETUP program copies the Word files to a directory of your choice. It will ask for the name of the directory, and the key here is to name a directory that is in your directory path, so no matter what drive or directory you are using when you type *word* or *spell*, your computer will find and start the named program. If you're updating from an earlier version of Word to version 3.0 or later, SETUP will ask if you want to remove the old version from your hard disk. Answer that you do, because this is the only way to remove hidden files that were part of the hard-disk copy-protection scheme prior to version 3.0.

If you're using a version prior to 3.0, SETUP will not prepare your hard disk for use with a mouse, because the program can't guess what directory you want the mouse software (MOUSE.SYS) to be in, nor does SETUP want to risk erasing an existing CONFIG.SYS file. Instead, you must pick a directory for MOUSE.SYS and either create a one-line CONFIG.SYS file, or add a line to an existing CONFIG.SYS file.

. . . And if all this sounds more than vaguely high-tech to you, take heart. Your DOS manual can help you out, and so can Chapter 28, "Using a Hard Disk."

WITHOUT SETUP

If you have a single-disk-drive system, such as an IBM PCjr, you cannot use SETUP. If your version of Word has a number lower than 2.0, you do not have the SETUP program. If you have Word 3.0 or higher, you don't really need SETUP, although it is convenient.

To set up a Word Program disk without the SETUP program, copy the DOS system and the file COMMAND.COM onto your Program disk. For example, if the DOS disk is in drive A and the Program disk is in drive B, from the A prompt, use the commands *sys B:* and *copy command.com b:.* Then put the Utilities disk in drive A and use the Copy command again to put the mouse software and whatever printer description file you need on the Program disk. For example, you could type *copy mouse.sys b:* and, if you have a Diablo 620 printer, *copy d620.prd b:.*

You'll need to create a CONFIG.SYS file containing the instruction DEVICE = MOUSE.SYS. You may also want to create an AUTOEXEC.BAT file to include such things as the Mode command (if you have a serial printer), or a Path command (if you have a hard disk). See your DOS manual and Chapter 28 for details.

If you have a high-capacity disk drive (IBM's is 1.2 megabytes), you can put DOS, Word, Spell, and other programs on it, too. Because all the programs you need are on one disk, you have some of the same advantages you get from running Word on a hard disk.

USING TWO MONITORS

Some people attach two displays (monitors) to their computer at once, typically one monochrome (for extra screen resolution) and one color. Each must be attached to an appropriate display adapter, and a computer will only use one of the monitors at a time.

To switch between monitors, you must have the DOS Mode program on your Word Program disk (or, if you are using a hard disk, somewhere in the DOS path). Before starting Word, type *MODE MONO* at the DOS prompt (A>). This activates the monochrome monitor. Or, type *MODE CO80* to activate the color monitor. (Note that CO80 contains both the letter *O* and the number zero, not two zeroes.)

Beginning with Word version 3.0, Word will use whichever monitor is active at the time Word is started.

In Word versions 1.15 and 2.0, Word always started on a color monitor when it had a choice, unless the word/m startup choice was used. (See the discussion of the word/m command below.)

STARTING WORD

Starting the program is as easy as typing *word* and pressing the Enter key. After starting, your screen should look much like this:

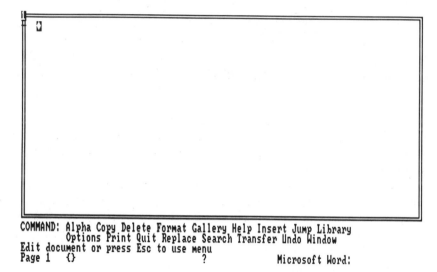

```
COMMAND: Alpha Copy Delete Format Gallery Help Insert Jump Library
          Options Print Quit Replace Search Transfer Undo Window
Edit document or press Esc to use menu
Page 1    {}                          ?              Microsoft Word:
```

Recall that the large, double-lined box surrounds the text area where your work will be displayed; the four lines at the bottom of the screen are the command area. In the upper left corner of the text area is the diamond-shaped end mark. It is always the last character in a document, but it is never printed by your printer. When (as now) there is no document on the screen or when the end mark is selected, the cursor-like selection is on the end mark, so it appears as a diamond in a highlighted square. At other times, the end mark itself is a diamond.

STARTUP CHOICES

After typing *word*, you have the option of typing a space and the name of a document you want Word to load immediately. You can also type a forward slash and one of several letters, which are switches that control one aspect or another of Word's behavior. A space before the slash is optional. Include one if you prefer.

word/l

When you type *word/l*, Word starts up and also loads the last document you were working on. It even scrolls the document to the last place you were working, and selects the same character(s) that were highlighted when you quit Word.

word/c

What happens when you type *word/c* depends on whether your computer has a monochrome or a color/graphics adapter. If you're using a standard IBM Monochrome Display and Printer Adapter, the /c has no effect other than to start Word. If you're using the IBM Color/ Graphics Monitor Adapter, Word starts in the "character" mode, which means that graphics capabilities (such as showing the mouse pointer as an arrow) aren't used, and the screen looks somewhat clearer.

If you're using a Hercules Graphics Card (or a copy), or if you're using an IBM Enhanced Graphics Adapter with a monochrome monitor, starting with word/c means Word is displayed as if a Monochrome Display and Printer Adapter is being used instead. No graphics show. There's not much point in doing this on a fast computer, such as the IBM PC AT, but on slower machines, such as the original IBM PC, turning off the graphics this way significantly increases the speed at which changes, such as scrolling, are reflected on the screen. Using word/c is a good way to start Word on the IBM PCjr, too.

word/m

Typing *word/m* has different effects depending on what version of Word you use.

With version 3.0, word/m has an effect only if you have an Enhanced Graphics Adapter (EGA) with just 64K of dedicated display memory, and you are using an IBM Enhanced Color Display (or compatible high-quality color monitor by a different manufacturer). The /m causes Word to operate in a high-resolution (640- by 350-pixel), black-and-white mode rather than the much lower, 640- by 200-pixel, color mode. (Adding more memory to the EGA allows high-resolution—640- by 350-pixel—color, and makes the /m switch unnecessary.)

In Word versions 1.15 and 2.0, typing *word/m* has an effect only if you have both the IBM Monochrome and Color/Graphics adapters installed at the same time, and hooked to separate displays (monitors). Word normally appears on the monitor attached to the color/ graphics card, but the /m option causes the monochrome card and display to be used instead.

word/h

In Word versions 1.1 and higher, typing *word/h* starts Word in a special condensed mode of 43 lines of 90 characters, instead of the normal screen size of 25 lines of 80 characters. This option only works when the Hercules Graphics Card or a compatible card (such as the AST Preview card) is installed. Beginning with Word version 3.0, typing *word/h* on a computer using an EGA card (or compatible) gives a Word screen with 42 lines of 80 characters. Of the two, the EGA card gives the more readable output in the /h mode.

word/x

The word/x choice is used only in Word version 2.0. Earlier versions (1.0 and 1.15) didn't have Library commands, so the /x option wasn't needed. Later versions (beginning with 3.0) are more sophisticated and don't need the /x option. So concern yourself with the next two paragraphs only if you have Word version 2.0.

In version 2.0, typing *word/x* excludes the Library Spell and Library Run commands for the duration of the Word session. Generally, you can ignore this switch unless you have between 256K and 320K of RAM in your computer, and you want to speed up Word's performance. If you have more than 320K, the /x switch has no effect. If you have 192K, the Library Spell and Library Run commands are automatically suppressed.

If the amount of RAM in your computer falls into the 256K-to-320K range, the /x switch lets you tell Word not to reserve any memory for the Library Spell and Library Run commands. Therefore it speeds up the rest of Word. (Technically, the question is whether you have 284K of usable memory after loading DOS and other "resident" programs, all of which use some of your computer's RAM. To see how much usable memory is available, run the DOS CHKDSK program. The last line of the CHKDSK message will tell you. The amount of memory is not reported accurately by CHKDSK if you are using Microsoft Windows.)

Combinations

Some startup choices, such as /c and /h, cannot be used at the same time, but other switches can be combined. For example, you can type *word/c/l* to start in color mode and load the last document that was used in the previous editing session. Word ignores switches that are inappropriate. If you use a switch and unexpectedly see the message *Enter Y to create file,* you probably mistyped the switch name. Word, not recognizing it, interpreted it as a document name. Then, not finding such a document, Word asked if you meant to create a new document by that name.

Quitting

Having started Word, you'll want to know how to quit. Either click a mouse button when the mouse pointer is on the word *Quit* at the bottom of the screen, or press the Escape key followed by the letter Q.

SETTING OPTIONS

Word will tailor itself to your needs and your equipment (your printer, for example), but you have to tell it what you want by setting some options with four commands: Print Options, Window Options, Options, and, for certain computer configurations, Transfer Options. (There is also a Library Spell Options command, but you needn't be concerned with it at first.) Word remembers your chosen options even when the computer is turned off, so you needn't set most options more than once for any particular computer setup. Word remembers the settings by storing them on the Program disk in a file called MW.INI. When you quit Word (with the Quit command), Word updates MW.INI. Whenever you start Word, it reads MW.INI, so it knows how to set options.

If you've used the Learning Microsoft Word tutorial disk or have experience with Word, you already know how to choose commands with the keyboard, the mouse, or both. For simplicity, this section shows only the keyboard method. Even if you know how to use the mouse, put it aside for a few minutes to avoid confusion.

PRINT OPTIONS

The Print Options command tailors Word to your printer.

1. Press the Esc key. This tells Word that you are going to use a command. Observe that the Alpha command is highlighted after you press Esc.

    ```
    COMMAND: Alpha Copy Delete Format Gallery Help Insert Jump Library
             Options Print Quit Replace Search Transfer Undo Window
    Select option or type command letter
    Page 1   {}                          ?              Microsoft Word:
    ```

2. You want to use the family of Print commands, so press the letter P to pick Print from the menu. Word responds by showing you a menu of the commands in the Print family. The Printer command is highlighted, because Word is "guessing" that you want to use the Print Printer command. However, its guess, called a *proposed response,* is wrong this time.

    ```
    PRINT: Printer Direct File Glossary Merge Options Queue Repaginate
    ```

3. You want the Print Options command, so press the letter O for Options. Word responds by displaying several categories of printing choices. Each choice is a *command field.* The first field, which is highlighted initially, is *printer.* Note that the message on the second-to-the-bottom line refers to the highlighted field.

    ```
    PRINT OPTIONS printer:
                  draft: Yes(No)     queued: Yes(No)     copies: 1
                  range:(All)Selection Pages     page numbers:
                  feed: Manual(Continuous)Bin1 Bin2 Bin3 Mixed
                  widow/orphan control:(Yes)No        setup: LPT1:
    Enter printer name or select from list
    Page 1   {}                          ?              Microsoft Word:
    ```

4. This is where you tell Word what printer you are using. *Enter printer name or select from list,* the message says, and that's what you dc. If you used the SETUP program, the printer description file (.PRD file) for your printer should be in the *printer* field already, and you can skip to step 6. Otherwise, press any of the four direction (arrow) keys to bring a list of printer names and abbreviations onto the screen.

5. Use the direction keys to move the highlight to the printer description file name that matches your printer make and model. If the .PRD file for your printer is not among those listed, you can use the TTY file (a "generic" printer description file) or the TTYWHEEL file (a "generic" printer description file with enhancements for daisy-wheel printers). In the following example, the .PRD file for the Diablo 630 printer has been selected. (This example shows a number of .PRD file names and is what you'll see if you have a hard disk. If you, or the SETUP program, copied only the .PRD files you need onto your Word Program disk, you probably have only one or two names showing on your screen.)

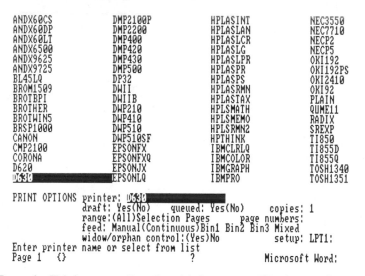

```
ANDX60CS       DMP2100P      HPLASINT      NEC3550
ANDX60DP       DMP2200       HPLASLAN      NEC7710
ANDX60LT       DMP400        HPLASLCR      NECP2
ANDX6500       DMP420        HPLASLG       NECP5
ANDX9625       DMP430        HPLASLPR      OKI192
ANDX9725       DMP500        HPLASPR       OKI192PS
BL45LQ         DP32          HPLASPS       OKI2410
BROM1509       DWII          HPLASRMN      OKI92
BROTBPI        DWIIB         HPLASTAX      PLAIN
BROTHER        DWP210        HPLSMATH      QUME11
BROTWIN5       DWP410        HPLSMEMO      RADIX
BRSP1000       DWP510        HPLSRMN2      SREXP
CANON          DWP510SF      HPTHINK       TI850
CMP2100        EPSONFX       IBMCLRLQ      TI855D
CORONA         EPSONFXQ      IBMCOLOR      TI855Q
D620           EPSONJX       IBMGRAPH      TOSH1340
D630           EPSONLQ       IBMPRO        TOSH1351

PRINT OPTIONS printer: D630
               draft: Yes(No)      queued: Yes(No)      copies: 1
               range:(All)Selection Pages      page numbers:
               feed: Manual(Continuous)Bin1 Bin2 Bin3 Mixed
               widow/orphan control:(Yes)No            setup: LPT1:
Enter printer name or select from list
Page 1   {}                            ?            Microsoft Word:
```

6. Press the Tab key once. Pressing this key causes Word to confirm the selection in the currently highlighted field and to move the highlight to the next field—in this case, *draft.* Now, Word is asking you whether you want printing to be in a high-speed "rough" draft mode, rather than a "final" polished form. Notice that Word's proposed response is *No.* Since you probably don't want draft printing, leave it set as is.

7. Press the Tab key once more, to move the highlight to the *queued* field. Note that when you leave the *draft* field, the highlight disappears and the word *No* is enclosed in parentheses.

Press the Tab key four more times. Observe that a proposed response is given in all of the fields you pass except for *page numbers*. The highlight should now be in the field labeled *feed*. (If you overshot the *feed* field, either hold the Shift key and press the Tab key to "tab" backward, or keep pressing the Tab key to bring the highlight full circle through the fields once more.) The *feed* field is where you tell Word whether you feed paper to your printer a sheet at a time (*Manual*) or you have form-feed paper that can be run continuously (*Continuous*) through your printer. Some printers, such as the Diablo 630, have an optional feeder that allows paper to be fed automatically a sheet at a time from bins. This is why there are also settings labeled *Bin1*, *Bin2*, *Bin3*, and *Mixed*.

8. The first time you ever use Word, the word *Continuous* is highlighted. You don't have to make any change if you are using continuous-feed paper. If you feed paper into your printer a sheet at a time, press the Spacebar until the word *Manual* is highlighted, as shown in the following example.

```
PRINT OPTIONS printer: A:D630
               draft: Yes(No)      queued: Yes(No)      copies: 1
               range:(All)Selection Pages      page numbers:
               feed: Manual Continuous Bin1 Bin2 Bin3 Mixed
               widow/orphan control:(Yes)No              setup: LPT1:
Select option
Page 1   {}                              ?              Microsoft Word:
```

9. Next, press the Tab key once or twice (depending on your version of Word) to move to the last field, *setup*. This is where you tell Word which port your computer will use to send information to your printer.

Depending on how your computer is configured, you can have one or two serial ports (COM1: and COM2:) and up to three parallel ports (LPT1:, LPT2:, and LPT3:). Determine what port your printer uses. If you're unsure, try LPT1: if you have a parallel printer, and try COM1: if you have a serial printer.

10. If the *setup* field already shows the proper port name, type nothing. Otherwise, type one of the following names precisely, including the colon at the end:

    COM1:   COM2:   LPT1:   LPT2:   LPT3:

In Word versions 1.15 and above, you don't need to type the name; you can pick the printer port name from a list. Press any direction key to display the printer port names on the screen, then use the direction keys to highlight the proper one.

11. Press the Enter key to execute the Print Options command. Word is now tailored to your printer.

12. Word guesses that you want to print something whenever you've finished using the Print Options command, so at this point the Print menu will be displayed again on your screen. Press the Esc key to return to the Edit menu—the one showing the alphabetic list of commands, from Alpha to Window.

WINDOW OPTIONS

The Window Options command lets you tailor the appearance of the text area (or areas, if you open more than one window). If you wish, you can turn on a ruler at the top of the text window to see paragraph indents and tab stops. Or, you can turn on a style bar to see one- or two-letter codes for styles you've assigned from style sheets. Or you can change the colors of the screen displays if you're using a color computer system. Or decide whether "hidden" text in a document—such as indexing instructions—shall be visible in a window or not. Or you can specify whether or not the view of a document in a window is in outline form or normal text form. If you split the text area into multiple windows, you can even tailor each window individually.

But we won't be so fancy. We're just going to turn on the ruler, since it's the one setting any Word user can try. Besides, it's handy for seeing where you have set tab stops and paragraph indents.

1. If the Edit menu isn't displayed, press the Esc key to tell Word you wish to use a command.

2. You want the family of Window commands, so press the letter W to pick Window from the Edit menu. Word responds by showing the Window menu. The Split command is highlighted—another guess by Word.

    WINDOW: Split Close Move Options

3. You want the Window Options command, so press the letter O for Options. (Don't press zero, press the letter O.) Word responds by showing the Window Options command fields, which in version 3.0 look like this:

    ```
    WINDOW OPTIONS window number: 1  outline: Yes(No) show hidden text:(Yes)No
                  background color: 0  style bar: Yes(No)            ruler:(Yes)No
    Enter number
    Page 1   {}                       ?                  Microsoft Word:
    ```

4. You don't want to change any of the fields except the last one, so press the Tab key until you reach the field labeled *ruler.*

    ```
    WINDOW OPTIONS window number: 1  outline: Yes(No) show hidden text:(Yes)No
                  background color: 0  style bar: Yes(No)            ruler: Yes No
    Select option
    Page 1   {}                       ?                  Microsoft Word:
    ```

What are you skipping? The bypassed *window number* field tells you which window you are working in when you have more than one open on the screen; the *outline* and *show hidden text* fields, which first appeared in Word version 3.0, control aspects of the view you get of a document in a window; the *background color* field lets you choose a background color if you have a color-display card installed in your computer and are using its color capabilities; the *style bar* field is used with style sheets. Details on these options are in Chapter 17, "The Family of Window Commands."

5. We want to turn the ruler on, so press the Spacebar once to move the highlight from *No* to *Yes*.

6. Press the Enter key to execute the Window Options command. Now the Edit menu should be displayed at the bottom of the screen again, and a ruler should be across the top.

```
COMMAND: Alpha Copy Delete Format Gallery Help Insert Jump Library
         Options Print Quit Replace Search Transfer Undo Window
Edit document or press Esc to use menu
Page 1   {}                                    Microsoft Word:
```

OPTIONS

The Options command lets you specify your preferences about several of Word's general qualities. We'll concern ourselves with one, a field called *visible*, which lets you tell Word to display certain spacing characters that it normally does not display. When you're learning Word, it's a good idea to make these characters visible, and one in particular is important to see. It is the paragraph mark, which you place in a document by pressing the Enter key when you want a paragraph to end. The mark acts as something of a "bank," too. Word "deposits" in it your instructions regarding paragraph formatting for the paragraph it ends. Once it is made visible, the paragraph mark looks like this: ¶.

The Options fields and their order differ slightly depending on the version of Word. The instructions for making characters visible vary slightly, too. Usually there are three choices in the *visible* field, but in early versions there are only two.

1. Press the Esc key. The Alpha command is highlighted.

2. Press the letter O for Options. Word responds by displaying the command fields for the Options command. Beginning in Word version 3.1, the command fields look like this (in version 3.0, the third line is not included):

```
OPTIONS visible: None Partial Complete  printer display: Yes(No) menu:(Yes)No
    default tab width: 0.5"    measure:(In)Cm P10 P12 Pt        mute: Yes(No)
    date format:(MDY)DMY       time format:(12)24    decimal character:(.),
```

In version 2.0, the menu of fields was similar except the *default tab width* field was not included. In still earlier Word versions, the menu looked like this:

```
OPTIONS mute: Yes No        measure:(In)Cm P10 P12 Pt
        overtype: Yes(No)    display mode:(Normal)Printer    visible: Yes(No)
```

3. If necessary, press the Tab key to move to the *visible* field.

4. Press the Spacebar once, so that either *Yes* or *Partial* is highlighted. (In versions of Word beginning with 2.0, the choice *Complete* lets you see all spacing characters, even Spacebar spaces and tab characters. *Partial* is less confusing, except when you're making critical spacing and tabbing decisions.)

5. Press the Enter key to execute the Options command.

Paragraph marks will now be displayed wherever you press the Enter key while writing or editing. If you find they annoy you, repeat the Options command and change the *visible* field back to *No* or *None*. Seeing the paragraph marks is useful, however, and makes Word easier to use at first. Once you know Word well, you may want to get rid of them, because they do clutter the screen somewhat.

TRANSFER OPTIONS

The final options command, Transfer Options, is the only setting Word does not automatically remember for you. Transfer Options lets you specify a disk drive other than the one where Word normally looks for and stores documents. It's a command that needn't concern many people though, because Word makes pretty good guesses about the drive you want. If you have a computer with two floppy-disk drives and the Word Program disk is in drive A, Word assigns drive B as the document disk. If you have a single floppy-disk drive or a hard disk with a single floppy drive, Word designates the drive you run the program from as both the program and the document drive. If you want Word to look on a different drive for documents or if you use different directories (especially on a hard disk), use this command. Otherwise, skip it.

1. Press the Escape key.

2. Press the letter T to see the Transfer menu.

    ```
    TRANSFER: Load Save Clear Delete Merge Options Rename Glossary
    ```

3. Press the letter O, for Options. Word responds by displaying *setup*, the sole field in the Transfer Options command.

    ```
    TRANSFER OPTIONS setup: B:
    ```

4. If the drive letter (or drive and directory) shown is not the one you want to use for documents, type in what you want. Remember to include the colon after the drive letter. You can omit the backslash unless you're specifying a directory.

5. Press the Enter key to execute the command.

The Simple Word

You can type and print your first Word document in a matter of minutes. The secret is not to get too fancy, or assume too much. This chapter shows the simplest side of Word. First, it illustrates how Word's built-in formats give you easy control over the appearance of documents. Second, it offers a tutorial exercise that shows you a trouble-free way to write, print, and save a good-looking document in a few minutes. Along the way you'll practice such things as selecting, deleting, and moving text.

This chapter is intended primarily for newcomers to Word. If you are an intermediate or advanced user, you may want to skim it for tips and skip the hands-on practice session.

BUILT-IN FORMATS

Word's built-in formats make creating attractive documents easy. By holding down the Alt key and pressing one or more of 21 other keys, you can specify a wide variety of looks for what you write or edit. Built-in formats can be combined for additional variety. In Part II of this book you'll discover even more ways to format documents (with the Format family of commands). But for the exercise in this chapter we will rely on built-in formats, because they're relatively flexible and quite simple to use. For many purposes, built-in formats are all you need.

Recall from Chapter 3 that there are three main types of formatting: division, paragraph, and character. Word has built-in formats for each.

The built-in division format

Division formatting controls the appearance of pages in a major section of a document (a chapter or a section full of tables, for example). But most people generally don't break documents into more than one division, so "division formatting" can usually be called "document formatting." Word has only one built-in division format. It is always in effect unless you change it, so there's literally nothing to using it: If you do nothing, the built-in division format will be used by Word. The built-in division format has these characteristics:

- Page length is 11 inches; page width is 8.5 inches.
- Automatic page numbering is turned off.
- If you turn on automatic page numbering, page numbers print 0.5 inch from the top of the page and 7.25 inches from the left edge of the page.
- Top and bottom page margins are 1 inch.
- Left and right page margins are each 1.25 inches, providing you with a 6-inch-wide writing space.

NOTE: If there's a different format you'd prefer Word to use automatically, you can define a Division Standard style in a NORMAL style sheet. This is an advanced feature, described in Chapter 23.

Built-in paragraph formats

Paragraph formatting guides the way lines are laid out on the page. It is called paragraph formatting because it is imposed on a whole paragraph at a time. In the absence of instructions from you, Word gives every paragraph a "normal" paragraph format. This built-in format has these characteristics:

- Text is aligned evenly on the left side. The right side of the paragraph is uneven (not justified).
- Text is not indented on either the right or the left side. In other words, text extends all the way to the page margins. (This is not to say the text extends to the edge of the page. The "page margins" are part of division formatting.)
- The first line of the paragraph has no special indentation.
- Lines are single spaced, six to the vertical inch.
- There is no extra space either above or below the paragraph.
- Tab stops are preset every 0.5 inch.

Word offers ten other built-in paragraph formats that alter the "normal" paragraph format. Each of these formats has its own Alt-key combination. An eleventh key combination, Alt-P, undoes all paragraph formatting and returns the selected paragraph or paragraphs to the "normal" built-in format.

The table in Figure 5-1 and the examples in Figure 5-2 show the built-in paragraph formats and their key combinations.

Any paragraph or paragraphs that contain the selection (cursor) when a paragraph key code is used will be formatted according to the corresponding built-in format. As little as a single character in a paragraph is all that needs to be selected. If the selection extends across two or more paragraphs, they will all be formatted.

To obtain this paragraph formatting (appearance)	Press Alt plus this key	If a style sheet is in use press Alt plus these two keys
Normal paragraph (undoes all formats)	p	x p
Centered	c	x c
Indent first line ½″	f	x f
Justified (right and left edges even)	j	x j
Flush left (only left edge even)	l	x l
Decrease left indent ½″ (undo nest)	m	x m
Increase left indent ½″ (nest)	n	x n
Open spacing (space before paragraph)	o	x o
Flush right (only right edge even)	r	x r
Hanging indent (simulates a tab)	t	x t
Double-spaced lines	2	x 2

Figure 5-1. Built-in paragraph formats and key codes

```
Alt - P: This paragraph is in the "normal" built-in
paragraph format used by Word. Note that it is flush left,
meaning that only the left edges of the lines are even.

Alt - C: Now the paragraph is shown in the centered built-in
    format. Center the lines in a paragraph by selecting any
    character or characters in it and hold down the Alt key
                while pressing the letter C.

      Alt - F: This paragraph shows the paragraph format that
indents the first line. The key combination for this format
is applied by holding down the Alt key and pressing F.

Alt - J: Now the paragraph has  been  justified.  Each  line
except the last is the same length. Extra spaces are  placed
in the middle of lines to make both ends line up.

      Alt - F, Alt - J: This paragraph has both a first  line
indent and justification. To do  this,  apply  one  built-in
format, and then the other.

Alt - L: This paragraph shows the flush left style. It looks
identical to the "normal" built-in paragraph format, but
differs because it can be added on top of other paragraph
formats, while the "normal" format replaces all other built-
in paragraph formats.                       (continued)
```

Figure 5-2. Examples of built-in paragraph formats

```
Alt - N: The combination Alt - N "nests" a paragraph
half an inch. That means its left indent increases a
half inch, relative to the way it was formatted before
the built-in format was applied.

Alt - M: The combination Alt - M is the opposite of Alt - N.
Holding down the Alt key and pressing the letter M reduces
nesting by one-half inch, relative to the way the paragraph
was before, or to the paragraph preceding it.

           Alt - N, Alt - N: You can nest a paragraph a full
           inch by using the combination Alt - N twice. Each
           use causes a half-inch indentation for the whole
           paragraph -- and all that follow it.

Alt - O: All of these paragraphs have open spacing --
meaning there is a blank space before them. To achieve this,
you use the built-in paragraph format Alt - O.

   Alt - R: This format is of less use than most. It lines up
     the right ends of lines, and leaves the paragraph "ragged
          left." It is called the flush right built-in format.

Alt - T:  This format simulates some fancy work with tabs.
     It is called a "hanging indent," because its first line
     has an outdent of 0.5 inches.  Each time you press the
     Alt-T combination, the outdent increases half an inch.
     (Prior to Word 3.0, the outdent was fixed at 1 inch.)

Alt - 2: Paragraphs can be double-spaced by using the built-

in format that has the key combination Alt - 2. Select any

spot in the paragraph--or select many paragraphs--and hold

down the Alt key at the same time you press the 2 key.

           Alt - N, Alt - F, Alt - J: This paragraph has been
           formatted with built-in paragraph formats  that  nested
           it, gave it a first line indent, and justified it.
```

Figure 5-2 (continued)

Built-in character formats

Character formatting determines how characters in your text appear when printed. Underlining and boldfacing are examples. If your computer equipment can display it, the formatting is shown on the screen. Key combinations are used to apply nine built-in character formats, singly and together. Since character formatting affects individual characters, you must select all the characters you want to format. This is the only way Word can identify the ones that require formatting.

The ten built-in character formats are shown in the table in Figure 5-3 and the examples in Figure 5-4. They affect the formatting of any typeface to which they are applied. The Alt-Spacebar combination listed as "normal" strips all special character formatting from the selected characters. As a practical matter, unless you're using a style sheet the normal character

To obtain this character formatting (appearance)	Press Alt plus this key	If a style sheet is in use, press Alt plus these keys
Normal character (undoes formats)	Spacebar	Spacebar
Bold	b	x b
Italic	i	x i
Underline	u	x u
Double underline	d	x d
Small capitals	k	x k
Strikethrough	s	x s
Superscript	+	x +
Subscript	−	x −
Hidden	e	x e

Figure 5-3. Built-in character formats and key codes

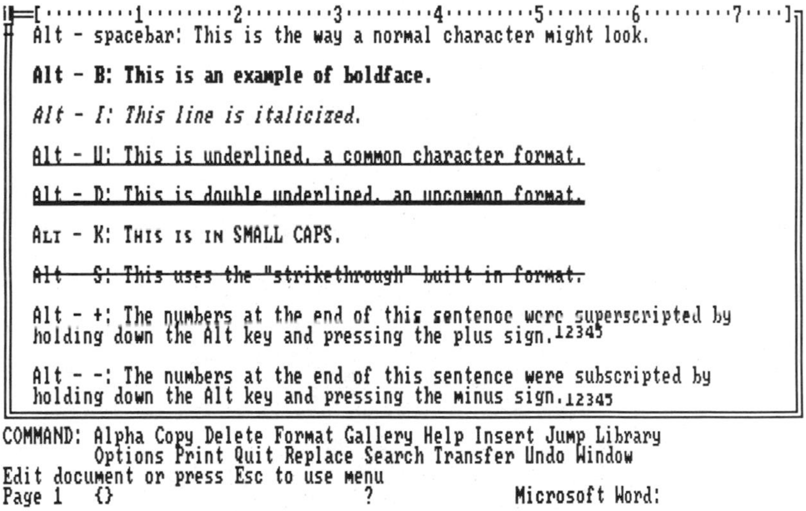

```
⊩═[ · · · · · · · · · ·1· · · · · · · · · ·2· · · · · · · · · ·3· · · · · · · · · ·4· · · · · · · · · ·5· · · · · · · · · ·6· · · · · · · · · ·7· · · · ]┐
  Alt - spacebar: This is the way a normal character might look.

  Alt - B: This is an example of boldface.

  Alt - I: This line is italicized.

  Alt - U: This is underlined, a common character format.

  Alt - D: This is double underlined, an uncommon format.

  Aʟᴛ - K: Tʜɪs ɪs ɪɴ SMALL CAPS.

  Alt - S: This uses the "strikethrough" built in format.

  Alt - +: The numbers at the end of this sentence were superscripted by
  holding down the Alt key and pressing the plus sign.12345

  Alt - -: The numbers at the end of this sentence were subscripted by
  holding down the Alt key and pressing the minus sign.12345

COMMAND: Alpha Copy Delete Format Gallery Help Insert Jump Library
         Options Print Quit Replace Search Transfer Undo Window
Edit document or press Esc to use menu
Page 1  {}                                ?               Microsoft Word:
```

Figure 5-4. Examples of built-in character formats (Characters formatted as "hidden" normally don't appear on the screen. When they do, they have a dotted or solid underline.)

probably will be Pica 12 point (known, somewhat confusingly, as Pica 10 by daisy-wheel type printers). Sometimes, however, the normal character is not Pica 12. On the HP LaserJet printer, for instance, it is Courier 12 point (Courier 10-pitch).

Built-in character formats can be combined with each other and also with built-in paragraph formats.

THE TUTORIAL

This tutorial teaches you how to take advantage of Word's built-in formats so you can easily give a polished appearance to your documents. You'll write a short, informal memo, revise and format it, then print and store it. So that you not only act, but also understand what you do, the steps in the tutorial are fully explained. If you want to gain a feel for uninterrupted activity with Word, go through the hands-on practice without stopping to absorb the discussion. Then come back and read it carefully while the exercise is still fresh in your mind.

If you followed the instructions in Chapter 4, the ruler will be displayed at the top of the screen, and normally invisible characters, such as paragraph marks, will be visible. If they are not displayed, turn them on if you want your screen to match the illustrations on the following pages.

If Word is not already on your screen, type *word* and press Enter. The only character in Word's text area should be the diamond-shaped end mark, highlighted because it shares the same spot as the selection (cursor).

Now, let's use Word to create and print this memo:

```
                              Memo


       TO:      Horatio Toad, supervisor

       FROM:    Ima Killjoy

       RE:      European Travel


          I've returned from a hectic trip to Europe, one I
       didn't request, you'll remember.  It was your idea to send
       me abroad on a scouting trip.  And it was on short notice.

          The streets were crowded.  There wasn't a shower in my
       room.  The sleeping car on the train to Amsterdam was a
       furnace.  It rained half the time.  I felt intimidated
       occasionally.

          So I have just one question, boss: How soon may I go
       back?  I loved it!
```

To ensure that we're starting from the same place, press the Esc key and then press the letter A for Alpha (if you are using a mouse, click the left button when the mouse pointer is on the word *Alpha* at the bottom of the screen).

Creating a buffer

Until you understand Word well, avoid the end mark, because it cannot be formatted. All writing and editing done at the location of the end mark (in other words, when it is selected) always has the "normal" built-in character and paragraph formats, so when the end mark is selected, efforts to change formatting are either futile or cause the end mark to move away from the selection.

If you're a beginner, the first thing you should do when creating any document is create a buffer of several blank lines between where you are working and the end mark. Ideally, put in enough blank lines to move the end mark beyond the last line of the screen.

The initial steps in this tutorial create just such a buffer of several blank paragraphs, and format these blank paragraphs with suitable built-in formats. By formatting all the paragraphs identically, you don't have to worry about the formatting changing on you if you move the selection from paragraph to paragraph.

Look before you type

Step 1. Look at the format of the letter you are about to create. Observe that all of the paragraphs have a blank space above them ("open paragraph spacing") and most have their first line indented a half inch.

Step 2. With the selection on the end mark, apply the built-in format for open paragraph spacing:

    Hold down the Alt key and press the letter O.

The end mark can't be formatted, so Word responds by pushing the end mark down a line below the selection. It also puts a paragraph mark at the location of the selection. Note also that the paragraph mark itself moved down one line. That's because the built-in format for open-paragraph spacing automatically puts a blank line before every paragraph.

Step 3. Apply the built-in paragraph format that indents the first line of the paragraph a half inch:

    Hold down the Alt key and press the letter F.

Word responds by indenting the paragraph mark and selection (cursor) a distance that will print as a half inch.

Step 4. Now you have a paragraph formatted with both open spacing and a first-line indent. Next:

    Press the Enter key once to create another paragraph.

Notice that the selection moved down two lines and now highlights the mark of the second paragraph. This second paragraph is formatted just like the first, since it was created from it.

```
║═[····¦····1·········2·········3·········4·········5·········]·········7·····┐
║                ¶
║                ⅈⅈ
║      ♦
```

NOTE: If you were now to press the up direction key once, the selection would move back up to the preceding paragraph. Anything you subsequently wrote in either paragraph would be formatted with open spacing and first-line indentation. However, if you were to press the down direction key once instead, the selection would move to the end mark, and anything you typed would assume the look of a "normal" paragraph. No indentation, no open spacing. If you didn't understand what had happened, you might think that Word had some-how lost your formatting instructions. On the contrary—the formatting would still be there, but you'd have to move your selection back up to a formatted paragraph in order to use it.

Step 5. With the selection on either of the paragraph marks on your screen:

Press the Enter key a dozen times.

This creates a dozen more paragraphs, all identically formatted. This is your buffer.

Step 6. Move back to the top of the document:

Hold down Ctrl and press PgUp.

Your screen will show a series of paragraphs, all of which are identically formatted, and the end mark will be nowhere in sight. Now you're ready to write.

Entering text

Step 1. First:

Type the word *Memo* and press the Enter key to signify the end of the para-graph (in this case a single line).

The word will not be centered, boldfaced, or underlined, although it will be before we're through. We'll come back later to do the formatting.

Step 2. To create a blank paragraph for extra space:

Press the Enter key again.

```
║═[····|····1·········2·········3·········4·········5·········]·········7·····┐
║                                                                             ║
║      Memo¶                                                                   ║
║      ¶                                                                       ║
║      ░¶                                                                      ║
║      ¶                                                                       ║
║      ¶                                                                       ║
```

Step 3. Type the next line:

```
║      TO:    Horatio Toad, supervisor█                                       ║
```

To type the example exactly, follow *TO:* with four spaces. If you make a typing error, use the Backspace key to back up and erase it, then retype it.

> Press the Enter key at the end of the line, to end the paragraph and create
> a new one.

Step 4. Type the next two lines, pressing the Enter key at the end of each:

```
║      FROM:  Ima Killjoy¶                                                    ║
║      RE:    European Travel¶                                               ║
```

Step 5. To give an extra space before beginning the body of the memo:

> Press the Enter key one extra time.

Step 6. Type the first paragraph of the memo, as shown here:

```
║         I've returned from a hectic trip to Europe, a trip I
║      didn't request, you'll remember.  It was your idea to send
║      me abroad on a scouting trip.  And it was on short notice.░
║
║      ¶
```

```
COMMAND: Alpha Copy Delete Format Gallery Help Insert Jump Library
         Options Print Quit Replace Search Transfer Undo Window
Edit document or press Esc to use menu
Page 1  {}                        ?                     Microsoft Word:
```

Do not press the Enter key at the end of each line. Word moves to the next line for you. Do press the Enter key once at the end of the paragraph. Observe that the paragraph's first line is indented as a result of the Alt-F built-in format you used when you started the document.

Step 7. Type the next paragraph. Remember to press the Enter key only at the end of the paragraph. Notice that when you reach the word *furnace,* the screen scrolls automatically to provide more space. When you're done, your screen should look something like this (it is possible that it will be scrolled to a different point):

```
=[·····!····1·········2·········3·········4·········5·········]·········7·····]
        RE:     European Travel¶

        ¶

        I've returned from a hectic trip to Europe, a trip I
    didn't request, you'll remember.  It was your idea to send
    me abroad on a scouting trip.  And it was on short notice.¶

        The streets were crowded.  There wasn't a shower in my
    room.  The sleeping car on the train to Amsterdam was a
    furnace.  It rained half the time.  I felt intimidated
    occasionally.▯



        ¶

        ¶

        ¶



COMMAND: Alpha Copy Delete Format Gallery Help Insert Jump Library
         Options Print Quit Replace Search Transfer Undo Window
Edit document or press Esc to use menu
Page 1    {}                                 ?          Microsoft Word:
```

Revise and format

Before you finish typing the memo, let's go back and practice revising and formatting what you've already typed. First you'll revise content, and then you'll change some formatting with built-in formats.

Step 1. Let's decide that the word *trip* is overused in the first paragraph. We'll eliminate the second use of the word.

Move the selection to the word *a,* as shown here.

```
║       I've returned from a hectic trip to Europe, ▯ trip I                    ║
```

You can move the selection either with the direction keys or by rolling the mouse until the mouse pointer is on *a* and then clicking the left mouse button.

Step 2. To see how Word operates:

Press the Del key once.

The Del key deletes whatever is selected—in this case, the word *a.* Note that when the selected text disappears from the text area it appears inside the scrap brackets on the bottom line of the screen. The scrap is handy for moving passages around in a document, because you can select a passage, delete it to the scrap, move the selection to a new location, and press the Ins key to put the contents of the scrap in that spot.

Step 3. Now that you've seen the scrap, use the Undo command to restore the *a* you just deleted:

> Press the Esc key, then press the letter U. Or move the mouse pointer to the Undo command in the menu at the bottom of the screen, and click the left mouse button.

The document and screen will look as they did before you used the Del key.

Step 4. Now we'll try something new and important. It's called "extending the selection." You can select any number of consecutive characters by this means. Right now, your selection should still be on the word *a*. We'll extend the selection to include both *a* and the word *trip*. You can use either the keyboard or the mouse.

With the keyboard:

> Press the F6 key while the selection is on *a*.

This key turns on the "extend selection" mode. Note the EX on the bottom line of the command area.

> Using either the Right direction key or the F8 key, extend the right edge of the selection to include the word *trip*.

If you go too far, use the Left direction key or the F7 key to fine-tune the size of the selection. The F7 and F8 keys move the selection a word at a time instead of a character at a time.

With the mouse:

> Position the mouse cursor on the *a* and hold down the left button as you roll the mouse until *trip* is selected, too. Then release the button.

The selection should look like this (note that the highlight includes the space after the word *trip*):

> ‖   I've returned from a hectic trip to Europe, a trip I   ‖

Step 5. Delete the selected phrase, sending it to the scrap. With the keyboard:

> Press the Del key, or use the Delete command by pressing the Esc key followed by the letter D.

With the mouse:

> Position the mouse pointer on the Delete command at the bottom of the screen and click the left mouse button.

Unless you use the Del key, Word responds with the message *DELETE to:* {}. The brackets in the message symbolize the scrap, the place to which Word is guessing you want to delete the selected text. Because the guess is correct:

> Press the Enter key, or click the left mouse button on the word *DELETE* in
> the message.

After the deletion, the selection stays in the same position but the remaining text in the paragraph re-forms to fill the space left by the deleted words *a trip:*

```
‖═[····¦····1·········2·········3·········4·········5·········]·········7····‖
‖       RE:     European Travel¶
‖
‖       ¶
‖
‖       I've returned from a hectic trip to Europe, ▌ didn't
‖ request, you'll remember.  It was your idea to send me
‖ abroad on a scouting trip.  And it was on short notice.¶
‖
‖       The streets were crowded.  There wasn't a shower in my
‖ room.  The sleeping car on the train to Amsterdam was a
‖ furnace.  It rained half the time.  I felt intimidated
‖ occasionally.¶
‖
‖       ¶
‖
‖       ¶
‖
‖       ¶
‖
COMMAND: Alpha Copy Delete Format Gallery Help Insert Jump Library
         Options Print Quit Replace Search Transfer Undo Window
Edit document or press Esc to use menu
Page 1   {a·trip·}                    ?              Microsoft Word:
```

Step 6. To complete the revision:

> Type the word *one* and put a space after it with the Spacebar.

The word is inserted at the selection, replacing the deleted words.

```
‖       I've returned from a hectic trip to Europe, one ▌          ‖
‖ didn't request, you'll remember. It was your idea to send        ‖
```

Step 7. Use the Undo command again. It will show you what the document looked like before you substituted the word *one* for the words *a trip.* If you use the Undo command yet another time, it will undo the undo. This procedure lets you compare two versions of a passage, to see which you like best. Try it. You'll see this:

```
‖       I've returned from a hectic trip to Europe, ▐a trip▌I          ‖
```

then this again:

```
‖       I've returned from a hectic trip to Europe, ▐one ▌I            ‖
```

Step 8. Next we'll try some character formatting. With the keyboard:

> Use the Down direction key to move the selection down one line.

Part of the sentence beginning *It was your idea* should be highlighted (selected).

> Press the F9 key to select the entire sentence.

With the mouse:

> Move the mouse pointer to any point in the sentence that begins *It was your idea* and click both mouse buttons at once.

Step 9. The key code U will let you underline whatever is selected — in this case, a whole sentence. To use the built-in character format for underlining:

> Hold down the Alt key and press the letter U.

To reveal the underlining:

> Move elsewhere in the document by pressing a direction key, or click a mouse button when the mouse pointer is away from the selected sentence.

```
‖  didn't request, you'll remember.  It was your idea to send             ‖
   me abroad on a scouting trip.  And it was on short notice.
```

Step 10. Paragraph formatting is next:

> Hold down Ctrl and press PgUp to move to the top of the document.

The capital *M* of *Memo* is selected. Now:

> Press and release the F6 key to turn on the extended selection mode, and then press the Down direction key four times.

This causes all the paragraphs from the beginning of the memo to the line *RE: European Travel* to be partly or entirely selected. (Recall that you don't have to select all of a paragraph in order to give it paragraph formatting.)

Step 11. We want to remove the first-line indent for each of these paragraphs, so first we'll use the built-in normal paragraph format:

> Hold down the Alt key and press the letter P.

Word responds by eliminating the indents and the open spaces between paragraphs. Note that the text remains selected. We want to retain the open spacing that was eliminated with the Alt-P combination, so we restore it with the built-in open-paragraph format:

> Hold down the Alt key and press the letter O.

Step 12. To center the word *Memo* on the page, apply the built-in paragraph format that centers:

> Move the selection to one or more characters in the word *Memo,* and then hold down the Alt key and press C.

Step 13. Character formatting is next. Select all of the characters in the word, *Memo* by pressing F7 or F8, or by placing the mouse pointer anywhere on the word and by clicking the right button. Now, boldface the characters:

> Hold down the Alt key and press B.

Finally, underline them:

> Hold down the Alt key and press U.

Step 14. Formatting is complete for that portion of the document you've typed so far, but you have one paragraph left to type. So:

> Move the selection to the paragraph mark below the last typed line. Type *So I have just one question, boss:* and stop. Make sure that you type a space after you type the colon.

Step 15. Now, underline the rest of the sentence as you type it:

> Hold down the Alt key and press U.

This key combination turns on the built-in underlining format at the space occupied by the selection.

Step 16. Finish the remainder of the sentence:

> Type *How soon may I go back?*

It is underlined as you type. (On some color monitors, and a few monochrome monitors, which are running in text rather than graphics mode, you will see reduced-intensity characters rather than underlining. But the underlining will be printed.)

Step 17. At the end of the sentence:

Hold down the Alt key and press the Spacebar.

This key combination applies the built-in "normal" character format, thereby turning off the underlining.

Step 18. Only the last three words of the memo remain to go:

Type *I loved it!*

```
‖     So I have just one question, boss: How soon may I go        ‖
‖  back?  I loved it!░                                            ‖
```

You're done.

Before you print the document, you may wish to experiment with the Copy, Delete, and Insert commands. If you wish to keep the memo in its current form, use the Undo command (press Esc and U) after each experimental change to the document. To try moving a passage from one place to another: Select the passage; delete it to the scrap by pressing Esc, D, and Enter; move the selection to the new location; and insert the deleted material by pressing the Ins key. Or, to copy a passage so that it appears more than once: Select the passage, copy it to the scrap (unlike Delete, the Copy command leaves selected text intact in the document), move the selection to a new location, and insert the passage from the scrap. The Del and Ins keys are shortcuts for the commands of the same names.

Printing

Because you already set up Word to work with your printer (in Chapter 4), printing what you've written is simple. The command is Print Printer. You can press the Esc key, P, and P again, or click the left mouse button with the pointer on the word *Print* and then, when the Print submenu appears, on the word *Printer.* Recall that the right mouse button often provides you with a shortcut. Here's an example: If you click the right button when the mouse pointer is on the word *Print,* you needn't click again on the word *Printer.*

If you're using a dot-matrix printer with continuous-feed paper, a laser printer, or a printer with an automatic sheet feeder, the document will print without delay. If you're using a printer that requires paper to be fed manually a sheet at a time, Word will pause before printing each page and display this message or a similar one:

```
Enter Y to continue or Esc to cancel
```

When the paper is in place, press the letter Y. Otherwise, press the Esc key.

If you're using a daisy-wheel printer, or any other that requires you to change typefaces manually, Word will pause before printing and ask you to mount the appropriate daisy wheel on the printer. A typical message is:

```
Enter Y after mounting Pica 10
```

Once the new typeface wheel is mounted on the printer, press Y to begin printing. If you have a daisywheel printer with manually fed paper, you'll get both *Enter Y* messages in succession.

Sometimes you want to count the pages in your document before printing. Or you may want Word to lay out the pages ("repaginate") electronically so you can see where the page breaks will occur. The Print Repaginate command tells you the number of pages, and shows you the tops of new pages with a symbol « displayed just left of the beginning of the line.

As a final step before printing, you may wish to select and delete any extra paragraph marks remaining in the buffer you created between the end of your document and the end mark. Word will "print" these paragraphs as blank lines if they're still in the document. Deleting the excess paragraph marks eliminates any paper waste.

Storing a document

To save a document onto disk, use the Transfer Save command. Press Esc, T, and S. Word responds this way:

```
TRANSFER SAVE filename: █                    formatted:(Yes)No
```

Type in a file name of up to eight characters and press the Enter key. Do not specify a file name extension (three letters after a period). Word assigns the extension .DOC automatically. For the practice memo, for example, you can type *memo* as the file name. When you press Enter, the document is saved, with the name MEMO.DOC, on the disk in the drive Word normally uses for documents (probably B), or in the drive you specified with the Transfer Options command. (If you wish, you can specify an alternate drive or a path name by typing it before the file name.)

After it is saved, a document remains on the screen. To clear the screen, use the Transfer Clear Window command: Press Esc, T, C, and W.

To load a document from disk storage onto the screen, use the Transfer Load command. Press Esc, T, and L. Word responds this way:

```
TRANSFER LOAD filename: █                    read only: Yes(No)
```

Type the file name of the document you want to load and press the Enter key. Word assumes the file name extension is .DOC. If you are not sure of the name of the document, press any direction key to see a list of all documents that have the extension .DOC. Move the highlight among the choices on the list with the direction keys, and press Enter when the desired choice is highlighted. You can also place the mouse pointer on your choice and click the left button, or else choose the file and load it in one step by clicking the right button.

Quitting Word

When you are finished with Word, press the Esc key and the letter Q. If there has been no new editing since you last saved the document, Word will quit directly. If the document on the screen has had even minor changes made to it since it was last saved, even if it's only been repaginated for printing, Word will ask whether you want to save the edited version. If so, you will see this message, or a similar one:

```
Enter Y to save, N to lose edits, or Esc to cancel
```

If you want to save the latest version of the document under its existing name, press Y. To lose the editing changes made since you last stored the document on disk, press N. If you decide you're not ready to quit after all, press the Esc key.

If you use the mouse to execute the Quit command, Word will save editing changes automatically if you click the right mouse button.

The Format Division commands

Recall that Word comes with a single built-in division format. Sometimes you may want to change such things as page size or margin width, or you may want to turn on automatic page numbering. To make such changes, select any character(s) in your document and use the Format Division commands.

In earlier versions of Word, there was a single command called Format Division. It let you set 19 different characteristics of page layout. Because confronting this number of choices was confusing to some people, beginning with Word 3.0 the same 19 choices are broken into three different commands: Format Division Margins, Format Division Page-numbers, and Format Division Layout.

For simplicity, at first concern yourself with only a few of the 19 choices. Assuming you have version 3.0 or later, use the Format Division Margins command by pressing Esc, F, D, and M. Word responds by displaying the following array of command fields.

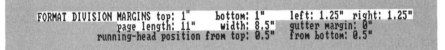

```
FORMAT DIVISION MARGINS top: 1"        bottom: 1"      left: 1.25"  right: 1.25"
                         page length: 11"        width: 8.5"    gutter margin: 0"
             running-head position from top: 0.5"    from bottom: 0.5"
```

The shading in the preceding illustration appears only in the book, not on the screen. In the beginning, concern yourself only with the fields that are *not* shaded. Use the Tab key to move from field to field, just as you did with the various Options commands in Chapter 4. Type in different measurements for margins and page size if you desire, then press the Enter key. A division mark (::::::) will appear across the width of the screen, just before the end mark. Try to stay away from the division mark—just as you tried to stay away from the end mark.

If you want automatic page numbering, pick the Format Division Page-numbers command. Initially, ignore all the fields except the first one, which gives you the *Yes No* choice of having automatic page numbers. By pressing the Spacebar, you can choose between *Yes* and *No*. Press the Enter key when you've made your choice.

If you're using a version of Word prior to 3.0, the general technique is the same. Pick the Format Division command by pressing Esc, F, and D, and then use the Tab key to move among the 19 fields.

```
FORMAT DIVISION break: Cont Column Page Odd Even
     page length: 11"        width: 8.5"       gutter width: 0"
     pg #: Yes(No)         from top: 0.5"      from left: 7.25"
     numbering:(Cont)Start       at:           format:(1)I i A a
     margin top: 1"         bottom: 1"         left: 1.25"        right: 1.25"
     # of cols: 1    space between: 0.5"       footnotes:(Same-page)End
     running head pos    from top: 0.5"        from bottom: 0.5"
```

You've learned "The Simple Word." There are much more complex capabilities that Word offers, but isn't it nice to know you can do so much, so easily?

Using Command Menus

Commands are at the heart of Word. Use them to give instructions, even complex or detailed instructions.

This chapter explores the general techniques of using commands. The chapters in Part II provide a detailed reference to the specific uses of each command.

COMMAND MENUS

Although commands perform different tasks, the ways they are used follow consistent rules. Word's commands are reached through one "primary" and one "secondary" menu. The primary menu is the Edit menu. It is displayed at the bottom of your screen whenever you write or edit. The secondary menu is called the Gallery menu and is used only to view, modify, or create styles in a style sheet. You reach it by choosing the Gallery command from the Edit menu.

The Edit menu

The Edit menu appears on your screen when you start Word and is used the majority of the time. Unless you turn it off with the Options command, it is displayed whenever you read, write, or edit text. The Edit menu looks like this:

```
COMMAND: Alpha Copy Delete Format Gallery Help Insert Jump Library
         Options Print Quit Replace Search Transfer Undo Window
```

Through the use of commands from the Edit menu, you create, edit, format, and print documents.

Single-word commands

Depending on your version of Word, you have 50 or more commands available from the Edit menu. Although most are part of large families of commands, 11 are single-word commands that you reach directly from the menu. They are: Alpha, Copy, Delete, Gallery, Help, Insert, Options, Quit, Replace, Search, and Undo.

As a brief example, let's look at the Delete command, which you use to place selected text either in Word's short-term storage place, the scrap, or in a longer-term storage place, the glossary. Here is a graphic representation of the way you choose the Delete command:

```
COMMAND: Alpha Copy Delete Format Gallery Help Insert Jump Library
         Options Print Quit Replace Search Transfer Undo Window
```

You pick the word *Delete* by pressing the Escape key, then pressing D.

The Edit menu disappears when you press D. In its place, a command field appears, asking you to specify where you want the selected text deleted to:

```
DELETE to: {}
```

Now, you can either type in a glossary name and press Enter to send the text to the glossary, or you can, just by pressing the Enter key, accept Word's proposed response—in this case, the scrap, symbolized by the scrap brackets, { }. Whichever you choose, the selected text will vanish from the document.

Command families

The remaining commands are members of various families that you reach by picking the appropriate family name from the Edit menu. The family names are: Format, Jump, Library, Print, Transfer, and Window, representing such commands as Format Character, Jump Page, Library Hyphenate, Print Printer, Print File, Window Split Vertical, and so forth.

For example, the name Format on the Edit menu represents commands having to do with the way a document looks. Picking the Format family, by pressing the Esc key and then the letter F, causes the Format submenu to appear:

```
COMMAND: Alpha Copy Delete Format Gallery Help Insert Jump Library
         Options Print Quit Replace Search Transfer Undo Window

FORMAT: Character Paragraph Tabs Footnote Division Running-head Style
```

Now, suppose you want to affect the appearance of your document by changing tab settings. You choose Format Tabs from the submenu by pressing the first letter (T) of the command you want:

```
FORMAT: Character Paragraph Tabs Footnote Division Running-head Style

FORMAT TABS: Set Clear Reset-all
```

Word shows you another submenu, so you can tell it whether you want to set, clear, or reset your tabs. For this example, let's say you want to set new tabs. You could press the letter S for Set, but since Word in this case is proposing the correct response, just press Enter.

```
FORMAT TABS SET position: █
           alignment:(Left)Center Right Decimal       leader char:(Blank). - _
```

The Format Tabs Set command ends in a collection of three command fields: *position,* *alignment,* and *leader char.* The first of these is a fill-in field, and the remaining two are menu-type fields. Fields are where you tailor a command to your own requirements. When fields are filled in or set as you desire, press the Enter key to execute the command. Press the Esc key if you want to cancel the command.

A few commands, such as Format Tabs Set, have three words in them. More often, they have two, such as Format Paragraph. Regardless, you pick the names from menus and submenus.

The Gallery menu

You reach the "secondary" menu, the Gallery menu, through the Edit menu's Gallery command. The Gallery is where you look at the styles of a style sheet, if there is one in use. When you are in the Gallery, your document is replaced on the screen by a style sheet and the Gallery menu appears at the bottom. This is the Gallery menu:

```
COMMAND: Copy Delete Exit Format Help
         Insert Name Print Transfer Undo
```

Observe that there are fewer command names in the Gallery menu than there are in the Edit menu. Many of the same names are used in both menus, but don't confuse them. The Gallery commands are used only for modifying and creating style sheets. Here is the way your screen looks when the first screen of a style sheet is in the Gallery:

```
I
I
 1  S/ Division Standard                        SEMI-BLOCK LETTER, 6" WIDTH
         Page break. Page length 11"; width 8.5". Folios Arabic. Top margin
         1.67"; bottom 1"; left 1.25"; right 1.25". Top running head at 1".
         Bottom running head at 0.5". Footnotes on same page.
 2  LH Paragraph 10                             ADJUSTABLE LETTERHEAD SPACE
         Modern b 12. Flush left, space after 2 li.
 3  RA Paragraph 14                          shift-◄┘ RETURN NAME, ADDR
         Modern b 12. Flush left, Left indent 3.2", space before 1 li (keep
         in one column, keep with following paragraph).
 4  DA Paragraph 7                              DATE
         Modern b 12. Flush left, Left indent 3.2", space after 1 li (keep
         in one column, keep with following paragraph).
 5  IA Paragraph 11                             INSIDE ADDRESS/Mr. Jim Smith
         Modern b 12. Flush left, Left indent 0.5" (first line indent -
         0.5"), right indent 2.8" (keep in one column, keep with following
         paragraph).
 6  SA Paragraph 13                             SALUTATION / Dear...
         Modern b 12. Flush left, space before 1 li (keep in one column,
         keep with following paragraph).

COMMAND: Copy Delete Exit Format Help
         Insert Name Print Transfer Undo
Edit style sheet or choose Exit to see document
GALLERY  {}                        ?              Microsoft Word: SEMI.STY
```

Note that the word *GALLERY* is displayed in the lower left corner. Note also that the file name extension in the lower right corner is .STY, for "style sheet," rather than .DOC, which you see when a document and the Edit menu are on the screen. You can disregard the Gallery menu until you're ready to use the substantial power of style sheets. (Press E for Exit to return to your document.)

USING COMMANDS

You've had a taste of Word's commands, and seen that a variety of editing, formatting, printing, and other options are available at the touch of a few keys. To tap this power effectively, you'll want to learn the finer points of using Word's command menus, submenus, and fields.

Choosing from menus

You make choices from the Edit and Gallery menus much as you do from restaurant menus. Word is your waiter and will deliver what you order. And just as you can either tell a waiter what you want or simply point to it on the menu, with Word you can type the first letter of your choice or point to its name with your mouse.

Choosing with the keyboard

To use the keyboard to choose a command from the Edit menu, first press the Esc key. This moves Word's attention from the text area to the command area. If you have turned off the menu with the Options command, it will reappear temporarily when you press Esc. Proceed with either of two methods:

- Press the first letter of the command or the command family you want.
- Or, use the Spacebar to move the highlight to the command you want, and press the Enter key when the command is highlighted.

Word automatically returns you to your document or to the Edit menu after you execute a command. You can have Word return you to the document at any time by pressing the Esc key followed by the letter A (for the Alpha command).

Choosing with the mouse

To use the mouse to select a command, roll the mouse on your desktop until the mouse pointer is on the name of the command. Then click the left mouse button.

You can select commands with the right button, too, but as a general rule, it is advisable to use the left mouse button, at least until you know the command menus and submenus well. Clicking the left button moves you a step at a time through menus, while clicking the right button often takes a shortcut and skips you ahead a step by accepting Word's proposed response for the next choice. But, of course, a shortcut is no advantage if it takes you someplace other than where you want to go. The right button is useful once you're experienced with Word and know where you're going.

To return from the Edit menu to the text area with the mouse, place the mouse pointer in the document at the place where you wish to resume writing or editing, and click the left button. If you're in a submenu or a command field, you must first click both mouse buttons when the mouse pointer is in the command area.

Alternatively, you can leave the command area whenever you want and return to your last position in the document by executing the Alpha command with the mouse. Again, you may need to click both mouse buttons first, to return to the Edit menu from a submenu or a field.

Submenus

When you pick the name of a family of commands, such as Format, Word presents you with a submenu of additional choices. Some may lead to still another submenu. The majority of commands conclude with one or more command fields, where you make choices about how the command will perform its work.

Think again about how you make choices from a restaurant menu—about how one set of choices can lead to another and another, until you've ordered just what you want, prepared as you like it. Suppose you decide to order prime rib. The waiter asks if you want rice or potato. Potato. Do you want it french fried, mashed, or baked? Baked. What about toppings: butter? sour cream? chives? The waiter has a broad range of offerings (submenus, if you will) but doesn't ask you for choices until they become relevant.

Similarly, Word offers you a comprehensive array of choices through its menus, but they aren't immediately apparent. Like a thoughtful waiter, Word doesn't bother you with questions about your intentions until you express an interest. This strategy simplifies and helps streamline the way you think about your work.

An example

To illustrate Word's menu/submenu system, let's explore the Format Paragraph command from the Edit Menu. When you choose Format, Word displays a submenu that asks what kind of formatting you want to do:

FORMAT: **Character** Paragraph Tabs Footnote Division Running-head Style

Unlike those on the main menus, the choices on submenus are not necessarily in alphabetical order. Instead, the first choices listed are those people make often.

You choose from submenus exactly as you do from the Edit menu. So, to pick Paragraph from the Format submenu, and thus specify the Format Paragraph command, you could:

♦ Press the letter P (for Paragraph).

♦ Or, press the Spacebar once to highlight the word *Paragraph*. Then press Enter.

♦ Or, roll the mouse on the desktop until the mouse pointer is positioned on the word *Paragraph*, then click the left mouse button.

Once the Format Paragraph command has been picked, a collection of command fields replaces the Format submenu. The Format Paragraph command fields look like this beginning with version 3.0 of Word:

```
FORMAT PARAGRAPH alignment: Left Centered Right Justified
     left indent: 0"         first line: 0"        right indent: 0"
     line spacing: 1 li      space before: 0 li     space after: 0 li
     keep together: Yes(No)  keep follow: Yes(No)  side by side: Yes(No)
```

These command fields let us control the physical dimensions of paragraphs.

The method of choosing the Format Paragraph command can be shown as a path from the Edit menu to the Format submenu to the Format Paragraph command:

```
COMMAND: Alpha Copy Delete Format Gallery Help Insert Jump Library
         Options Print Quit Replace Search Transfer Undo Window


FORMAT: Character Paragraph Tabs Footnote Division Running-head Style


FORMAT PARAGRAPH alignment: Left Centered Right Justified
     left indent: 0"         first line: 0"        right indent: 0"
     line spacing: 1 li      space before: 0 li     space after: 0 li
     keep together: Yes(No)  keep follow: Yes(No)  side by side: Yes(No)
```

Command fields

Simply picking a command sometimes doesn't give Word enough information about what you want to do. When it needs more details, it asks for them by displaying a set of command fields. The fields let you tailor the effect of a command to suit precise needs. They are the last specifications you make before executing a command, and all of them appear at once at the bottom of the screen.

Here are examples of command fields. In each case, you are expected to make a choice or enter some information in the space following the colon.

The Delete command ends in a single command field:

```
DELETE to: {}
```

The Transfer Save command ends in two command fields:

```
TRANSFER SAVE filename: ▮                          formatted:(Yes)No
```

The Format Paragraph command ends in ten command fields:

```
FORMAT PARAGRAPH alignment: Left Centered Right Justified
     left indent: 0"         first line: 0"        right indent: 0"
     line spacing: 1 li      space before: 0 li     space after: 0 li
     keep together: Yes(No)  keep follow: Yes(No)  side by side: Yes(No)
```

Command fields come in two basic forms: *fill-ins,* and *menus* of two or more specific choices, from which you pick one.

When a command has more than one field, you move from one to the other by pressing the Tab key to move forward and Shift-Tab to move backward. With a mouse, you can move directly to any field by clicking the left mouse button when the pointer is on the name of, or in, the desired field.

Once you're in a command field, you can make a choice. To help you out, Word usually proposes a response. The suggestion is highlighted when you are in the particular field. If it is a menu-type field, the proposed response is surrounded by parentheses when a different field is highlighted. If there is no proposed response in a command field, that means:

♦ Word has no clue to what you might want (such as what to name an unnamed document, or what pages to print when you are printing only parts of a document).

♦ Or, you are using a Format command to change the appearance of selected text, but different parts of the selected text are formatted in different ways (for example, some of it is underlined and some isn't).

If you try to execute a command but have failed to make a choice in a field where there is no proposed response and where a choice is required, Word bleeps its alarm and gives you the message *Not a valid file* or *Command field requires response.* It also highlights the command field requiring a response.

How does Word decide what response to propose? It usually simply endorses the status quo. But Word's proposed responses are only suggestions. You are free to change them. For an example of how to make changes, let's look at the fields of the Format Character command in version 3.0 of Word.

```
FORMAT CHARACTER bold: Yes No    italic: Yes(No)          underline: Yes(No)
          strikethrough: Yes(No)    uppercase: Yes(No)       small caps: Yes(No)
          double underline: Yes(No) position:(Normal)Superscript Subscript
          font name:              font size:               hidden: Yes(No)
```

The first eight fields are menus; the next two, *font name* and *font size,* are both the fill-in type, and the last field, *hidden,* is a menu.

Menu-type fields

To make a choice from a particular command-field menu, move to the field by using the Tab key or mouse, and then use any of the usual three menu methods:

1. Press the Spacebar until your choice is highlighted.

2. Or, press the first letter of your choice, for example, Y for *Yes* or N for *No.*

3. Or, position the mouse pointer on your choice and click the left mouse button.

Fill-in fields

The two fill-in fields in the Format Character command, *font name* and *font size,* let you pick a typeface (font) and type size for whatever text is selected.

There are several ways to respond to a fill-in field. The obvious way, and one that always works, is to type in a response. Sometimes you don't have to type, because fill-ins often have proposed responses, just as menu-type fields do. For example, for most printers Word usually proposes Pica (Modern a) as the font name and 12 (points) as the font size in the Format Character command. These look like this in the fill-in fields of the Format Character command fields:

```
font name: Pica          font size: 12
```

You can edit a proposed fill-in response with the following keys:

- ◆ F7 moves the highlight one word to the left.
- ◆ F8 moves the highlight one word to the right.
- ◆ F9 moves the highlight one character to the left.
- ◆ F10 moves the highlight one character to the right.
- ◆ Backspace deletes a character to the left of the highlight.
- ◆ Del deletes all highlighted characters.

If you type any characters without first pressing one of these keys, the proposed response will vanish and be replaced with what you type. But once you press F7, F8, F9, or F10, then the character keys—as well as the Del and Backspace keys—can be used to edit a response.

In addition, many fill-in fields let you pick a response from a list. Generally, Word tells you when a list is available by including in its message the words . . . *or select from list*. Lists have the virtue of telling you of appropriate responses, and eliminate the need to type. You can request a list regardless of whether there is a proposed response.

To display a list of possible responses, select the appropriate field by pressing the Tab key, and then press any direction key. Or, place the mouse pointer on or after the field name, and click the right mouse button. The list will temporarily replace the text area of the screen. The list for the *font name* field, when you are using the Diablo 630 printer, looks like this:

```
Pica (modern a)          Courier (modern b)
Elite (modern c)         Prestige (modern d)
LetterGothic (modern e)  GothicPS (modern f)
CubicPS (modern g)       Titan (modern h)
OCR-A (modern o)         OCR-B (modern p)
BoldPS (roman a)         TrendPS (roman b)
RomanPS (roman i)        Script (script a)
ScriptPS (script b)      Narrator (decor a)
Emphasis (decor b)       Kana (foreign b)
Hebrew (foreign c)
```

To pick from the list with the keyboard, press the appropriate direction key until the choice you desire is highlighted. Then, to tell Word you've made your choice, press the Tab key to move to the next command field.

To pick from the list with a mouse, position the mouse cursor on your choice and click the left mouse button. When you've made your choice in that field, move the mouse pointer to a different field. (If you click with the right button, you'll both pick from the list and execute the whole command.)

Executing a command

The final step is "executing," or "carrying out," the command—two names for the same thing. This is the step in which you tell Word: "Okay, everything's set up just the way I want it, so put the command into effect now."

A few commands are executed automatically as soon as they are picked. These are straightforward commands, like Alpha, that do not require choices to be made through the use of command fields. But most commands offer choices through fields, and you must carry out these commands manually after you've made your choices. With the keyboard, you execute such a command in only one way—by pressing the Enter key once the command fields are set as you want them. With the mouse, you click the left button while the mouse pointer is on the all-capital name of the command at the far left side of the command area. For example, you execute the Format Character command by clicking the left button while the mouse pointer is anywhere on the words *FORMAT CHARACTER* in the array of Format Character command fields.

You can also carry out a command by clicking the right mouse button after making your final choice in any menu or field. For example, when using the Format Character command to specify underlining, you can position the mouse on the word *Yes* in the *underline* field, and then click the right mouse button. This picks *Yes* for the underline and simultaneously carries out the whole Format Character command.

Backing out of a command

It's easy to back out of a command before executing it. If you're in the Edit menu, press the Esc key or click both mouse buttons simultaneously when the mouse pointer is anywhere in the command area. If you're in the Gallery menu, use the Exit command (Edit, in early versions).

If you do back out of a command, none of the changes you may have made in command fields will take effect, nor will they be remembered by Word. It will be as though you never chose the command at all.

COMMANDS IN SUMMARY

You've been acquainted with the fine points of using commands. Here's a quick look at the commands and command families, and where you'll find details on each.

Use the Alpha command to move from the Edit menu to the text area, to write or edit. *See Chapter 9, "The Simplest Commands: Alpha, Quit, Undo."*

Use the Copy command to copy selected text either to the scrap or to the glossary. *See Chapter 10, "The Scrap and Glossary Commands: Copy, Delete, Insert."*

Use the Delete command to delete selected text from a document and send it either to the scrap or to the glossary. *See Chapter 10.*

Use the family of Format commands to control the appearance of a document's characters and its layout and to use previously defined styles from style sheets. *See Chapter 12, "The Family of Format Commands."*

Use the Gallery command to view the individual styles that comprise the style sheet, if any, that is in use. *See Chapter 11, "The Efficiency Commands: Gallery, Help, Options, Replace, Search."* (The Gallery command is also the gateway to the Gallery menu, a separate collection of commands used to modify or create style sheets. This is an advanced use of Word, covered in Chapter 24, "Power Tools: Style Sheets .")

Use the Help command to read instructions on the use of Word. *See Chapter 11.*

Use the Insert command to place the text from the scrap or the glossary into a document. *See Chapter 10.*

Use the family of Jump commands to move almost instantly to a particular page of a document, or to jump back and forth between footnotes and footnote reference marks in the main body of a document. *See Chapter 13, "The Family of Jump Commands."*

Beginning with version 2.0 of Word, use the family of Library commands to hyphenate or check the spelling of words in a document or to use other software without leaving Word. Beginning with version 3.0, you can also use Library commands to alphabetize lists, re-number lists, and create indexes and tables of contents. *See Chapter 14, "The Family of Library Commands."*

Use the Options command to tailor the way in which Word performs, to meet your needs. *See Chapter 11.*

Use the family of Print commands to prepare a document for printing and to print it. You can print a document directly, or merge a document with a file of data and print the result. You can also print a document to a file on disk so that it can be used by other programs, including telecommunications packages. *See Chapter 15, "The Family of Print Commands."*

Use the Quit command to end an editing session. *See Chapter 9.*

Use the Replace command to substitute one word or phrase for another word or phrase, either once or repeatedly. *See Chapter 11.*

Use the Search command to rapidly locate a word or phrase. *See Chapter 11.*

Use the family of Transfer commands to load, save, and combine documents and to perform other tasks that involve an entire document or file. *See Chapter 16, "The Family of Transfer Commands."*

Use the Undo command to reverse the effect of your last deletion or editing act. *See Chapter 9.*

Use the family of Window commands to tailor the appearance of a text window to your needs, and to create, move, and eliminate multiple windows on your screen. The Window Option command is one way to turn on and off Word's powerful outlining feature. *See Chapter 17, "The Family of Window Commands."*

Using Windows

Some people are amused that Word lets them divide the screen into as many as eight windows, and that different documents—or parts of the same document—can be loaded into each window and edited. Impressive technology? Yes, they'll concede. But who would need *eight* windows? And how could anyone use a screen that was divided up so much?

Eight does seem to be more windows than most people would want, which is why it's a good number to have possible. In its windowing capability, as in so many aspects of Word, there is power to spare.

Chapter 21, "Power Tools: Multiple Windows," explores the *why* of multiple windows and suggests effective ways to use up to four, or even more, at once. In this chapter, we'll concentrate on the rudiments of *how*, limiting ourselves to just three windows.

With Word, you can:

♦ Divide an existing window with the Window Split Horizontal, Window Split Vertical, and Window Split Footnote commands. Window Split Horizontal divides the selected window from left to right, and Window Split Vertical creates a new window with the boundary running up and down. The Window Split Footnote command partitions off the bottom of a text window and displays footnote text, if any, for the document that is in the upper window.

♦ Remove a window from the screen, with the Window Close command.

♦ Change the size of two or more windows at a time, by shifting the common borders they share, with the Window Move command.

♦ Set a few basic characteristics of text windows, one window at a time (as you saw in Chapter 4), with the Window Options command.

Almost every function of the family of Window commands is performed more quickly and easily with a mouse, but the direction keys can be used with the Window commands to partially simulate the way a mouse marks a spot on the screen. For details on the commands, see Chapter 17, "The Family of Window Commands."

Windows are a highly *visual* feature of Word, so an easy way to learn the Window commands is simply to follow along step by step as we create, move, and eliminate windows. The first series of steps and illustrations demonstrates using multiple windows without a mouse;

the second series accomplishes the same things with a mouse. If you want practice, treat these examples as tutorials.

CONTROLLING MULTIPLE WINDOWS
WITH COMMANDS

Step 1. We begin with a single text window containing a simple document; its only formatting is the built-in format Alt-O, which places a blank line before each paragraph. This is what the screen looks like after the document has been saved with the name FIRST:

```
‖═[·········1·········2·········3·········4·········5·········]·········‖·····7·····╖
‖
‖  This is document 1.
‖
‖  It contains a series of single-spaced paragraphs. The built-
‖  in format Alt-O places a blank line before each paragraph.
‖  If the window is split either horizontally or vertically,
‖  the document can occupy both windows--but scrolling in each
‖  window is independent, so you can look at two parts of the
‖  document at once, or look at different documents.
‖
‖  Seeing more than one part of a document is helpful when you
‖  are moving a passage from one place to another, because you
‖  can see both the origin and the destination.
‖
‖  When a window is split, Word gives the new window the next
‖  available number. The number appears in the upper left
‖  corner. Only one window at a time can contain the selection.
‖  The selection moves to the newest window that is created,
‖  but it will return to the first one if you press F1.█

COMMAND: Alpha Copy Delete Format Gallery Help Insert Jump Library
         Options Print Quit Replace Search Transfer Undo Window
Edit document or press Esc to use menu
Page 1   {}                          ?              Microsoft Word: FIRST.DOC
```

Step 2. Prepare to divide the window into two text windows, using the Window Split Vertical command (press Esc, W, S, and V). When the command is picked, Word proposes to split the window from top to bottom at the location of the selection—in this case, at column 52. Beginning with version 3.0, Word also asks if we want the new window to be cleared. Initially, we want the same document in the new window as was in the old window, so leave the *clear new window* field set to No.

```
‖═[·········1·········2·········3·········4·········5·········]·········‖·····7·····╖
‖
‖  This is document 1.
‖
‖  It contains a series of single-spaced paragraphs. The built-
‖  in format Alt-O places a blank line before each paragraph.
‖
⌐  The selection moves to the newest window that is created,
‖  but it will return to the first one if you press F1.█

WINDOW SPLIT VERTICAL at column: 53█   clear new window: Yes(No)

Enter number
Page 1   {}                          ?              Microsoft Word: FIRST.DOC
```

Step 3. Press the Enter key to carry out the Window Split Vertical command. Note that the new window is labeled in the upper left corner with a highlighted 2, which indicates that it is the active (or "selected") window.

```
1═0 · · · · · · · · 1 · · · · · · · · 2 · · · · · · · · 3 · · · · · · · · 4 · · · · · · · · 5┌2═ · · · · · ] · · · · · · · · 7 · · · · ·┐
  This is document 1.

  It contains a series of single-spaced paragraphs. T║  uilt-
  in format Alt-O places a blank line before each par║  ph.
  If the window is split either horizontally or verti║  y,
  the document can occupy both windows--but scrolling ║  each
  window is independent, so you can look at two parts ║  the
  document at once, or look at different documents.

  Seeing more than one part of a document is helpful   ║  you
  are moving a passage from one place to another, bec  ║  you
  can see both the origin and the destination.
```

Step 4. Window 2 appears to be mostly blank, but it actually contains the same document as Window 1. It's just "looking" at the right side of the document. To adjust the area at which Window 2 looks, press the Home key. This moves the selection to the beginning of a line and forces Word to show it. Suddenly, more of the document appears.

```
1═0 · · · · · · · · 1 · · · · · · · · 2 · · · · · · · · 3 · · · · · · · · 4 · · · · · · · · 5┌2═[ · · · · · · · · 1 · · · · · · · · 2┐
  This is document 1.                                    This is document 1.

  It contains a series of single-spaced paragraphs. T║  It contains a series
  in format Alt-O places a blank line before each par║  in format Alt-O place
  If the window is split either horizontally or verti║  If the window is spli
  the document can occupy both windows--but scrolling ║  the document can occu
  window is independent, so you can look at two parts ║  window is independent
  document at once, or look at different documents.      document at once, or

  Seeing more than one part of a document is helpful     Seeing more than one
  are moving a passage from one place to another, bec    are moving a passage
  can see both the origin and the destination.           can see both the orig

  When a window is split, Word gives the new window t    When a window is spli
  available number. The number appears in the upper      available number. The
  corner. Only one window at a time can contain the s    corner. Only one wind
  The selection moves to the newest window that is cr    The selection moves t
  but it will return to the first one if you press F1    but it will return to

COMMAND: Alpha Copy Delete Format Gallery Help Insert Jump Library
         Options Print Quit Replace Search Transfer Undo Window
Edit document or press Esc to use menu
Page 1   {}                                 ?              Microsoft Word: FIRST.DOC
```

Step 5. We want to create a fresh document in Window 2. We'll use the Transfer Clear Window command to wipe the existing document out of the window: First make sure the selection is in the window you want to clear (Window 2), then press the key sequence Esc, T, C, and W. Because Window 2 is selected, once it is cleared, the name FIRST.DOC vanishes from the lower right corner of the screen, but the document named FIRST remains, at this point in Window 1.

```
1═0·········1·········2·········3·········4·········5┐2═[·········1·········2┐
║                                                    ║║      ◊                 ║
║This is document 1.                                 ║║                        ║
║                                                    ║║                        ║
║It contains a series of single-spaced paragraphs. T║║                        ║
║in format Alt-O places a blank line before each par ║║                        ║
║If the window is split either horizontally or verti ║║                        ║
║the document can occupy both windows--but scrolling  ║║                        ║
║window is independent, so you can look at two parts  ║║                        ║
║document at once, or look at different documents.    ║║                        ║
║                                                     ║║                        ║
║Seeing more than one part of a document is helpful   ║║                        ║
║are moving a passage from one place to another, bec  ║║                        ║
║can see both the origin and the destination.         ║║                        ║
║                                                     ║║                        ║
║When a window is split, Word gives the new window t  ║║                        ║
║available number. The number appears in the upper l  ║║                        ║
║corner. Only one window at a time can contain the s  ║║                        ║
║The selection moves to the newest window that is cr  ║║                        ║
║but it will return to the first one if you press F1  ║║                        ║
└─────────────────────────────────────────────────────┘└────────────────────────┘
COMMAND: Alpha Copy Delete Format Gallery Help Insert Jump Library
         Options Print Quit Replace Search Transfer Undo Window
Edit document or press Esc to use menu
Page 1    {}                            ?              Microsoft Word:
```

If we were to move the selection to Window 1—by pressing the F1 key or by clicking either mouse button when the pointer is in Window 1—the name FIRST.DOC would reappear in the lower corner of the screen (assuming the document had at some point been saved with the Transfer Save command).

Step 6. Window 2 is too small to be very useful, so we'll enlarge it by moving to the left the border between the windows with the Window Move command. Windows are moved by specifying a new location for the lower right corner of a window.

When the Window Move command is picked, Word always proposes the current location of the lower right corner of the selected window—in other words, it proposes no change at all. In our example, we see this proposed:

```
WINDOW MOVE lower right corner of window #: 2█     to row: 20   column: 79
```

So, to resize a window, we often end up moving the corner that is adjacent to, rather than part of, the window we're actually trying to resize. In other words, we sometimes resize a window by changing the shape of its neighbor.

Step 7. Moving the lower right corner of Window 2 would do us no good, and it's impossible in this case anyway because it is at the edge of the screen. We want to make Window 2 bigger, but we'll do it indirectly, by moving the right border of Window 1 to the left. To do this, we type a *1* in the *window #* field:

```
WINDOW MOVE lower right corner of window #: 1█     to row: 20   column: 79
```

Vertical borders are moved right and left by changing column numbers, so we press the Tab key twice to jump to the *column* field:

```
WINDOW MOVE lower right corner of window #: 1     to row: 20   column: 79█
```

Step 8. We could type a column number, but instead let's mark a column with the direction keys. By pressing the Left direction key we cause a special marker that looks like a cursor to move across the bottom border of the text window. As it moves, its position is reflected in the *column* field. We'll stop when we reach 8:

```
1═0·········1·········2·········3·········4·········5═2═[·········1·········2═
║                                                    ║  ▯
║ This is document 1.                                ║
║                                                    ║
║ It contains a series of single-spaced paragraphs. T║
║ in format Alt-0 places a blank line before each par║
║ If the window is split either horizontally or verti║
║ the document can occupy both windows--but scrolling ║
║ window is independent, so you can look at two parts║
║ document at once, or look at different documents.  ║
║                                                    ║
║ Seeing more than one part of a document is helpful ║
║ are moving a passage from one place to another, bec║
║ can see both the origin and the destination.       ║
║                                                    ║
║ When a window is split, Word gives the new window t║
║ available number. The number appears in the upper l║
║ corner. Only one window at a time can contain the s║
║ The selection moves to the newest window that is cr║
║ but it will return to the first one if you press F1║
WINDOW MOVE lower right corner of window #: 1     to row: 20   column: 8

Enter number
Page 1   {}                         ?          Microsoft Word:
```

Step 9. Press the Enter key to carry out the Window Move command and reposition the window border. Now the blank Window 2 fills most of the screen, and gives plenty of space for writing or editing.

```
1═0····2═[·········1·········2·········3·········4·········5··········]·····═
║     ║  ▯
║ This║
║     ║
║ It co║
║ in fo║
║ If th║
║ the d║
║ windo║
║ docum║
║     ║
║ Seein║
║ are m║
║ can s║
║     ║
║ When ║
║ avail║
║ corne║
║ The s║
║ but i║
COMMAND: Alpha Copy Delete Format Gallery Help Insert Jump Library
         Options Print Quit Replace Search Transfer Undo Window
Edit document or press Esc to use menu
Page 1   {}                         ?          Microsoft Word:
```

Step 10. We type a second document, this time in Window 2. We use the built-in formats Alt-2 and Alt-F to make the paragraphs double-spaced with indented first lines.

```
1═0····─2═[····¦····1·········2·········3·········4·········5·········]······─
 This              This is Document 2. No name is displayed in the lower

 It co       right corner of the screen because it hasn't been saved yet.
 in fo
 If th              This document is a series of double-spaced paragraphs
 the d
 windo       with the first line of each paragraph indented. By moving
 docum
             the window border back and forth you can compare the
 Seein
 are M       contents of this window with the document in the other one.
 can s
                    Want to see a footnote window?█
 When        ♦
 avail
 corne
 The s
 but i
─────────────────────────────────────────────────────────────────────
COMMAND: Alpha Copy Delete Format Gallery Help Insert Jump Library
         Options Print Quit Replace Search Transfer Undo Window
Edit document or press Esc to use menu
Page 1   {}                          ?               Microsoft Word:
```

Step 11. Create a footnote window with the Window Split Footnote command (Esc, W, S, and F). Word proposes that we split the window at the present line number of the selection, in this case, line 14:

WINDOW SPLIT FOOTNOTE at line: **14**█

We want the split farther down, so press the down direction key to move a special marker along the left border of the window. As the marker moves, the line number ("row" number in the earliest versions of Word) shown in the command field reflects the marker's position. At line 16, we stop:

```
 If th              This document is a series of double-spaced paragraphs
 the d
 windo       with the first line of each paragraph indented. By moving
 docum
             the window border back and forth you can compare the
 Seein
 are M       contents of this window with the document in the other one.
 can s
                    Want to see a footnote window?█
 When        ♦
 avail ║█
 corne
 The s
 but i
─────────────────────────────────────────────────────────────────────
WINDOW SPLIT FOOTNOTE at line: **16**

Enter number
Page 1   {}                          ?               Microsoft Word:
```

Step 12. Press the Enter key to execute the Window Split Footnote command. A special upper border of hyphens appears—the border of a footnote window. (If the original window had a ruler displayed, there will be numbers, along with hyphens, in the footnote window border.)

```
Seein │││ contents of this window with the document in the other one.
are M │││
can s │││      Want to see a footnote window?█
      │││
When  │││   ♦
avail ║3--0---------1---------2---------3---------4---------5---------6------
corne ║    ♦
The s ║
but i ║

COMMAND: Alpha Copy Delete Format Gallery Help Insert Jump Library
         Options Print Quit Replace Search Transfer Undo Window
Edit document or press Esc to use menu
Page 1   {}                         ?              Microsoft Word:
```

NOTE: If we had used the Window Split Horizontal command, a new document window, rather than a footnote window, would have been created in the same location.

Step 13. If we use the Format Footnote command to place a footnote reference mark, such as an asterisk or a superscripted 1, in the text in Document 2, the corresponding footnote text can be typed—and viewed—in the footnote window. When the footnote text has been typed, the Jump Footnote command returns us to the footnote reference mark in the upper window.

```
1═0····⌐2═[····¦····1·········2·········3·········4·········5·········]······⌐
This │││     This is Document 2. No name is displayed in the lower
     │││
It co │││ right corner of the screen because it hasn't been saved yet.
in fo │││
If th │││     This document is a series of double-spaced paragraphs
the d │││
windo │││ with the first line of each paragraph indented. By moving
docum │││
     │││ the window border back and forth you can compare the
Seein │││
are M │││ contents of this window with the document in the other one.
can s │││
     │││      Want to see a footnote window?⌐!
When  │││   ♦
avail ║3--[---------1---------2---------3---------4---------5---------]------
corne ║ ¹This is a footnote, appearing in the footnote window. The
The s ║ "1" is the "footnote reference mark."  It has been formatted
but i ║ to be superscripted, using the Format Character command.

COMMAND: Alpha Copy Delete Format Gallery Help Insert Jump Library
         Options Print Quit Replace Search Transfer Undo Window
Edit document or press Esc to use menu
Page 1   {}                         ?              Microsoft Word:
```

Step 14. Any of the three windows can be removed with the Window Close command. Once a window is closed, its screen space is taken over by adjoining windows. We close Window 1, the original window, by using the Window Close command (Esc, W, and C) and typing the number 1. The following illustration shows how the screen appears before we press the Enter key:

```
1═0····╥2═[····¦····1·········2·········3·········4·········5··········]······╖
║                                                                             ║
  This  ║║        This is Document 2. No name is displayed in the lower        ║
        ║║                                                                     
  It co ║║    right corner of the screen because it hasn't been saved yet.     
  in fo ║║                                                                     
  If th ║║        This document is a series of double-spaced paragraphs        
  the d ║║                                                                     
  windo ║║    with the first line of each paragraph indented. By moving        
  docum ║║                                                                     
        ║║        the window border back and forth you can compare the         
  Seein ║║                                                                     
  are m ║║    contents of this window with the document in the other one.      
  can s ║║                                                                     
        ║║        Want to see a footnote window?█                              
  When  ║║    ♦                                                                 
  avail ║3--[---------1---------2---------3---------4---------5---------]------
  corne ║  ¹This is a footnote, appearing in the footnote window. The          
  The s ║  "1" is the "footnote reference mark."  It has been formatted         
  but i ║  to be superscripted, using the Format Character command.            
```

WINDOW CLOSE window number: 1█

Enter number
Page 1   {}   ?   Microsoft Word:

Step 15. Once we press the Enter key, what had been Window 1 vanishes and the remaining two windows expand to full width. The windows are renumbered automatically by Word.

```
1═[····¦····1·········2·········3·········4·········5··········]·········7·····╖
║                                                                             ║
         This is Document 2. No name is displayed in the lower                
                                                                              
     right corner of the screen because it hasn't been saved yet.             
                                                                              
         This document is a series of double-spaced paragraphs                
                                                                              
     with the first line of each paragraph indented. By moving                
                                                                              
     the window border back and forth you can compare the                     
                                                                              
     contents of this window with the document in the other one.              
                                                                              
         Want to see a footnote window?█                                      
     ♦                                                                        
2--0---------1---------2---------3---------4---------5---------6---------7-----
  ¹This is a footnote, appearing in the footnote window. The                   
  "1" is the "footnote reference mark."  It has been formatted                 
  to be superscripted, using the Format Character command.                    
```

COMMAND: Alpha Copy Delete Format Gallery Help Insert Jump Library
         Options Print Quit Replace Search Transfer Undo Window
Edit document or press Esc to use menu
Page 1   {}   ?   Microsoft Word:

CONTROLLING MULTIPLE WINDOWS WITH A MOUSE

The same things can be accomplished more rapidly with a mouse. In this series of steps, the Window commands aren't used at all. The order of some steps has been changed to demonstrate additional techniques. NOTE: The following illustrations show the mouse pointer as it appears with a computer using graphics capabilities. Otherwise, the mouse pointer is a blinking square or rectangle.

Step 1. Our first objective is to split the original window vertically, but this time with the border far enough to the left that Window 2 is large to begin with. To do this, position the mouse pointer on the top border of the window, above the word *is* in the first sentence. At this place on the screen, the pointer appears as a box, symbolizing the potential to manipulate a window.

```
⊩=[····□···1·········2·········3·········4·········5·········]·········7·····]
║ This is document 1.
║
║ It contains a series of single-spaced paragraphs. The built-
║ in format Alt-O places a blank line before each paragraph.
║ If the window is split either horizontally or vertically,
║ the document can occupy both windows--but scrolling in each
║ window is independent, so you can look at two parts of the
║ document at once, or look at different documents.
║
║ Seeing more than one part of a document is helpful when you
║ are moving a passage from one place to another, because you
║ can see both the origin and the destination.
║
║ When a window is split, Word gives the new window the next
║ available number. The number appears in the upper left
║ corner. Only one window at a time can contain the selection.
║ The selection moves to the newest window that is created,
║ but it will return to the first one if you press F1.■
COMMAND: Alpha Copy Delete Format Gallery Help Insert Jump Library
        Options Print Quit Replace Search Transfer Undo Window
Edit document or press Esc to use menu
Page 1   {}                        ?            Microsoft Word: FIRST.DOC
```

Step 2. Click the left mouse button to create a new text window at the location of the mouse pointer. If you click the right button, the window will be cleared (beginning with version 3.0). We don't want that yet. After clicking with the left button, there are two windows containing the same document, but the beginnings of the lines don't show in Window 2.

```
1=0···╥2=1·········2·········3·········4·········5·········]·········7·····]
║ This ║║ ocument 1.
║ It co ║║ ns a series of single-spaced paragraphs. The built-        ▶
║ in fo ║║   Alt-O places a blank line before each paragraph.
║ If th ║║ ndow is split either horizontally or vertically,
║ the d ║║ ent can occupy both windows--but scrolling in each
║ windo ║║    independent, so you can look at two parts of the
║ docum ║║ at once, or look at different documents.
```

We solved this problem without a mouse by pressing the Home key. We'll solve it now by moving the mouse pointer to the bottom border of the text window and clicking the left mouse button, which scrolls the document horizontally, and brings words into view from beyond the left window border. At this place on the screen the mouse pointer becomes a double-headed arrow (if you have graphics capabilities).

```
1═0····╥2═[·············1·········2·········3·········4·········5·········]·····╥
║       ║                                                                       ║
║ This  ║║  This is document 1.                                                 ║
║       ║║                                                                      ║
║ It co ║║  It contains a series of single-spaced paragraphs. The built-        ║
║ in fo ║║  in format Alt-0 places a blank line before each paragraph.          ║
║ If th ║║  If the window is split either horizontally or vertically,           ║
║ the d ║║  the document can occupy both windows--but scrolling in each         ║
║ windo ║║  window is independent, so you can look at two parts of the          ║
║ docum ║║  document at once, or look at different documents.                   ║
║       ║║                                                                      ║
║ Seein ║║  Seeing more than one part of a document is helpful when you         ║
║ are m ║║  are moving a passage from one place to another, because you         ║
║ can s ║║  can see both the origin and the destination.                        ║
║       ║║                                                                      ║
║ When  ║║  When a window is split, Word gives the new window the next          ║
║ avail ║║  available number. The number appears in the upper left              ║
║ corne ║║  corner. Only one window at a time can contain the selection.        ║
║ The s ║║  The selection moves to the newest window that is created,           ║
║ but i ║║  but it will return to the first one if you press F1.                ║
╨───────╨──────────────────────────────────────────┼──────────────────────────╨
COMMAND: Alpha Copy Delete Format Gallery Help Insert Jump Library
         Options Print Quit Replace Search Transfer Undo Window
Edit document or press Esc to use menu
Page 1    {}                              ?              Microsoft Word: FIRST.DOC
```

Step 3. We could edit the document now, but instead let's erase it from Window 2 with the Transfer Clear Window command. Click the left mouse button with the pointer on the command names Transfer, Clear, and Window, in sequence.

```
║ When  ║║  When a window is split, Word gives the new window the next          ║
║ avail ║║  available number. The number appears in the upper left              ║
║ corne ║║  corner. Only one window at a time can contain the selection.        ║
║ The s ║║  The selection moves to the newest window that is created,           ║
║ but i ║║  but it will return to the first one if you press F1.                ║
╨───────╨──────────────────────────────────────────────────────────────────────╨
TRANSFER CLEAR: ▓▓▓ Window

Select option or type command letter
Page 1    {}                              ?              Microsoft Word: FIRST.DOC
```

NOTE: When there is only a single window on the screen, it can be cleared by positioning the mouse pointer on the top or right window border, and clicking both buttons.

Step 4. After the window is cleared, we type Document 2. Then, we position the mouse pointer on the right border of the text window. We can click the left mouse button to create a horizontal text window, click the right mouse button to create a horizontal text window that is already cleared of content, or hold down the Shift key and click either mouse button to create a footnote window. NOTE: Prior to version 3.0 of Word, clicking the right mouse button created a footnote window.

```
1═0····┐2═[·····¦·····1··········2··········3··········4··········5··········]······┐
 This   ║     This is Document 2. No name is displayed in the lower          ║
 It co  ║  right corner of the screen because it hasnt been saved yet.       ║
 in fo  ║                                                                    ║
 If th  ║     This document is a series of double-spaced paragraphs          ║
 the d  ║                                                                    ║
 windo  ║  with the first line of each paragraph indented. By moving         ║
 docum  ║                                                                    ║
        ║  the window back and forth you can compare the contents of         ║
 Seein  ║                                                                    ║
 are m  ║  this window with the document in the other one.                   ║
 can s  ║                                                                    ║
        ║     Want to see a footnote window?█                                ║
 When   ║  ♦                                                                 ║
 avail  ║                                                                    ║
 corne  ║                                                                 □  ║
 The s  ║                                                                    ║
 but i  ║                                                                    ║
COMMAND: Alpha Copy Delete Format Gallery Help Insert Jump Library
         Options Print Quit Replace Search Transfer Undo Window
Edit document or press Esc to use menu
Page 1   {}                              ?              Microsoft Word:
```

Step 5. We hold down the Shift key and click the right mouse button to create a footnote window at line 16, indicated by the mouse pointer. We enter footnote text as we did without the mouse, using the Format Footnote and Jump Footnote commands. When done, we use the Jump Footnote command to select the footnote reference mark in the document.

Step 6. Finally, we place the mouse pointer on the right border of Window 1.

```
1═[····┐2═[·····¦·····1··········2··········3··········4··········5··········]······┐
 This   ║     This is Document 2. No name is displayed in the lower          ║
 It co  ║  right corner of the screen because it hasnt been saved yet.       ║
 in fo  ║                                                                    ║
 If th  ║     This document is a series of double-spaced paragraphs          ║
 the d  ║                                                                    ║
 windo  ║  with the first line of each paragraph indented. By moving         ║
 docum  ║                                                                    ║
        ║  the window back and forth you can compare the contents of         ║
 Seein  ║                                                                    ║
 are m  ║  this window with the document in the other one.                   ║
 can s  ║                                                                    ║
        ║     Want to see a footnote window?!█                               ║
 When   ║  ♦                                                                 ║
 avail 3--[----------1---------2---------3---------4---------5---------]------
 corne  ║  ¹This is a footnote, appearing in the footnote window. The        ║
 The s  ║  "1" is the "footnote reference mark." It has been formatted       ║
 but i  ║  to be superscripted, using the Format Character command.          ║
COMMAND: Alpha Copy Delete Format Gallery Help Insert Jump Library
         Options Print Quit Replace Search Transfer Undo Window
Edit document or press Esc to use menu
Page 1   {}                              ?              Microsoft Word:
```

When we click both mouse buttons with the pointer in this position, Window 1 closes, and the other windows widen and are renumbered. That's how the mouse does the job of the Window Close command.

Step 7. We haven't yet moved a window border with the mouse. The concept is the same as with the Window Move command: Specify a new location for the lower right corner of a window. But with the mouse pointer we just pull the corner to where we want it. You must have more than one window on the screen. Start by positioning the pointer on the lower right corner of the appropriate window. If you are running Word with graphics, the mouse pointer looks like four arrows pointing in different directions.

```
║╪[····¦····1·········2·········3·········4·········5·········]·········7·····╫
║
          This is Document 2. No name is displayed in the lower

   right corner of the screen because it hasnt been saved yet.

          This document is a series of double-spaced paragraphs

   with the first line of each paragraph indented. By moving

   the window back and forth you can compare the contents of

   this window with the document in the other one.

          Want to see a footnote window?▌
 ♦
2--0---------1---------2---------3---------4---------5---------6---------7----⟨⊕⟩
#  ¹This is a footnote, appearing in the footnote window. The
   "1" is the "footnote reference mark." It has been formatted
   to be superscripted, using the Format Character command.
```
COMMAND: Alpha Copy Delete Format Gallery Help Insert Jump Library
         Options Print Quit Replace Search Transfer Undo Window
Edit document or press Esc to use menu
Page 1   {}   ?   Microsoft Word:

Step 8. Now, press and hold down either mouse button. Roll the mouse on the desktop so that the pointer moves. When you release the button, the window border will move to that position.

As you'll discover in Chapters 17 and 21, there are more efficient ways to manipulate windows than the steps outlined in the preceding tutorials. However, the steps you've just used are an easy way to start.

If you're still among the skeptics, or if you suspect there's something frivolous about such an abundance of windowing features, you can always ignore the capabilities you don't think you need. Someday, when you face some special problem or opportunity, you may discover you can use them after all.

CHAPTER EIGHT

Keep in Mind

As you leave Part I, you embark on a journey—the itinerary of which you may design for yourself—through the features of Word. It is an odyssey of many rewards. But before you know Word well, you may find yourself in situations from which you don't know how to escape. You may feel you've taken the wrong turn in a labyrinth. Don't panic. Don't pull out the plug. Don't reboot your computer. Chances are nothing is wrong, even if nothing at the moment seems right.

This chapter is a collection of miscellany with one purpose: to help you cope with situations that may be confusing. If you get lost during your exploration of Word, refer back to this chapter to see if a tip here doesn't help you. The first four tips give specific advice, the next four are more conceptual, and the last one helps you recover files you believe you've lost.

Tip #1: An escape plan

The following steps offer a contingency plan that will free you from almost any situation you don't understand and deposit you back in your document, so you can return to writing or editing. Not all the steps are necessary in every situation, but followed in the order presented here, they are almost an all-purpose escape plan. Even if you don't understand the steps, you can follow them blindly back to safe ground. Usually you can omit the first two steps unless your problem involves one of the Print commands:

1. If your printer is off, turn it on. If your printer is on, turn it off and back on.
2. Hold down Ctrl and press Scroll Lock. Wait a moment and repeat.
3. Press Esc twice.
4. Press E (for Exit).
5. Press Esc twice.
6. If the lower left corner of the screen says *OUTLINE*, *Level*, or *Text*, hold down the Shift key and press the F2 key.
7. Press A (for Alpha).
8. Press the Left direction key, then the Right direction key.

Don't worry about the bleeping alarm sound that may accompany some of the steps. The alarm means only that you're attempting something that's not possible. As alarms go, it's unalarming.

NOTE: If you are using Library Spell (in other words, running the spelling checker through Word instead of separately) and can't get free, press Esc, then press Q, followed by Y. (If you're using a floppy-disk version, you'll be prompted to swap the Word disk for the Spell disk and press Y again.)

Tip #2: Make invisible characters visible

This tip was part of setting options in Chapter 4, "Setting Up." It will help you if you are a beginner. If you have Word version number 2.0 or higher, set the Options command's *visible* field to *Partial*. If you have an earlier version of Word, set the Options *visible* field to *Yes*. Normally invisible characters, such as paragraph marks, will then be visible on the screen.

Visible paragraph marks clutter the screen, so Word gives you the choice of seeing them or not. But out of sight shouldn't be out of mind, because the marks are the storage places for paragraph formatting. And until you're experienced with Word, it's easy to inadvertently delete a paragraph mark that you can't see.

What happens when a paragraph mark is deleted? The paragraphs immediately preceding and following the mark merge into a single paragraph. This merging poses little problem if the two paragraphs were formatted identically before the mark was deleted. But if they were not, eliminating the mark causes a sudden change in text appearance, as the newly combined paragraph takes on the format of the original second paragraph. If you encounter this problem, try the Undo command (press Esc, followed by U). Better to avoid the problem altogether, though, by keeping paragraph marks visible so they won't be deleted inadvertently.

Tip #3: Keep modes off

Recall from Chapter 2 that six keys and key combinations turn special modes on and off. Because they affect the way Word operates, they should all be turned off except when you have reason to use them. Look at the screen's bottom line, just left of *Microsoft Word:*, and make sure none of these codes is displayed: CS, EX, NL, SL, CL, or OT. Some computers also have lights on the keyboard that indicate when some of these special mode keys are turned on. Turn these modes off (or on) as follows:

- ◆ *CS, the Column Select mode.* Hold down the Shift key and press the F6 key.
- ◆ *EX, the EXtend selection mode.* Press the F6 key.
- ◆ *NL, Numeric Lock.* Press the Num Lock key.
- ◆ *SL, Scroll Lock.* Press the Scroll Lock key.
- ◆ *CL, Caps Lock.* Press the Caps Lock key.
- ◆ *OT, OverType mode.* Press the F5 key.

The CS mode is new, beginning with version 3.0 of Word. Also beginning with version 3.0 is an outlining feature that amounts to a mode. Unless you mean to use it, turn off outlining if it is on by holding down the Shift key and pressing the F2 key. The outlining mode is on when any of the following words appear in the lower left corner of the screen: *OUTLINE*, *Level*, or *Text*.

Tip #4: Move away from the final division mark

A double line of dots that extends across the width of the text window is a division mark, which contains page-layout information for the text preceding it. This formatting can be changed with the Format Division command(s) or by applying a division style from a style sheet. If you select any part of a division mark, the whole line of dots is highlighted. That's because, wide as the division mark is on the screen, Word considers it a single character.

Sometimes a division mark may appear at the end of a document, just before the diamond-shaped end mark. It may cling to the end of the document's final paragraph. Adding text at the location of one can be unnerving to newcomers. If you don't want to bump into the mark, select it and press the Enter key several times.

NOTE: When a document ends in a division mark, write and edit only before the mark. The mark controls the page layout of the paragraphs above it, so any writing you do below the division mark may not have the division (page) formatting.

The next four tips are more conceptual. Keeping them in mind will help you understand and control Word.

Tip #5: Distinguish between margins and indents

In Word:

♦ A left or right *margin* is part of division formatting and applies to all text on the page except running heads. Margins help shape page design and are controlled with the Format Division Margins command (or, in older versions of Word, the Format Division command).

♦ An *indent* is part of paragraph formatting, and hence can be changed at your will from paragraph to paragraph. Use indents when you want to insert more space to the left or right of a paragraph than page (division) formatting provides. Indents are of three types, left, right, and first-line, and are controlled with the Format Paragraph command. (Left and right indents apply to every line of a paragraph, while the first-line indent affects only a paragraph's first line.)

If you let the differences between margins and indents become fuzzy in your mind, or if you think of margins when you mean indents, you might use the wrong command to format your text or do more work than you need to. Pay special attention if you're coming to Word from a word processor that doesn't distinguish between margins and indents. With some programs you must change margins even when you want only a single paragraph indented. Word is conceptually different—and much more flexible.

Tip #6: Distinguish between points and pitch

If you use a daisy-wheel printer or otherwise manually change typefaces, learn to distinguish between the two ways—points and pitch—Word measures type size. Both measurements are based on the inch, but approach it differently:

♦ Typographically, a point is $\frac{1}{72}$ of an inch. The higher the point number, the taller the characters.

♦ Pitch is a unit of width, as in 10 pitch or 12 pitch. The number tells how many characters will fit side by side in an inch of space. The higher the pitch number, the more characters to the inch, and generally the smaller the width of each character.

If you are used to thinking in terms of typewriters, you may know that "normal" 10-pitch type is called Pica, and "normal" 12-pitch type is called Elite. Pica type is taller and wider than Elite. Keep this in mind, and remember that for most printers Word assumes:

> Pica is 12 point, but 10 pitch.
> Elite is 10 point, but 12 pitch.

When you are formatting documents, you pick type size by specifying a *point* size in the *font size* field of the Format Character command. Word prompts you with the message *Enter font size in points or select from list.* Although you format in points, for your convenience Word uses pitch in its messages that refer to type sizes on a daisy-wheel printer. For example, the "normal" typeface with most printers is 12-*point* Pica, which is the same as 10-*pitch* Pica. When you check the character formatting of the document with the Format Character command, Word displays the type size in points:

```
font name: Pica          font size: 12
```

But when Word reminds you to mount the proper daisy wheel on your printer, it asks for the type in pitch, just as the daisy wheel itself is labeled:

```
Enter Y after mounting Pica 10
```

Tip #7: Tabbing and spacing in tables

When you are using type that is proportionally spaced, justified, or of more than one pitch (width), characters all show on the screen as if they're the same width, even if they aren't. This can cause a table that is created with Spacebar spaces to be printed as a ragged mess, even though it looks well ordered on the screen. In this case, consider lining up tabular text using the Tab key and the Format Tabs Set command (or, better yet, a style-sheet style).

If you use only one typeface throughout a document, and it is neither proportionally spaced nor justified, the screen's accuracy limitation isn't a problem. You can use the Spacebar to line up tabular material, because a Spacebar space will be printed the same width as every other space in the document—from a lowercase *i* or a period to a capital *M* or *W*.

Tip #8: Disks, files, and Word

With most word processors, you choose between long documents and speedy editing: The more words in a document, the more slowly the computer responds to instructions. In contrast, because of the unusual way it stores documents, Word can manipulate five pages or 100 with equal speed. But, editing slows when you haven't saved your document recently. While other word processors reward you for keeping documents short, Word rewards you for saving periodically—always a wise practice anyway.

The following paragraphs offer you a descent into the inner world of Microsoft Word. The information here is for the experienced user who is curious about what happens when a document is saved, why Word sometimes hesitates before responding, and what it means when Word displays a message that begins with the words *Enter Y to retry access.*

What happens when you work

Suppose you have a computer with two floppy-disk drives. You load Word into the computer's memory from the Program disk in drive A, and you load an existing document into memory from a document disk in drive B. Then, suppose you add editing changes with the keyboard. When you finish editing, you save the updated document back on the disk in drive B, with the same document name. All these activities involve transferring information from one place to another, and are pretty obvious after you've used Word for a while. But some other, invisible, transfers also take place:

♦ *Drive A.* When you first start Word, it loads into memory a file called MW.INI from the Program disk in drive A. This file tells Word how options were set the last time the program was used. One of the options is the printer you use, the name of which is stored in MW.INI and reflected in the Print Options command's *printer* field. Word loads the corresponding printer description file (such as EPSONRX.PRD) from the Program disk. If you are using a hard-disk system, the directory in which the Word program is stored (or, prior to version 3.0, a directory called MSTOOLS), replaces the Program disk.

♦ *Drive B.* When you load a document for editing, Word may automatically load a matching style sheet (a file with the extension .STY) and, when you first start Word, a glossary file called NORMAL.GLY from the disk in drive B. If you're using a hard-disk system, Word will look for these files in the logged directory—that is, the directory that appears in the Transfer Options command's *setup* field.

♦ *Overlays.* If your computer has less than 320K of available memory, certain parts of Word, called overlays, are loaded into the computer's memory when needed, and are discarded when unneeded. If, when you issue a command or press a key that hasn't been used for a while, Word hesitates for a moment and drive A spins, chances are an overlay is being loaded. Overlays don't slow Word much if you have a hard disk.

♦ *Scratch file.* As you write and edit, Word gathers new characters in groups of 1,024 and sends them to a temporary "scratch file" on the Program disk. These transfers explain why, on floppy-drive systems, drive A periodically turns on for a few moments.

During those moments, Word may lag behind and not display new text as fast as you type it. (And on a PCjr, you can't type at all during those times.) Word creates the scratch file—and occasional other files with similar functions—and gives them names beginning with MW, followed by six numerals and the extension .TMP. Word automatically deletes these files when you quit the program. Normally, you are unaware of these .TMP files, but they're important, as you'll see in the next tip.

♦ *Memory.* The content of the original document on the disk in drive B (or whatever drive shows in Transfer Options) is unaffected during editing. Changes in document content and format are reflected on the screen and kept in memory, but they aren't recorded in the document file until the document is saved on disk. Because alterations are made only in the computer's memory, Word rapidly handles even massive editing changes—such as justifying or unjustifying a 200-page document—in just a few seconds. When a lot of the computer's memory fills up, the bottom line of the screen warns you to save the document. Depending on your version of Word, either the word *SAVE* appears or the indicator of available (*% Free*) memory drops to 60% or less. You should then use the Transfer Save command.

♦ *Saving.* Editing changes aren't transferred from memory to the document file until the document is saved. Prior to version 3.0, this meant Word took longer to save documents than many word processors, but now—due to improved programming—it is among the fastest. Here's what happens when you use the Transfer Save command. First, Word changes the file name extension of the original document on the disk in drive B from .DOC to .BAK. Then, it combines a copy of the original document with both the editing changes in the computer's memory and the new text stored in the scratch file. As these three sources are integrated, they are recorded on the disk in drive B with a special temporary name. When the saving is complete, Word changes the name to that of the original document, with the file name extension .DOC.

Word stores most of the formatting information about a document at the end of the file, and this is the last part of the document to be recorded on disk during a Transfer Save operation. When Word is nearly through saving, there is a moment, maybe longer, when the computer is deathly still: The drives aren't turning and nothing on the screen is changing. During this time, Word figures out the document's formatting. When the drive comes alive again, it is only for a moment, while formatting is recorded. The save is complete.

Saving your work

Saving frees a lot of the computer's memory. On versions of Word beginning with 1.15, it also resets the scratch file so that it doesn't grow indefinitely as you type in keystrokes. But to stop the growing scratch file in versions 1.0 and 1.1, you must either quit or execute the Transfer Clear All command (but only after saving any documents, style sheets, or glossary entries that have unsaved editing changes).

One way or another, you must reset your scratch file periodically, because the Program disk has only so much room on it, and in any case the file can't grow to more than about 64,000 characters. This should present no problem if you use the Transfer Save command periodically and your version of Word is 1.15, 2.0, 3.0 or higher. But if your version is 1.0 or 1.10 and if you're a fast typist, you need to deliberately clear the scratch file every three hours or so—sooner if the directory of the Program disk shows you have less than 64K of free space on it (before you start Word). If the scratch file isn't cleared, eventually a *Disk Full* or *Program Disk Full* message will bring editing to a screeching halt.

Enter Y...

When Word can't find a disk file (such as a .TMP file) where it expects to, it pauses and displays the name of the needed file at the end of the message *Enter Y to retry access to FILENAME*.

This message can mean a disk file has been damaged and is unreadable, but usually the message is routine. You often see it when you've switched document disks during the editing session. In this case, it means Word needs a file on a disk that's been removed. You can be pretty sure this is what's happening if the file name in the message has the extension .DOC, .BAK, or .TMP. Other times, the message means you have requested on-screen help and the MW.HLP file is not on the Program disk, or it means you've specified a printer, but the corresponding printer description (.PRD) file isn't on the Program disk.

If you see this message, locate the disk with the needed file, insert it in the proper drive, and press the letter Y. Later—sometimes only a moment later—you may get another *Enter Y...* message prompting you to swap disks again. This is normal, too.

When your disk is full

When you fill up a document disk, you can use the Transfer Delete command to eliminate unneeded files, as long as the files haven't been used since Word was started. Often, however, you may prefer to save the document you're editing on a different disk. Remove the document disk, put another *formatted* disk in the appropriate drive, and use the Transfer Save command. This procedure is bound to generate a slew of *Enter Y...* messages prompting you to switch back and forth between the full disk, which contains needed documents with the extensions .DOC and .BAK, and the new disk, on which Word is saving the new file with a temporary name.

A final note

A document disk fills up faster than you might expect, because Word maintains on it a complete backup copy of every document you edit, and because Word sometimes also records temporary files on the document disk during the course of editing. These temporary files are erased before you return to DOS, but meanwhile they eat up disk space. Try to use a disk that has at least three times as much free space as you expect the document length to reach. Erase .TMP files that remain on the disk by accident. And if you need an excuse for the capacity and speed of a hard disk, look no further.

Tip #9: Salvaging files with Debug

Have you ever "lost" part of a document to your computer? You can sacrifice a considerable amount of unsaved work if the power fails during an editing session, or if you're forced to reboot the computer for some reason (such as failing to use the Transfer Save command when the *SAVE* message appears). However, you may be able to salvage much or most of what you thought you'd lost by using the Debug program that comes with DOS.

First, here's a word of warning for people using version 2.0: If you hope to recover lost work, do not restart Word right away after you reboot your computer. Your work might be held in a .TMP file and, in version 2.0 only, restarting Word erases all .TMP files. (Quitting with the Quit command in any version of Word also erases .TMP files.) Because you're attempting to recover lost work, this discussion assumes you didn't quit in an orderly way. If you do restart Word 2.0, you may still be able to recover the .TMP files if you have a program, such as the Norton Utilities NU.COM or UNERASE.COM, that restores erased files.

To use Debug, instead of starting Word check the document disk or your Word Program disk for one or more files with the extension .TMP. A typical one might be MW412803.TMP. If there are several, look for those with a date and time matching that of the editing session in which you had difficulties.

Although this .TMP file may contain some of the lost information, you can't load it directly into Word. If you try, Word may crash or display one of these messages: *Not a valid file* or *Enter Y to create file.* Instead, use Debug as follows to edit some coded information at the beginning of the .TMP file, changing it from a *formatted* Word file, but one with a defect that makes Word unable to use it, to an *unformatted* file that Word can use.

Now, assuming the DOS disk containing the program DEBUG.COM is in drive A and the file MW412803.TMP is on the disk in drive B, follow these steps:

1. Use the DOS Copy command to copy the file to the DOS disk, at the same time changing the name so that it does not end in .TMP. For example, you can copy the file and change its name to TRYSAVE.DOC in one step by typing, at the DOS prompt: *copy b: mw412803.tmp trysave.doc.* NOTE: If you are using a hard disk and DEBUG.COM is in a subdirectory that is specified in the path, merely rename MW412803.TMP to TRYSAVE.DOC, using the DOS Rename (REN) command.

2. Type *debug* followed by a space, type the name of the file (*trysave.doc*), and then press Enter. The computer responds with a hyphen, which is Debug's prompt.

3. After the hyphen, type *e100* and press Enter. This command tells Debug to edit the file, beginning with the first character. Debug will display a cluster of characters on the next line.

4. Type *0* (zero) and then press the Spacebar. Repeat the *0-Spacebar* combination seven times, for a total of eight; then press Enter.

5. At the hyphen, type *w* and press Enter. This command tells Debug to write to the disk the changes (the zeroes you typed) you made to the file. You'll see a *Writing (number of) bytes* message, followed on the next line by another hyphen.

6. Type *q* to quit Debug.

You're through with Debug, and your screen should record the story of what you've done so far—something like this:

```
A)copy b:mw412803.tmp trysave.doc

A)debug trysave.doc
-e100
1241:0100  00.0    00.0    00.0    00.0    20.0    20.0    4D.0    50.0
1241:0108  4C.
-w
Writing 0C00 bytes
-q

A)
```

NOTE: The zeroes you type are the zeroes following the double digits in the fourth line of the preceding screen illustration. The odd-looking numbers, such as 4D and 0C00, are numbers in the base-16 (hexadecimal) system often used by computers.

7. Restart Word and load the backup (.BAK) copy, if there is one, of the document you lost work from. For example, if you were writing a document called GOODLUCK.DOC when the power failed or you rebooted, it is gone. But if you saved the document at some point before losing it, you should load the file GOODLUCK.BAK. This file contains your document as it was the last time you saved it. Use the Transfer Rename command to change the extension from .BAK to .DOC.

8. Open a second window, and load into it the document you modified with Debug— in this case, TRYSAVE.DOC. In it will be many bizarre-looking characters that aren't understandable to you (or me). Ignore them, and look for passages of text you typed and want to recover. When you find such a passage, move it from TRYSAVE.DOC to the earlier version of the document (GOODLUCK.DOC) that's in the other window.

Move as many desired passages as you can find from the recovered file to the backup file. Piecing the (renamed) .BAK and .TMP files together this way often restores much or most of the "lost" text.

NOTE: Beginning with version 3.0, Word no longer deletes .TMP files when you first start the program. This is because now Word can be used on a network of several computers, and if Word deleted .TMP files whenever one person started the program, it could wipe out information needed by other users. For this reason, every few weeks (or more often), you may want to check your Word program disk or hard-disk directory for unneeded .TMP files. (You may not find any, because when you use the Quit command, Word erases the .TMP files it created in that particular editing session.)

II

Using

Much of Word's flexibility comes from the
diversity of its commands. Here, you learn
the ins and outs of using each of them.

The Simplest Commands: Alpha, Quit, Undo

Three of Word's commands are particularly simple to use. Two of them, Alpha and Quit, are essential. The third, Undo, soon seems essential. Word carries out each command as soon as you choose it from the Edit menu. They have no submenus, and there is no need to press the Enter key for any of them.

ALPHA

```
COMMAND: Alpha Copy Delete Format Gallery Help Insert Jump Library
         |Options Print Quit Replace Search Transfer Undo Window
       ┌─┘
       │
```
(Carried out as soon as it is picked)

Alpha, the first command in the Edit menu, has only one purpose: to move you from the command area to the text area. Pick Alpha when you have finished using other Edit-menu commands and wish to resume writing or editing. Alpha is the *functional* opposite of the Esc key, which jumps you from the text area to the command area.

When using a mouse, you generally don't need either the Alpha command or the Esc key. Clicking both mouse buttons at the same time with the mouse pointer in the command area works like the Alpha command, and, when the menu is turned off, moving the mouse pointer to the bottom of the screen and clicking one button works like the Esc key.

Returning to the text area from the Gallery menu is a different matter. If you're using the keyboard, first press E to pick the Gallery menu's Exit command (called the Edit command in Word versions prior to 2.0) to return to the Edit menu. Then, use the Alpha command as usual. To use the mouse to return from the Gallery menu, place the mouse pointer on Exit and click the left button.

QUIT

```
COMMAND: Alpha Copy Delete Format Gallery Help Insert Jump Library
         Options Print Quit Replace Search Transfer Undo Window
```

QUIT: (Carried out as soon as it is picked if no editing or text entry has taken
       place; otherwise, requests confirmation of the command)

Use the Quit command to end a session with Word and return to DOS. If no information will be lost as a result of quitting immediately, that's what Word will do. If there are any
unsaved editing changes to the document, Word will highlight the document and display
the message *Enter Y to save, N to lose edits, or Esc to cancel*.

To save the latest editing changes on disk, press Y. If the document has never been saved
on disk, pressing Y causes Word to display the message *Not a valid file* and return you to the
text area. Use the Transfer Save command, then quit again.

If the document has been saved before, Y causes it to be saved again, with the recent
editing changes. To throw away the editing changes and quit, press N. If you decide not to
quit after all, press the Esc key. The document remains highlighted, because all of it is selected. To eliminate the highlighting, press the Up or Left direction key to move to the first
character in the document; press the Down or Right direction key to move to the end mark.
With the mouse, reduce the selection to a single character by clicking the left button when
the mouse pointer is on the desired character. (If you don't have a mouse, and you want to
return the selection to the position it had before you used the Quit command, try using the
Undo command twice, followed by the Left direction key and then the Right direction key.)

If different text windows contain different documents, using the Quit command causes
Word to highlight, in turn, each document that has unsaved editing changes. For each, Word
prompts you to press Y, N, or the Esc key. When all documents are taken care of, Word carries out the Quit command.

If there are unsaved changes to a style sheet that is being used to format a document,
Word highlights the corresponding document when you use the command, and displays the
message *Enter Y to save style sheet, N to lose edits, or Esc to cancel*.

Just as for a document, press Y to save the style sheet with its changes. Press N to throw
away the changes to the style sheet. Or press the Esc key to cancel the Quit command.

If you want to save the style sheet under a different name, press the Esc key to cancel
the command, and press G (for Gallery). Then press T and S (Transfer Save), type in the new
name, and press the Enter key. Finally, press E to return to the Edit menu. If desired, use the
Quit command again.

You'll see a similar message if your glossary has new entries that will be lost. Pressing
Y will cause the entries to be saved to the glossary file NORMAL.GLY. To save them to
a different glossary file, use the Transfer Glossary Save command.

Quitting with the mouse

Clicking the left mouse button when the mouse pointer is on the word Quit is the same as pressing Esc, followed by Q. Clicking the right mouse button causes Word to automatically save all documents, style sheets, and glossary entries that have unsaved changes, and then to quit. There is no confirmation message and no opportunity to change your mind. Word's swiftness in this instance can be annoying, because it is easy to quit accidentally when, instead, you meant to click the right mouse button with the pointer on one of the menu names surrounding Quit.

If this happens, and you catch yourself before releasing the right mouse button, move the mouse pointer out of the command area before releasing the button. Once you release it with the pointer on Quit, Word quits. You can't stop it.

If, however, Word saves changes you don't want saved, the prior (backup) version of the document should still be on the disk, with the same file name and the extension .BAK. You can delete the new .DOC version, and then recover the .BAK file by using the Transfer Load command and typing the document's full name, including the .BAK extension. Then you can use Word's Transfer Rename command to restore the .DOC extension. Or, you can use the DOS Rename command to change the extension to .DOC before loading the re-named document into Word.

UNDO

```
COMMAND: Alpha Copy Delete Format Gallery Help Insert Jump Library
         Options Print Quit Replace Search Transfer Undo Window
```

(Carried out as soon as it is picked)

The Undo command reverses (undoes) your last editing action. It is the *functional* complement of the F4 key, which repeats your last editing action.

If you accidentally delete some text—from a single letter to an entire document—the Undo command will restore it. Or, if you type in a continuous string of text characters and decide you don't want them after all, the Undo command eliminates them. Furthermore, if you underline a passage or make any other formatting change, you can undo what you just did.

You can even undo the Undo command by using it twice in a row. This lets you change your mind or do a before-and-after comparison.

There's another clever wrinkle. If you select and delete text and then type new text at the same location, Word remembers *both* the deletion and the insertion, and the Undo command reverses the combination. For instance, if you select the word *tomboy*, delete it all at once (not a character at a time), and type in the words *lively little girl*, the Undo command will eliminate the phrase *lively little girl* and return the word *tomboy* to the document.

However, if you invert the process, inserting text (*lively little girl*) in your document and then deleting the original text (*tomboy*), only the last editing act—the deletion—can be reversed with the Undo command.

Finally, the command will undo a "global" change to a document as long as the change was the result of a single command, used just once. For example, the Undo command will take out *all* hyphens placed in a document with one use of the Library Hyphenate command, or it will revoke any number of replacements made with one use of the Replace command.

You can predict how much the Undo command will do if you remember the following rules:

- The Undo command reverses only editing acts (in other words, actions that change the content or format of a document). For example, it will reverse the effect of a Format command, but will not do the same for the Options command or one of the Print commands.

- The Undo command reverses only the last editing act. Word begins a new editing act whenever you change the location of the selection *without* changing the content of the document. For example, suppose you type a few words, move the selection (cursor) a few spaces with the direction keys or the mouse, and then type a few more words. At this point, the Undo command can affect only the words typed after you moved the selection, because that move signaled the start of a new editing act. However, if you had moved the selection with the Spacebar or the Backspace key, a new editing act would not have been started because these keys change the content of the document by adding or deleting characters. The selection happens to move when these keys are pressed, but that is merely a by-product of their primary function, which is to change a document's content.

- There is an exception to the "last editing act" limitation: As in the earlier "tomboy" example, Undo will reverse the combination of the deletion of text followed by the typing of text in the same document location.

The Scrap and Glossary Commands: Copy, Delete, Insert

The Copy, Delete, and Insert commands are closely related. You use them to delete, move, reproduce, store, or retrieve text passages, using the *scrap* and the *glossary,* two special storage areas Word sets aside.

Word temporarily stores one selected passage from a document in the scrap. The glossary, on the other hand, can hold any number of text selections. And unlike the contents of the scrap, entries in the glossary can be saved in a file on disk—a permanent holding area for "boilerplate" text you use again and again, in different documents.

The Copy and Delete commands move text from a document on the screen to the scrap or the glossary; the Insert command retrieves text from storage and inserts it into a document. Three keys—Del, Ins, and F3—provide shortcuts. The F2 key, when used with the Ins key or the Insert command, lets you perform mathematical functions, such as addition, and insert the results into a document.

This chapter briefly explains the scrap and the glossary, then presents detailed explanations of each of the commands. But before we begin, an analogy may give you an intuitive sense of why Word uses both a scrap and a glossary. Think of the scrap as the part of your mind that registers fleeting information, such as a phone number you must remember just long enough to dial. Think of the glossary as a pad of paper where you can jot an assortment of phone numbers—later filing any numbers you want to keep for permanent reference.

THE SCRAP

The scrap can hold anything from a single character to a long document. Depending on the length of the selected text, all or part of the scrap's contents is shown inside brackets, { }, on the bottom line of the screen.

Word automatically proposes the scrap as the destination for text affected by the Copy and Delete commands. This means text is copied or deleted to the scrap if you carry out the Copy or Delete command when the scrap brackets appear in the command field *COPY to:* { } or *DELETE to:* { }. Similarly, Word proposes the scrap as the source of text to be inserted in a document with the Insert command. If you try to insert the scrap's contents when the scrap is empty, your computer just bleeps at you and Word displays the message *Scrap is empty.* A selection sent to the scrap is "killed" when you replace it by sending another selection to the scrap.

There are shortcuts. You can use the Del and Ins keys to move text to and from the scrap. You can kill a selection by holding down the Shift key and pressing the Del key. This will delete the selection without sending it to the scrap.

To use the mouse to store and retrieve text with the scrap, click the right button when the mouse pointer is on the Copy, Delete, or Insert command name.

THE GLOSSARY

The glossary can hold many entries of any length, each with a different name. A glossary entry created from one document can be inserted in the same document or another, as long as you do not quit Word or use the Transfer Clear All command. You can make a collection of glossary entries permanent, so that each can be used in the future, by saving the collection on disk as a glossary file. Or, you can erase glossary entries with the Transfer Glossary Clear command.

As with the scrap, you use the Copy and Delete commands to send selected text to the glossary, and you use the Insert command to retrieve the text you want. The difference is that you don't accept Word's proposed response for the commands. The proposed response is the scrap, symbolized by the scrap brackets { }. Instead, you give the text a *glossary name* by typing one in the command field, or you pick an existing name from a list Word displays at your request. Glossary names can have up to 31 letters — no spaces or punctuation marks allowed, though for ease of reading you can separate words in a name by capitalizing the first letter of each or (in versions of Word higher than 1.1) inserting the underline character between them. Make the names descriptive, because Word displays only the names, not the glossary entries themselves, when you press a direction key to request a list.

For example, when you choose the Copy command, and Word displays:

        COPY to: {█}

you can replace the proposed scrap brackets with a glossary name:

        COPY to: my_glossary_name█

and then simply execute the command.

Or, if you wish to see a list of glossary names, press any direction key when Word is displaying the command field *COPY to:* { }, *DELETE to:* { }, or *INSERT from:* { }. Or, place the mouse pointer to the right of the colon and click the right button.

Beginning with version 3.0 of Word, the Print Glossary command will give you a paper copy of the glossary names and the text you have stored as an entry with each name. (See Chapter 15, "The Family of Print Commands.")

Six glossary names are reserved: *page, footnote, date, dateprint, time,* and *timeprint.* You cannot store text in the glossary under any of these names.

The F3 key is a shortcut for retrieving text from the glossary, much as the Ins key is a shortcut for retrieving text from the scrap. If you know the glossary name, type it where you want the glossary entry to appear in the text, and press F3. The name will be replaced by the glossary entry it represents.

Figure 10-1 may help you conceptualize the various ways the commands can be used together to move text from a document into the scrap or glossary and then back into a document again.

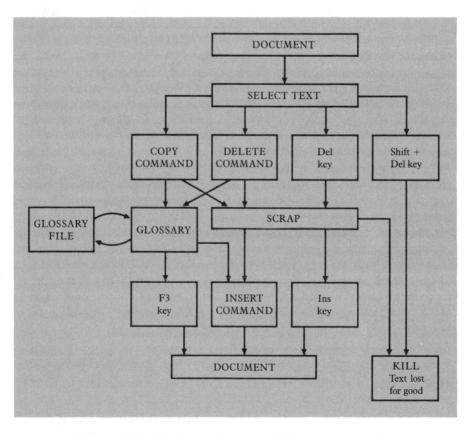

Figure 10-1. *Ways to use the scrap and glossary commands*

COPY

```
COMMAND: Alpha Copy Delete Format Gallery Help Insert Jump Library
         Options|Print Quit Replace Search Transfer Undo Window


COPY to: {}
```

The Copy command lets you copy any amount of text—a character, a word, a phrase, a paragraph, even several pages—either to the scrap or to the glossary. Text is not affected by being copied.

Copying to the scrap

To copy to the scrap, first select the text you want to copy. Then pick the Copy command and execute it by pressing the Enter key. If you use the mouse, instead, click the left button to cause Word to display the proposed response, the scrap brackets: { }. Click the right button to skip the proposed response and copy the selected text directly to the scrap.

Once text has been copied to the scrap, the first and last few characters of the passage appear as a reminder inside the scrap brackets on the bottom line of the screen.

To retrieve the contents of the scrap for use in the same document (or in a document in a different window), place the selection where you want the material to appear and either execute the Insert command or press the Ins key.

This Copy-Insert combination is a way to reuse the same words, phrases, paragraphs, or even long passages over and over in one or several documents without retyping. For example, you might copy a paragraph to the scrap and then immediately insert it back into a document two or three times in a row, so that you can edit each differently, compare them, and eventually keep only the best version.

But remember: The scrap's content is replaced every time something new is copied to it, and usually whenever text is deleted from a document, too. In other words, the scrap is merely a temporary holding area for text, a last stop before it vanishes forever. If you copy (or delete) text into the scrap with the idea of inserting it somewhere else in a document, use the Ins key or Insert command immediately. If you do other editing first, you might inadvertently replace the scrap contents.

Copying to the glossary

The other destination for text is the glossary, where any number of passages can be stored with different names.

The first step in creating a glossary entry is to select text. Then, pick the Copy command from the Edit menu just as if you were copying the passage to the scrap—but, if you use a mouse, click the left button rather than the right, so Word will stop and ask for a destination instead of copying directly to the scrap.

Once you've selected the text and picked the Copy command, make up a glossary name and type it. The name will replace the scrap brackets in the command field. Before typing a name, review the list of existing glossary names, if you wish, by pressing a direction key.

Recall that the glossary name may be up to 31 letters and numbers long, and may not contain spaces or symbols other than an underline. Try to limit names to 20 letters or fewer, however, because you'll only see the first 20 characters of each glossary name anyway when you pick from a list.

During any single editing session, new glossary entries exist only in your computer's memory. When you quit Word, you lose the glossary. If you want, you can make your glossary permanent by saving its full contents in a glossary file on disk. If you do this, glossary entries can be used during different editing sessions, and frequently used phrases, paragraphs, and even long sections of text can be reused day after day, week after week, without being re-typed. (Chapter 16, "The Family of Transfer Commands," tells you how to save and reuse the glossary with the Transfer Glossary commands.)

A tip: You can include paragraph formatting with a paragraph destined for the glossary by selecting the paragraph mark (normally invisible) along with the appropriate text. When the paragraph mark is part of the glossary entry, Word will insert the text into any document, with the lines laid out as they were originally (centered, justified, indented, and so on).

DELETE

```
COMMAND: Alpha Copy Delete Format Gallery Help Insert Jump Library
         Options Print|Quit Replace Search Transfer Undo Window

   ┌─────────────────┘
   │
DELETE to: {}
```

The Delete command is most commonly used to eliminate selected text from a document or, when used with the Insert command, to move text from one location to another.

The Delete command is identical to the Copy command in all but one respect: Delete eliminates the selected text from the document, while Copy doesn't. Refer to the section on the Copy command for details on using the Copy or Delete command with the scrap and the glossary, and for tips on naming glossary entries.

The Del key automatically deletes text to the scrap. Clicking the right mouse button when the mouse pointer is on the Delete command has the same effect.

If you want to delete to the glossary, instead, pick the Delete command. (With the mouse, click the left mouse button when the mouse pointer is on Delete.) Then, type the glossary name you want, and carry out the command.

Copy versus Delete

To illustrate the different applications of Copy and Delete, let's play around with the word *ballistocardiograph*—a word no one would want to type twice.

♦ To eliminate *ballistocardiograph* from a document, we select it and then use the Delete command (or the Del key) to send it temporarily to the scrap. The contents of the scrap perish when something new is sent to it, so *ballistocardiograph* probably won't hang around long in the scrap. That's fine, unless we want to reuse the word. If you think there's an outside chance you will later want to resurrect the word (or some other deletion), delete it to the glossary instead of the scrap.

♦ To move *ballistocardiograph* to a different location, we select it, delete it to the scrap, select the new location, and then insert it with the Insert command or the Ins key. We could move the word between documents or windows this way, too.

♦ To reuse *ballistocardiograph* repeatedly without retyping it, we select it and delete (or copy) it into the glossary, then use the Insert command each time we want to use the word. If we give *ballistocardiograph* the glossary name *bal,* we can easily reuse the word by typing *bal* and then pressing the F3 key. (That's what I did when writing this section.)

Delete but preserve the scrap

It is possible to delete text without placing it in the scrap: Hold down the Shift key and press the Del key. This capability is helpful when the scrap contains a word or passage you want to preserve for later insertion into the text, but meanwhile you have deleting to do. Another method of preserving the scrap is to delete unwanted text to the glossary, using a name you know you can ignore.

If you accidentally replace the scrap with new text but discover your error before you do any other editing whatsoever, the Undo command returns the scrap to its former condition.

INSERT

```
COMMAND: Alpha Copy Delete Format Gallery Help Insert Jump Library
         Options Print Quit Replace Search Transfer|Undo Window
         ┌─────────────────────────────────────────────┘
         │
   INSERT from: {}
```

The Insert command inserts the contents of the scrap or a particular glossary entry into a document at the selection. If necessary, text in the document moves to the right and down to make room for the inserted material, just as it does when you type new text. Before text can be inserted, it must be placed in either the scrap or the glossary with the Copy or the Delete command or the Del key.

If the selection is wider than a single character (if it is highlighting a word or sentence, for example), the contents of the scrap or glossary are inserted at the position of the first highlighted character of the selection.

The Insert command has a single command field, *INSERT from:* { }, which proposes the scrap brackets as the source of material for the insertion.

If you execute the Insert command without altering this proposed response, the command automatically inserts the contents of the scrap. If you type in the name of a glossary entry before executing the command, the named glossary entry is inserted instead of the contents of the scrap.

If the name you type isn't exactly the same as that of a glossary entry, Word tells you *Glossary name not defined*. For this reason, you may want to pick the glossary name from a list of existing names. Just as with the Copy and Delete commands, press one of the four direction keys when the command field is displayed, or place the mouse pointer to the right of the colon in the command field and click the right button. A list like this appears on the screen:

```
page                footnote           123Go           BasketballLadder
CodeOfEthics        courage            DraftOutline    EthicsOfLobbying
ExampleOfGrid       ExplanationOfDuties happy          ListOfWORDfeatures
PossibleFlowersMom  ReasonsNotToSwimAtla Recollections  RentalBoilerplate
ReturnAddress       s
```

Use the direction keys to move around the list until the name you want is highlighted, or place the mouse pointer on the glossary name you want and click the left mouse button to highlight it. Once the name is highlighted, it will also appear after the colon in the *INSERT from:* field near the bottom of the screen.

As you can see in the preceding example, space limitations allow only the first 20 letters or numbers of a glossary name to show up on the list. The full name, however, appears in the command field. For instance, in the example, the first 20 letters of this name appear: *ReasonsNotToSwimAtla*. But if you highlight the listing, this shows up in the command field:

```
INSERT from: ReasonsNotToSwimAtlanticOcean
```

When the glossary name you desire is highlighted, execute the command by pressing the Enter key or by clicking the right mouse button. The glossary entry associated with the name you picked will be inserted into the document at the beginning of the selection.

If you are using the mouse to pick from a list of glossary names, you can move the mouse pointer to the desired glossary name and click the right button to execute the command immediately.

Retrieving glossary entries from disk

You've seen that the Copy and Delete commands can be used to put text into the glossary so it can be inserted later somewhere else in a document.

It's also possible to put text into the glossary from special glossary files on disk. These files, which have the file name extension .GLY, can be whole collections of glossary entries. For more information, refer to the Transfer Glossary Save, Transfer Glossary Merge, and Transfer Glossary Clear commands in Chapter 16, "The Family of Transfer Commands."

The Ins and F3 keys

The Ins and F3 keys are shortcuts. The Ins key inserts from the scrap. Press the key when the selection is at the location in the document where you wish to insert the scrap's contents. The F3 key inserts glossary entries at the location of the selection. To use the glossary this way, type the name of the glossary entry, make sure the selection is in the space immediately following the end of the name, and press F3 or, if the glossary name is at least two characters long, select the name and press F3. Either way, the glossary name will vanish and be replaced by the associated glossary entry.

If the alarm bleeps and nothing happens when you press the F3 key, you are not in Alpha (text-entry) mode, *or* the selection is not the name or not in the space immediately to the right of the name, *or* the name you are giving isn't that of a current glossary entry. Press the Esc key and the letter A, and check the selection, or use the Insert command and a direction key to see a list of current glossary names.

The permanent glossary names

The entries *page, footnote, date, dateprint, time,* and *timeprint* are permanently recorded in the glossary. (Prior to version 3.0 of Word, only *page* and *footnote* were available.)

The glossary name *page* causes the number of the current page to be printed. The *page* entry is handy to use with running heads ("headers" or "footers" at the tops or bottoms of pages), where you may want a page number in a particular position on every printed sheet of paper. To use *page,* type the word *page* and press the F3 key. You see *(page)* on the screen, but the correct page number will be printed.

If you want to precede the page number with the word *Page*—Page 1 on the first sheet, Page 2 on the second, and so forth—type the words *Page page* and press the F3 key. You will see *Page (page)* in the running head on the screen, but it will print as *Page,* followed by the page number. (See the Format Running-head and the Format Division commands in Chapter 12 for more information on running heads and page numbers.)

The glossary name *footnote* is generally used in one special case: If you accidentally delete the reference mark for an automatically numbered footnote from the footnote part of a document, typing *footnote* and pressing F3 will restore the special auto-number character. It appears as a number on the screen.

The *footnote* glossary name doesn't work when a footnote reference mark is deleted accidentally from the main body of a document, because the deletion causes the corresponding footnote text to be deleted, too.

The remaining four permanent names in the glossary allow you to put the date and time in your documents automatically. These names were introduced in Word version 3.0.

The glossary name *date* causes the current date, or the date your computer believes to be current, to be inserted into your document. Simply type the word *date* and press the F3 key. The date appears in your document in this form: November 27, 1986. Beginning with version 3.1, if you change the *date format* field of the Options command to *DMY,* the date will be inserted in this form: 27 November, 1986.

If you want the date to be updated automatically each time the document is printed, use the glossary name *dateprint*, instead of *date*. Type *dateprint* and press the F3 key. The Word screen will show *(dateprint)*, but any document will be printed with the current date. This is handy in correspondence (and form letters) you send often.

The glossary names *time* and *timeprint* are similar in use to *date* and *dateprint*, except they show the time your computer believes it to be. With *timeprint,* the screen shows *(timeprint)* but the document is printed with the actual time, expressed in this form: 7:57 PM. To switch to a 24-hour clock, set the *time format* field of the Options command to *24*. The time then is expressed as 19:57.

By using both *dateprint* and *timeprint* in a document that is frequently updated in content and printed, you can "stamp" all your copies with the date and time they are printed.

By using the *date* and *time* glossary names, you needn't check your office calendar or clock. For instance, if you type the word *time* and press the F3 key, you see the time. You can delete it by either pressing the Backspace key a few times or else using the Undo command (Esc and U) followed by the Del key.

Please note that Word relies on DOS to tell it the time. DOS will only know the correct time if you have a clock/calendar built into your computer, or if you type in the correct time when you start or reboot the computer. (Many people don't bother to type in the date and time.) If you don't have a built-in clock/calendar and you use an AUTOEXEC.BAT file, you may want to be sure the lines *date* and *time* are included so that DOS prompts you to tell it the date and time whenever you start or reboot your computer. (See Chapter 28, "Using a Hard Disk".)

You can intentionally mislead the computer, by using the DOS Date and Time commands to reset the computer's understanding of the date and time. Imagine it's November 27, 1986, and you want a document to be dated one day earlier. Use Word's Library Run command (Esc-L-R), followed by the DOS Date command, followed by a space and the date you want to tell the computer. Type the date in the form 11-26-86, and then press Enter.

```
LIBRARY RUN: date 11-26-86█

Enter DOS command
Page 1   {}                          ?              Microsoft Word:
```

On a hard-disk system the command will be executed almost instantly, and a message will tell you to *Press a key to resume Word.* Press any key, such as the Spacebar, and continue your work with Word. If Word is on a floppy disk, you'll see the message *Replace Word program disk if necessary. Enter Y when ready.* Assuming the DOS COMMAND.COM program is on the same floppy disk as Word, simply press Y. Later, if you want to correct the date (or time), repeat these steps.

Inserting mathematical answers

Beginning with version 3.0, Word performs simple mathematical operations: addition, subtraction, multiplication, division. Conveniently, you don't have to retype numbers, because Word performs math on numbers already on the screen, regardless of whether the figures are arranged horizontally or in a column.

First select the numbers, then press the F2 key. The mathematical answer appears in the scrap, so you can insert it into a document with the Insert command or Ins key. If you want to perform a calculation but don't want to lose the previous contents of the scrap, use the Undo command immediately after pressing the F2 key.

To select a column of numbers, first select one corner of the rectangular area that makes up the column, then hold down the Shift key and press the F6 key. This will activate Word's Column Select mode, and the letters *CS* will appear on the bottom line of the screen. Expanding the selection (by moving the selection or clicking with the mouse) causes a rectangular shape to be highlighted on the screen. (See Chapter 27, "Power Tools: Creating Tables.") When you press the F2 key, Word will add, subtract, multiply, or divide the highlighted numbers.

Word will add each number it encounters to the previous total, unless a number is preceded by a minus sign ($-$) or is inside parentheses, in which case it is subtracted. When a number is preceded by an asterisk ($*$) it is multiplied by the previous total, and when a number is preceded by a division sign ($/$) it is divided into the previous total. All other letters and characters are ignored, except for the percent sign (%), which causes the number preceding it to be divided by 100.

For example, pressing F2 when this is selected:

|| `he had 157 but then he got 97 more` ||

causes the result *254* to appear in the scrap at the bottom of the screen. Selecting *157 + 97* or *157 97* would have the same effect, because numbers are always added unless there are contrary instructions.

Pressing F2 when this is selected:

|| `12+10/2(3)*4+200%` ||

causes the result *34* to appear in the scrap. Word always works from left to right (or from top to bottom if computing a column). It reaches the result of 34 by adding 12 plus 10, for 22, then dividing by 2, for 11, then subtracting 3, for 8, then multiplying by 4, for 32, and then adding 200%, which Word interprets as 2 (because 200 divided by 100 is 2). The final result is 32 plus 2, or 34.

Several points should be kept in mind when using Word's math functions:

♦ These functions are not sophisticated. The math feature was developed primarily to make it easy for people preparing financial reports and other documents that contain columns of numbers to add them. Consequently, Word does not recognize any precedence among operators. It will not, for instance, automatically perform multiplication and division before addition and subtraction, nor does it recognize parentheses as a means to control which numbers are to be combined first in a series that mixes multiplication or division with addition and subtraction.

♦ The percent sign affects only the number immediately preceding it, dividing it by 100. Word performs this before adding, subtracting, multiplying, or dividing any other numbers inside the selection.

♦ The answer Word gives has as many decimal places to the right of the decimal point as does the number contained in the selection that has the most decimal places. This means that dividing 5.00 by 6 gives the answer 0.83, because 5.00 has two decimal places. Dividing 5.0 by 6 gives the answer .8, and dividing 5 by 6 gives the answer 0. (However, even though Word expresses a result as .8 or 0, it "knows" the total is really 0.83333333333..., so the selection $5/6*6$ gives the correct result of 5, rather than 0.)

♦ Use of the plus sign (+) for addition is accepted, but is unnecessary because Word always adds numbers unless it sees a symbol indicating the contrary.

♦ Results of up to 14 digits appear in the scrap. If an answer contains more than 14 digits, the message *Math overflow* appears.

♦ Your result will contain commas if at least one of the numbers in the selection contains a comma. However, your answer will not contain a $ sign even if one of the selected numbers is expressed in dollars. You must add $ signs manually.

♦ You can replace a series of selected numbers with the result that appears in the scrap, by holding down the Shift key and pressing the Insert key. For example, if you select *3 + 4* and press the F2 key, the result *7* appears in the scrap. But the *3 + 4* remains selected. Holding Shift and pressing the Ins key causes the selected numbers to be deleted and replaced with the contents of the scrap—in this case, the number 7.

Inserting from the thesaurus

Word includes a 220,000-word thesaurus that you use somewhat like the glossary to insert text into a document. Select a word, but instead of pressing F3, hold down the Ctrl key and press F6. This brings to the screen a list of synonyms. Pick one and press Enter to insert it into the document in place of the selected word. Or press Esc to cancel the thesaurus.

The thesaurus was new beginning with Word version 3.1. Even in its details, it is simple to use.

Select a word

Spot a word in your document for which you want to see a list of words with similar meanings. Either select the whole word or the space immediately following it.

Press Ctrl-F6. Half of the Word screen will be replaced temporarily with a list of synonyms. Nouns will be listed together, as will verbs and adjectives (adj). So will adverbs (adv), prepositions (prep), and connectives (conv). Within each of these categories there may be alphabetized subgroups, reflecting different shades of meaning. Subgroups are separated from each other with semicolons.

For example, the word *bomb* can be either a noun or an adjective. If you select it and press Ctrl-F6, you'll see four subgroups—two for nouns, two for verbs.

```
bomb:
noun bust, disaster, dud, failure, fiasco, flop, turkey;
     bombshell, explosive, mine, missile, payload, rocket, rocketry,
     warhead.
verb fail, flop, stumble, trip;
     blitz, bombard, cannonade, shell.
```

Some words have several dozen synonyms. If there are more than can fit in the thesaurus window at once, Word will notify you to use the PgDn key to scroll through a longer list. Once you've scrolled down, you can scroll back up with the PgUp key.

If Word doesn't know any synonyms for the word you've selected, it will show you synonyms for a similarly spelled root word. For instance, if you ask to see synonyms of the word *coldness*, it will show synonyms for *cold*. If it fails to find synonyms for a root word, Word shows you a list of alphabetically similar words. If you select one and press Enter, you'll be shown the synonyms of that word.

Once a list of synonyms is on the screen, you have several choices:

♦ To return to your document without inserting a synonym, press Esc. This works at any time.

♦ To pick a synonym, use the direction keys to select it on the list, then press Enter. This removes the synonym list from the screen, and replaces the selected word in the document with your new choice. The newly inserted word will have the same capitalization, punctuation, and formatting as the original word.

♦ Alternatively, broaden your search for the perfect word by requesting the synonyms of any word on a synonym list. Select a synonym and press Ctrl-F6 to see a new list. For instance, when looking for synonyms of the word *bomb*, you can select the word *flop* from the synonym list and press Ctrl-F6 to see a list of words with similar meanings. You can link up to 10 synonym lists in this way, moving to a new list each time by pressing Ctrl-F6, or moving back through previous lists by pressing Ctrl-PgUp.

As a bonus, you can use the thesaurus dictionary as a fast (but sometimes inconclusive) way to check the spelling of a word. Select the word in question, then press Ctrl-F6. If the word is recognized, you'll know it is spelled correctly. If it isn't in the dictionary, you may be able to spot it on the list of alphabetically similar words. (Of course, it may be that the word is spelled correctly but isn't in the thesaurus dictionary. Don't give up. Word's Library Spell command uses a completely different dictionary, better suited to checking spelling and suggesting alternatives.)

Similarly, you may be able to refine your understanding of the meaning of a word by requesting a list of synonyms. Be aware, however, that a good thesaurus and dictionary in book form are more comprehensive and ultimately more useful than the synonym and spelling dictionaries that come with Word. (You have to flip a few pages, but come on! It doesn't take *that* long to look up a word!)

A few final details

If you have a hard disk, copy the thesaurus disk into the *same* directory (or subdirectory) as the Word program. If you have doubts, look for the file WORD.COM and copy the large file on the thesaurus disk into the same directory. You'll never have to worry about the thesaurus again. Just use it.

If you are running Word from a floppy disk, you'll have to insert the thesaurus disk in the B drive (or other document drive) each time you request a synonym. Word will tell you to *Replace document disk with thesaurus disk. Enter Y when ready.* Remove your document disk, insert the thesaurus disk, and press Y. After you've finished with the thesaurus, Word will prompt you to swap the two disks again.

The Efficiency Commands: Gallery, Help, Options, Replace, Search

The commands in this chapter aren't vital to your use of Word. You can create, revise, format, print, and store documents without them. But don't ignore these five commands. Just because they're not essential doesn't mean they're not useful. The Gallery, Help, Options, Replace, and Search commands can increase your efficiency—and isn't efficiency one reason you're using a word processor?

This is what the efficiency commands do:

- The Gallery command lets you look at English-language descriptions of the individual styles of a style sheet attached to a document.

- The Help command provides on-screen assistance in the use of Word. You can request help that is "context sensitive"—in other words, Word will tailor the information to whatever task you're attempting when you use the command. Beginning with version 3.0, you can also use tutorials from the Learning Microsoft Word disk.

- The Options command gives you choices about the way Word operates. You can control such things as how closely the on-screen appearance of a document matches its printed appearance.

- The Search command quickly scans a document for any specified character or characters, word or words.

- A closely related command, Replace, goes one step further, both searching for and replacing specified text with any other character, characters, word, or words.

For details on the subleties and more exotic uses of both the Replace and Search commands, see Chapter 22, "Power Tools: Search and Replace."

GALLERY

```
COMMAND: Alpha Copy Delete Format Gallery Help Insert Jump Library
         Options Print Quit Replace Search Transfer Undo Window


COMMAND: Copy Delete Exit Format Help
         Insert Name Print Transfer Undo
```

Whenever you use the Gallery command, the Gallery menu replaces the Edit menu and the text area is transformed into a viewing area—not for art, as in some galleries, but for English-language descriptions of the formatting styles in a style sheet. You can disregard the Gallery command if you're not using style sheets. To learn more about them, read Chapter 24 of this book, "Power Tools: Style Sheets," and *Microsoft Word Style Sheets,* which I co-authored with JoAnne Woodcock (Microsoft Press, 1987).

Just as there are three types of formats—division, paragraph, and character—there are three corresponding types of styles. A division style, for example, controls page layout. Here's an example:

```
 3    S/ Division Standard                    STANDARD MARGINS, LETTER DIV
         Page break. Page length 11"; width 8.5". Page # format Arabic. Top
         margin 1.67"; bottom 1"; left 1.25"; right 1.25". Top running head
         at 1". Bottom running head at 0.83". Footnotes on same page.
```

Here is an example of a paragraph style that might appear in the Gallery:

```
 1    SP Paragraph Standard                    STANDARD PARAGRAPH (STND ¶)
         Modern b 12. Flush left (first line indent 0.5"), space before 1
         li.
```

A paragraph style controls paragraph formatting (line layout and spacing) and establishes a "normal" format for the characters in a paragraph. You can override "normal" character formatting by applying a character style to selected text. This is an example of a character style, as it might appear in the Gallery:

```
 5   UC Character 1                            UNDERLINED CHARACTER
         Modern b 12 Underlined.
```

What's the difference between formatting conventionally and using styles in style sheets? The question is discussed at length in Chapter 24, but a partial answer is that a style lets you name a particular format so that you can, with just two or three keystrokes, apply that "style" to one or many parts of a document or documents. For example, if you frequently use a centered, underlined heading with extra blank spaces above and below it, you can define a paragraph style with that formatting and use the style each time you want a heading.

Any document can have one style sheet at a time "attached" to it—"attached" meaning that the styles in the style sheet are available for formatting the document. The Gallery displays the various styles of whatever style sheet is attached to the document. When you want to return from the Gallery to the Edit menu and your document, press E or click the mouse with the pointer on Exit in the Gallery menu. (In versions of Word prior to 2.0, the Exit command was called Edit.)

If the Gallery is blank

When I taught myself Word in the fall of 1983, I was vexed by a blank Gallery. I didn't know what to do about it. Every hour or so I'd pick the Gallery command, hoping that something would magically appear, but . . . no luck. Is this is a familiar frustration for you, too?

A blank Gallery simply means there is no style sheet attached to the document on the screen. Styles don't magically appear in the Gallery; they must be put there. To associate a style sheet with a document, so that the style sheet will appear in the Gallery, either:

♦ Begin creating styles with the Gallery menu's Insert command.

♦ Or, return to the Edit menu, attach an existing style sheet to the document with the Format Style Sheet command, and pick the Gallery command once again.

It is also possible to look at or edit a style sheet temporarily, without associating it with a document, by loading it with the Gallery's Transfer Load command.

When a style sheet in the Gallery is associated with a document, the styles in the style sheet may be applied to a document with the Edit menu's Format Style commands or with key codes. You *cannot* format a document with styles when you are in the Gallery. You must return to the Edit menu for that.

HELP

```
COMMAND: Alpha Copy Delete Format Gallery Help Insert Jump Library
         Options Print Quit Replace Search|Transfer Undo Window


HELP: Resume Next Previous
      Introduction Commands Editing Keyboard Mouse Selection Tutorial


TUTORIAL: Lesson Index
```

The Help command transforms the text area into a viewing area for information about Word. More than 100 different screens of information are available. Generally, information provided by the Help command is better as a reminder of how to do something than it is as an instruction tool for a beginner.

Word gets its help information from a file named MW.HLP on the Program disk. If you've deleted this file to make more room on the disk, you'll see the message *Enter Y to retry access to MW.HLP* if you use the Help command. If you see this message, insert a disk containing MW.HLP into the disk drive and press Y, or press the Esc key to cancel your request for help.

Browsing

If you seek general information or want to browse through screens of information to find what you want, pick Help as you do any other command. First you'll see an introduction and some instructions on using the help information, and from there you can go on to search for the details you desire. All help screens include a special menu at the bottom:

```
HELP: Resume Next Previous
      Introduction Commands Editing Keyboard Mouse Selection Tutorial
```

Search through the help screens with the commands on this menu, either by pressing the initial letter of the command name (do not press the Esc key first), or by clicking either button when the mouse pointer is on the command name. This is what the commands allow you to do:

- ♦ R, *Resume,* returns you to your document. It bypasses the Edit menu entirely, letting you resume work exactly where you left off. (As an alternative to using the Resume command to return to your document, you can place the mouse pointer in the command area and click both buttons. With the keyboard, pressing the Esc key will take you from the Help command to the Edit menu.)

- ♦ N, *Next,* moves you to the next screen of information. (The PgDn key does, too.)

- ♦ P, *Previous,* backs you up to the previous screen of information. (PgUp does, too.)

- ♦ I, *Introduction,* gives you an overview of the help feature and tells you what Help commands to use to find particular information.

- ♦ C, *Commands,* introduces the methods by which commands and command fields are used, and gives a brief explanation of each command.

- ♦ E, *Editing,* gives pointers on how to perform common editing tasks.

- ♦ K, *Keyboard,* takes you to the first of 15 screens of information on what you can do with particular keystrokes and combinations of keystrokes.

- ♦ M, *Mouse,* covers the major uses of the mouse.

- ♦ S, *Selection,* tells you the basics of selecting text and scrolling with either the keyboard or the mouse.

- ♦ T, *Tutorial,* lets you use the Learning Microsoft Word lesson disk without quitting the Word program. Picking Tutorial gives you a second choice: Lesson or Index. Lesson lets you use a specific lesson that addresses whatever kind of task you were involved in when you picked the Help command. Index gives you an index of all available lessons. (If you have a hard disk and the Learning Microsoft Word disk has been copied onto it, the tutorial will appear as soon as you request it. On a floppy-disk computer system, Word will ask you to swap disks—first inserting the Learning Microsoft Word disk, later replacing it with the Word Program disk again.)

Looking for specifics

If you need assistance with a specific command or command field, don't use the Help command right away. First, use the Edit menu to highlight the command or command field about which you're seeking information; then, without executing the command, use the Help command in one of these ways:

♦ Press Alt, followed by H, if no style sheet is in use.

♦ Press Alt, followed by X, followed by H, if a style sheet is in use.

♦ If you have installed a mouse, you may place the mouse pointer on the question mark (the Help mark) in the bottom line of the screen, and click either mouse button.

Any of these three methods also works if you're in the midst of using a command and need help, so the help feature is "context sensitive." Word senses the context in which you are working when you request assistance, and tries to oblige you.

OPTIONS

```
COMMAND: Alpha Copy Delete Format Gallery Help Insert Jump Library
         Options Print Quit Replace Search Transfer Undo Window


OPTIONS visible: None Partial Complete  printer display: Yes(No) menu:(Yes)No
        default tab width: 0.5"     measure:(In)Cm P10 P12 Pt           mute: Yes(No)
        date format:(MDY)DMY        time format:(12)24    decimal character:(.),
```

You use the Options command to tailor Word's operation to your preferences in several ways. Each field controls a different option. Fields have been added in recent versions of Word. Prior to version 2.0, the fields looked like this:

```
OPTIONS mute: Yes No      measure: In Cm P10 P12 Pt
        overtype: Yes No  display mode: Normal Printer     visible: Yes No
```

If you compare the two Options menus, you will see that the *menu* field replaced the old *overtype* field, the *display mode* field was changed to *printer display,* and the *visible* field became a three-choice, rather than two-choice, option.

Making a choice in an Options command field affects the documents in all windows. Between editing sessions, Word stores your Options choices on disk in a file called MW.INI, so each time you use Word your previous choices remain in effect until you change them.

The command fields of the Options command are straightforward, although the *printer display* and *measure* fields interact subtly, as you'll see in the section titled "Interactions."

Let's begin with three fields introduced in version 3.1.

date format. Leaving this set to MDY causes Word to insert the date in the *month-day-year* format when you use the *date* or *dateprint* glossary entries. Changing the setting to DMY causes Word to use the *day-month-year* format (see pages 102 and 103).

time format. When set to 12, Word uses a 12-hour clock when it inserts the time in a document or printout. When set to 24, Word uses a 24-hour clock—so 3:05 PM becomes 15:05. Insert the time with the *time* or *timeprint* glossary entries (see pages 102 and 103).

decimal character. Shall the decimal point be a period or a comma? Leave this set to period unless you are in France, Germany, or Scandinavia, or are writing to those countries.

If you change it to comma, Word will no longer recognize the comma as a separator of entries in lists. Instead, semicolons must be used. For example, the *page number* field of the Print Options command will require semicolons instead of commas, as will data files and header paragraphs in form-letter documents to be merge printed.

The remaining fields are also available in versions of Word preceding 3.1.

visible. Which normally invisible (nonprintable) characters, if any, shall be displayed on the screen?

Picking *None* (*No* in versions before 2.0) keeps all nonprintable characters invisible on the screen. Picking *Partial* (*Yes* in versions before 2.0) causes the paragraph mark (¶), the new-line character (↓), and the optional (nonrequired) hyphen (-) to be shown on the screen. Beginning with version 3.0, picking *Partial* also causes a double-headed arrow (↔) to be shown, indicating the presence of hidden text. Picking *Complete* (beginning with version 2.0) causes Spacebar spaces (·) and tab characters (→) to be shown, too.

What are these characters, and what do they do?

- The paragraph mark indicates the end of a paragraph. A paragraph mark stores the paragraph formatting for the preceding text. Insert it by pressing Enter.

- The new-line character appears at the end of a line of text and indicates an intentional break to begin a new line. To insert a new-line character, hold Shift and press Enter. It does not cause a new paragraph (or new paragraph formatting).

- The optional hyphen is a hyphen that is not required to separate two words. The hyphen in *talk-ing*, for example, is optional because you normally insert it only when the word breaks at the end of a line. Insert optional hyphens by holding Ctrl and pressing the hyphen key, or using the Library Hyphenate command.

- A Spacebar space separates words or characters in a document. It is the character you insert whenever you press the Spacebar.

- The tab character tells Word to move to the next tab stop. You create a tab character by pressing the Tab key. The tab character is just a single character, but when you select it, a highlighted bar extends from the actual tab character to the location of the tab stop to which it corresponds.

- The double-headed arrow reveals that hidden text has been inserted into the document at that point. When hidden text has been made visible (with the Window Options command), the arrow doesn't appear. Instead, the "hidden" text is underlined (the underline is a series of fine dots when you are using Word in a graphics mode).

Keeping some or all of these characters invisible helps keep the screen uncluttered, but it also can make them easy to forget. And overlooking the existence of these characters can lead to such results as the unwitting deletion of paragraph marks, with a consequent sudden change in paragraph formatting.

In versions of Word numbered 1.15 and higher, all normally invisible characters are displayed inside the scrap brackets when you have deleted them to the scrap.

menu. Shall the menu at the bottom of the screen be displayed during text entry?

Picking *Yes* causes the Edit menu to be displayed during text entry. Picking *No* turns off the Edit menu during text entry.

If you are an intermediate or advanced user of Word, you probably will want to choose *No,* because removing the menu increases the text area by three lines. The bottom line of the command area remains the same, except that Word's messages temporarily take over the space when necessary.

The Edit menu returns when you want to use a command: Just press Esc or place the mouse pointer on the bottom line of the screen and click either button.

overtype. Shall new characters typed into a document replace existing characters? This field was removed beginning with version 2.0. Now, the choice is made only by pressing the F5 key.

mute. Do you want to hear about it when you attempt the impossible? Word sounds the audible alarm on your computer as a reminder. Think of the alarm as a friendly toot, rather than a blaring honk of warning. Turn it off if you wish by setting *mute* to *Yes.*

default tab width. Word assumes you want tab stops half an inch apart, which gives five spaces between stops with pica-size type (10-pitch, or 10 characters to the inch). Beginning with Word version 3.0, you can change this assumption of half an inch (0.5") to anything you like. If, for instance, you want five spaces of elite-size type, change *default tab width* to 0.42". For greater control, refer to the Format Tabs Set command.

printer display (or display mode). A printed line is composed of both *content* (characters) and *format* (appearance). The printed copy shows both the content and the format of each line properly, and in most cases the screen does, too. There are exceptions on the screen, however, and you tell Word how to handle them with the *printer display* field.

When your on-screen documents have conventional formats, Word can usually display each line's content and format on the screen just as it will appear when printed. But when you change type sizes within a document or use type other than 10-pitch (pica) or 12-pitch (elite), Word may only be able to display either the exact characters that will be printed on a particular line or the format of that line—but not both at the same time. If you choose to see format, the content of the document will be shown accurately, but possibly will not appear on the same lines as in the printed version.

The *printer display* field asks, in effect, "Do you want the *characters* in the lines on your screen to match, line for line, the way they'll be printed?"

Picking *Yes* (*Printer* in versions before 2.0) tells Word to show which line each character will print on, even if it means the format of the document will be distorted on the screen. For instance, picking *Yes* might cause some justified text to appear unjustified on the screen, even though it will still print properly.

Picking *No* (*Normal* in versions before 2.0) tells Word to forgo accuracy in line content, if necessary, in order to represent paragraph formats accurately. In this case, justified text is justified both on the screen and on the printout, but a particular word might appear in different lines in the two versions.

When you use the Library Hyphenate command and set its *confirm* field to *Yes,* Word temporarily switches the *printer display* field to *Yes,* unless you already have.

measure. Which unit of measure do you want Word to use to express distances and measurements in various Format command fields? Possibilities are inches (*In*), centimeters (*Cm*), 10-pitch characters (*P10*), 12-pitch characters (*P12*), and points (*Pt*).

Word displays text slightly differently, depending on the size of type it believes you are using. When you pick *In, Cm,* or *P10,* Word assumes you're using pica-sized (10-pitch) characters. When you pick *P12* or *Pt,* Word assumes you're using elite-sized (12-pitch) characters. Use inches and centimeters when you want the convenience of common units of measure. Use *P10* when you want to specify measurements in pica-sized characters. Use *P12* when you want to specify measurements in elite-sized characters. Use points when you want the precision of units that are ½2 of an inch. (Actually, Word accepts instructions as exact as ½0 of a point— ½440 of an inch— but unless you're using Word with typesetting equipment, you probably can't take full advantage of this degree of precision.) The following diagram shows you the relationships among these units of measure:

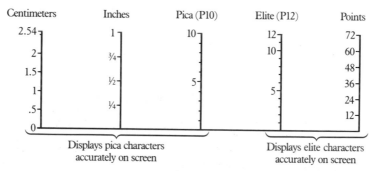

By way of example, let's see how these units of measure are reflected in the Format Paragraph command. First, set the *measure* field of the Options command to *In* and your Format Paragraph command fields might look like this:

```
FORMAT PARAGRAPH alignment: Left Centered Right Justified
        left indent: 1"          first line: 0.5"      right indent: 0.75"
        line spacing: 1 li      space before: 1 li       space after: 0 li
        keep together: Yes(No)  keep follow: Yes(No)  side by side: Yes(No)
```

Set the *measure* field to *Cm,* and, for the same paragraph, the Format Paragraph indent fields would look like this:

```
left indent: 2.54 cm    first line: 1.27 cm    right indent: 1.9 cm
```

Set *measure* to *P10* and the fields would change to:

```
left indent: 10 p10    first line: 5 p10    right indent: 7.5 p10
```

Choose *P12* and the fields would become:

```
left indent: 12 pl2     first line: 6 pl2     right indent: 9 pl2
```

Or, choose *Pt* and you would see:

```
left indent: 72 pt     first line: 36 pt     right indent: 54 pt
```

In each example, the measurements stayed the same—they were just expressed in different units.

One final note: You probably think in terms of inches or centimeters. Don't worry about having to convert them to Word's other units of measure. Enter your measurement in inches (1″, 2″, and so on) or centimeters (2.54 cm, 5.0 cm), and when you execute the Format commands, Word will convert your measurement to whatever unit you have specified in the Options *measure* field. (For related information, see the section "Specifying locations" in Chapter 12, "The Family of Format Commands.")

Interactions

As you've seen, achieving complete agreement between what is displayed on the screen and what is printed on paper is sometimes impossible. To achieve agreement when it *is* possible, you may need to consider the interaction of these three elements: the character pitch (width) you use, the setting of the *printer display* field, and the setting of the *measure* field. If you're troubled by disagreement between your screen and printout, review the preceding pages of this chapter and bear the following points in mind:

♦ When you use characters with different pitches (widths) in the same document, total agreement is impossible, because Word, like most other word processors, cannot display the text layout for more than one pitch at a time. (The simple word processor Microsoft Write, which works with Microsoft Windows, accepts Word documents and shows characters of different sizes.)

♦ If you're using pica-sized type exclusively, set the *measure* field for *In, Cm,* or *P10* and be assured the display will match your printout.

♦ If you're using elite-sized type exclusively, set the *measure* field for *P12* or *Pt*.

♦ If the screen display does not match the formatting you specified, try setting the *printer display* field to *No*. You may, however, need to reset the field to *Yes* to see exact agreement in the content of lines between screen and paper, and you may need to set the field to *Yes* when text is wider than the text window.

♦ If you're using different character sizes in the same document and want to see how the different sizes will print, you can set *printer display* to *Yes*, and switch the *measure* setting back and forth (as between *P10* and *P12*).

♦ If you use other than 10- or 12-pitch type, expect some inconsistency between the screen display and your printout, unless you are using the same pitch throughout.

♦ If you use tab characters in a document, double-check the *measure* field to be sure it is set appropriately for the pitch you are using.

♦ If a previously created document mysteriously seems to have lost its formatting, check to see if you have changed the *measure* field's setting and make sure that you've installed the same printer description (.PRD) file you used originally. And if you used a style sheet to format the document, make sure it is still on the disk.

REPLACE

```
COMMAND: Alpha Copy Delete Format Gallery Help Insert Jump Library
         Options Print Quit Replace Search Transfer Undo Window
         ┌─────────────────────────────────────┐

REPLACE text:                          with text:
        confirm:(Yes)No  case: Yes(No) whole word: Yes(No)
```

The Replace command lets you substitute new characters for old. If the selection is highlighting a single character on the screen, the Replace command searches from there to the document's end. So, if you want Word to look through an entire document, move the selection to the beginning of the document. If you expand the selection to encompass a passage, Replace will search through the selection, rather than the whole document.

When the Replace command is finished (or when you stop it by pressing the Esc key), Word tells you the number of replacements made. If, after you use the Replace command, you decide you like the original way better, the Undo command will put everything back as it was.

The Replace command acts on "hidden" text only when the Window Options command has been set so that hidden text appears on the screen.

Fields of the Replace command

There are five fields in the Replace command. The first two tell Word what to substitute; the other three let you fine tune the command.

text. In the *text* field you enter the word, words, or characters you wish to replace. Word will accept up to 40 characters, including numbers and punctuation marks. You can use a question mark (?) as a "wildcard" to represent any character. For example, *fo?l* causes Word to find such character combinations as *foil, fool, foul, foal,* and *fowl.*

If you've used either the Replace or Search command previously during the same editing session, Word proposes the previous *text* entry again. To accept this proposed response, move to the next field.

The ^ symbol (the shifted 6 key on the IBM PC keyboard) tells Word that the next character is a special symbol. These are the possibilities:

♦ ^? represents question marks (since Word interprets ? without the ^ as a wildcard).

♦ ^- (hyphen) represents optional (nonrequired) hyphens you have inserted (with the Library Hyphenate command or the Control-hyphen key combination). To Word, an optional hyphen is a character like any other, so it must be specified in the *text* field, even though the hyphen itself may not show on the screen.

♦ ^d represents either division marks or new-page marks, both formatting characters.

♦ ^n represents new-line marks, which you insert into a document with the Shift-Enter key combination, and which force a new line to begin within a paragraph.

♦ ^p represents paragraph marks, which you insert into a document with the Enter key.

♦ ^s represents nonbreaking spaces, which you place between words with the Control-Spacebar key combination when you want to ensure that a new line won't begin between the words.

♦ ^t represents tab characters, which you create with the Tab key.

♦ ^w represents any *and all* spaces and spacing characters in your document, including Spacebar spaces, tab characters, paragraph marks, new-line characters, division marks, new-page marks, and nonbreaking spaces. Be careful with ^w—if you give Word the following command:

```
REPLACE text: ^w                    with text:
        confirm: Yes NO  case: Yes(No) whole word: Yes(No)
```

you will remove every bit of white space between the words in your document. (If you happen to do this inadvertently, you may appreciate the Undo command.)

with text. In this field, you enter the word, words, or characters that will replace the material in the *text* field. Again, you can specify up to 40 characters, and you can use the preceding list of ^ symbols, except for ^w and ^? (in this field, the question mark is treated as a question mark, not as a wildcard).

If you have used the Replace command earlier, Word will propose the previous *with text* entry again. To accept the proposed response, move to the next field.

confirm. Shall Word ask you to confirm each replacement?

If you choose *No,* Word makes all replacements and then notifies you. The effects won't be displayed until then.

If you choose *Yes,* Word will stop each time it finds the text to be replaced, highlight it, and ask you with the message *Enter Y to replace, N to ignore, or press Esc to cancel* to confirm that particular replacement.

If you press Y, Word makes the replacement and continues searching. But if you press N, Word leaves the original text unchanged and continues searching. And if you press the Esc key, you both reject the proposed replacement and cancel the Replace command.

case. Shall Word seek only text that matches the capitalization (or lack of capitalization) of characters you've typed in the *text* field?

If you choose *Yes,* Word ignores all but exact matches—in other words, if you've typed *Dog* in the *text* field, Word ignores *dog* in its search. When Word finds an exact match, it replaces the text with exactly the combination of upper- and lowercase letters you've typed in the *with text* field. In other words, it replaces *Dog* with *Cat, cAt, CAt,* or *CAT*—however you typed "cat" in the *with text* field.

On the other hand, if you choose *No,* for *case,* Word shows some intelligence. It ignores case during the search (it will find both *Dog* and *dog,* regardless of how you've typed it in the *text* field). But, when replacing text, Word will mimic the case of the text being replaced—in other words, *Dog* will be replaced with *Cat,* and *dog* will be replaced with *cat,* and *DOG* will be replaced with *CAT,* and so on—no matter how you've typed *cat* in the *with text* field.

whole word. Shall Word search for whole words only?

If you choose *Yes,* Word stops only at matching text it interprets as a whole word (that is, a collection of characters with spaces or punctuation marks at both ends).

If you choose *No,* Word highlights the characters you specify, even if they are fragments of other words. For example, if you've specified *valid* in the *text* field and have chosen *No* for *whole word,* Word will display not only the word *valid,* but the same letters in the words *invalid* and *validity,* as well.

SEARCH

```
COMMAND: Alpha Copy Delete Format Gallery Help Insert Jump Library
         Options Print Quit Replace Search Transfer Undo Window
              |_____
              |
SEARCH text:
        direction: Up(Down) case: Yes(No) whole word: Yes(No)
```

The Search command is much like the Replace command, but it only highlights the text being sought—it does not replace the text. Like Replace, Search only finds "hidden" text if it has been made visible with the Window Options command. Refer to the Replace command for details on the *case* and *whole word* fields, but note these exceptions, which apply to Search:

♦ The *direction* field lets you move either *Up* (toward the beginning) or *Down* (toward the end) of the document, relative to the position of the selection.

♦ You can search for another occurrence of the same text by holding down the Shift key and pressing the F4 key. This "repeat the previous search" key works even if you've done other editing since you last used the Search command. In other words, you can use Shift-F4 twenty minutes later.

The Family of Format Commands

If Word has a specialty, it is formatting: giving you the means to make documents look the way you want them to. Word is adept at helping you shape and reshape the appearance of your document, both before and after you've written it. Content and form are distinct from one another, and even dramatic changes generally can be made to one without affecting the other.

Word's Format commands let you control the appearance of printed text. They let you manipulate everything from the layout of your document's pages to the format of footnotes, page numbers, even the typeface, size, and attributes (such as underlining) of a single character. Formatting is cumulative, so you can apply more than one format to the same text. With the Format commands, you describe to Word the design you want by filling in fields or choosing from submenus.

The Format commands aren't your only formatting options. Two shortcuts—built-in formats and style sheets—are at your disposal, too. The built-in formats, discussed in Chapter 5, "The Simple Word," give you quick and easy access to a variety of popular designs, such as various paragraph indentations and character underlining. Style sheets, discussed in Chapter 24, "Power Tools: Style Sheets," are similar to built-in formats, but more flexible because, in a sense, each style sheet is a set of built-in formats ("styles") created for a particular purpose.

This chapter includes a brief overview of formatting, but focuses on the use of Format commands, especially Format Character, Format Paragraph, and the Format Division commands. These correspond to the three types of formatting that govern every part of a document:

- Character formatting—the appearance of letters, numbers, and symbols.
- Paragraph formatting—the rules used by Word to lay out the lines of a paragraph. (Think of this as "line formatting.")
- Division formatting—the layout (design) of pages throughout a document or a major section ("division") of a document.

A "family tree" of sorts shows you how to reach all of the Format commands from the Edit menu:

```
COMMAND: Alpha Copy Delete Format Gallery Help Insert Jump Library
         Options Print Quit|Replace Search Transfer Undo Window
                 ┌─────────┘
FORMAT: Character Paragraph Tabs Footnote Division Running-head Style
          ┌──────────────────┘
FORMAT TABS: Set Clear Reset-all
        ┌───────────────────────┘
FORMAT DIVISION: Margins Page-numbers Layout
     ┌──────────────────────────────────────┘
FORMAT STYLE: Character Paragraph Division Sheet
```

FORMATTING AND THE SELECT-DO CONCEPT

Like all of Word's commands, the formatting techniques and combinations you can use are governed by the Select-Do concept described in Chapter 3, "Thinking About Word." First, you select the text to be formatted or the place where you wish to begin formatting, and then you act on the selection with Format commands, built-in formats, or styles from a style sheet.

You can "select" your text and "do" your formatting either after the text is complete or as you write. You'll probably do some of both, but let's consider the two methods individually.

Formatting after writing

To format existing characters in a document, select the text you want to format, as in the following example:

```
‖ This is a sample sentence written with Microsoft Word.                    ‖
```

Then, apply the formatting. In this case, underline the selected text with the Format Character command:

```
FORMAT CHARACTER bold: Yes(No)      italic: Yes(No)         underline: Yes No
                 strikethrough: Yes(No)   uppercase: Yes(No)      small caps: Yes(No)
                 double underline: Yes(No) position:(Normal)Superscript Subscript
                 font name: Pica          font size: 12              hidden: Yes(No)
```

Press the Enter key and move the selection to the right to reveal the result:

‖ This is a <u>sample sentence written with Microsoft Word.</u>█   ‖

(In this example, as in the next, underlining could also be applied to the selection with the built-in underlining format, Alt-U, or a style for underlining from a style sheet.)

Formatting while writing

Now, let's see how a similar sentence is underlined during writing. This time, enter text as usual, until you reach the point at which you want underlining to begin:

‖ This is a █   ‖

Note that the diamond end mark is not on the line. This is intentional and important, because if you try to format characters while the selection is on the end mark, Word refuses and displays the message *End mark cannot be edited.*

To begin formatting, select the character or space where you want underlining to begin and format it with the Format Character command, the built-in Alt-U format, or a style sheet. Continue typing, and the result is:

‖ This is a <u>second sample</u>█   ‖

‖ This is a <u>second sample written with</u>█   ‖

‖ This is a <u>second sample written with Word.</u>█   ‖

The formatting appears on the screen a letter at a time, as you type. Everything you type continues to be underlined until you move the selection away from the formatting (with a direction key or the mouse), or remove the formatting from the selection (by pressing the Alt-Spacebar key combination). Alternatively, you can turn off underlining with the Format Character command or by applying a different style from a style sheet.

Here are some pointers on formatting as you type:

1. Select an area of the document, as small as a single character or as large as the whole document, and format it as desired.
2. Then do all your writing inside this formatted area. The area will grow as you type, and everything in it will be formatted as you want.
3. But be careful when scrolling or moving the selection. You can inadvertently move beyond the formatted area and suddenly seem to lose your formatting.

COMMAND FIELDS

Word's Format commands lead you, either directly or via a submenu, to the command fields, where you specify the formatting you want to apply to your document. Some of these command fields are of the fill-in type; most of them are of the menu type, offering you a set of options from which to choose. In either case, Word generally displays a proposed response that shows you the formatting currently in effect for selected text. For example, if you select all or part of a paragraph that is single spaced, with a first-line indent of ½ inch and a blank line between it and the preceding paragraph, this is what Word displays when you choose the Format Paragraph command:

```
FORMAT PARAGRAPH alignment: Left Centered Right Justified
     left indent: 0"          first line: 0.5"      right indent: 0"
     line spacing: 1 li      space before: 1 li      space after: 0 li
     keep together: Yes(No)  keep follow: Yes(No)  side by side: Yes(No)
```

As you can see, these command fields tell you even more. The paragraph is also flush left, it is not set off by any indent on either the right or left side (except the first-line indent already mentioned), and it creates no following extra line of space. (We won't worry about the *keep together*, *keep follow*, and *side-by-side* fields for now—they're niceties described later in this chapter.)

The Format command fields can be a valuable aid, not only in applying formatting to your document, but often in checking on the current formatting.

Word displays proposed responses in Format command fields *unless* the selected text is formatted inconsistently—for instance, some of it is underlined and some isn't. In those cases, Word does not know what to show you in the command fields.

As with a menu-type field, you can ignore fill-in fields if you do not wish to change a particular aspect of formatting. A field you leave blank, or with its proposed response unchanged, has no effect on the selected text.

Specifying locations

Many Format command fields allow you to specify a location for text in terms of some unit of measure. Word understands six units of measure: inches, centimeters, 10- and 12-pitch characters, points (1/72 of an inch), and "lines" (1/6 of an inch). These units can be used interchangeably, and fractions are permitted when expressed as decimals (not ½ or ¾, but .5 or .75).

Word is shipped with inches set as the usual unit of measure, but as described in Chapter 11, you can pick a different measure with the Options command. For the most part, Word assumes that all numbers you enter in Format command fields are in the usual unit of measure. But:

♦ You can use any unit of measure you want in a field, as long as you type in its abbreviation when specifying a measurement. That is, even if you specify centimeters in the Options command's *measurement* field, you can still express an inch as *1"* in a particular command field and Word will convert the inch to 2.54 centimeters for you.

♦ Vertical measurements in Format Paragraph command fields always are presumed to be in lines (*li*), unless you specify a different unit. One line is 1/6 inch, or 12 points. Since six lines to an inch is the usual line-space setting on typewriters and typewriter-like printers, the number of lines is a convenient way to specify vertical measurements in the Format Paragraph command fields. But while vertical measurements are usually specified in inches or lines, using points provides potentially greater flexibility as well as conformity with professional printing terminology. For instance, if you want eight lines to an inch instead of six, type *9 pt* in the *line spacing* field of the Format Paragraph command.

♦ If you are accustomed to using the typographical unit of measure called a "pica"— ⅙ of an inch—you can use lines, instead. The abbreviation is *li*, so if you want a 7-pica left margin for a brochure, type *7 li* in the *left* field of the Format Division Margins command.

THE FORMAT COMMANDS

Now we come to the commands that make up the Format family. The remaining sections of this chapter describe the commands and command fields in detail.

FORMAT CHARACTER

```
FORMAT: Character Paragraph Tabs Footnote Division Running-head Style

FORMAT CHARACTER bold: Yes No      italic: Yes(No)          underline: Yes(No)
           strikethrough: Yes(No)   uppercase: Yes(No)       small caps: Yes(No)
           double underline: Yes(No) position:(Normal)Superscript Subscript
           font name: Pica          font size: 12                   hidden: Yes(No)
```

The Format Character command lets you specify type and character attributes such as underlining, boldfacing, or italicizing for the selected text. It also lets you "hide" text, beginning with Word version 3.0. If you don't specify character formatting in the Format Character command fields (or through built-in formats or style sheets), characters are "normal"—on most printers, Pica 12 point (generally 10-pitch) with no special attributes.

Whether or not you can see character formatting on your screen depends on the capabilities of your computer and screen. If your equipment can't display a particular character attribute (italics, for example), it probably substitutes underlining or some other distinctive on-screen "look" to indicate that the formatting isn't normal. The formatting will still print as you intend, however, if your printer is capable of reproducing it. If your printer cannot handle a particular character size or attribute, Word makes an appropriate substitution or, as a last resort, omits the formatting and uses normal characters instead. If you later print the same document on a printer with sufficient capabilities, all character formatting will be reproduced. In other words, Word won't forget character formatting, even if your computer and screen can't show it or your printer can't print it.

Fields of the Format Character command

bold: Yes No. Shall the selected text be in boldface? If you pick *Yes*, Word instructs your printer to boldface or double strike the selected characters.

italic: Yes No. Shall the selected text be in italics? If you pick *Yes*, Word instructs your printer to italicize the selected characters if it can. If you have a daisy-wheel printer, Word stops printing and requests that you mount an italic font.

underline: Yes No. Shall the selected text be underlined? Think a moment on this one. Picking *Yes* means Word will underline blank spaces too. If you want only words to be underlined, first select and underline one word, then select subsequent words individually with the F7 or F8 key, underlining each with the F4 key (which repeats the last editing act). In other words, after underlining the first word, press F8-F4 as many times as needed.

strikethrough: Yes No. Shall the selected text have a horizontal line struck through it? This attribute is useful for showing proposed deletions—for example, in legal documents.

uppercase: Yes No. Shall the selected text be displayed and printed in all CAPITAL LETTERS?

small caps: Yes No. Shall the selected text be displayed and printed as smaller-than-normal CAPITAL LETTERS?

double underline: Yes No. Shall the selected text have two underlines, one right below the other?

position: Normal Superscript Subscript. Shall the selected text be positioned normally, or shall it be printed slightly above[abc] or below[xyz] the line? Superscripting is useful in footnote references, and both sub- and superscripting are useful in scientific and mathematical notation.

font name. What font (shape of type) do you want for the selected text? You can either enter a font name or choose from a list. The list you see and choose from varies according to the printer you're using. To understand why, briefly look at the relationship of fonts, printers, and Word itself.

You link Word to a printer through the Print Options command (or, beginning with version 2.0, also by running the SETUP program). Word can use any of a large number of printers with differing capabilities and requirements. When you use the Print Options command or the SETUP program to tell Word which printer you are using, what you're actually doing is installing the appropriate printer description file in Word. This customizes the program and gives it specific information relating to your particular printer—information such as what fonts and sizes of type are available. That's why the font list varies according to the printer you have designated.

font size. After picking a font name, you may pick a font size (height of type). You specify the font size in points, and can pick from a list of choices, just as for *font name.* The size list, however, varies according to both the printer description file and the font name you've specified. Three points to remember:

- If you've installed the printer description files TTY.PRD or PLAIN.PRD, the only combination of font name and size available is Pica 12.

- As explained in Chapter 8, font size is measured in *points* during formatting, but for daisy-wheel and certain other printers is expressed in *pitch* during printing. When you're using a printer that emulates a typewriter, you're probably using pica type, which is 10-pitch and 12-point (10 characters to the inch that normally need a vertical space 12 points high), or elite type, which is 12-pitch and 10-point (12 characters to the inch that normally need a vertical space 10 points high). This means that if you format characters as Pica 12 and print them on a daisy-wheel printer, when Word instructs you to mount the proper daisy wheel, it will say Pica 10. The distinction can be confusing at first.

♦ If the font name is followed by PS, as in ROMANPS, the font you've chosen is proportionally spaced and on most printers has a designated font size of 12.

hidden: Yes No. Shall the selected text be hidden? If you pick *Yes*, Word will neither show the text on the screen nor send it to the printer to be printed. The exception to this is when the Window Options command's *show hidden text* field has been set to *Yes*, in which case hidden text appears in the text window and also prints. In this case, however, hidden text appears with an underline or in a special color, or, if your computer has graphics capabilities, with a tiny dotted underline. (Also, depending on how the Options command is set, the presence of hidden text may be indicated on the screen with a double-headed arrow (↔) in lieu of any actual "hidden" characters.

Hidden text, which was a new feature in version 3.0 of Word, is useful for annotating documents with temporary or private comments, and is a vital element in using the Library Index and Library Table commands to create indexes and tables of contents for documents. For details, see Chapter 14, "The Family of Library Commands," and Chapter 26, "Power Tools: Hidden Text and Indexing."

As explained in Chapter 5, "The Simple Word," there is a built-in format for hidden text: Press the Alt key and the letter E. (If a style sheet is in use, either press the Alt key and the letter X followed by E, or else use a style that includes the hidden attribute.)

FORMAT PARAGRAPH

```
FORMAT: Character Paragraph Tabs Footnote Division Running-head Style


FORMAT PARAGRAPH alignment: Left Centered Right Justified
        left indent: 0"         first line: 0"      right indent: 0"
        line spacing: 1 li    space before: 0 li    space after: 0 li
        keep together: Yes(No)  keep follow: Yes(No)  side by side: Yes(No)
Select option
Page 1    {}                        ?              Microsoft Word:
```

The preceding diagram shows the Format Paragraph command fields, as they are beginning with version 3.0. If you have an earlier version, some of the Format Paragraph command fields will not appear, or they will appear in a different order. The *side by side* field was new in version 3.0, and the *keep follow* field was new in version 2.0. Prior to 2.0, the *keep together* field was called *keep.*

The Format Paragraph command lets you specify such line formatting as indentation, spacing, and alignment. The command affects whole paragraphs at a time, and applies to as many paragraphs at once as you have selected. On-screen, paragraph formats generally look much like the way they'll print, although accuracy decreases when you format characters in more than one size, because the screen shows all characters as the same size.

It's important to understand that Word somewhat redefines the meaning of the word *paragraph*. As writers, we're accustomed to thinking of a paragraph in terms of content—as a cohesive block of text devoted to a single theme or point. But Word manipulates format as well as content, so a "paragraph" to Word is a cohesive unit of formatting, too. Word considers a paragraph to be whatever lies between two paragraph marks. Since any paragraph (by Word's definition) can be formatted distinctively, you can start a new paragraph for formatting reasons as well as for content. For example:

♦ To center a single line, make it a separate paragraph and then format it to be centered. The same goes for titles, running heads, and footnotes.

♦ To construct a table in which different lines have different tab stops (an impossibility with many word processors), make each line a separate paragraph.

In some senses, the Format Paragraph command could be called the Format Line command, because you can give any single line a distinctive design just by making it a paragraph in itself. When formatted thoughtfully, a paragraph created for formatting purposes needn't look like a traditional, separate-block-of-text paragraph to your readers.

Word's "normal" (built-in) paragraph format is flush-left (ragged-right non-justified) alignment, no indentations, and single-spacing with no extra blank lines before or after the paragraph. Additionally, there are no restrictions on where normal paragraphs split from one page to the next during printing, except that Word never strands a single line by itself at the top of a page unless it is a one-line paragraph. (However, this "widow/orphan control" can be turned off with the Print Options command.) Paragraphs are "normal" until you change them by making choices in the Format Paragraph command fields, or by using built-in paragraph formats or paragraph styles from a style sheet. (You can redefine what is "normal" paragraph formatting by designating a "Paragraph Standard" style in a style sheet.)

The paragraph mark

Understanding the role of the paragraph mark is crucial to understanding paragraph formatting. Whenever you press the Enter key, a paragraph ends and several things happen:

♦ Word marks the end of the paragraph with a paragraph mark. This mark is as much a real character as is any letter, number, or punctuation mark, so it can be selected, copied, or deleted.

♦ Within each paragraph mark, Word stores the formatting instructions for the paragraph it ends.

♦ Word moves you to a new line and begins a fresh paragraph, giving it the same formatting as the preceding paragraph. This paragraph formatting prevails unless you change it.

How does this affect you? Imagine you've written two paragraphs and have formatted each differently. During editing you inadvertently delete the mark that ends the first paragraph. You just deleted the first paragraph's identity as a separate paragraph. The result?

The two paragraphs join at the position where the mark used to be, and the formatting instructions of the second paragraph take control of the newly unified paragraph. The formatting of the first paragraph disappeared with its paragraph mark. Annoying? Confusing? Quite possibly, if you don't understand. All is not lost, of course; there's always the Undo command. And if the two paragraphs had the same formatting to begin with, just insert a new paragraph mark to break them apart again.

Changing indentation within a paragraph

Beginning with version 3.0, you can trick Word into letting you change the indentation of lines within a paragraph. This is useful when you want to wrap text around a photograph, illustration, or other element such as a heading. The strategy is to "hide" extra paragraph marks inside paragraphs, using hidden-text character formatting. Each of these extra paragraph marks can be formatted with different left and right indents so that line length can be changed repeatedly. Interestingly, this was not an intentional feature of Word, and was unknown to Microsoft until I discovered it during my experimentation for the second edition of this book. The technique is best suited to advanced users, and is described and illustrated in Chapter 26, "Power Tools: Hidden Text and Indexing."

Fields of the Format Paragraph command

alignment: Left Centered Right Justified. This field gives you a menu of four ways to lay out the individual lines of a paragraph:

Left is normal typewriter format, in which the left margin is flush and the right margin is ragged. Left alignment is common in correspondence because, with a letter-quality printer, it has a more "personalized" typewritten look than the obviously computer-generated or typeset appearance of left- and right-justified text. Often, the first line of a left-aligned paragraph is indented. This book is set with "left" alignment—also called "ragged right."

Centered causes every line of the paragraph to be centered within the margins of the page. Centering is useful for formatting titles, headings, and running heads, where the paragraph is a single distinctive line. When using centered alignment, you probably want to set the *first line* indent to 0 to avoid offsetting the line to the right of center.

Right, not surprisingly, is the opposite of *Left*. This choice makes lines align flush right, with a ragged left margin—an uncommon formatting choice.

Justified makes each line fill all available space between the left and right edges; in other words, the left and right edges of the text line up vertically. Only the final line of a justified paragraph doesn't have to line up. Newspapers and most magazines and books (but not this one), have justified type. As a further refinement, with most printers Word automatically prints justified paragraphs with microspacing (that is, finely adjusted spacing between letters and words), even though microspacing does not show on the screen. Type fonts that are proportionally spaced automatically print with microspace justification, if the printer is capable of it and if the *alignment* field is set to *Justified*. You can avoid microspace justification by setting the Print Options command's *draft* field to *Yes*. (For more information, see Chapter 15, "The Family of Print Commands.")

Indent fields

Three indent fields control to what extent, if any, the paragraph or its first line is indented beyond the page margins you establish with the Format Division command. The *first line* indent gives you a way to indent the beginning of a paragraph automatically without pressing the Spacebar or using the Tab key. The *left indent* and *right indent* fields let you put additional blank space to the left or right of a paragraph—as when you want a quoted passage to be printed in lines shorter than those of surrounding text.

The ruler, which you can turn on and off with the Options command or by clicking with the mouse in the upper-right corner of a text window, displays across the top of the window and shows the location of indents (and tab stops) for whatever paragraph is selected.

Running heads (see the section later in this chapter) are a special case, because margins do not apply to them. When you are using the Format Paragraph command to design a running head, the *left indent* and *right indent* fields specify distances from the edges of the pages rather than from the (division) margins. Now, let's look at the three indent fields, as they apply to all paragraphs except running heads.

left indent. How far from the left page margin shall the selected paragraph or paragraphs be positioned? The normal setting, 0, aligns the left edge of the paragraph with the left margin of the page.

first line. How far in from the paragraph's left indent shall the first line begin? A popular setting is 0.5 inch, which indents the first line half an inch in from the left edge of the other lines of the paragraph. The 0.5-inch setting gives five blank spaces of pica-size type at the beginning of the paragraph. However, if you're using smaller, elite-size type and want an automatic five-space indentation, specify *.42"* or *5 p12* instead. Negative settings (− .5") are allowed.

right indent. How far from the right page margin shall the selected paragraph or paragraphs be? The normal setting, 0, means a full-length text line reaches the right margin.

Vertical spacing fields

Vertical spacing between lines of a paragraph and between paragraphs is established in three fields: *line spacing, space before,* and *space after.* Word's ability to show line spacing on the screen is limited, but it will print fractional line settings, such as 1.5 lines, to the best ability of the printer.

line spacing. How much space shall there be between the lines of a paragraph? The normal setting is *1 li*. If you specify *2*, the lines will be double spaced. Although Word assumes six lines to an inch, measures other than lines are permitted. So, for example, you could increase the space between lines slightly by specifying *13 pt* in the *line spacing* field.

Beginning with Word version 3.0, you can type the word *AUTO* in the *line spacing* field. This causes Word to readjust line spacing on a line-by-line basis, so that lines of small type are closer together than lines of large type. The rule Word follows is that line spacing will be equal to the point size of the largest type on a line. This works well generally, although you may need to add some *space before* when a line of small type directly follows a line of substantially larger type.

space before. How much extra vertical space, if any, shall be placed immediately above the paragraph?

space after. And how much extra vertical space, if any, shall be placed immediately below the paragraph?

Remember that the extra space between two paragraphs is the sum of the *space after* the first paragraph and the *space before* the second. When adding spaces between paragraphs, it's advisable to consistently create any blank lines with either *space before* or *space after,* but not both. This standardizes your formatting and minimizes the possibility of inadvertently "stacking" extra spaces—as when a paragraph with *space after* is followed by a paragraph with *space before.* I recommend using *space before,* the same convention used in Word's built-in format (Alt-O) for open paragraph spacing, and the convention I follow in the style sheets that come with my book *Microsoft Word Style Sheets.*

Keep fields

Word generally follows this rule when breaking a paragraph across two pages during printing: Unless a paragraph is a single line, Word never prints only one line of it at either the bottom of one page or the top of another. Instead, Word arranges pages so there are at least two lines of the paragraph on each. You can eliminate the rule by setting the *widow/orphan control* field of the Print Options command to *No,* and you can strengthen and supplement the rule with the Format Paragraph *keep* fields: *keep together* and *keep follow.*

keep together: Yes No (or *keep: Yes No* in early versions). If a paragraph falls near the end of a page, shall the entire paragraph be printed on one page or, in the case of multi-column pages, in the same column? If you pick *Yes,* Word moves the whole paragraph to the next page or column rather than splitting it. This option is valuable in circumstances such as keeping all of a table together.

keep follow: Yes No (not in versions prior to 2.0). Shall the page be laid out so that the last line of the paragraph is printed on the same page as the first two lines of the next paragraph? Setting this field to *Yes* for a heading ensures that it prints on the same page as the beginning of the text to which it refers. Setting it to *Yes* in the last paragraph in the body of a letter guarantees that part of the paragraph is printed on the same page as the letter's complimentary closing.

To make sure that all of two consecutive paragraphs are printed on the same page, pick *Yes* for both *keep together* and *keep follow* in the first paragraph, and *Yes* for *keep together* in the second. You'll discover that by using the keep attributes effectively throughout a document, there is often little need before printing to preview page breaks with Word's Print Repaginate command. Page breaks needn't be monitored; unacceptable ones are automatically avoided.

side by side: Yes No (not in versions prior to 3.0). Shall paragraphs be printed beside each other in separate columns whenever possible? Word lets you print paragraphs of text next to each other in two or more columns, provided that each of the paragraphs involved has been formatted with the *side by side* field set to *Yes,* and that the paragraphs would not overlap each other if they were printed on the same lines.

For example, to print two paragraphs beside each other, you might format the first one with a wide right indent and the second one with a wide left indent, and set the *side by side* field to *Yes* for both paragraphs. Specifically, if a page is 8.5 inches wide and the right and left margins are 1.25 inches each, you have 6 inches of printable width. You could set the Format Paragraph command's *right indent* field to *3.5"* for the first paragraph, and its *left indent* field to *3.5"* for the second paragraph. As long as *side by side* was set to *Yes* for both paragraphs, they would print beside each other, with a 1-inch gutter between them.

If, instead, you wanted to print a series of five paragraphs beside five other paragraphs, you would set *side by side* to *Yes* for each of them, and format them with a wide indent on whichever side of the paper you did not want them to be printed. When printing, Word would put each paragraph on the appropriate side, and position it as high in the column as possible. The same technique can be used to print three or more columns.

There is quite a bit you can learn about the side-by-side feature. Among other things, it gives you a way to change the number of columns on a page, in the middle of the page. (See Chapter 27, "Power Tools: Creating Tables.")

Although paragraphs will show on the Word screen in the appropriate horizontal position, columns do not appear side by side on the screen. They only print that way.

THE FORMAT TABS SUBMENU

```
FORMAT: Character Paragraph (Tabs Footnote Division Running-head Style
         └─────────────────────┐
FORMAT TABS: Set Clear Reset-all
```

Normally, Word presets a tab stop every half inch: Press the Tab key, and the cursor jumps half an inch to the next predetermined stop. This built-in formatting meets many basic needs and requires no setting up. But as you'll see here, when you're ready to set your own tabs, Word offers a formidable array of tab features.

For one thing, you can change the distance between preset tab stops by altering the setting of the *default tab width* field of the Options command (beginning with version 3.0 of Word). For much greater flexibility, you will want to use the three Format Tabs commands.

Picking Format Tabs brings to the screen the Format Tabs submenu—Set, Clear, and Reset-all—shown above. The Format Tabs Clear and Format Tabs Reset-all commands are used only to eliminate tab stops. There's almost nothing to learn about them. The Format Tabs Set command, on the other hand, allows several formatting choices and requires learning.

Content versus format

Recall the distinction between a document's content and format. When setting and using tabs, bear in mind that a tab *character* is content, but a tab *stop* is format.

When you press the Tab key, a tab character is inserted into the text at the location of the selection. The tab character keeps blank the space between its insertion point and the location of the next tab stop in the same line. Though it can blank out many consecutive spaces, the tab character is a single character and therefore is selected, deleted, and copied like any other single character.

Normally, the tab character is invisible, but beginning with version 2.0, you can display it on the screen as a small, right-facing arrow by setting the *visible* field of the Options command to *Complete.*

On the other hand, when you use the Format Tabs Set command, you create formatting—a tab stop containing instructions on how any tab character that comes in contact with it will affect the appearance of the document. A tab stop is part of paragraph formatting, though it is applied with the Format Tabs Set command rather than the Format Paragraph command. You can vary tab stops between different paragraphs. One way to create tab stops that apply throughout a document is to select the entire document before using the Format Tabs Set command.

FORMAT TABS SET

```
FORMAT TABS: Set Clear Reset-all


FORMAT TABS SET position: █
              alignment:(Left)Center Right Decimal        leader char:(Blank). - _
```

With the Format Tabs Set command you can create, move, and even delete tab stops. In addition to giving you control over the locations of tab stops, the Format Tabs Set command lets you choose two features called *alignment* and *leader character* that allow you to align text at a tab stop in a variety of ways and, if you wish, to lead up to a tab stop with a series of dots, hyphens, or underlines.

Word always displays a ruler at the top of the text window when you are making choices with this command. The ruler (described in Chapter 17 in the section "Window Options") shows the location, alignment, and leader characters (if any) of tab stops for the selected paragraph(s).

Because people often want tab stops left-aligned and without leader characters, *Left* and *Blank* are the proposed responses in the Format Tabs Set fields. Word's preset tab stops are always left-aligned and without leader characters, too.

Preset tab stops are similar to the tab stops on a typewriter, in that any tab stop is ignored when it is left of the selection (or, in the case of a typewriter, left of the place you are typing on a line). Tab stops created with the Format Tabs Set command are the same way, beginning with version 3.0 of Word.

But in earlier versions, tab stops you create remain in effect regardless of the content of the line or the existence of other tab stops. This is important, because it means earlier versions of Word never ignore a tab stop you've created with the Format Tabs Set command. The first time you press the Tab key in a line, Word tries to move to the first tab stop you've formatted into the line. If the tab stop is to the left of the selection, the selection stays where it is, but for clarity it appears to move one character to the right on the screen. If the tab stop is to the right of the selection, the selection moves to the stop. (If there are no tab stops that you've created, Word moves to the next preset tab stop to the right, as it would on a typewriter.) You can ignore all of this if you're using version 3.0 or later.

position. How far from the left margin (not the left edge of the page) shall the tab stop be located? You can use any of Word's units of measure. Alternatively, you can press the Right direction key and watch a special highlight work its way across the ruler to any position you desire. (If you overshoot, use the Left direction key to move back.) If you use the direction keys, the *position* field displays the numeric location of the special highlight, using whatever unit of measure you have specified with the Options command. The mouse can be used to point to the location for a tab stop, too.

alignment: Left Center Right Decimal. What part of the text shall line up with the tab stop? Its left end? Center? Right end? Decimal point? (When *Decimal* is picked, text without a decimal point is aligned as if you'd picked *Right*—that is, the text runs from the tab stop to the left.) Note the tab-stop information in the ruler above the text in these examples of each type of alignment:

```
╟═[····L····1·········2·········C·········4······D·5·········6··R·]····7·····┐
║
║       Left-aligned      A column         99.95      Right
║       text looks        centered          1.005      for
║       like this.     under the "C."   1,588.00   poetry!
```

leader char: Blank . - _. Which leader character, if any, do you want displayed in the otherwise blank space leading to the tab stop? (Leaders are often used in tables of contents.) Here are examples (again, note how information is displayed in the ruler):

```
╟═[·········1·········2···L····3···-L····4····L···5·········]·········7·····┐
║
║  Leader characters:   .....Dot  -----Dash  ____Underline
```

Using Format Tabs Set

Unless you want a left-aligned tab stop with no leader characters, consider choosing from the *alignment* and *leader char* menu fields and then filling in a tab *position*. By filling in the tab position last, you keep all of these possibilities open:

♦ You can press the Enter key to carry out the command. The choices in the *position*, *alignment*, and *leader char* fields are accepted, and the tab stop is created.

♦ Or, you can press the Ins key to designate an initial tab stop, then change the *position* field and specify another location by pressing Ins again. You can do this repeatedly; the location and attributes of each stop will be marked on the ruler. All such tab stops take effect when the command is finally carried out.

♦ Format Tabs Set can delete a tab stop, too. Make sure the *position* field is highlighted, then use the Right (or Left) direction key to move the special ruler highlight to the unwanted tab stop. Press Del, then Enter, and the tab stop is gone.

When you use a mouse to set tab stops, place the mouse pointer on the ruler at the desired position. Then:

♦ Click the left mouse button to designate the spot as a tab stop to be formatted according to your settings in the *alignment* and *leader char* fields.

♦ Or, click both mouse buttons to eliminate a tab stop at that location.

♦ Or, press and hold down the left mouse button when the mouse pointer is at the position of a tab stop you want to move. Move the mouse pointer to the new position before releasing the mouse button.

You can mark, move, or delete several tab stops with the mouse before actually executing the command.

Here's a shortcut for mouse users. If tab stops you wish to set are left-aligned and have no leader characters, choose the Format Paragraph command, position the mouse pointer on the ruler at the location of the desired tab stop, and click the left button. You can designate as many tab stops as you wish; they will be created when you execute the Format Paragraph command. To eliminate one or more tab stops, use the same procedure, but click both mouse buttons at once. (Note to creators of style sheets: The same shortcuts work in the Gallery.)

For other tips on creating tables and other tabular material, see Chapter 27, "Power Tools: Creating Tables." In general, the easiest way to format tab stops is by setting up a style in a style sheet.

FORMAT TABS CLEAR

```
FORMAT TABS: Set Clear Reset-all
                ┌──────┘
FORMAT TABS CLEAR position: █
```

The Format Tabs Clear command does nothing you can't do with Format Tabs Set. You use the Clear command to eliminate one or more tab stops in the selected text.

The Format Tabs Clear command has only one field, *position*. Use it to type in the position of a tab stop to be cleared, or use the Right direction key to move the special highlight along the ruler to the desired (or rather, undesired) tab stop. With the mouse, you can eliminate several tab stops by moving the mouse pointer to each, clicking both mouse buttons, and finally carrying out the command.

If you type in the position of a tab stop to be cleared, you may have to type in the unit of measure, too. For instance, to clear a tab stop at 2 inches, you'd type 2″.

FORMAT TABS RESET-ALL

```
FORMAT TABS: Set Clear Reset-all
                       ┌──────┘
(Carried out as soon as it is picked)
```

The Format Tabs Reset-all command eliminates all tab stops at once, thereby restoring the preset tab stops.

The command acts only on paragraphs that are selected in whole or in part when the command is executed. There are no command fields; Format Tabs Reset-all executes automatically whenever it is picked from the Format Tabs submenu.

FORMAT FOOTNOTE

```
FORMAT: Character Paragraph Tabs Footnote Division Running-head Style
       ┌──────────────────────────────────────┐
FORMAT FOOTNOTE reference mark: ▮
```

The Format Footnote command places a footnote reference mark at the selected location in the document and allows you to create corresponding footnote text. Picking the Format Footnote command produces a single command field, *reference mark.* Respond to this field in one of two ways:

♦ Type in a character of your choice (an asterisk is common) and execute the command. The character you type is the reference mark for the footnote and is inserted into the text at the selection. You can type more than one character.

♦ To have Word automatically number footnotes, execute the command without responding to the field. Word assigns the next available numeral to the footnote. If the footnote is the first in a division, the number assigned to it is 1. The next footnote is 2, the next 3, and so on.

When you execute the Format Footnote command, Word immediately jumps to the end of the document, where it stores all footnote text. The footnote reference mark appears again, and you can type corresponding footnote text after it. When you are through, use the Jump Footnote command to return to the footnote reference mark in the text. (Conversely, if you are working in the main part of a document and want to see a certain footnote, select the appropriate reference mark and use the Jump Footnote command to jump in the other direction, to the text of that footnote.)

Word will print footnotes either at the bottoms of respective pages or collected together at the end of a document or division of a document. It depends on how the Format Division Layout command's *footnotes* field is set.

♦ If the field is set to *Same-page,* Word will print all of the footnote on the same page as the footnote reference, if there is room. If there is not room, beginning with version 3.0, Word will wrap footnote text to successive pages, as necessary.

♦ If the field is set to *End,* Word will gather together all of the footnotes contained in a division and print them at the end of the division. If you want the footnotes to appear on a page by themselves, insert a new-page character (Ctrl-Shift-Enter) at the end of the division. Most documents have only a single division, which means that *End* refers to the end of the document, practically speaking.

If you delete a footnote reference mark to the scrap or the glossary, the associated footnote text is deleted, too. If you reinsert the reference mark, the footnote text is reinserted, too. If you're using automatic footnote numbering, Word renumbers and reorders the footnotes when you move or delete footnote reference marks.

If while editing footnote text you accidentally delete an automatically numbered footnote reference mark, you can't retype it. If the Undo command doesn't work, Word has a special-purpose, permanent *footnote* entry in the glossary specifically designed to get you out of this jam. Select the location of the missing reference mark, type the word *footnote,* and press the F3 key. The automatically numbered reference mark will be restored. (NOTE: This feature restores reference marks at the beginning of the *footnote text,* not footnote reference marks accidentally deleted from the main body of the document.)

Footnote windows and superscripting

By opening a special footnote window as described in Chapter 7, "Using Windows," and Chapter 17, "The Family of Window Commands," you can write, edit, or view footnote text without jumping back and forth to the end of your document. The footnote window shows the footnote text corresponding to any footnote reference mark displayed in the main window. As reference marks are scrolled on and off the screen in the main window, the corresponding footnote text appears and disappears from the footnote window.

To visually set off footnote reference marks from your text, you may want to superscript them. To do so, select the reference mark and then use either the Format Character command described earlier in this chapter or the built-in superscript character format (hold down the Alt key and press the $\pm$ key twice to use the built-in superscripting format on a single character). When you're comfortable with style sheets, you can superscript footnote references automatically by creating a "footnote ref" character style and format it to be superscripted. (Style sheets are covered in Chapter 24, "Power Tools: Style Sheets.")

Footnote limitations

Impressive as Word's footnoting capabilities are, you should be aware of two limitations:

♦ Auto-numbering restarts with the number 1 at every division mark. If you want sequential footnote numbering across two or more divisions (sections of a report, for example), you must type the footnote numbers in all but the first division. On the other hand, if you want auto-numbered footnotes reset to 1 in the middle of a document, a new-division mark will do the job.

♦ Word's Format Division commands won't allow you to collect and print all footnotes at the end of a multi-division document. If you specify *End* in the *footnotes* field of the Format Division Layout command, the footnotes are printed at the end of the division, not the end of the document. To overcome this limitation after you've finished writing a document, combine the footnote text from the end of every division and place it at the end of the main document, or make it a separate document. If you've used automatically numbered footnotes in the document, the footnote reference numbers probably will change; you'll then have to correct them manually.

THE FORMAT DIVISION SUBMENU

```
FORMAT: Character Paragraph Tabs Footnote Division Running-head Style
                                          |
        _____|
       |
FORMAT DIVISION: Margins Page-numbers Layout
```

There are three Format Division commands: Format Division Margins, Format Division Page-numbers, and Format Division Layout. Use them to design pages or page columns. If the document has a single division, you can use the commands to set up page design throughout. But if the document has two or more divisions, you can use the commands to format the pages of each division differently.

The boundary between the divisions is indicated by a *division mark* (created with the Ctrl-Enter key combination). Technically, the division mark is a single character, even though it stretches the width of the text window as a series of colons (::::::).

It's important to remember that the mark contains the division formatting for the text that precedes it—not the text that follows. The first time any Format Division command is used with a document, a division mark automatically appears at the end of the document. The division mark at the end of a document, like the end mark, can be puzzling to newcomers who try to write or format at its position, or below it. Best not to work too near a final division mark if you don't understand it.

The Format Division commands between them generate 19 command fields. Prior to version 3.0 of Word, there was a single command, called Format Division, that combined the features of what are now three separate commands. There is no difference in function among the versions, but the features are less intimidating when split into thirds, as they are beginning with version 3.0. The single Format Division command fields, prior to 3.0, made an imposing array:

```
FORMAT DIVISION break: Cont Column Page Odd Even
       page length: 11"        width: 8.5"      gutter width: 0"
       pg #: Yes(No)        from top: 0.5"      from left: 7.25"
       numbering:(Cont)Start      at:           format:(1)I i A a
       margin top: 1"         bottom: 1"        left: 1.25"      right: 1.25"
       # of cols: 1   space between: 0.5"       footnotes:(Same-page)End
       running head pos    from top: 0.5"       from bottom: 0.5"
```

Although these fields are now broken into three commands, the values shown in the fields continue to reflect Word's "normal" division formatting. This "default" design gives you a single-column, 8½- by 11-inch page, with 1-inch margins at the top and bottom and 1¼-inch left and right margins. Page numbers, if any, are consecutive Arabic numerals, beginning with 1, printed ½ inch from the top and 7¼ inches from the left edge of the page. Footnotes, if any, are printed at the bottom of the page, and running heads, if any, are ½ inch from the top or bottom of the page, depending on whether they are "headers" or "footers." Any of the normal settings can be changed by altering the proposed responses in the fields of the Format Division commands (and the overall definition of what is a "normal" division can be changed by creating a *Division Standard* style in a Normal style sheet).

FORMAT DIVISION MARGINS

```
FORMAT DIVISION: margins Page-numbers Layout
    ┌────────────────────┐
    │
FORMAT DIVISION MARGINS top: 1█      bottom: 1"     left: 1.25"  right: 1.25"
                 page length: 11"     width: 8.5"   gutter margin: 0"
          running-head position from top: 0.5"   from bottom: 0.5"
```

Page margins govern the amount of blank space around your text. They are equivalent to the frame around a picture, and border everything except running heads, which are unique in that they are printed *in* the top or bottom margin, and they can extend into the left and right margins.

The distinctions between division margins and paragraph indents can be confusing at first, so continue the frame analogy and think of indents as optional matting inside the frame. Most paragraphs print right up to the page margins, but sometimes a paragraph or passage needs what we commonly think of as "wider margins." Rather than forcing us to actually change page (division) margins, Word lets us create paragraph indentation. In other words, we add matting around our picture rather than changing the width of the frame.

margin top. Enter a measurement in any accepted unit of measure for the distance from the top of each page to the first line of text. Word proposes 1 inch. Remember to leave room in the margin for a running head, if you intend to use one.

bottom. Enter a similar measurement for the distance from the end of text on each page to the bottom edge of the paper. Word proposes 1 inch. Leave room for a running head, if you intend to use one.

left. Enter a measurement for the left margin—the distance from the left edge of the paper to the left edge of text. Word proposes 1.25 inches. If you specified a gutter margin (see below), Word will automatically measure from the edge of the gutter on odd-numbered pages. Remember, if a left indent is specified in paragraph formatting, actual text may be farther from the edge of the page than the margin measurement alone indicates.

right. This is the same as for *left*, but measured from the right edge of the paper to the rightmost edge of text.

NOTE: If you feed paper into your printer a sheet at a time, the top margin of your printed page may come out about five lines too large and the bottom margin about five lines too small. To adjust the *top* and *bottom* fields, try reducing the top margin by .83" and increasing the bottom margin the same amount. (You can set up a division style in a style sheet to take care of this for you.)

page length. Enter the length of your paper in inches (″), centimeters (cm), points (pt), or lines (li). The proposed length is 11 inches; the maximum permitted is 22 inches.

width. Enter the width of your paper, using any of Word's accepted units of measure. Pica-size characters (P10) are equivalent to tenths of an inch; elite-size characters (P12) are equivalent to twelfths of an inch. The proposed width is 8.5 inches; the maximum permitted is the smaller of 22″ or 254 characters.

gutter margin. When formatting pages that will be reproduced on both sides of the paper and bound, specify a gutter (extra margin) allowance for the binding. A gutter margin of ½ inch typically is suitable for pages that are to be inserted into three-ring notebooks. Word puts this extra space on the left side of odd-numbered pages and on the right side of even-numbered pages. If pages are to be printed on just one side, leave the gutter margin at 0 and add any width required for binding by increasing the left margin, instead.

The vertical placement of running heads (*running head position*) on a page is controlled by two fields: *from top* and *from bottom*. Measurements in these fields do not obligate you to have running heads; they simply indicate how far from the top or bottom of the page running heads will be printed if used. Running heads are printed in the margins of a document, and are repeated page after page. None of the margin fields, including *left* and *right*, apply to running heads.

from top. How far from the top of the page shall running heads be printed? This field applies only when you have a running head formatted to appear in the top margin of a page. Word proposes 0.5 inch, but printers in which you hand-feed paper may not be able to print a running head that close to the top of the page.

from bottom. How far from the bottom of the page shall running heads be printed when *Bottom* is specified with the Format Running-head command? Word proposes 0.5 inch, but some laser printers, such as the Hewlett-Packard LaserJet, can't print quite that close to the bottom of a page.

FORMAT DIVISION PAGE-NUMBERS

```
FORMAT DIVISION: Margins Page-numbers Layout


FORMAT DIVISION PAGE-NUMBERS: Yes NO     from top: 0.5"    from left: 7.25"
                numbering:(Continuous)Start     at:           number format:(1)I i A a
```

You can number pages in either of two ways:

♦ Set the Format Division Page-numbers command's first field to *Yes,* to print page numbers in the location specified in the *from top* and *from left* fields. You do not see the numbers as you edit.

♦ Print the current page numbers with the reserved glossary name, *page,* which automatically numbers. Most often, this glossary name is typed into a running head, and it can be given a label or other accompanying text, such as the word *Page*. The use of *page* is described with the Format Running-head command later in this chapter, and at the end of Chapter 10.

No matter which method you use, you set the starting number and its printed form (Arabic, Roman, or alphabetic) with the following fields of the Format Division Page-numbers command.

PAGE NUMBERS: Yes No (or, prior to Word version 3.0, *pg #: Yes No*). Set this field to *Yes* to turn on automatic page numbering in the selected division. Choosing *No* means page numbers won't be printed unless you use the glossary name *page*.

from top. If *PAGE NUMBERS* is set to *Yes,* how far from the top of the page shall the number be printed? Use any of the accepted units of measure. The proposed distance is 0.5 inch.

from left. If *PAGE NUMBERS* is set to *Yes,* how far from the left edge of the page shall the number be printed? Again, use any accepted unit of measure. Word proposes 7.25 inches. If you've specified a gutter margin, Word allows for the gutter in computing the horizontal position of the page number.

numbering: Cont Start. Word's proposed response, *Cont*, starts numbering at 1 in the first (or only) division in a document, or continues previous numbering if the division follows another. Picking *Start* informs Word you will specify the starting page number. This field also controls numbering printed with the special glossary entry *page*.

at. If you pick *Start* in the *numbering* field, specify the starting number here. Word accepts only numbers, not letters, so if you pick lettering in the *format* field and want to start with E, type 5 for the fifth letter. The *at* field controls page numbers in running heads, too.

format: 1 I i A a. These five choices represent the five ways Word can print page numbers. Keep the proposed *1* for Arabic numerals (1, 2, 3); pick *I* or *i* for upper- or lowercase Roman numerals (I, II, III or i, ii, iii); pick *A* or *a* for upper- or lowercase alphabetic lettering (A, B, C or a, b, c).

FORMAT DIVISION LAYOUT

```
FORMAT DIVISION: Margins Page-numbers Layout


FORMAT DIVISION LAYOUT footnotes: Same-page End
        number of columns: 1        space between columns: 0.5"
            division break:(Page)Continuous Column Even Odd
```

Word lets you print two or more columns on a page. It also lets you place footnote text either on the same page as its reference mark or at the end of the division.

footnotes: Same-page End. Choose where you want footnotes to be collected for printing: at the bottoms of pages or the ends of divisions. (For more details, refer to the Format Footnote discussion earlier in this chapter.)

number of columns. Word proposes one column, and that's probably all you want on a single page. If not, type in the number of columns you need. The text will print as you instruct, but on the screen you'll see a single, narrower column of type. (To print different numbers of columns on the same page, use the side-by-side feature described in Chapter 27.)

space between columns. When there are several columns on a page as a result of division formatting, how much blank space shall be printed between them? Word proposes ½ inch.

division break: Page Continuous Column Even Odd. This field controls the effect of a division mark on the pages in a division. If the field is set to *Page,* which is Word's proposed response, a division mark forces the printer to begin a new division on a new page. The *division break* field offers you advanced control of division formatting; skip it unless you need one of the four settings other than *Page.*

NOTE: To control the transition from one division to another with the *division break* field, change the setting of the division following the division mark.

Page, the proposed response, begins printing the new division on the next page.

Continuous instructs Word to delay changing to the new division format until it reaches the top of the next page. In other words, it just ignores the division mark until it naturally reaches the top of the next page during printing, at which time the new division formatting takes hold. You pick *Continuous* to control the division following, not preceding, the relevant division mark. This setting is useful when you don't want a division mark to immediately force a new page—as, for example, when you want the second page of a newsletter to have two columns instead of one, but you don't care exactly where in the text the transition from one to two occurs.

Column, like the remaining two settings, tells Word to begin the new division immediately, at the division mark. *Column* starts printing the new division at the top of the next column. If there is only one column to a page, *Column* begins a new page.

Even is similar to *Page,* but tells Word to start the new division on the next even-numbered (left-hand) page.

Odd is similar to *Even,* but begins printing on the next odd-numbered page, leaving a blank even-numbered page if necessary. One use for *Odd* is to ensure that new sections of documents that are printed on both sides of the paper always start on a right-hand (odd-numbered) page.

FORMAT RUNNING-HEAD

```
FORMAT: Character Paragraph Tabs Footnote Division Running-head Style
        ┌──────────────────────────────────────────────────┐

FORMAT RUNNING-HEAD position: Top Bottom
        odd pages:(Yes)No  even pages:(Yes)No  first page: Yes(No)
```

A running head, often called a "header" or a "footer," is one or a few lines of text printed in the margin at the top or bottom of one or more pages. A title is often printed at the top of each page of a chapter or report, for example, and a page number or other message may be repeated at the top or bottom of each page. Sometimes, different running heads appear on odd- and even-numbered pages, and often running heads are omitted on the first page of a document. All these situations, and more, are accommodated with the Format Running-head command, which turns any paragraph in which it is executed into a running head, and lets you choose generally where it will be printed. Just select the paragraph, pick the Format Running-head command, fill in the command fields as desired, and execute the command.

Fields of the Format Running-head command

position: Top Bottom. Shall the running head be printed at the top or the bottom of the page? (This is linked to the *running head position* fields of the Format Division Margin command, as explained shortly.)

odd pages: Yes No. Shall the running head be printed on odd-numbered (right-hand) pages? Generally, the answer to this is *Yes*, unless different running heads are being used on odd- and even-numbered pages.

even pages: Yes No. Shall this running head be printed on even-numbered pages? Generally, the answer to this, too, is *Yes*, unless different running heads are being used on even- and odd-numbered pages.

first page: Yes No. Shall this running head be printed on the first page of the division? Often as not, the answer here is *No*, because running heads usually don't appear on title or cover pages. If you choose *Yes*, make the running head the first paragraph in the division.

Understanding running heads

Running heads print from the page at which the Format Running-head command is put into effect until the end of the division, or until Word encounters another running head with the same combination of *position*, *odd pages*, *even pages*, and *first page*. To keep a running head from printing beyond a particular page, either create a new division or replace the running-head paragraph with a new paragraph that has no printable characters in it (some spaces and a paragraph mark, for instance).

If you want a running head to print on the same page on which it exists in the text, it must be the first text on the page. A running head can be more than one line or paragraph long, but if it is deeper than the page margin, Word won't print it.

If you execute the Format Running-head command without changing any of the settings Word proposes, the running head will appear at the top of all pages except the first. Choosing *No* in the three *page* fields transforms a running-head paragraph into normal text.

Format Running-head and other commands

You use the Format Running-head command in conjunction with the Format Division Margins, Format Paragraph, and, sometimes, the Format Character and Format Tabs Set commands. Jointly, they provide remarkable flexibility, but their use is relatively complex. Understanding how the commands relate to each other is the key to success:

♦ Format Running-head turns a selected paragraph into a running head and specifies where and on what pages it is printed. It does not control the appearance of the running head, or the exact position of the running head on the page.

- Format Division Margins (the *running-head position* fields) lets you specify the exact positions reserved for running heads at the tops and bottoms of pages. But specifying these positions has no effect until paragraphs are converted into running heads with the Format Running-head command.

- Format Paragraph controls the layout of the line or lines that make up the running head. The Format Paragraph command is the only way you can control the horizontal placement of a running head.

- Format Character can be used to boldface, underline, or otherwise format the characters within the running head.

- Format Tabs Set is often used to create tab stops in running heads, because running heads frequently contain words or phrases separated by tab characters. For example, the running head of a report may have a title printed flush left and a page number printed flush right, courtesy of a tab character and a right-aligned tab stop. (If you want the page numbers always on the "outside" and the titles always on the "inside" of double-sided pages, use different running heads for odd- and even-numbered pages.)

Margins and indents

A useful feature of running heads is that they are exempt from the left and right margins you set with the Format Division Margins command. Until you understand this, you may be mystified if your running heads print well out into a document's margins. At least, I was.

Think about the picture frame analogy mentioned in the discussion of the Format Division Margins command. Running heads are unconstrained by the margin "matting" at the sides of your page because you may sometimes want a running head to start or finish outside a document's left or right margins. But more often, you may want a running head to adhere to the margin rules of the rest of a document. What then? The answer's easy, though not obvious: Use the Format Paragraph command on the running-head paragraph to specify a left paragraph indent equal to the division's left margin, and specify a right paragraph indent equal to the division's right margin. Generally, you will probably also want to set the first-line paragraph indent to 0 for a running head. If you use a gutter in your division formatting, you will have to use separate running heads (though possibly with the same text) for odd- and even-numbered pages.

Running-head symbols

On-screen, running heads can be spotted quickly in a document because a caret (^) appears in the selection bar just left of the first line of the running-head paragraph.

In addition, if the style bar is on, a one- or two-letter code appears to the left of the caret. The code shows the type of running head: A *t* or a *b* indicates whether the running head will appear at the top or the bottom of the page. If only one of these letters appears, the running head is printed at that location on both odd and even pages, or on the first page plus either or both the odd and even pages. If the *t* or *b* is followed by an *f,* the running head is printed only on the first page. If the *t* or *b* is followed by an *o,* the running head appears only on odd pages. If the *t* or *b* is followed by an *e,* the running head appears only on even pages.

Page numbers and the glossary

Word's automatic page-numbering feature is actually a special character stored permanently in the glossary. It can be inserted into the text at any time by typing the word *page* and pressing the F3 key. The page character is represented as *(page)* on the screen, but it prints the current page number.

The *(page)* character is useful in running heads and gives superior flexibility compared to the automatic-numbering feature of the Format Division Page-numbers command. The *(page)* character can be linked with a label, such as the word *Page,* so that typing *Page page F3,* for example, causes *Page (page)* to appear in the text of the running head, but *Page 5* to appear on the printed page five.

THE FORMAT STYLE SUBMENU

NOTE: You can skip this section for now if you don't use style sheets.

```
FORMAT: Character Paragraph Tabs Footnote Division Running-head STYLE
                                                               |
        ┌──────────────────────────────────────────────────────┘
        |
FORMAT STYLE: Character Paragraph Division Sheet
```

Four commands govern the way existing style sheets are used with documents: Format Style Character, Format Style Paragraph, Format Style Division, and Format Style Sheet. Of these, Format Style Sheet is the most important because it controls which style sheet, if any, is attached to a document. The other three Format Style commands primarily offer you alternate ways to do the same things you can do by pressing an Alt-key combination: attach character, paragraph, and division styles to selected text. These commands are not used to create or to modify style sheets, but to apply formatting instructions from existing style sheets to specific documents. Chapter 24, "Power Tools: Style Sheets," explains the relationship between documents and style sheets.

The Format Style Sheet command is the same in all versions of Word. The other three Format Style commands differ slightly in versions prior to 2.0, but this discussion of the 2.0 and 3.0 commands should provide sufficient guidance for earlier versions, too.

FORMAT STYLE CHARACTER

```
FORMAT STYLE: Character Paragraph Division Sheet
              |
      ┌───────┘
      |
FORMAT STYLE CHARACTER: █
```

Use the Format Style Character command to identify or switch the style currently controlling the format of the selected character(s). Picking the command produces a single field, *FORMAT STYLE CHARACTER,* which identifies the current character style, if any, that is formatting the selected character (or the first—leftmost—character if more than one is selected). The command identifies the style by its *variant* number or name. For example:

```
FORMAT STYLE CHARACTER: Character 3█
```

(In versions of Word prior to 2.0, the *FORMAT STYLE CHARACTER* command field shows usage and variant.)

Because the Format Style command fields reflect only formatting governed by a style, if the first character of the selection has been shaped by any direct formatting—that is, by the Format Character command or a built-in character format—the *FORMAT STYLE CHARACTER* command field is blank.

Switching a character style

When the *FORMAT STYLE CHARACTER* field is displayed, you can replace the current style (if any) with any other character style in a style sheet. Or you can apply a style where there is none. A new style dislodges any previous character style. The new style affects the entire selection. When the field is displayed you can switch to a new character style in any of three ways:

♦ Type the key code of the desired character style (such as Alt-BC if you want a bold character style and that is the key code).

♦ Type the name of the character style you desire (such as Character 3 in the preceding example).

♦ View a list of available character styles, highlight the style of your choice, and execute the command to apply it to the selection. If you request a list, you may note that each listing generated by the Format Style Character, Format Style Paragraph, and Format Style Division commands is cut at the 39th letter. That's so two lists can appear side by side on an 80-column screen.

FORMAT STYLE PARAGRAPH

```
FORMAT STYLE: Character Paragraph Division Sheet


FORMAT STYLE PARAGRAPH: █
```

Use the Format Style Paragraph command just as you use the Format Style Character command, but to identify or switch the paragraph style that controls the format of the selected paragraph or paragraphs. Picking the command produces the field *FORMAT STYLE PARAGRAPH*.

When the command is picked, the command field shows the name of the paragraph style of the selection, provided that the entire selection has the same style. The field is blank if the selection contains more than one paragraph style or if it contains any direct paragraph formatting accomplished with the Format Character command or a built-in format.

Change to a different paragraph style in a style sheet by using any of the methods described for the Format Style Character command.

FORMAT STYLE DIVISION

```
FORMAT STYLE: Character Paragraph Division Sheet
```

```
FORMAT STYLE DIVISION: ▮
```

Use the Format Style Division command to identify or switch the division style that controls formatting of the selected division(s). Picking the command produces the field *FORMAT STYLE DIVISION*.

You use the Format Style Division command as you do the Format Style Paragraph command, except that selecting a single character in a division selects the entire division.

FORMAT STYLE SHEET

```
FORMAT STYLE: Character Paragraph Division Sheet
```

```
FORMAT STYLE SHEET: ▮
```

Use the Format Style Sheet command to look at the name of the style sheet, if any, that is attached to the entire current document, or to assign or switch a document's style sheet. Because more than one style sheet can be applied to a document (though not at the same time), it is possible to dramatically change the appearance of a document simply by swapping one style sheet for another. Step by step, this is how you attach a different style sheet to a document:

1. Select any character(s) within the document.

2. Pick the Format Style Sheet command.

3. When the name of the presently attached style sheet, if any, is displayed in the *FORMAT STYLE SHEET* field, type in the name of a different style sheet (you can omit the .STY extension), or pick the name of a style sheet from a list.

4. Execute the command. The new style sheet will replace the former one, and the appearance of the document may change immediately, if new formatting rules are imposed by the new style sheet.

NOTE: Beginning with version 3.0 of Word, the full path name leading up to a style sheet is displayed when you pick the Format Style Sheet command and a style sheet already is attached to the document. Because there is almost always a style sheet attached (even if it is NORMAL.STY), you'll find that when you pick the command the drive letter and path, such as B:\LETTERS\NORMAL.STY, will appear. To change the style sheet, you do not need to worry about the drive letter or the pathname. Just type the name of the style sheet (assuming that the style sheet is on the default drive and in the default directory, as shown in the Transfer Options command). For more information, see the Transfer Save and Transfer Options commands in Chapter 16, "The Family of Transfer Commands," or the discussion of pathnames in Chapter 28, "Using a Hard Disk."

The Family of Jump Commands

The Jump commands hop you from one place to another in a document—either to a page you specify, or back and forth between footnote reference marks and footnote text. There are two Jump commands: Jump Page and Jump Footnote.

```
COMMAND: Alpha Copy Delete Format Gallery Help Insert Jump Library
         Options Print Quit Replace Search Transfer Undo Window


JUMP to: Page Footnote
```

(A third command, Jump Running-head, was eliminated after Word version 1.0. The command no longer is necessary because running heads are now placed in the main text portion of a document. In version 1.0, they were stored at the end of a document, much as footnote text is. Hence the former need for a Jump Running-head command.)

JUMP PAGE

```
JUMP to: Page Footnote


JUMP PAGE number: ▮
```

The Jump Page command causes the selection to move to the first character of a specified page. It works only after breaks between pages have been calculated for a document. This calculation occurs when a document is printed (with the Print Printer command) or repaginated (with the Print Repaginate command). Beginning with version 3.0, the Library Index and Library Table commands also cause Word to repaginate a document.

When you pick the Jump Page command, the *number* command field is displayed at the bottom of the screen. Type the desired page number. Whether you are moving forward or backward, one page or a hundred, the command almost instantly moves you to the new page. Once there, you see the new page and the last few lines of the page preceding it. In the selection bar to the immediate left of the text, a special mark, » (the new-page mark), shows the beginning of the page; the page number is displayed in the lower left corner of the screen.

The Jump Page command jumps to a new-page mark, but it will not jump to a new-column mark, which is a new-page mark preceded by a number representing a column on a page. Nor will the command jump to a new-page character, except to the extent that new-page marks and new-page characters coincide.

```
This is a new-page character:
...............................................................................

This is a new-page mark:  »

This is a new-column mark:  2»
(The 2 indicates the start of the second column on a page.)
```

In documents that have been formatted to have more than one division, a particular page number may appear more than once. Word jumps to the *next* page that has the number you specify. To jump to a particular page in a particular division, follow the page number with a *D* and the number of the division. For instance, typing *3D2* would jump you to the third page of the second division. (If you wish to jump to a level of heading rather than to a known page number, you can use outline view. See Chapter 25, "Power Tools: Outlining.")

Nonexistent pages

If you attempt to use the Jump Page command before the document has been printed or repaginated, Word displays the message *Pagination is required*. Use the Print Printer or Print Repaginate command, then try the Jump Page command again.

If you specify a page number higher than any in the document, Word jumps to the beginning of the last page.

You see the message *No such page* when the new-page mark for the desired page has been deleted since the document was last printed or repaginated. It's easy to inadvertently delete the new-page marks: Each is tied to the final character of the preceding page, which happens to be the final character of the preceding line. Whether this final character is visible or whether it is a spacing character, deleting it may cause the new-page mark to vanish, too. Not only that, the Undo command will not restore the new-page mark.

If you get the *No such page* message, either repaginate the document and then try the Jump Page command again, or jump instead to the next-highest or next-lowest page number and scroll to the desired position.

JUMP FOOTNOTE

```
JUMP to: Page Footnote
```

(Carried out as soon as it is picked)

The Jump Footnote command executes as soon as it is picked. It moves you directly to the next footnote reference mark in the active document, or back and forth between a footnote reference mark and the corresponding footnote text. Where it jumps to depends on where the selection is when you execute the command.

Jump to next reference mark

When text (not a footnote reference mark) is selected, using the Jump Footnote command moves the selection to the next footnote reference mark. If you are at the beginning of a document, for example, and the first footnote reference mark is on page 3, using the command will move the selection to the reference mark on the third page.

In this context, Word always jumps toward the end of the document. When there are no footnote reference marks between the selection and the end of the document, this message appears: *No more footnote references.*

When the selection contains many characters and one of them (but not the first one) is a footnote reference mark, the Jump Footnote command reduces the size of the selection to the single character that is the actual footnote reference mark.

Jump to footnote text

When only a footnote reference mark is selected, or when a mark is the first character of a larger selection, the Jump Footnote command hops you to the footnote text corresponding to the mark. If a footnote window is open, the selection moves to it. Otherwise, Word almost instantly scrolls to where footnote text is stored at the end of the document.

Jump back to reference mark

When footnote text is selected, the Jump Footnote command returns you to the corresponding reference mark in the document. Use this command when you finish writing a footnote and want to pick up where you left off in the document.

The Family of Library Commands

Check your spelling, hyphenate the words in a document, sort and renumber lists, compile indexes and tables of contents, even run another program—all with the family of Library commands available beginning with version 3.0 of Word—and in limited form in version 2.0. There are seven commands in the Library family: Autosort, Hyphenate, Index, Number, Run, Spell, and Table. Each enhances Word's power and flexibility.

```
COMMAND: Alpha Copy Delete Format Gallery Help Insert Jump Library
         Options Print Quit Replace Search Transfer Undo Window

LIBRARY: Autosort Hyphenate Index Number Run Spell Table
```

Most of the Library commands are self-contained on the Word Program disk. An exception is Library Spell, which works in conjunction with a separate Spell disk that contains not only the spelling checker but five additional spelling-utility programs. These five utilities are described at the end of this chapter.

When Library Spell or Library Run is used, Word is held in your computer's memory and the other program has available to it whatever memory remains. So to use the Library Run command to access major programs such as Multiplan or Lotus 1-2-3, you need ample memory—often 512K or more of RAM.

Unless you are using a hard-disk system, your Word Program disk must contain the DOS program COMMAND.COM in order for you to use Library Spell or Library Run. If you run a program frequently through Library Run, you may want to add it to the Program disk, too. However, don't crowd your Program disk.

Since Library commands were new with version 2.0 of Word, in earlier versions you'll see the message *Library reserved for future use* when you pick Library from the Edit menu. These earlier releases of Word make no provision for automatic hyphenation, but you can check spelling with the separate Spell disk. Version 2.0 includes only three of the Library commands—Spell, Hyphenate, and Run.

LIBRARY AUTOSORT

```
LIBRARY: Autosort Hyphenate Index Number Run Spell Table
         |
         |
LIBRARY AUTOSORT by: Alphanumeric Numeric    sequence:(Ascending)Descending
                case: Yes(No)                column only: Yes(No)
```

With the Library Autosort command you can alphabetize or put in numeric order lists and columns of words and numbers. Word will sort in either ascending (*1, 2, 3* or *a, b, c*) or descending (*9, 8, 7* or *z, y, x*) sequence. The Library Autosort command was introduced in version 3.0 of Word.

Before picking the Library Autosort command, you must select (highlight) the text to be sorted. The selection can be whole paragraphs or a column from a table. Generally, Word reorders the selected text according to the letters or numbers that begin each paragraph, but if you set the Library Autosort's *column only* field to *Yes,* Word will sort by individual lines instead of by paragraphs. As you'll see in a tutorial in this section, with a little cleverness it is also possible to alphabetize items such as names within a paragraph.

If you complete a sort and decide you made a mistake, immediately using the Undo command will restore the selected text to its form before you sorted it.

Fields of the Library Autosort command

There are four fields in the Library Autosort command.

by: Alphanumeric Numeric. Shall Word put the selected elements in alphanumeric order or in numeric order? If you choose *Alphanumeric,* Word alphabetizes the paragraphs or lines, putting special characters (such as * and #) first, followed by numbers and then by letters. If you choose *Numeric,* Word orders the elements by numeric value, and will recognize only numerals 0 through 9 and the following characters associated with numbers: decimal point (.), dollar sign ($), percent sign (%), minus sign (–), comma (,), open parenthesis (( ), and close parenthesis, ( )).

An example of the difference between alphanumeric and numeric sorting is instructive. If you select a column of numbers that contains 12, 2, 112, and .12, you obtain different results sorting it alphanumerically than if you sort it numerically. An alphanumeric sort considers the digits in a number from left to right, just as if it were alphabetizing a word, and so it returns the numbers in this order: .12, 112, 12, and 2. The first number is .12 not because it is the smallest number, but because it starts with a special character, in this case a decimal point. The number 2 comes last because its first digit has a higher value than the first digit of any of the other numbers.

In contrast, the numeric sort looks at all the digits in a number at once, and assigns the number a priority dependent on its overall numeric value, and so it returns the numbers in lowest-to-highest order: .12, 2, 12, 112.

A valuable use of a numeric sort is to reorganize a document by numbering its paragraphs according to the order in which you want them to appear. Selecting the document (or portion of a document) and executing the Library Autosort command with the *by* field set to *Numeric* will cause the document to be restructured in the numbered order. Because a numeric sort recognizes decimals, it is possible to give a paragraph a number between two existing numbers. For instance, if you want to put a paragraph between two paragraphs already numbered 7 and 8, you can give the paragraph to be inserted the number 7.5. These numbers must be typed at the beginning of the paragraphs, and can be removed later by selecting the whole document (or relevant portion), setting the *NUMBER* field of the Library Number command to *Remove,* and executing the command.

A characteristic of this method is that every paragraph to be moved must be numbered. If you want to move two consecutive paragraphs, you cannot number the first one and assume the one following it will move with it. (However, this kind of move is possible by numbering paragraphs using Word's outline mode. See Chapter 25, "Power Tools: Outlining," and the example of combining indexes in Chapter 26, "Power Tools: Hidden Text and Indexing.")

sequence: Ascending Descending. Picking *Ascending* causes Word to alphabetize from *A* to *Z* and to number from *0* to *9*. Picking *Descending* instructs Word to reverse the sequence.

In an alphanumeric sort with the *sequence* field set to *Descending,* paragraphs starting with special characters (such as & or #) would come last instead of first.

case: Yes No. Picking *Yes* causes Word to put words beginning with capital letters before words beginning with lowercase letters when performing an alphanumeric sort in an ascending sequence. Picking *No* causes Word to ignore case in sorting.

column only: Yes No. This field has two uses. First, it allows you to sort the elements in one column of a table without affecting the order of the other columns. Second, it permits you to sort selected text by line rather than by paragraph.

To understand the sorting of individual columns, recall that it is possible to select individual columns of text using Word's Column Select mode. (This method was introduced at the end of Chapter 10, "The Scrap and Glossary Commands," and is reviewed in the tutorial below.)

Once a column in a table is selected, you can sort its order with the Library Autosort command. The question becomes whether the new order determined by the sort should be applied only to the selected column or to the entire table. For instance, if you were sorting a table that contained last names in one column and addresses and phone numbers in another column, you probably would not want Word to reorganize the order of the names without also reorganizing the order of the corresponding addresses and phone numbers. In this case, you would pick *No* in the *column only* field, because you would want all the columns to be reordered. Picking *Yes* would cause Word to reorganize the order of the selected column without affecting any of the other columns at all. Regardless of what you pick, the order is determined by the contents of that column alone.

If you want to sort a table by more than one column, you do so consecutively, sorting first by the least-important column and last by the most-important column. For example, if you wanted to alphabetize a table of people by the city in which they live, and then by family names within the various cities, you would first sort the column containing family names and then you would sort the column devoted to city names. The city names in this case are the objects of the "primary sort," and the family names are the objects of a "secondary sort."

The other purpose of the *column only* field is to sort by line instead of by paragraph. This is useful when you have a table or list that assigns a new element to every line, but doesn't start a new paragraph for each line. Generally, this applies only when each line ends with a new-line character (created by holding down the Shift key and pressing the Enter key).

A tutorial

The following tutorial illustrates how several techniques can be combined to do sophisticated sorting. In this example, we have a list of seven names that are contained in a paragraph, with the given name preceding family name and commas separating the names. If we want to organize these names in alphabetic order, we are challenged, not only because the names are neither on separate lines nor in separate paragraphs, but also because we want family names to be alphabetized before given names.

Here is the list of names:

> John Smith, Jean Jones, Ima Smiling, Barry Smith, Pam Powers, Petty Powers, Larry Adams.

Our technique will be to temporarily make each name a separate paragraph in which the given name is separated from the family name by a tab character, then to alphanumerically sort the list of paragraphs twice—first by given name, and second, using Word's Column Select mode, by last name. Finally, we will remove the tab characters and paragraph marks to restore the list of names to its original, non-tabular format.

NOTE: Before beginning, pick the Options command and change the *default tab width* field to 0.8″. After you have finished the sort, you can change it back to 0.5″, but for now the extra space between tab stops will be needed to create proper separation between names.

1. Select the list of names, and choose the Replace command. In the *text* field type a comma followed by a space, then press the Tab key to move to the *with text* field, where you type a comma followed by ^*p* (Shift-6 and *p*, which stands for a paragraph mark). Tab to the *confirm* field and press the Spacebar once to highlight the word *No*. This is what your text should look like before you press the Enter key to execute the Replace command:

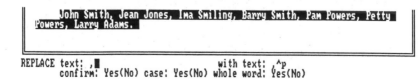

2. When you press Enter, your screen shows each name as a separate paragraph and the collection is selected (highlighted). Pick the Replace command again, and this time put a space (press the Spacebar once) in the *text* field and type ^*t* (Shift-6 and *t*, which represents a tab character) in the *with text* field. Press the Tab key to move to the *confirm* field, and press the Spacebar once to set it to *No*. Now press the Enter key and the space representing a tab and character will appear between each first and last name:

```
John        Smith,
Jean        Jones,
Ima         Smiling,
Barry       Smith,
Pam         Powers,
Petty       Powers,
Larry       Adams.
```

3. While the entire list is selected this way, pick the Library Autosort command. Accept the default settings of the command: the *by* field set to *Alphanumeric*, the *sequence* field set to *Ascending*, the *case* field set to *No*, and the *column only* field set to *No*. Execute it by pressing the Enter key.

This has the effect of alphabetizing the list by the given (first) names of the people on it. Recall that secondary sorts (such as alphabetizing by first names) are performed before primary sorts (such as alphabetizing by last names).

Now we will alphabetize the list by last names, using Word's Column Select mode and its ability to sort by column.

4. Select the first letter of the initial last name on the list, in this case the *S* of *Smith*. Hold down the Shift key and press the F6 key to turn on the Column Select mode. Observe that the letters *CS* appear on the bottom line of the screen.

5. Using the direction keys or the mouse, extend the selection to beyond the last character of the last family name on the list. Because the Column Select mode is on, the selection will be rectangular and the given names will not be selected. Be sure that the rectangular selection extends beyond the last character of the longest name on the list.

```
Barry       Smith,
Ima         Smiling,
Jean        Jones,
John        Smith,
Larry       Adams.
Pam         Powers,
Petty       Powers,
```

6. Pick the Library Autosort command again, and accept the same settings in the fields as before. Press the Enter key to execute the command. Word will alphabetize the names by family name, because only family names were selected when the command was executed. Given names will remain alphabetized within the context of the alphabetization of the last names, so that Jean Powers will come before John Powers, and Pam Smith before Petty Smith.

The alphabetization is complete, but the names are still in a tabular form. The entire block of names remained selected after the completion of the last sort. We will now use the Replace command twice to return them to paragraph form.

7. Pick the Replace command and type $^\wedge t$ (Shift-6 and *t*, representing tab characters) in the *text* field. Press the Tab key to move to the *with text* field, and press the Spacebar once to put a single space in the field. Press the Tab key to move to the *confirm* field, and press the Spacebar once to set it to *No*. Execute the command, and the tab characters between the given and last names are replaced by single spaces.

8. Pick the Replace command again, and type $^\wedge p$ (Shift-6 and *p*, representing paragraph marks) in the *text* field. Press the Tab key to move to the *with text* field, and press the Spacebar once to put a single space in the field. Press the Tab key to move to the *confirm* field, and press the Spacebar once to set it to *No*. Execute the command, and the names will return to paragraph structure, as they were in the beginning— only now they are alphabetized.

```
‖    Larry Adams, Jean Jones, Pam Powers, Petty Powers, Ima                   ‖
‖ Smiling, Barry Smith, John Smith,
```

9. The only remaining task is to change the period after Adams into a comma, and the comma at the end of the sentence into a period. Do this manually.

LIBRARY HYPHENATE

```
LIBRARY: Autosort Hyphenate Index Number Run Spell Table
        ┌──────────────────┐
        │
LIBRARY HYPHENATE confirm: Yes No            hyphenate caps:(Yes)No
```

For manuscripts, screenplays, and certain other documents, hyphenation generally isn't appropriate. On the other hand, for justified text or narrow columns, hyphenation is desirable because it increases the average number of characters per line, thereby reducing unnecessary white space between words and letters. Use the Library Hyphenate command to have Word hyphenate any amount of text, from a single word to a whole document.

Hyphens inserted with the Library Hyphenate command are of the *optional* or *non-required* variety, meaning they are displayed and printed only if needed to break a word at the end of a line. (You can also insert optional hyphens manually, without the Library Hyphenate command, by holding down the Control key and pressing the hyphen key.) When such a hyphen is not at the end of the line, it does not normally display on the screen. If you select an invisible optional hyphen, the selection seems to vanish. Pressing any direction key moves the selection to an adjacent visible character, causing it to reappear. You can display optional hyphens on the screen by setting the Options command to make normally invisible characters visible.

At your option, the Library Hyphenate command either inserts hyphens automatically or shows you where each hyphen would be placed and lets you accept or change the suggestions individually. Word finds the correct places to hyphenate multisyllabic words by using a sophisticated formula and a substantial amount of data on the Program disk. It does not place a hyphen at every possible break between syllables: It ignores words that already contain hyphens and it ignores words in which the addition of an optional hyphen won't affect the present layout of the document. In the following example, a sentence is repeated twice, the second time hyphenated. Observe that in the unhyphenated version, the word *seating* is at the beginning of the second line, and there is some space at the end of the preceding line. In the hyphenated version, the first syllable of *seating* has been moved up to use the space.

```
⊩[·········1·········2·········3·········4·········5·········]·········7·····⌐
 Library Hyphenate doesn't place an optional hyphen in
 seating unless the presence of the hyphen lets the word be
 split between two lines.

 Library Hyphenate doesn't place an optional hyphen in seat-
 ing unless the presence of the hyphen lets the word be split
 between two lines.
```

What is hyphenated?

You can choose to hyphenate a word, sentence, paragraph, or section of a document by selecting the appropriate text before executing the Library Hyphenate command. The command follows the same rules as the Replace command regarding what text is acted upon:

♦ If the selection is a single character, all words from that point forward are candidates for hyphenation, provided they don't already contain hyphens. This means an entire document is hyphenated if only the first character of it is selected.

♦ If the selection covers more than one character, hyphenation is confined to the words that are partly or totally selected.

Remove existing optional hyphens

Word won't look for a new hyphenation point in any word that already contains a hyphen. Consequently, to achieve the most effective hyphenation, first remove existing optional hyphens with the Replace command: Type ^- (Shift-6, followed by the hyphen key) in the Replace command's *text* field, tab past the *with text* field, and, to save time, set *confirm* to *No*. If you set *confirm* to *Yes*, first set Options to display normally invisible characters.

Inserting or deleting a large number of hyphens uses up a lot of computer memory, so for best performance on large jobs, use the Transfer Save command immediately after inserting hyphens with Library Hyphenate or removing hyphens with Replace.

Upon completion of the Library Hyphenate command, a Word message tells you the total number of words hyphenated.

If used immediately, the Undo command removes all the hyphens that have been inserted with the Library Hyphenate command. Because you can execute the Undo command repeatedly, you can compare the hyphenated and the unhyphenated document. For an accurate reflection of how the document will look when printed, set the Options command *printer display* field to *Yes* before comparing.

Fields of the Library Hyphenate command

There are only two fields in the Library Hyphenate command, *confirm* and *hyphenate caps.* Either can be set to *Yes* or *No.*

confirm: Yes No. Choosing *No* causes Word to execute the command without asking you to confirm each hyphen. This is the faster choice, because *Yes* makes you approve each suggested hyphen. If you pick *Yes,* the following sequence occurs:

1. Word temporarily turns on the Option command's Printer Display mode, so the screen shows the lengths and content of lines as they will print. This mode gives you the information needed to review potential hyphenation points intelligently.

2. Each time Word finds a multisyllabic word that can be hyphenated, it highlights the character that would follow the hyphen, and displays the message *Enter Y to insert hyphen, N to skip, or press Esc to cancel.*

Press Y to accept the proposed hyphenation point. If you want to hyphenate the word at a different letter, change the proposed point by pressing the Left or Right direction key to move the highlight a character at a time, or press the Up or Down direction key to jump the highlight left (Up key) or right (Down key) to the next point in the word that Word recognizes as acceptable for hyphenation. Then press Y.

Press N to skip the word but to continue hyphenating. Press the Esc key to cancel further hyphenation but to keep the hyphenation of any words up to that point.

3. Finally, Word turns off the Printer Display mode if it was off before the Library Hyphenate command was executed.

hyphenate caps: Yes No. Pick *Yes* to tell Word to consider hyphenating words that start with a capital letter. Pick *No* to protect names and other such words from hyphenation.

LIBRARY INDEX

```
LIBRARY: Autosort Hyphenate Index Number Run Spell Table

LIBRARY INDEX entry/page # separated by:  ■    cap main entries:(Yes)No
                 indent each level: 0.2"        use style sheet: Yes(No)
```

Once a document has been prepared for indexing, you can use the Library Index command to actually compile the index. Word will place the index at the end of the document, separated from the rest of the text by a division mark. (A division mark looks like a series of colons (::::::::::) across the width of the text window. In this case, creating a new division allows you to use the three Format Division commands to format the pages on which the index will print differently than the other pages in your document.)

Preparing a document for indexing involves designating index entries throughout the text with some simple coding that is formatted as hidden text. For details on these preparations, see Chapter 26, "Power Tools: Hidden Text and Indexing."

An index created with the Library Index command is an alphabetized list of all the previously designated index entries from the document, complete with page numbers. When the same index entry appears on more than one page of your document, duplicate listings are automatically eliminated from the index, and page numbers are combined.

The Library Index command will create an index with up to five levels of entry—the main entry and four sublevels. Rudimentary formatting of the levels is possible with the Library Index command, and sophisticated formatting is possible by telling the command to use a style sheet.

Before using the Library Index command, make sure hidden text is invisible in the text window—that is, make sure the *show hidden text* field of the Window Options command is set to *No*. This is advisable because the command repaginates the document before assigning page numbers, and the temporary presence of otherwise hidden text can render the pagination of the document inaccurate.

Word assembles an index that begins with a line of hidden text that says *.Begin Index.*, and ends with a similar line that says *.End Index.* You can delete these lines, but generally there's little reason to, since they are hidden and won't print (unless you've made hidden text visible with the Window Options command). However, one reason to delete the lines is if you want to index your document more than once, keeping each version of the index at the end of your document for reference.

If the *.Begin Index.* and *.End Index.* lines are in the document when you execute the Library Index command, Word will replace the old index with the new one. However, before making this substitution, Word displays the message *"Enter Y to replace existing index or Esc to cancel,"* giving you a chance to change your mind.

Fields of the Library Index command

The Library Index command has four fields, each pertaining to how the index compiled by the command will be formatted.

entry/page # separated by. Unless you change the setting in this field, Word will insert two blank spaces between the index entry and the first of its page numbers. You can, if you prefer, change this setting to a single space, multiple spaces, or characters such as hyphens. You can also specify a tab character, by typing $^\wedge t$ (Shift-6 and *t*). Word will move the other fields aside (or even to another line) to make room if you type more than four characters in the *entry/page # separated by* field.

cap main entries: Yes No. Shall Word capitalize the first word of each main (first-level) entry in the index? Generally you'll want to leave this field set to *Yes*, although for some scientific and other indexes the use of lowercase letters is preferred, in which case you should change the setting to *No*.

indent each level. Unless you use a style sheet *and* set the next field (*use style sheet*) to *Yes,* the *indent each level* field controls how far each subentry should be indented relative to the entry that precedes it. The default setting is .2″, which corresponds to two spaces of pica-size (10-pitch) typewriter type. This means that a first-level index entry will not be indented (unless you format it later), but that a subentry (a second-level index entry) will be indented .2″, a third-level entry will be indented another .2″, and so forth. Word will accommodate up to five levels of entries, each indented more than the level above it by the amount specified in the *indent each level* field. If you want each level indented three pica-size (p10) spaces instead of two, change the field from *.2″* to *.3″*. If you want two elite-size (p12) characters, change the field to *.17″* (or *2 p12*), and if you want three elite-size characters, change it to *.25″* (or *3 p12*).

use style sheet: Yes No. Shall Word use the special *Index level* styles in a style sheet to individually control the formatting of each level of entry? This is an advanced but extremely powerful feature of Word, combining the features of indexing and style sheets. If you don't understand style sheets yet, you may want to skip the following. If you want more details, see Chapter 24, "Power Tools: Style Sheets," and Chapter 26, "Power Tools: Hidden Text and Indexing."

If you pick *No,* Word will ignore any style sheet attached to the document when it carries out the paragraph formatting of the index. Instead, it will follow the indentation instructions given in the preceding field, *indent each level.* (However, if there is a style sheet attached to the document, Word will format the characters of the index entry according to the *character* formatting of the Standard Paragraph style in the style sheet, even though it will not follow the *paragraph* formatting of the style.)

If you pick *Yes* in the *use style sheet* field, Word will disregard the *indent each level* field of the Library Index command, and will format the index according to both the character and paragraph formatting in the style sheet attached to the document. If the style sheet contains the special styles *Index level 1, Index level 2, Index level 3,* and *Index level 4,* Word will follow the formatting of the appropriate style when formatting the various levels of the index. If any of these special index styles is not in the style sheet, Word will substitute the formatting of the Paragraph Standard style for the missing style(s). If you add the missing index style(s) later, Word automatically will update the format of the index to reflect the presence of the new style(s).

Word can accommodate five levels of index entry and there are only four index styles, so in the rare event there is a fifth level in an index you create, entries on the fifth level are formatted with the Paragraph Standard style—unless you later change the formatting by applying a different style manually, or by using direct formatting.

If you pick *Yes* and there is no style sheet attached to the document, the levels of entry in the index will not have relative levels of indentation until an appropriate style sheet is attached.

A great deal more can be said about indexing. Again, see Chapter 26, "Power Tools: Hidden Text and Indexing."

LIBRARY NUMBER

```
LIBRARY: Autosort Hyphenate Index Number Run Spell Table


LIBRARY NUMBER: Update Remove              restart sequence:(Yes)No
```

Use the Library Number command to renumber lists, paragraphs, headings, or sub-headings. The command, which recognizes and updates a variety of numbering (and lettering) schemes, can also remove numbering. Generally, the command affects only text that is selected. However, when a single character is selected, the entire document is subject to the command. With the exception of numbering performed when Word is in Outline mode, elements that are not numbered (or lettered) before the Library Number command is executed will not be numbered or lettered by the command. In other words, Word renumbers or removes numbering, but doesn't add numbering on its own to unnumbered elements (except in Outline mode).

In some senses, the Library Number command is related to the Library Autosort command. For instance, either command can be used to update a series of numbered paragraphs in which the numbers are out of sequence. But while the Library Autosort command rearranges paragraphs to put the numbers in order, the Library Number command updates the numbers but leaves the paragraphs in their original order.

Beginning with version 3.0, Word recognizes several kinds of characters as "numbers," and can update any of them:

- ◆ Arabic numerals (1, 2, 3).
- ◆ Roman numerals (I, II, III).
- ◆ Lowercase Roman numerals (i, ii, iii).
- ◆ Capital letters (A, B, C).
- ◆ Lowercase letters (a, b, c).
- ◆ Double numeration (1, 1.1, 1.2, 1.3).

Word recognizes and updates a number or letter provided it is followed by a period (.) or a close parenthesis ( )), in turn followed by a space or tab character and some text. The Library Number command won't update a number that isn't followed by punctuation and text. Also, the number or letter must begin a paragraph, except that it may be preceded by spaces, tab characters, and/or an open parenthesis (( ).

As examples, Word recognizes and updates all of these: 4, 4), (4), IV., IV), (IV), iv., iv), (iv), A., A), (A), a., a), (a), 2.3, 2.3), and (2.3).

Word renumbers using the numbering scheme (such as Roman or Arabic) and punctuation that it first encounters. A number that Word puts at the beginning of a paragraph has the same character formatting (font type and size, and attributes such as underlining) as the first printable character in the paragraph.

When you want to renumber several lists within the same document, one way is to select each set of elements to be renumbered and to execute the Library Number command once for each list. In this way, different lists can be numbered using different schemes—for instance, Arabic numerals for one list and Roman numerals for another.

But Word can handle several renumbering tasks simultaneously, with a single execution of the Library Number command, as long as the different lists are at discrete levels of indentation in a document. The best example of a document with suitable levels of indentation is an outline (whether viewed in Word's outline mode or not). Each level of heading in an outline is indented a different amount, and each can have a separate numbering scheme (such as Arabic or Roman). Subheads that are indented one level could be in Arabic numerals while main headings could be in Roman numerals, with each numbered independently. This only works when the indentation has been created with paragraph formatting, such as the *indent* fields of the Format Paragraph command, the built-in format Alt-N, or paragraph styles from a style sheet. (When apparent indentation has been achieved by pressing the Spacebar or the Tab key, the effect reflects the content of the document rather than its formatting, and so Word ignores it for purposes of renumbering. This is because the Library Number command disregards spaces or tab characters that lead up to a number.)

Two notes on renumbering outlines:

- For each level of heading that is indented farther to the right than the level that preceded it, Word automatically restarts its renumbering (from I or 1 or A or a). This is useful, because it means that subheadings will be numbered in relation to the heading they follow. In other words, the Library Number command is smart enough to not just continue counting at each level of indentation; in any level of heading, it starts counting over again when the structure of the outline suggests this is appropriate.

- When Word is in outline mode, the Library Number command will *number* as well as *renumber* an outline's levels of heading. In document mode, Word won't do this (even for a document that has levels of indentation and appears to be an outline) because the program can't assume that you want every paragraph numbered. But in Outline mode, Word knows it is dealing with an outline, and will assign appropriate numbers to every paragraph. By default, Word will assign a standard system of outline numbering, following this pattern: I., A., 1., a), (1), (a), i. You can alter this pattern of numbering, and even have Word intelligently assign a double numeration system (1.1, 1.2, 1.3, and so on) to an outline. For details, see Chapter 25, "Power Tools: Outlining."

Also note that the double numeration system works differently in Word's normal document mode than it does in outline mode. Normally, the Library Number command uses double numeration by updating the digits to the right of the final decimal point. For instance, if a list begins with 1.1, the successive numbers assigned by Word will be 1.2, 1.3, 1.4, and so on. However, in outline mode the double numeration system is considerably more powerful, and automatically updates each digit and assigns new digits as it encounters changes in levels of indentation. For an example, see Chapter 25, "Power Tools: Outlining."

The double numeration system, which is appropriate for some scientific, technical, and legal documents, is called *legal format* in the Word 3.0 manual.

If you don't like the consequences of the Library Number command, the Undo command will return the document to its previous condition. This technique works only when the Undo command is used immediately after the Library Number command.

Fields of the Library Number command

Although the Library Number command has great flexibility, it takes many of its cues as to how to renumber by mimicking what it already finds in a document. Consequently, the command has only two fields in which you give it explicit instructions.

NUMBER: *Update Remove*. Leave this set at *Update,* unless you want to remove all the numbers/letters that start paragraphs in a document (or a selection from a document). The *Remove* setting is handy when you want to convert an outline into a document that no longer has paragraph numbering, or when you want to eliminate numbers you have temporarily added to the beginnings of paragraphs.

restart sequence: *Yes No*. Shall renumbering begin at 1 (or I or i or A or a)? If you pick *Yes,* Word restarts the sequences of numbers. If you pick *No,* Word accepts the first number in the selection (or document, if only a single character is selected) and continues the sequence upwards.

LIBRARY RUN

```
LIBRARY: Autosort Hyphenate Index Number Run Spell Table

LIBRARY RUN: ▮
```

You can run other programs or use DOS commands by putting Word temporarily on hold with the Library Run command. Your computer must have sufficient memory for both the other program and Word.

On a floppy-disk system, each time you leave or return to Word with the Library Run command, it will instruct you to enter Y when the program disk is ready. This is your opportunity to switch disks to put a needed program in place. You needn't switch disks if the software you need is already on the Word Program disk.

When Word is being run from a hard disk, the transition from Word to the other program and back is momentary, so the message doesn't appear.

When you're done with the other program, you see the message *Press any key to resume Word.* When you press a key, the Word screen returns, just as you left it when you picked the Library Run command.

Even if your computer doesn't have enough spare memory to run major programs through the Library Run command, you can use such DOS commands as Chkdsk, Comp, Copy, Date, Dir, Format, Mkdir, Rename, and Time without quitting Word. You can also use the Spell utility programs discussed at the end of this chapter, as well as BASIC and utility programs that do not require large amounts of memory. For instance, you can format a disk without leaving Word—something that can be a big help if you have a full Program disk. And the Norton Utilities FF (File Find) and LD (List Directories) programs let you find what you want on a hard disk without exiting from Word.

Test the Library Run command by requesting a directory of your disk. Choose the command (Esc, L, R), type *dir,* and press Enter.

Library Run can be put to many good uses when a *batch file* is executed. See Chapter 18, "Speed."

NOTE: It is dangerous to run DOS-resident programs *for the first time* through Library Run, because the RAM these programs set aside interferes with Word's ability to function once you want to resume word processing. For instance, while it may be okay to load Sidekick before starting Word, don't load it into RAM with Library Run. Similarly, don't use the DOS Mode command through Library Run.

Returning temporarily to DOS

You can run a succession of programs through the Library Run command by "returning" temporarily to DOS. Type *COMMAND* instead of a command or program name. You see the DOS prompt (A> or C>, etc.)—just as if you'd quit Word. In fact, it is the same as quitting, except that the Word program, your document, and any other files you've been using are still in your computer's memory. You're in a position that is equivalent to being at the DOS prompt in a computer with less memory. To return to your previous place in Word, type *Exit* and press the Enter key. (It's best to type Exit rather than start Word a second time through the Library Run command.)

LIBRARY SPELL

LIBRARY: Autosort Hyphenate Index Number Run Spell Table

COMMAND: Dictionary Help Options Proof Quit

COMMAND: Add Correct Help Ignore Mark Options Quit
         Resume Next Previous

The Library Spell command is one of two ways to use Microsoft Spell, the spell-checking program tailored for Word. The other way is to use Spell separately from Word, by typing *spell* at the DOS prompt and specifying the document name when Spell asks for the file name.

In either case, like spelling-checker programs in general, Spell compares a document's words with entries in an electronic dictionary and shows you the words that it does not recognize. These may be misspellings, or they may be legitimate words that just aren't in the dictionary.

Spell comes with a basic dictionary that contains more than 80,000 words. You can add words that you use repeatedly—your name, for instance. Add any number of words, up to the capacity of the disk, but beware: Adding too many words will slow Spell's performance by giving it an excessive number of entries to examine. Strike a balance between speed and completeness.

You could, given enough time and disk space, create an enormous dictionary containing almost all existing English (or French, or German) words, but even a computer would take a long time to search this enormous dictionary, and such a complete dictionary could mask errors by including obscure words that matched your misspellings. For example, if you meant to type *buttering, father,* and *sleepiness,* but actually typed *butterine, fother,* and *steepiness,* a sufficiently complete dictionary wouldn't catch the typos because it would recognize the spellings as legitimate words.

Unless you're using Word on a hard disk or a high-capacity floppy that also contains Spell, you'll need to swap disks when you execute the Library Spell command. Word gives the message *Enter Y when Spell disk is ready,* prompting you to press the letter Y after you've removed the Word disk and replaced it with the Spell disk. When you're through using Spell, you see a message telling you to *Enter Y when Program Disk is ready.* This is your cue to replace the Spell disk with the Word Program disk once again, press Y, and resume using the document—now with its spelling corrected.

The simple approach

Spell provides several options and fancy, helpful features, but at first you'll probably want to use the spelling checker in its least elaborate way.

There are two phases to correcting spelling. In the *proofing* phase the words in the document are checked against one or more dictionaries on the Spell disk, and the unrecognized words are compiled into a list. In the *review* phase Spell displays each listed word, in turn, in context. You can then:

♦ Tell the program to ignore the word. This is appropriate if it's correctly spelled but not in the dictionary.

♦ Type the correct spelling if you know it.

♦ Ask for some possible spellings based on entries in a dictionary.

♦ Instruct Spell to mark the word for later attention.

The proofing phase

When you start Spell, you encounter a main menu with the commands Dictionary, Help, Options, Proof, and Quit. The only command that concerns you at first is the Proof command, which is Spell's proposed response. Execute it as you do any Word command, by pressing Enter or clicking with the mouse pointer on the word *Proof.*

If you entered Spell through the Library Spell command and a document is active in Word, proofing begins as soon as you pick the Proof command.

If you use Spell independently of Word, you'll be asked to specify a file name after you pick the Proof command. You may have to include a drive letter (and a path if you're using subdirectories on a hard disk). Once you give the file name, press the Enter key and proofing begins. From this point on, your use of Spell is the same regardless of how you started it.

While Spell proofs your document, take a moment to look at the screen. It is divided into three horizontal windows, plus a command area at the bottom. The three windows are blank during the proofing phase, but when proofing ends and the review phase begins, each window springs to life.

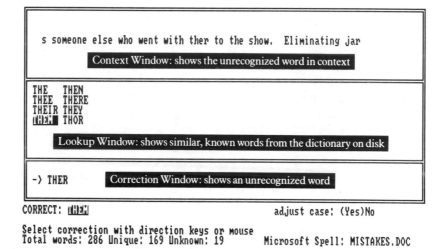

The bottom box, the *Correction Window,* shows you unrecognized words one at a time. Simultaneously, the top box, the *Context Window,* shows a line of the document containing the word. The middle box, the *Lookup Window,* is blank until you request a list of possible words spelled somewhat like the word in question.

The review phase

After Spell compiles the list of words that it doesn't recognize, the review phase begins. Another menu appears:

```
COMMAND: Add Correct Help Ignore Mark Options Quit
          Resume Next Previous
```

and the "misspelled" words are presented, one at a time, in alphabetical order in the Correction Window. You review these words, and determine what you want to do with each. The menu offers ten choices. For the moment we'll ignore the Help and Quit commands, which are self-explanatory once you know Word, and the Add and Options commands, which are discussed later in the sections "Setting Spell options" and "Adding words to dictionaries."

Ignore. If the spelling of the word in the Correction Window is fine, pick Ignore from the menu to tell Word to disregard it. This is Spell's proposed response, so you need only press the Enter key.

Mark. Pick the Mark command to insert a special mark, usually an asterisk, immediately before each occurrence of the word in question throughout the document. The mark tags the word for your later attention when you are editing. If you wish, you can use Spell's Options command to change the mark from an asterisk to a different character.

Why mark a word for later correction? Perhaps you've accidentally split a word into two pieces: For example, you've typed the word *factual* as *fact ual*. Spell recognizes *fact* but considers *ual* a misspelling. You see the problem in the Context Window when *ual* is displayed, but you need to edit the document to correct it, so you pick the Mark command to tag the error. Upon returning to Word, find the mark with the Search command, and correct it.

Correct. To change the spelling of the displayed word, choose Spell's Correct command. If you know the correct spelling, type it. The program looks up the word, and if it can't recognize your new spelling, it asks if you want to try again: *Not in Dictionary; Retype? (Y/N).*

The Correct command has a single field, *adjust case,* which is normally set to *Yes,* telling the program to give the corrected word the same combination of upper- and lowercase letters as the original word. If you change it to *No,* the correction is made exactly as you type it.

When using the Correct command, you can request help with spelling. Press any direction key or click the right mouse button to see a list of words from Spell's dictionary that are similar to the unrecognized word. Spell creates the list by assuming the first letter of the misspelled word is correct, but that one other letter is missing, wrong, transposed with an adjacent letter, or included when it shouldn't be. It compares these possibilities with a dictionary, and displays the list of possible alternatives in the midscreen Lookup Window. If you see the word you want, pick it from the list with the direction keys or the mouse. If none is suitable, press the Esc key.

If you know only the first few letters of the word you want, type them, type an asterisk, and press a direction key. Spell will let you pick from among all the words that begin with the letters you typed. If you know only the last few letters of the word, type an asterisk, type the letters, and press a direction key. You can also use a question mark to represent any single letter that you don't know.

Resume, Next, and Previous. Use these commands to move around in the list of unrecognized words. The Previous command moves you one word at a time back toward the beginning of the list. Use it to reconsider a decision you made about an earlier word on the list. The Next command moves you forward a word at a time, but will not take you beyond the point where you last used the Previous command. Resume, a sort of super Next command, jumps you directly to where you were when you picked the Previous command.

Once you have ignored, marked, or corrected all the unrecognized words, Spell tells you *REVIEW DONE* and asks you to press Y to carry out the changes. Until you press Y, none of the changes you've specified will actually be incorporated in your document. If you press N, the changes are discarded and the document is left unchanged. You face the same choice if you use the Quit command before completing your review of the words.

This is all you may need to learn about using Spell, but several additional features enhance its power. Read on when ready.

Setting Spell options

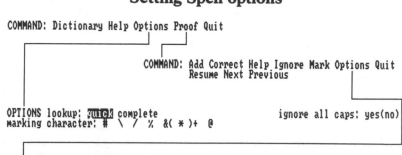

Spell's Options command, which can be reached either from the main (proofing) menu or from the secondary (review) submenu, gives you choices about how the program operates. Three command fields, *lookup, ignore all caps,* and *marking character,* can be set with the Options command from the proofing menu, but usually only one of them, *lookup,* can be set with the Options command from the review submenu.

NOTE: In the earliest version of Spell, all three options are available from both menus. This slight difference doesn't affect operation of the program.

lookup: quick complete. Picking *quick* tells Spell to assume the first two letters of an unrecognized word are correct when you call for a list in the Lookup Window. Picking *complete* tells Spell to assume none of the letters is necessarily correct. This offers more words, but takes longer.

ignore all caps: yes (no). Pick *yes* if you want the program to ignore words composed entirely of capital letters—IBM, UNICEF, NATO, and the like. Unless you've added such words to the dictionary, they will probably be displayed as misspellings. Pick *no* if all words must be examined.

marking character: # \ / % & * + @. Change this field if you don't want the marking character to be an asterisk. The asterisk has other common uses, notably as a footnote reference mark, so to keep the Spell marking character unique you may want to pick a different choice from the menu. Press the Spacebar to pick one that is unlikely to appear naturally in the document. Only one marking character is permitted for each review of a document.

Using supplemental dictionaries

So far you've seen how to use Spell with the main dictionary. The dictionary's file name is MAINDICT.CMP. There is a second file, called HIGHFREQ.CMP, which is part of the main dictionary. HIGHFREQ.CMP, as its name implies, contains many common words. When Spell checks a document of fewer than about 350 words, it uses HIGHFREQ.CMP to save time, and uses MAINDICT.CMP only for words it can't locate in HIGHFREQ.CMP.

Another file, called UPDICT.CMP, is also treated by Spell as if it is part of the main dictionary. It is called the *standard* dictionary, and is a list of words *you* create to expand the main dictionary. You will probably put your name in the standard dictionary, for example, so that each time Spell checks a document, it ignores your name.

There are also two other kinds of supplemental dictionaries, called *document* dictionaries and *user* dictionaries, to which you can add words. Although there is only one main dictionary and one standard dictionary, you can create any number of document and user dictionaries, and use different ones for different documents.

A document dictionary is a special list of words for a *single* document. If you're writing a report that uses technical terms, for instance, you can place them in a document dictionary and not have to clutter your other dictionaries with words that you rarely, if ever, use. When you create a document dictionary, Spell assigns it the same file name as the document with which it is associated, but gives the dictionary the extension .CMP rather than .DOC. If your document is called REPORT.DOC, for example, Spell names the corresponding document dictionary REPORT.CMP.

A user dictionary is a list of words related to a *group* of documents. For example, three people who use the same Spell disk might each create a personal user dictionary to supplement the main and document dictionaries with unusual words they use. But even if you're the only person who uses the Spell disk, you might create any number of user dictionaries and apply each to different kinds of documents. For instance, if you're a physician whose hobby is bird-watching and you produce the church newsletter, you might create three separate user dictionaries for medical, ornithological, and ecclesiastical terms.

You can give a user dictionary any file name you wish, as long as it has the extension .CMP. If you create a user dictionary without giving it a name, Spell gives it the name SPECIALS.CMP. Later, you can change SPECIALS to any other name with Word's Transfer Rename command, or by using the DOS Rename command through DOS or through the Library Run command.

Naming the user dictionary

```
COMMAND: Dictionary Help Options Proof Quit
         |
         |
DICTIONARY: ▮
```

Specify a user dictionary for use during a particular Spell session by picking the Dictionary command from the main (proofing) Spell menu. When the *DICTIONARY* field is displayed, type in the name of an existing user dictionary, pick one from a list, or make up a new name. You can omit the .CMP extension; Spell assumes it.

If you specify an existing user dictionary, Spell checks it along with other dictionaries when proofing a document. If you execute the Dictionary command without typing in a name, Spell creates the user dictionary named SPECIALS.CMP. Of course, in this case SPECIALS.CMP has no content—until you give it some. Which brings us to the Add command . . . .

Adding words to dictionaries

```
COMMAND: Add Correct Help Ignore Mark Options Quit
         │Resume Next Previous
         │
       ──┘
ADD word to: Standard Document User
```

You can create dictionaries from scratch by typing lists of words, but generally it's more efficient to use the Add command to create or augment a special dictionary as a by-product of reviewing the unrecognized words of a document.

Choose Add whenever you wish to add the word in the Correction Window to a dictionary. The Add command has one command field, *word to,* which offers a menu of three dictionaries: *Standard, Document,* and *User.* Picking *Standard* puts the word in the update dictionary of the main dictionary; picking *Document* puts the word in a dictionary with the same name as the document, but with the extension .CMP; and picking *User* puts the word in the user dictionary SPECIALS.CMP, unless you've specified a different name for the user dictionary with the Dictionary command. (The words are added in such a way that the alphabetical order of the respective dictionaries is preserved. Spell won't function properly if its dictionaries aren't in alphabetical order.)

Be careful when adding words, especially to the standard dictionary; if a misspelling gets on the list, the spelling checker won't catch the same misspelling in future documents.

You can look at a dictionary with the DOS Type command, or by loading it into Word with the Transfer Load command. (Use its full name, including the extension .CMP.)

Creating dictionaries from scratch

You can create a dictionary from scratch by typing a list of words, each as a separate paragraph (followed by a paragraph mark). Create such a list with Word, by saving it in un-formatted form (set the *formatted* field to *No* in the Transfer Save command). Give the list a name with the extension .CMP. For example, a user dictionary of slang could be SLANG.CMP. Dictionary words must be in alphabetic order. If you enter them in a different order, or if you already have a non-alphabetic file you want to turn into a dictionary, use the Library Autosort command to put them in order.

It is possible to create a new main dictionary from scratch, just as you can create a supplemental dictionary. Such a main dictionary, if it is very long, cannot be accessed as quickly as the MAINDICT.CMP dictionary that comes with Spell, because the original is compacted for high-speed operation. However, you might need to create a new main dictionary in order to use Spell with a foreign language or with any special subset of English. For instance, if you write or edit children's literature, you might include only simple words in the new main dictionary. Doing this would convert Spell into a filter that would draw inappropriate words to your attention.

LIBRARY TABLE

LIBRARY: Autosort Hyphenate Index Number Run Spell Ⓣⓐⓑⓛⓔ

```
LIBRARY TABLE index on: ▓      entry/page # separated by: ^t
          indent each level: 0.4"        use style sheet: Yes(No)
```

Once a document has been appropriately prepared with hidden coding, executing the Library Table command generates a table of contents, table of illustrations, or other lists of elements in the document. Tables can have relatively sophisticated formats, including sub-headings, and the command can be used successive times to create several different tables.

The Library Table command arranges the references it compiles according to page number, from first to last. (In contrast, the related Library Index command arranges references in alphabetical order, from *A* to *Z*, and combines duplicates into single entries followed by multiple page numbers.)

Before executing the Library Table command, you must designate table entries throughout the text, using simple coding that is hidden in the document. For details on these preparations, see Chapter 26, "Power Tools: Hidden Text and Indexing."

The Library Table command will create a table with any number of levels of entry, each indented from the preceding level. Rudimentary formatting of the levels is possible with fields of the Library Table command, and sophisticated formatting of the first four levels (which is a greater number than most people will need) is possible by instructing the Library Table command to consult a style sheet.

Before using the Library Table command, make sure hidden text is invisible in the text window—that is, make sure the *show hidden text* field of the Window Options command is set to *No.* This is advisable because Library Table repaginates the document before assigning page numbers, and the temporary presence of otherwise hidden text can render the pagination of the document inaccurate.

Like Library Index, the Library Table command places its compilations at the end of the document, separating each table from the other text with a division mark (:::::::). After the division mark, Word starts a table with a line of hidden text that says *.Begin Table.*, and ends it with a similar line that says *.End Table.* If you keep these hidden lines in your document, any new table you create with the Library Table command will replace the existing table (after displaying the message *Enter Y to replace existing table or Esc to cancel*). If you delete the hidden lines *.Begin Table.* and *.End Table.*, running the Library Table command causes a new table to be added after the previous one, as a separate division.

Once a table has been compiled, you may change its location in the document. However, be aware that moving the table can change the pagination (page numbering) of the document. Often this is not a problem, because the tables in the front of a book or other formal document frequently are on pages numbered separately (typically in lowercase Roman numerals) from the main pages of the text (which typically are numbered with Arabic numerals). For tips on how to move tables and yet keep pagination consistent, see Chapter 26.

NOTE: The name of the Library Table command may be misleading at first. This command does not create general tables of information, such as statistical tables you might want to incorporate into a report. Word does allow you to format simple or sophisticated statistical and similar tables, but that is accomplished with styles from a style sheet or with the Format Tabs Set command.

Fields of the Library Table command

The Library Table command has four fields, the last three of which are identical to the fields of the Library Index command.

index on. The default entry in this field is *C.* Unless you change the setting, the Library Table command will search through the document for table entries that start with the hidden text *.C.* (or *.c.*). The *C* of *.C.* stands for *Contents,* but you can employ any letter. Unlike Library Index, which always looks for the hidden text *.i.* to identify index entries in the text, the Library Table command will seek any letter of your choice that is set off between periods. You might use *.P.* to compile a list of photographs in a document, for instance. And because you can run the command several times using a different letter to compile a different set of entries each time, a variety of tables can be appended to a single document. (Remember, however, that you must delete the hidden line *.Begin Table.* in order to add a second or successive table to a document that already has a table generated by the Library Table command.)

entry/page # separated by. The default setting in this field is ^{t}, which stands for a tab character. It causes the Library Table command to place a tab character between the name of each table entry and the corresponding page number. Generally, the command also automatically incorporates a right-aligned tab stop into the table's paragraph formatting. This combination of the tab character and right alignment causes table entries to print on the left, with indentation as appropriate, and the page numbers for each entry to print on the right.

You can change the *entry/page # separated by* field to something else, such as a few spaces, or a comma and a few spaces. If you do not include a ^{t} (a tab character) in the field, a right-aligned tab stop will not be automatically added to the formatting of the table.

Although it appears there is only room to type about 20 spaces in this field, Word will wrap what you type to another line and move fields aside to make room for longer entries.

indent each level. Unless you use a style sheet *and* set the next field (*use style sheet*) to *Yes,* the *indent each level* field controls how far each subentry should be indented relative to the entry that preceded it. The default setting is 0.4", which corresponds to four spaces of pica-size (10-pitch) typewriter type. This means that a first-level table entry will not be indented (unless you format it later), but that a subentry under it (a second-level table entry) will be indented .4", a third-level entry will be indented another .4", and so forth. Word will accommodate virtually any number of levels of entry, each indented more than the level above it by the amount specified in the *indent each level* field. If you want each level indented five pica-size (p10) spaces instead of four, change the field from *.4"* to *.5"*. If you want four elite-size (p12) characters, change the field to *.33"* (or *4 p12*), and if you want five elite-size characters, change it to *.42"* (or *5 p12*).

use style sheet: Yes No. Shall Word use the special *Table level* styles in a style sheet to individually control the formatting of each level of entry? If you pick *No,* Word ignores any style sheet attached to the document when it carries out the paragraph formatting of the table. Instead, it follows the indentation instructions given in the preceding field, *indent each level.* (However, if there is a style sheet attached to the document, Word formats the characters of the table entry according to the *character* formatting of the Standard Paragraph style in the style sheet, even though it will not follow the *paragraph* formatting of the style.).

If you pick *Yes* in the *use style sheet* field, Word disregards the *indent each level* field of the Library Table command, and formats the table according to both the character and paragraph formatting in the style sheet attached to the document. If the style sheet contains the styles *Table level 1, Table level 2, Table level 3,* and *Table level 4,* Word follows the appropriate style when formatting the various levels of the table. If any of these special table styles are not in the style sheet, Word substitutes the formatting of the Standard Paragraph style for the missing style(s). If you add the missing table style(s) later, Word automatically will update the format of the table to reflect the presence of the new style(s).

Word can accommodate more than a dozen levels of table indentation, and there are only four table styles, so if a table contains more than four levels of entry, the additional levels will be formatted initially with the Standard Paragraph style.

If you pick *Yes* and there is no style sheet attached to the document, the levels of heading in the table will not have relative levels of indentation until you attach a style sheet that contains appropriate *Table level* styles. For more information, see Chapter 26, "Power Tools: Hidden Text and Indexing."

THE SPELL UTILITIES

The five utility programs discussed here come on the Microsoft Spell disk. They are ANAGRAM, WORDFIND, LOOKUP, WC, and WORDFREQ, and they range from handy to fun. Execute them either from DOS or through the Library Run command.

ANAGRAM

ANAGRAM unscrambles letters and lists the words they can form. Put your Spell disk in the disk drive, type *anagram,* a space, and the letters you want unscrambled, and pause a moment for the results. For example, if you type *anagram rehsot,* the computer lists the words *others* and *throes.* Add the wildcard character ?, and you find matches in which the wildcard character can be replaced by any letter, in any position in the word.

WORDFIND

WORDFIND is a blessing for crossword-puzzle fans and poets who don't mind some electronic help. (The earliest version of Spell called this program FIND.) It locates all the words in Spell's main dictionary that conform to a particular arrangement of letters and the wildcard characters ? (representing one letter) and * (representing any number of letters).

For example, imagine that your crossword puzzle needs a ten-letter word; the third letter is *O* and the sixth letter is *T*. Type *wordfind ??o??t????* and the program lists dozens of possibilities, from *abolitions* to *violations*. Too many choices. You continue working the puzzle, and realize the last two letters of the word are *N* and *G*. Type *wordfind ??o??t??ng* and the response narrows to *shoestring*.

For entertainment, use WORDFIND to discover the letters that complete this four-by-four grid. (Hint: Try *wordfind U?O?* first.)

S H E D
L O R E
U ? O ?
M ? S ?

LOOKUP

LOOKUP checks Spell's main dictionary to find words with spellings similar to the word you specify. Type *lookup mispell*, for example, and the computer lists the word *misspell* for you—very handy with Library Run on a hard disk.

WC

WC, the word-count program, tallies the number of words in a document. Type *wc* followed by a space and the name of the document. The program promptly gives an answer. If you want to count the number of words in the document on which you are actively working, use the Transfer Save command before using Library Run and WC. This ensures an up-to-date count, because WC counts the words on the document disk.

WORDFREQ

WORDFREQ counts the words in a document and lists the number of different words and the number of words that appear only once. Execute the command, either from DOS or (after saving the document) through the Library Run command, by typing *wordfreq*, a space, and the file name of the document.

As a byproduct, WORDFREQ writes to disk a list of all the words in the document and the number of times each appears. This is invaluable if you're trying to monitor your use (or rather overuse) of certain words. For example, if you find the word *very* is among your most common, you may wish to vary your vocabulary.

The frequency list is stored in a specially created file with the same name as the document, but with the filename extension .FRQ. So, for example, if the document is WINDSURF.DOC, the frequency list is WINDSURF.FRQ. The list begins with the most frequently used word, but you can force the list into alphabetic order if you type a space followed by *$a* after the name of the document when you use WORDFREQ: type *wordfreq windsurf $a*.

The Family of Print Commands

Though the name doesn't suggest both purposes, members of the family of Print commands are used to produce paper copies of documents and to prepare Word files for use with other programs. Except for the Print Options command, which ends in several fields, and the Print File command, which offers many possibilities, the Print commands are quite straightforward. The Print Printer command, for example, prints a document. Period. Many people really need only three of the eight commands: Print Printer, Print Options, and Print Repaginate.

```
COMMAND: Alpha Copy Delete Format Gallery Help Insert Jump Library
         Options Print Quit Replace Search Transfer Undo Window

PRINT: Printer Direct File Glossary Merge Options Queue Repaginate
```

This is what the Print commands do:

- ♦ Print Printer prints the document displayed in the active text window (the window containing the selection).

- ♦ Print Direct lets you use the computer and printer in typewriter fashion. Keystrokes are sent directly to the printer.

- ♦ Print File lets you store a document on disk either for later printing with DOS, or for use with other software.

- ♦ Print Glossary prints the names and associated glossary entries (text) that are active in Word's glossary (memory) at the time the command is picked. This command was new beginning with Word version 3.0.

- ♦ Print Merge is the command you give to merge data from a separate file into the document displayed in the active window, and print the result. This command replaces the Print Printer command when you print form letters and other mass-produced, but "personalized," documents.

♦ Print Options lets you tell Word about your printer and what you want done, so the other Print commands are carried out in accordance with your needs.

♦ Print Queue lets you stop and start the printing of documents that you've "queued up" to be printed in the background—that is, to print while Word is being used for other tasks.

♦ Print Repaginate lets you see and control where new pages will start if the document is printed in its current form.

PRINT PRINTER

PRINT: Printer Direct File Glossary Merge Options Queue Repaginate

PRINT PRINTER (Carried out as soon as it is picked)

Think of the Print Printer command as Word's print button. "Push" it whenever you want a paper copy of your work. There are no fields to fill in, and Word executes the command immediately. If you're using a mouse and the Edit menu is displayed, clicking the right button when the mouse pointer is on *Print* executes the Print Printer command without stopping at the Print submenu.

Whenever you use the Print Printer command, Word looks for specific printing instructions (type of printer, number of copies, and so on) in the fields of the Print Options command. If your printer automatically changes typefaces as needed, and you don't feed pages to it by hand, Word prints the whole document without delay. If you manually feed single sheets of paper to your printer, Word pauses to display this message before printing each page: *Enter Y to continue or Esc to cancel.* When you insert a new sheet of paper and press Y, printing continues.

Printing with daisy-wheel printers

If you change typefaces on your printer manually, Word pauses when a change in character formatting requires a different daisy wheel (or other printing element). Word tells you to mount the new typeface by displaying a message such as *Enter Y after mounting Prestige 12.* This message appears at the beginning of the printing of a document, and each time a new daisy wheel or other element is required. The name and pitch of the font (Prestige 12 in the example) reflect the character formatting contained in the document. Bear in mind here that the font size Word requests is the *pitch* number shown on the daisy-wheel element—not the font *point* size used during formatting.

There is no actual requirement to change the daisy wheel when Word requests you to. When you press Y, Word assumes you've made the change and it resumes printing with whatever daisy wheel is in the printer.

There are two instances in which Word does not pause, even if the document contains one or more different fonts. If you've specified TTY.PRD, TTYFF.PRD, TTYBS.PRD, or PLAIN.PRD in the *printer* field of the Print Options command, Word disregards changes in font type and size because they cannot be used with those printer description files. Similarly, if the Print Options command's *draft* field is set to *Yes*, Word gives you a high-speed draft without font changes.

Problems with printing

Word may be unable to execute the Print Printer command for any of several reasons. The printer may be turned off or disconnected. It may be offline, or not be connected to the port you specified in the Print Options command's *setup* field. If it is a serial printer, the DOS mode may be set incorrectly, or the printer may be jammed, out of paper, or out of ribbon.

Whatever the reason, if Word is unable to print, it pauses and then displays the message *Printer not ready*, followed by this message or a similar one: *Enter Y to continue or Esc to cancel*. The pause is usually momentary, but may last as long as a minute. If you are impatient, try pressing the Esc key, or the "break" key (on the original IBM PC keyboard, hold down the Ctrl key and press the Scroll Lock key), or try turning the printer off and then on again, or switch it on- and offline.

PRINT DIRECT

```
PRINT: Printer Direct File Glossary Merge Options Queue Repaginate
       |-----------------|
       |
PRINT DIRECT:
```

The Print Direct command sends your keystrokes directly to the printer. As with a typewriter, remember to enter a carriage return (with the Enter key) to end each line. When you finish, press the Esc key to return to the Edit menu. The Print Direct command is handy for such things as addressing one envelope, and it gives some flexibility, because it can even be used when you are writing or editing something else. Daisy-wheel printers use whatever wheel is mounted when the command is issued; dot-matrix and laser printers use their "normal" characters.

Although interesting, you may find the Print Direct command of doubtful value. The screen doesn't show what you've typed, so unless the printer is next to you, you cannot see the result. You can't correct mistakes, because no "word processing" takes place. And, depending on the printer, your characters may be printed as you type, or in spurts as you pause between phrases, or when you press the Enter key at the ends of lines.

PRINT FILE

```
PRINT: Printer Direct FILE Glossary Merge Options Queue Repaginate
        ┌───────────────────┐
        │
PRINT FILE name:
```

When you use the Print File command, you cause Word to "print" a document to a file on disk instead of to a printer. Later, the disk file can be used as input to other programs. One such program is DOS, which lets you print out the file on a printer, regardless of whether you're still using Word. Other programs that can use a Word disk file include most word processors and spreadsheets. You can transfer a disk file to another program by swapping disks, by transmitting the file with a telecommunications program and modem, or through an electronic-mail system.

Because Print File stores a document on disk, it is a cousin of the Transfer Save command. But Print File is more flexible. Whenever a document is printed to disk with Print File, its form is determined by whatever printer description (.PRD) file is installed in the Print Options command's *printer* field. By changing the .PRD file, you can print the same document to disk in several forms, for use with different kinds of programs.

There are four steps to transferring a document or other file from Word to other software with the Print File command:

1. Determine whether you really need the Print File command; the correct choice may be the Transfer Save command.
2. Determine which .PRD file is appropriate.
3. Execute the Print File command after specifying a name for the disk file.
4. Use the resulting disk file with other software.

Let's take the steps one at a time.

Print File or Transfer Save?

If you simply want to save your document so that you can use it later with Word, use the Transfer Save command rather than the Print File command. Similarly, use Transfer Save if you're going to use the document with the Microsoft word processor called Write, which is made especially for use with Microsoft Windows. And use Transfer Save if you're going to transfer a document to the simplified version of Word that comes in "Microsoft Works" hand-held computers, such as the Tandy 600 and the Zenith ZP-150. In each of these instances, the *formatted* field of Transfer Save should be left on *Yes*.

If you want to save a computer program you've written with Word, also use the Transfer Save command. (Computer programs include CONFIG.SYS files, and AUTOEXEC.BAT and other batch files, as well as instructions written in BASIC or another computer language.) When you save a computer program, set the Transfer Save command's *formatted* field to *No*.

There is another instance in which you may need to use Transfer Save (with *formatted* set to *No*), rather than Print File. Some word-processing programs do not use a carriage return at the end of each line. Instead, they need returns only at the ends of paragraphs. To create a file for use with such a program, use Transfer Save (*formatted* set to *No*) instead of Print File.

If you use Transfer Save and discover that the other word processor shows only the first line of each paragraph, you should use Print File, instead. If you use Print File and discover a paragraph mark (or other unwanted symbol) showing up at the end of every line, you should use Transfer Save, instead.

Which .PRD file?

You must install an appropriate .PRD file before executing the Print File command. Determine the .PRD file you use by the purpose to which you intend to put the disk file.

If you're storing the file on disk so that it can be printed later with DOS, use the .PRD file for the printer. (Usually this will already be installed in the Print Options command's *printer* field. If you don't have an appropriate .PRD file for your needs and printer, see the tip on modifying .PRD files in Chapter 18, "Speed.")

If the file is for use with supplemental software written specifically to enhance Word's formatting powers, use the .PRD files supplied with the supplemental software. One example of this kind of software is Scriptor, by Screenplay Systems, which prints a Word file in the peculiar, demanding format required by screenplays. Another example is Fancy Word, by SoftCraft, which prints Word files in many new fonts and type sizes, at low speed and medium resolution, on an Epson or Toshiba dot-matrix printer, or on an HP LaserJet printer. (This program is a version of Fancy Font.)

Most software, however, must receive files in a universal set of characters known as ASCII. An ASCII file contains only the symbols that represent numbers, letters, spaces, line feeds, and the like. Word's formatting characters and special printer codes are stripped out.

There are two steps to creating an ASCII file with the Print File command:

1. Install the PLAIN printer description (.PRD) file in the *printer* field of the Print Options command.

2. Set the *top, bottom, left,* and *right* fields of the Format Division Margins command to 0, and the *width* field to correspond to the maximum number of characters you want in each line. There are 10 characters to the inch with PLAIN installed, so a 70-character line would require you to type 7″ in the *width* field.

If you have more than one division in your document, select the whole document (Shift-F10) before making the changes in the Format Division Margins fields.

TIP: If you frequently prepare disk files with the Print File command, consider creating a style sheet with a division style that has 0-inch margin settings and the page *width* field set to the line width. You can use the Format Style Sheet command to attach the special style sheet temporarily to any document you are about to print as a file.

If you don't have PLAIN.PRD use TTY.PRD and then select the whole document (Shift-F10) and reset characters to "normal" with Alt-Spacebar. (PLAIN treats characters as "normal" automatically, but you have to do it yourself with TTY. By using Alt-Spacebar, you're sure no characters have underlining, boldfacing, italicizing, or any other special character formatting. Again, this isn't necessary if you're using PLAIN.PRD.)

Execute the Print File command

Once you have installed the appropriate .PRD file and made any necessary changes in the Format Division Margins fields (or chosen an appropriate division style from a style sheet), pick the Print File command. Word responds: *PRINT FILE name.* To avoid overwriting the original, formatted version of your document, type a name that is different from that of the document, or use an extension other than .DOC. You might use the extension .FIL, .TXT, or .ASC. For instance, if your document is called T-BIRD.DOC, you could type *T-BIRD.FIL* in the *name* field.

Before carrying out the command, consider what disk you want the file to be on or what directory you want it to be in. For example, if you're preparing a file for use with a telecommunications program, you may want to put a particular disk in your computer, or precede the name of the file with the name of a communications directory on your hard disk.

Press the Enter key to carry out the command. If Word responds with the message *Enter Y to overwrite file,* it means you've already stored a file under the same name and extension. If you don't mind losing the old version, press Y. To retain the old version, press the Esc key and pick the Print File command again, this time specifying a different name or extension.

Afterward, remember to change the .PRD file in the Print Options *printer* field so that it matches your printer, and reset the fields of the Format Division Margins command if you want to print the document later with the Print Printer command.

Using the disk file

The way you use a disk file created with the Print File command is determined by the software for which you created the file. If you've used PLAIN.PRD or TTY.PRD to create an ASCII file, checking for the entry *ASCII* in the index of the other software's manual often can lead you to the information you need. If you're using Scriptor, Fancy Word, or a similar program adapted specifically for use with Word, check the instructions with the software.

If you created a disk file with the .PRD file for your printer, you can copy the file to your printer from DOS. For example, if your disk file is called REPORT.FIL and your printer is connected to LPT1:, issue the command *copy report.fil lpt1:*.

Diablo, Toshiba, and certain other printers require a variation on this. If nothing happens when you follow the previous example, add a space and a /b after the name of the file: *copy report.fil /b lpt1:*.

You can use the DOS Print command to automatically print a queue of up to 10 disk files. First create the queue with the DOS Print command, then exit Word (or use Library Run) and execute the Print command at the DOS level. See your DOS manual for details. You can return to editing while DOS prints your files. This method gives better computer performance than using Word's own queue feature—the feature explained in the Print Options and Print Queue portions of this chapter.

Tips on Print File

Bear these two final tips in mind when using Print File.

♦ It is possible, but not easy, to edit the contents of a disk file by loading it into Word, making changes, and storing it again with the Transfer Save command (*formatted* field set to *No*). For example, you can often change the width of the ruled line that prints above footnote text. (This is easier with the files created by some .PRD files than it is with others.) Once it is edited, you can send the file to the printer with the DOS Copy or Print command.

♦ Even if a friend doesn't have Word, you can send him or her a fully formatted Word file to print. When you use Print File, install the .PRD file corresponding to your friend's printer. Send the file by disk or modem. He or she can print it perfectly with the DOS Copy or Print command.

PRINT GLOSSARY

PRINT: Printer Direct File **Glossary** Merge Options Queue Repaginate

PRINT GLOSSARY: (Carried out as soon as it is picked)

Print Glossary is one of the simplest of commands. New beginning in version 3.0 of Word, it prints each name in the glossary and the text associated with the name. For instance, let's say you've used the Copy or Delete commands to assign the name *thanks* to the phrase *Thank you for your attention to this matter*. When you pick the Print Glossary command, the word *thanks* will be printed, followed by the sentence it represents.

The Print Glossary command only prints the names and text entries that are in the glossary at the time the command is picked. To print the content of glossary files on disk (filename.GLY), first you must load them into the glossary with the Transfer Glossary Merge command.

PRINT MERGE

PRINT: Printer Direct File Glossary **Merge** Options Queue Repaginate

PRINT MERGE: (Carried out as soon as it is picked)

The Print Merge command lets you print form letters or other multiple-version documents by merging text or information from a second file (a data file) into your main document when—and as—you wish. It even allows you to use "if this, then that" instructions that tailor your documents to fit specific situations. These instructions are called *conditionals,* because the way they execute during the printing of a particular document depends on the condition (value) of a corresponding record in the data file.

The Print Merge command executes directly, like Print Printer. If you use multiple windows, be certain that the selection is in the appropriate document when you pick the Print Merge command.

While the command is easy to execute, Print Merge can be used successfully only after the document and data file have been properly prepared. This requires some thought and can be a relatively sophisticated task. The techniques are described in Chapter 23, "Power Tools: Merge."

PRINT OPTIONS

```
PRINT: Printer Direct File Glossary Merge Options Queue Repaginate
       ┌─────────────────────────────────────────────┘
PRINT OPTIONS printer: █
              draft: Yes(No)      queued: Yes(No)      copies: 1
              range:(All)Selection Pages       page numbers:
              feed: Manual(Continuous)Bin1 Bin2 Bin3 Mixed
              widow/orphan control:(Yes)No           setup: COM1:
```

It isn't enough just to tell Word to print to a printer, or file, or merge a document with data. Before these commands can be carried out successfully, the fields of the Print Options command must be set to reflect your computer equipment and needs. Once they are set, however, you may find little reason ever to make changes, because Word remembers most Print Options settings between editing sessions.

If you followed the step-by-step instructions for the Print Options fields in Chapter 4, "Setting Up," you've already made the most important choices. The Word SETUP program (beginning with version 2.0) can set some of the fields, too.

Fields of the Print Options command

Word remembers the choices you make in all of the Print Options fields except *copies, range,* and *page numbers.* If you have several printers connected to your computer, you can switch among them without leaving Word by making the appropriate changes in the *printer, feed,* and *setup* fields.

printer. Type the name of the printer description (.PRD) file that matches your printer. You can choose a printer description file from a list, by pressing a direction key. The list shows only the .PRD files you copied from the Word Utilities disk onto the Word Program disk during your setup procedures, unless you have a hard disk.

If the .PRD file in the *printer* field doesn't match the printer you use, the accuracy of the Print Repaginate, Library Hyphenate, Library Index, and Library Table commands, as well as the layout of the document on the screen, may be adversely affected. A serious mismatch between the .PRD file and the printer will cause a lot of what seems to be gibberish to be printed. The gibberish is embedded coding particular to a specific printer, telling the printer when to change line spacing, type fonts, and so forth. (Most of these instructions are known as "escape codes" or "escape sequences.") When a printer can't recognize coding intended for a different printer, it prints the coding as gibberish rather than following its instructions. Correctly matching a .PRD file to a printer solves the problem.

Word versions beginning with 3.0 use different .PRD files than earlier versions of the program. The name of the printer description file may be the same (such as HPLASPS.PRD), and the apparent operation may be the same, but the content is different technically. Use a .PRD file that came with the version of Word you are using. If in doubt, a .PRD dated 1986 or later should work with the most recent versions of Word. (You can tell which version of Word you are using by executing the Options command and reading the message line.) It is possible to convert an "old" .PRD file for use with the "new" Word, or even create a .PRD file from scratch. See the MAKEPRD tip in Chapter 18, "Speed."

One function of a .PRD file is to notify Word of which fonts and type sizes a particular printer can handle. The lists from which you pick in the Format Character command's *font name* and *font size* fields vary according to the .PRD file installed. Word can actually accommodate 64 different fonts at a time, in many sizes. The program thinks of the fonts in generic terms, calling them such things as *modern a, modern b, decor e,* and *roman i.* There's a full list of generic font names in the Word manual, just as there's a list of .PRD files and corresponding printers. Beginning with Word version 3.0, there is a separate manual on printers.

When a particular .PRD file is installed, it tells Word which of the 64 font types are available on the printer, and in which sizes. For example, the generic *modern a* is Pica on a Diablo 630 printer, but is Courier on an HP LaserJet printer. If you format characters as Pica when the Diablo .PRD file is installed, Word considers the characters to be *modern a.* It shows them as Pica for your convenience as long as it thinks you'll be printing the document on a Diablo printer. But if you install the LaserJet .PRD file HPLASCR, Word starts calling the Pica characters Courier. If you prefer, you can type the generic font names in the *font name* field of the Format Character command. Which actual font is used will depend on the .PRD file and printer.

If none of Word's .PRD files matches your printer model, use one with a name beginning with TTY (such as TTY.PRD, TTYWHEEL.PRD, TTYFF.PRD, or TTYBS.PRD). One of these printer description files will work on virtually any printer, because TTY files contain almost no escape codes. They have only the vital instructions that any printer understands: letters and numbers, line feeds, carriage returns, and not much more. Even a teletype understands these instructions, which is why the drivers are called TTY.

Use TTYWHEEL.PRD for a daisy-wheel printer and TTY.PRD for any other variety. If underlining doesn't work, try TTYBS.PRD, and if you're using a cut-sheet feeder on a printer that doesn't have its own .PRD file, try TTYFF.PRD. The TTY printer description files allow only 12-point/10-pitch printing. And, except for TTYWHEEL.PRD, they allow only *modern a* (usually Pica) printing. TTYWHEEL, however, lets you format documents with a variety of font names, and it causes Word to make the printer pause at appropriate times so that you can change daisy wheels.

Generally you change the printer description file when you change from one printer model to another. Likewise, you change it temporarily to PLAIN.PRD (or TTY.PRD) before using the Print File command.

Word version 3.0 automatically loads downloadable fonts for certain printers, such as the Hewlett-Packard LaserJet Plus, the IBM Pageprinter, and (beginning with version 3.1) the Apple LaserWriter. (A downloadable font is a set of instructions the computer sends to the printer to tell it how to shape and size characters.) Word will examine a document and automatically load the font information from the subdirectory of a hard disk, provided the font information is in the same subdirectory that contains Word. On a floppy-disk system, Word prompts you, with a message, to put the disk containing the fonts in a disk drive.

draft: Yes No. Setting this field to *Yes* tells Word to print in a high-speed "draft" mode that shows page and line placement but eliminates unusual character formatting. Also pick *Yes* when you wish to print a justified document without microspace justification.

queued: Yes No. Placing one or more documents in a queue by choosing *Yes* lets you print documents while continuing to use Word. Once queued printing is turned on in this field, executing the Print Printer command transfers the current document to a special queue that resides on, and is then printed from, the Program disk. The disk file is automatically erased at the end of printing, but in the meantime substantial free space on the Program disk is needed. You can queue any number of documents, but if you fill the disk you'll get a *Program disk full* message. Transferring the document to disk in a printer-ready form takes a few seconds per page, and during that time you cannot use the computer. While it is printing from the queue, you can use Word for editing, although performance slows. Once queued printing begins, you control it with the Print Queue command.

copies. How many copies do you want printed? If you request more than one copy of a multiple-page document, Word collates automatically by printing the entire document and then repeating.

range: All Selection Pages. When you want the Print Printer command to print the whole document, pick *All.* When you want to print just the selected text, pick *Selection.* When you want to print only certain pages, pick *Pages.*

page numbers. If you've picked *Pages* in the *range* field, this is where you list the page numbers you want printed. Use commas (2,4,6,8) to separate individual page numbers and use a hyphen (3-6) or a colon (3:6) to indicate a range of consecutive pages to print. (You can also combine the methods: 3-6,8.) To print to the end of a document when you don't know the final page number, pick a number you know is substantially higher than the final number. If you want to print a range of page numbers in a document that has several divisions, after the page number you can type *D* and a division number. For instance, *3D1-5D2* would tell Word to print all the pages from the third page of the first division to the fifth page of the second division. (If the decimal character has been set to comma, you must use semicolons instead of commas to separate page numbers. This is relevant beginning with version 3.1.)

feed: Manual Continuous Bin1 Bin2 Bin3 Mixed. Tell Word how paper is fed to your printer. *Manual* means you feed in a sheet at a time by hand; this setting prompts Word to pause at the end of every page and ask you to press Y to continue. *Continuous* indicates you have fanfold paper or you're using a laser printer or other printer that doesn't require manual feeding; when you pick *Continuous,* Word doesn't pause between pages. *Bin1, Bin2, Bin3,* and *Mixed* refer to printers with cut-sheet feeders or dual-bin sheet feeders that automatically load individual sheets from one or two trays. Picking *Bin1* or *Bin2* means every sheet will be printed on paper from the bin specified, presuming there are two bins. The *Mixed* setting lets you print the first page of a document from *Bin 1* and the remaining pages from *Bin 2*. This setting is handy, for example, if you have letterhead stationery in the first bin and non-letterhead paper, for additional pages of a multi-page letter, in the second bin. *Bin3* lets you use an envelope feeder on certain printers, such as the Diablo 630.

   widow/orphan control: Yes No. Don't take pity on widows and orphans, take interest. This field, new beginning with version 3.0 of Word, lets you decide whether Word will permit a document to be paginated in such a way that single lines of text are stranded at the tops or bottoms of pages. A widow line is the final line of a paragraph that is printed by itself at the top of a page, the beginning of the paragraph having been printed on the preceding page. An orphan line is the first line of a paragraph, printed by itself on the bottom of a page, with the remainder of the paragraph printed on the next page. Widow and orphan lines generally are considered unattractive.

   If you leave the *widow/orphan control* field set to *Yes*, Word will readjust the lengths of specific pages as needed to eliminate widow lines and orphan lines. If you pick *No*, Word will always print as many lines on a page as are allowed by the page's formatting, regardless of whether this results in widows and orphans.

   If you pick *Yes*, you can extend your control further over how page length is adjusted automatically to keep blocks of text on the same page. See the *keep together* and *keep follow* fields of the Format Paragraph command, described in Chapter 12, "The Family of Format Commands." Also, see the Print Repaginate command, below.

   setup. Tell Word which port your printer is connected to. There are five possibilities, though you may not necessarily have all installed in your computer. If you have a parallel printer, the possibilities are LPT1:, LPT2:, and LPT3:. If you have a serial printer, the possibilities are COM1: and COM2: (with these serial choices, you must also tell DOS that a printer is connected to the port; if you haven't already done so, use the Mode command as described in your DOS manual). Be sure to include the colon when typing the name of one of these settings. Beginning with version 1.15 of Word, you can pick from among the five port names by pressing a direction key or by clicking the right mouse button.

PRINT QUEUE

```
PRINT: Printer Direct File Glossary Merge Options Queue Repaginate
      |
      |
PRINT QUEUE: Continue Pause Restart Stop
```

   Queued printing refers to printing one or more documents while you keep Word available for continued use. You start it by setting the Print Options command's *queued* field to *Yes* and executing the Print Printer command. Once queued printing begins, the Print Queue command gives you control over it.

   The Print Queue command has one field, *PRINT QUEUE*, which has four options: *Continue, Pause, Restart,* and *Stop.*

Pause causes queued printing to be temporarily suspended. During the lull caused by Pause, you can proceed with other editing without the slowed performance usually associated with queued printing.

Continue resumes queued printing that has been paused.

Restart begins the printing of the document over again, repeating pages already printed.

Stop cancels queued printing, erasing the temporary disk file in which the queue is stored.

PRINT REPAGINATE

```
PRINT: Printer Direct File Glossary Merge Options Queue Repaginate
```

```
PRINT REPAGINATE confirm page breaks: Yes No
```

The Print Repaginate command repaginates a document, calculating where new pages will start if the document is printed in its current form. Page tops are shown with a » symbol to the left of the beginning of the line. The tops of columns are shown with the same symbol preceded by the number of the column on the page—2» is the top of the second column, 3» the top of the third.

The Print Repaginate command, like the Print Printer command, tells Word to lay out a document a page at a time. This task can be complex, because Word's unusual flexibility permits a page to have such intricacies as multiple columns, footnotes, different sizes of type, variable line spacing, and multiple-line running heads. Unlike Print Printer, the Print Repaginate command does not take the final step of sending the document to the printer.

But the Print Repaginate command allows you a special opportunity. Beginning with Word version 2.0, Print Repaginate lets you add new-page characters as a document is repaginated. (You can also enter them manually before repagination by pressing Shift-Ctrl-Enter.) A new-page character is an actual part of a document that is displayed as a series of dots across the text window; it forces Word to begin a new page.

If you want to preview page breaks, and possibly adjust the lines at which pages start, pick *Yes* in the *confirm page breaks* field. When Word reaches a page-break location, it pauses and asks you to confirm or change the choice: *Enter Y to confirm or use direction keys.* Accept the proposed location by pressing Y, or use the Up direction key to pick a point higher on the page. It is impossible to pick a point lower than that proposed by Word, but you can use the Down direction key to move the break back down after having moved it up. Once you've found the line at which you want the break to occur, press Y. Word inserts a new-page character (the row of dots) at that point.

What happens if there are new-page characters already in a document when you pick Print Repaginate? They automatically start new pages, unless you're confirming page breaks. In this case, you can pass judgment on new-page characters, too. Word stops as it encounters each, and advises you to *Enter Y to confirm or R to remove.*

There is a subtle but important improvement in this command, beginning with version 3.0 of Word. In version 2.0, adding a new-page character in the middle of a paragraph caused the paragraph to become two paragraphs. This meant, for instance, that if the original paragraph was formatted to have a first-line indent, the indent also would appear at the new page break. Word 3.0 is revised so that splitting a paragraph with a new-page character doesn't force a new paragraph to be created. This is true regardless of whether the new-page character is created with the Print Repaginate command or by holding down the Ctrl and Shift keys and pressing Enter.

A freshly repaginated document lets you see how it will print, but don't jump to the conclusion you need to repaginate frequently—or at all. Wise use of the *keep together* and *keep follow* fields of the Format Paragraph command helps ensure that text will not break across pages in visually undesirable ways. And when you're comparing a printed copy of a document with a heavily edited on-screen version, the Jump Page command is more useful if the on-screen version has not been repaginated since the paper copy was printed.

Three final notes:

♦ Be sure hidden text is invisible before you repaginate, unless you intend eventually to print the document with hidden text showing. Otherwise, the accuracy of the pagination will be suspect.

♦ Don't confuse a new-page mark (» near the left border of a window) with a new-page character (. . . . . . . dots across the screen). The mark just shows you where a page happened to begin as of the last printing or repagination, while the character is part of the document's content, and forces a new page to begin at that point.

♦ When tops of columns are shown (with 2» or 3» or 4»), they are the tops of columns created through multiple-column division formatting, *not* the tops of columns created with side-by-side paragraphs.

The Family of Transfer Commands

You transfer information between the disk drives and the screen with the family of Transfer commands. They are among your most important tools. Save a document on disk with the Transfer Save command, and later reload it from the disk with the Transfer Load command. Clear the screen or a text window with the Transfer Clear Window command, or clear everything—the screen, computer memory, and the temporary files Word creates on disk—with the Transfer Clear All command.

Erase a document or other file from disk with the Transfer Delete command. Change the name of the document on which you are working with the Transfer Rename command. Combine a document stored on disk with a document on the screen with the Transfer Merge command, or use the Transfer Options command to tell Word to change the disk drive or directory on which it looks for and stores information. Finally, use the Transfer Glossary commands to save, recall, and eliminate glossary files.

This describes the relationship of the Transfer commands to each other:

```
COMMAND: Alpha Copy Delete Format Gallery Help Insert Jump Library
         Options Print Quit Replace Search Transfer Undo Window
       |                                            |
       |                                            |
TRANSFER: Load Save Clear Delete Merge Options Rename Glossary
       |                                            |
       |                                            |
TRANSFER CLEAR: All Window                          |
       |                                            |
       |                                            |
TRANSFER GLOSSARY: Merge Save Clear
```

NOTE: The relationships of disks, files, and Word are described near the end of Chapter 8 "Keep in Mind."

LISTS AND WILDCARDS

Several of the Transfer commands let you pick a file name from a list of the files on your document disk. After choosing the command, call for a list and pick from it as usual, by pressing a direction key or clicking the right button when the mouse pointer is in the command field. To see a list of documents or other files stored on disk in a different drive, type the letter of the desired drive and a colon before using the direction key or the mouse.

The lists vary by command: Transfer Delete lists all files; Transfer Load and Transfer Merge list only files with the extension .DOC; Transfer Glossary Merge lists only files with the extension .GLY. (Note to users of style sheets: The Transfer commands in the Gallery menu list files with the extension .STY.)

You can limit your request and see a narrower range of file names. For instance, if you type *M* in the Transfer Load command's *filename* field before requesting a list, Word shows only the documents beginning with the letter *M*. This capability is useful if, for example, you make a practice of giving all memos a name starting with *M*, and want to list only them.

Two wildcard characters, ? and *, also let you tailor a list to your specifications. Use a question mark to represent any single character that can vary and an asterisk to represent any number of characters. For example, to see just those file names that have *E* as their second letter, you would type *?E** in the command field before requesting a list. To list every file, regardless of extension, type *.* in the command field, then press a direction key.

TRANSFER LOAD

```
TRANSFER: Load Save Clear Delete Merge Options Rename Glossary
      ┌─
TRANSFER LOAD filename: ▮                    read only: Yes(No)
```

Use the Transfer Load command to load an existing document from a disk into a text window.

Type the name of the document in the *filename* field or choose the file name from a list. You can type a period and an extension of up to three more letters, but this isn't usually necessary because Word assumes an extension of .DOC when it saves and loads documents. However, if you're loading a document or file created by some other program and it does not have the extension .DOC, you must type both name and extension. If you're loading a file that does not have an extension, type a period after the name.

If you request a name that isn't on the disk (or in the current directory of a hard disk), Word responds with the message *Enter Y to create file*. If you are trying to load an existing document, this message means you somehow got the name wrong. If you press Y, Word will clear the text window (if necessary) and create a new document with the name you gave. If you press the Esc key instead, Word will still clear the text window, but you can use the Transfer Load command again—this time, perhaps, picking the name from a list to ensure you're looking in the right place and that you don't misspell it.

Setting the *read only* field to *Yes* protects you from accidentally changing a document that you want only to read. If you try to edit such a "read-only" document, Word causes the computer to bleep and display the message *Read only: document may not be edited.*

After the Transfer Load command has been executed, Word displays the number of printable characters in the document. Word versions 2.0 and later also show in parentheses the number of bytes free on the disk.

You can load a document without using the Transfer Load command, at the time you start Word. Type *word* and then the name of the document. For example, at the A> or C> prompt, you could type *word park* to load a document called PARK.

Or, to start Word and simultaneously load the document that was in use when you quit the previous editing session, you can type *word/l*.

TRANSFER SAVE

```
TRANSFER: Load Save Clear Delete Merge Options Rename Glossary
         ┌──────────┐
         │          │
TRANSFER SAVE filename: █                    formatted:(Yes)No
```

The Transfer Save command is Word's "save" button. Use it to store an updated copy of a document on disk. You should use Transfer Save frequently—at least every half hour or hour.

The first time you save a new document, the *filename* field is blank. Type in a name of up to eight letters, and press the Enter key. Optionally, you can add a period and a file name extension of your own, but this isn't recommended if your document will be used again by Word. The Transfer Save command automatically adds the extension .DOC, and the Transfer Load command looks only for documents with the extension .DOC, unless you specify a different extension when using the commands.

Once you have saved a document with the Transfer Save command, Word proposes its name in the *filename* field whenever you re-save the document. Pick the command and press the Enter key, or click either mouse button while the pointer is on the words *TRANSFER SAVE*, to update the copy on disk. Updating the document causes Word to rename the old version as a backup copy with the extension .BAK. In turn, the old version of .BAK, if there is one, is erased. To clear a document from the screen after it has been saved, use the Transfer Clear Window command. Or just load a new document.

Beginning with version 3.0 of Word, once you have named a document, the drive and full pathname leading to the document will be displayed in the Transfer Save field. This may seem a little confusing at first, but the information is valuable to people who are storing documents using more than one drive or using more than one directory. For example, imagine you are using a hard disk assigned the drive letter C, and you have started Word in a directory called BIZ (for *Business*). You write and keep all your business correspondence in this directory. The first time you save a document, you give it the name OFFER:

```
TRANSFER SAVE filename: OFFER█              formatted:(Yes)No
```

Later, after you've made changes to the document, you pick the Transfer Save command to save it in its edited form. This time, however, the name of the document is shown preceded by the drive (C:\ in this case) and the path (BIZ\ in this case):

TRANSFER SAVE filename: `C:\BIZ\OFFER.DOC`   formatted:(Yes)No

If you wanted to give the document a different name, you would just begin typing and the name *C:\BIZ\OFFER.DOC* would vanish to make room for the new name. You wouldn't have to type the path name, because Word would add the default path name for you automatically. (To specify a different path for a document, you can type the path preceding the document name, like this: *C:\PROPERTY\OFFER*. To change the default path, use the Transfer Options command. For information on paths, see Chapter 28.)

It is also possible to use the Transfer Save command to change the name of a document, although the result is somewhat different than using the Transfer Rename command. The Transfer Rename command changes nothing except the name of the document. But saving a document under a new name with the Transfer Save command creates a new file with the new name—while the original version remains with its original name and contents. This is helpful if you have a letter or other document that you use repeatedly in different forms. Save it numerous times with different names, and modify the individual copies as needed.

If you make editing changes to a document and then save the document with a new name, thereby creating two copies of the document, consider whether you want the original copy of the document to have the editing changes, too. If you do, you must save the document *twice* (using the Transfer Save command), once with its original name and once with the new name.

After the Transfer Save command has been executed, Word displays the number of printable characters in the document and, in parentheses, the number of bytes free on the disk.

Creating unformatted files

The *formatted* field of the Transfer Save command is set to *Yes* unless you change it, and most of the time you should leave it that way. Changing it to *No* causes the document to be stored without the hidden formatting characters that control its appearance. This "unformatted" form is necessary when you save computer programs you've written with Word, and sometimes it is used instead of Print File to convert a Word document into a file for use by a different computer program.

If the program that's going to use the file needs carriage returns at the end of every line, you should use Print File. This is the most common case. But if the program needs carriage returns only at the ends of paragraphs, use Transfer Save and set the *formatted* field to *No*. You may have to try saving your Word file both ways to see which form the other program accepts.

NOTE: If you're using a telecommunications program to send a Word document by telephone or through a network to a receiving computer that doesn't use Word, it is the software at the receiving end—not the telecommunications software—that determines what form the Word file needs to be in. (See the discussion of the Print File command in Chapter 15.)

If the receiving software requires that you strip out all the "funny" characters, such as nonbreaking spaces, tabs, and new-line marks, consider using the Replace command to replace spacing characters of every type ($^\wedge$W) with Spacebar spaces (see Chapter 22).

Because reformatting a document can take a lot of work on your part, Word asks you to reconsider your request with the message *Enter Y to confirm loss of formatting* before it saves with *formatted* set to *No*. If you press Y, the formatting characters are cast aside. If you wish to save a document in an unformatted form, consider saving it twice: first, formatted, and then unformatted with a different name or a different extension.

When you save a document with *formatted* set to *No,* it is stored on the disk without formatting, but it remains formatted on the screen.

NOTE: Depending on your version of Word, you may have a Transfer Save choice that lets you save documents in Rich Text Format (RTF). "External" output in RTF lets Word documents be read by other word-processors that allow extensive character formatting. It also makes it easier to use Word with Microsoft Windows. If your version of Word can save in RTF format, it also reads RTF files.

THE TRANSFER CLEAR SUBMENU

TRANSFER: Load Save **Clear** Delete Merge Options Rename Glossary

TRANSFER CLEAR: **All** Window

Two commands, Transfer Clear All and Transfer Clear Window, clear documents from the screen and out of the computer's memory. When you pick either of these commands, Word warns you if as a result you will lose editing changes not yet on disk.

TRANSFER CLEAR ALL

TRANSFER CLEAR: **All** Window

TRANSFER CLEAR ALL:

This command gives you a clean sheet of paper. It returns Word to a single blank text window with no style sheets or glossaries in memory except those named NORMAL. Like quitting and restarting Word, the Transfer Clear All command erases the scrap, as well as the scratch file on the Program disk. But unlike Quit, the Transfer Clear All command doesn't erase Word's knowledge of changes you have made with the Transfer Options command.

If all the information you've entered with Word has been safely stored on disk, Word executes the Transfer Clear All command immediately. If there are unsaved editing changes to a document, style sheet, or the glossary, the program highlights the appropriate document (useful when you have several documents in different windows) and warns you of the potential loss. For any document with unsaved editing changes, the message is *Enter Y to Save, N to lose edits, or Esc to cancel.* (Prior to version 3.0, the message was *Enter Y to confirm loss of edits.*)

Even a tiny change to the document since it was last saved will cause Word to display a warning. Even printing the document is considered an editing change if the repagination moves the location of any page breaks. If you see the warning message in version 3.0, press the Esc key to cancel the command, press Y to save the editing changes and complete the command, or press N to lose the editing changes and complete the command. If you see the warning in versions prior to 3.0, press Y to lose the editing changes and complete the command, or press Esc to cancel the command.

If a style sheet attached to a document has unsaved editing changes, Word highlights the document and offers a slightly different message: *Enter Y to save style sheet, N to lose edits, or Esc to Cancel*. (Prior to version 3.0, the message was *Enter Y to confirm loss of edits to style sheet*.) A similar message appears if there are unsaved changes to the glossary.

To update and save the style sheet, use the Gallery's version of the Transfer Save command, then return to the Edit menu and retry the Transfer Clear All command. To save the glossary, use the Transfer Glossary Save command.

TRANSFER CLEAR WINDOW

```
TRANSFER CLEAR: All Window
     ┌─────────────────┘
TRANSFER CLEAR WINDOW:
```

Transfer Clear Window wipes the selected text window clean. It does not save the document in the window; you have to do that first with Transfer Save.

Like the Transfer Clear All command, Transfer Clear Window warns you when completing the command means you are going to lose editing to either a document or a style sheet. Unlike Transfer Clear All, Transfer Clear Window doesn't highlight the document to identify it. It doesn't need to, because the text window in which the command is executed always contains the document in jeopardy. If the same document is also in another window, the Transfer Clear Window command is carried out immediately, without messages, because the document is not in jeopardy as long as it remains in one of the windows.

It isn't necessary to clear a window before loading another document into it with the Transfer Load command.

TRANSFER DELETE

```
TRANSFER: Load Save Clear Delete Merge Options Rename Glossary
    ┌──────────────────────────┘
TRANSFER DELETE filename: █
```

Erase a document or other file from a disk with this command. The Transfer Delete command lets you make room for a new document on a full disk by erasing a file you don't need. If you can't sacrifice any documents, consider deleting the .BAK version of a little-used one.

To use this command, enter the appropriate file name in the *filename* field or choose from a list that shows every document on the disk. If you prefer, narrow the list as described in the section "Lists and wildcards" at the start of this chapter.

If the file you attempt to delete has been loaded or saved during the editing session, Word refuses to erase it and gives the message *Cannot delete file.* You can use the Transfer Clear All command to start a new editing session, so that you can subsequently delete any file. But remember that the Transfer Clear All command also erases everything from memory, so it is inappropriate if you're trying to save an unsaved document onto a full disk. In this case, disk swapping is a better option. (See Chapter 8, "Keep in Mind," for notes on disk swapping.)

TRANSFER MERGE

```
TRANSFER: Load Save Clear Delete Merge Options Rename Glossary

TRANSFER MERGE filename: █
```

Merge the full contents of a file on disk into the active document on the screen with this command. Word inserts the text at the beginning of the selection.

Calling up a list from the *filename* field shows you all files on the document disk ending with the extension .DOC.

The Transfer Merge command doesn't combine documents in the sense that files lose their individual identities. The command copies the contents of the document on disk and places them in the document on the screen, but leaves the document on the disk unaffected.

The Transfer Merge command acts on a whole document at a time. You cannot use it to merge only part of one document into another. To copy or move passages from one document to another, use the Copy or Delete command with the Insert command.

TRANSFER OPTIONS

```
TRANSFER: Load Save Clear Delete Merge Options Rename Glossary

TRANSFER OPTIONS setup: B:█
```

Transfer Options changes the default drive—the drive where Word expects to find and store documents, style sheets, and glossary files. If you have a computer with two floppy-disk drives, it is unlikely you'll use this command much, if at all. On such a system, the default drive is B when the Word Program disk is used from drive A. On a hard-disk system or a single-drive system, the drive from which Word is started is the default drive for documents.

To change the default drive, type the letter of the desired drive, followed by a colon, in the *setup* field. The field also accepts path names to different directories. Path names are of interest primarily to users of hard-disk computer systems. For more details, see Chapter 28, "Using a Hard Disk."

TRANSFER RENAME

```
TRANSFER: Load Save Clear Delete Merge Options Rename Glossary
         ┌─────────────────────────────────────────┘
TRANSFER RENAME filename: █
```

Use the Transfer Rename command to change the name of the document on which you are working. The name is changed both on the disk and in the bottom right corner of your screen.

If the new name you propose duplicates a name already on the disk, Word cancels the command and displays the message *Cannot rename file.* It displays the same message if you specify a drive other than the one on which the document is stored.

You can also rename a document by using the Library Run command to return to DOS, and then using the DOS Rename (ren) command.

THE TRANSFER GLOSSARY SUBMENU

```
TRANSFER: Load Save Clear Delete Merge Options Rename Glossary
         ┌──────────────────────────────────────────────┘
TRANSFER GLOSSARY: Merge Save Clear
```

The Transfer Glossary commands manipulate glossary entries. They become useful after you've become adept with the Copy, Delete, and Insert commands.

Realizing the full potential of Word's glossary feature requires a clear understanding of the differences among some similar-sounding terms and ideas:

♦ The *glossary* is a temporary storage area in computer memory. It holds passages of text, and any number of them can be stored there.

♦ A stored passage is a *glossary entry.* You create it by selecting text and storing it in the glossary with the Copy or Delete command.

♦ Each glossary entry has a *glossary name.* You assign the name at the time you use the Copy or Delete command.

♦ A glossary entry is copied from the glossary into a document with the Insert command (or the F3 key). You identify the entry by its name, which you can either type or pick from a list.

♦ The entire contents of the glossary can be stored on disk in a special *glossary file.* You create and name the file with the Transfer Glossary Save command. Word automatically assigns it the file name extension .GLY. A glossary file lets you keep collections of glossary entries permanently or semipermanently.

♦ During a later editing session you can load a stored glossary file into the glossary to make its glossary entries available for use. You specify a glossary file by name, and load it into the glossary with the Transfer Glossary Merge command. The command is called "merge" because the contents of the glossary file are added to those already in the glossary.

♦ A special glossary file called NORMAL.GLY can be used to save glossary entries you use frequently. Word automatically loads this file into the glossary when you start a session, so its glossary entries are always available for use. Different document disks (and directories on a hard disk) can have different glossary files named NORMAL.GLY. This makes it easy to dedicate disks (or directories) to different purposes and always have the appropriate glossary entries instantly available for each. Of course, you can give a glossary file any name you like, but if the name isn't NORMAL.GLY, the file won't load automatically. You'll have to load it with the Transfer Glossary Merge command.

TRANSFER GLOSSARY MERGE

```
TRANSFER GLOSSARY: Merge Save Clear
         ┌─────────────────
TRANSFER GLOSSARY MERGE filename: ▊
```

Add the contents of a glossary file (on disk) to the glossary (in memory) with the Transfer Glossary Merge command. If a glossary entry in a file has the same name as one which is already in the glossary, the new entry replaces the old one.

If you wish, you can call up a list of available glossary files when the Transfer Glossary Merge *filename* field is displayed.

TRANSFER GLOSSARY SAVE

```
TRANSFER GLOSSARY: Merge Save Clear
                    ┌──────────
TRANSFER GLOSSARY SAVE filename: ▊
```

Save on disk all glossary entries in a single glossary file with Transfer Glossary Save. For instance, you might save all the glossary entries for a particular report in a glossary file dedicated to the report. Type the name you want for the new glossary file. No list is available for this command. If you need to see a list of names already given to glossary files, pick the Transfer Glossary Merge command and call up a list—then press the Esc key to cancel the merge command.

The Transfer Glossary Save command can be used to replace or update the contents of existing glossary files. First, merge the contents of the glossary file into the glossary with the Transfer Glossary Merge command. Then, add new entries (with the Copy or Delete command), or delete existing entries (with the Transfer Glossary Clear command). Finally, save the entries in the glossary as a glossary file, using the same name as the glossary file you are updating.

TRANSFER GLOSSARY CLEAR

```
TRANSFER GLOSSARY: Merge Save Clear


TRANSFER GLOSSARY CLEAR names: █
```

Erase glossary entries you no longer need with the Transfer Glossary Clear command. If you want to erase entries from a glossary file on disk, load the appropriate glossary file into the glossary with the Transfer Glossary Merge command, eliminate unwanted entries with the Transfer Glossary Clear command, and use Transfer Glossary Save to record the amended version back on disk with the same name.

When using the Transfer Glossary Clear command, if you leave the *names* field blank and press the Enter key, all glossary entries are erased, but Word will first ask for your confirmation with the message *Enter Y to erase glossary names.*

You can eliminate a single entry from the glossary by typing its name or choosing from a list. In order to eliminate several glossary entries at once, separate the names with commas—don't leave any space after the commas. To pick several names from a list, highlight one, press the F10 key, type a comma, highlight another, and so on.

There is one instance in which you use semicolons instead of commas to separate glossary entries. Beginning with version 3.1, the Options command lets you pick the comma as the decimal character, instead of a period. (In France, Germany, and certain other countries, the decimal number 1.5 is expressed 1,5.) When the comma has been made the decimal character, it no longer can be used to separate entries in a list. Therefore, you must use semicolons (;) between glossary names when you are eliminating several glossary entries at once with the Transfer Glossary Clear command. (Similarly, you use the semicolon between page numbers in the *page numbers* field of the Print Options command.)

The Family of Window Commands

Window commands let you manage the screen's text area.

When you have and want only one text window, Window Options is the only applicable command from this family. The remaining commands let you create, eliminate, and move additional windows. (For an overview and tutorial, see Chapter 7, "Using Windows.")

```
COMMAND: Alpha Copy Delete Format Gallery Help Insert Jump Library
         Options Print Quit Replace Search Transfer Undo Window

WINDOW: Split Close Move Options

WINDOW SPLIT: Horizontal Vertical Footnote
```

There are certain rules that apply to all normal windows, but not necessarily to footnote windows:

♦ A new window is allowed only if both it and the window from which it is split have room for at least one character of text. Any window always takes up more than one character of screen space, however, because it has borders, a selection bar, and possibly a style bar.

♦ When a window is split, normally the two resulting parts initially have everything in common. Both contain the same document and the same options settings (as determined with the Window Options command), although they may show different parts of the document. However, beginning with version 3.0 of Word, it is possible to split a window and have the new window be blank.

♦ Though windows may begin alike, once they are split, either can be changed independently. Windows can show different parts of the same document, or they can show unrelated documents.

♦ You may clear a window of text at any time, as long as another window on the screen shows some part of the same document. If you attempt to clear a window or replace the document in it with another, and the document has unsaved editing and appears in just the one window, Word warns you with the message *Enter Y to save, N to lose edits, or Esc to cancel*. (Prior to version 3.0, the message was *Enter Y to confirm loss of edits*.)

♦ The F1 key moves you from window to window in numerical order. Holding down the Shift key and pressing F1 moves you in reverse order. Or, you can move from window to window in any order with a mouse by clicking either button when the mouse pointer is inside the desired window. These methods work for footnote windows, too.

♦ Word will not allow you to create more than eight windows, including footnote windows. If you try, you'll see the message *Too many windows*.

♦ Once a normal window has a footnote window, no additional windows can be split from either of them. If you try, you'll see the message *Not a valid window split*.

♦ Moving or copying text is accomplished with equal ease regardless of whether you are passing the text from one window to another or within the same window.

THE WINDOW SPLIT SUBMENU

WINDOW: **Split** Close Move Options

WINDOW SPLIT: **Horizontal** Vertical Footnote

There are really only two kinds of windows—normal windows and footnote windows. However, three Window Split commands exist because there are two ways to form a normal window: You can split an existing window horizontally, from left to right, or vertically, from top to bottom. The Window Split Footnote command creates a horizontal footnote window in the lower portion of a normal window.

WINDOW SPLIT HORIZONTAL

WINDOW SPLIT: **Horizontal** Vertical Footnote

WINDOW SPLIT HORIZONTAL at line: ▮   clear new window: Yes(No)

Use the Window Split Horizontal command to divide the window containing the selection into two windows. The new borders created by the command run from left to right.

When you choose this command, Word will propose the line containing the selection (or the end of the selection, if more than one line is selected) as the place for the split to occur. If you want the split to be at a different place, type the number of the line at which you wish to divide the window. You can also use the Up and Down direction keys to mark a spot on the screen for the horizontal split.

If you pick *Yes* in the *clear new window* field, the new window will be blank. This is a new field in Word version 3.0.

Create a new horizontal window with the mouse by positioning the mouse pointer on the right border of the existing window and clicking the left button. If you click the right button, the new window will be blank. (Prior to version 3.0, clicking the right button created a footnote window. See Window Split Footnote.)

WINDOW SPLIT VERTICAL

```
WINDOW SPLIT: Horizontal Vertical Footnote

    ┌──────────┘
    │
WINDOW SPLIT VERTICAL at column: ▮    clear new window: Yes(No)
```

Use the Window Split Vertical command to divide the window containing the selection into two windows. The new borders created by the command run up and down. You can have, at most, two vertical splits across the width of the screen. This means you can have no more than three side-by-side windows.

As with the Window Split Horizontal command, Word will propose a location for the split. In this case, Word proposes the column containing the selection (or the last character of the selection). Accept the proposed response or type in the number of the column at which you wish the split to occur. You can also use the Right and Left direction keys to mark a spot on the screen for the vertical split.

If you pick *Yes* in the *clear new window* field, the new window will be blank. This is a new field in version 3.0 of Word.

Create a new vertical window with the mouse by positioning the mouse pointer on the top border or ruler of the existing window and clicking the left button. If you click the right button (beginning with version 3.0), the new window will be blank.

WINDOW SPLIT FOOTNOTE

```
WINDOW SPLIT: Horizontal Vertical Footnote

  ┌──────────────────────────────┘
  │
WINDOW SPLIT FOOTNOTE at line:
```

Use the Window Split Footnote command to partition off a special footnote area at the bottom of a document window. The selection location is proposed as the line for the partition, but you can change it easily.

Type the number of the line at which you wish to split the footnote window from the document window above it, or, with the Up or Down direction key, mark the spot on the screen. With a mouse, position the mouse pointer on the right border of the text window at the line you desire, hold down the Shift key, and click either button. (In versions of Word prior to 3.0, just click the right button. There is no reason to hold down the Shift key.)

Because a footnote window is subsidiary to a regular text window, the only border separating the two is a dashed line like this (the numbers appear if you have turned on the ruler in the regular window with the Window Options command):

```
2--0---------1---------2---------3---------4---------5---------6---------7-----
```

The footnote window displays any footnotes for the passages currently in view in the document window. As you scroll through a document, footnote text appears and disappears as corresponding reference marks scroll past in the main text window. When no footnote reference mark appears in the document, the footnote window is blank.

Unless a document is heavily footnoted, consider keeping the footnote window small, perhaps only a single line, to keep the maximum text area available for your document. When a reference mark appears on the screen, the one-line footnote window fills with text, alerting you to increase its size temporarily to read a multiple-line footnote.

Editing actions are limited when you work with footnote text, so you may encounter the message *Not a valid action for footnotes.* If the message appears when you attempt to delete footnote text, it means the paragraph mark at the end of the footnote is among the characters you've selected. Word won't let you delete any selection that contains the paragraph mark. This is a tricky and important rule, because the paragraph mark is invisible unless you've made it visible with the Options command. You can delete footnote text freely as long as the selection does not extend beyond the final printable character in the footnote. To delete the footnote paragraph mark, you must delete the footnote reference mark in the main text of your document. This deletes the entire footnote.

When using a footnote window, keep these rules in mind:

♦ A footnote window can be closed with the Window Close Footnote command, or by clicking both mouse buttons when the pointer is on the right border of the window. But a footnote window cannot be cleared with the Transfer Clear Window command.

♦ Closing a footnote window does not delete or otherwise jeopardize footnote text. Word stores the text at the end of the main document and you can always view it there, by scrolling to the end of the document or using the Jump Footnote command.

♦ You can open a footnote window at any time, but it is impossible to write in one until you have used the Format Footnote command to place a footnote reference mark in the main text.

♦ You cannot load a document into a footnote window with the Transfer Load command.

♦ You cannot footnote a footnote, nor can you start a new division in a footnote.

Examples of footnote windows and their use can be found in Chapter 7, "Using Windows," and also in the section on the Format Footnote command in Chapter 12, "The Family of Format Commands."

WINDOW CLOSE

```
WINDOW: Split Close Move Options
      ┌──────────┘
WINDOW CLOSE window number:
```

Close normal and footnote windows with the Window Close command. If there is only one window on the screen, it cannot be closed.

Each window has its number displayed in its upper left corner. This number may change as other windows are closed. When you pick the Window Close command, Word proposes the number of the window that contains the selection. Accept the proposed response, or type the number of the window you wish to close. If the window you are closing is the only one on the screen containing unsaved editing changes, Word displays the message *Enter Y to save, N to lose edits, or Esc to cancel.* (Prior to version 3.0, the message was *Enter Y to confirm loss of edits.*) Save the changes with the Transfer Save command if you do not wish to lose them, then try the Window Close command again.

You can close a normal window — but not a footnote window — by clicking both mouse buttons when the mouse pointer is on the top window border (or the ruler, if it is displayed). Either normal or footnote windows can be closed by clicking both mouse buttons when the mouse pointer is on the right window border.

WINDOW MOVE

```
WINDOW: Split Close Move Options
      ┌───────────────┘
WINDOW MOVE lower right corner of window #:        to row:      column:
```

You can move a border between windows to make one larger and the other smaller. This is accomplished by repositioning the lower right corner of a window in such a way that the window borders are where you want them. Repositioning the corners of windows is the job of the Window Move command, or of the mouse.

Before picking the command, determine which window or windows need to be resized. Then, in the *lower right corner of window #* field, type the number of the window whose lower right corner needs repositioning to accomplish your aims. Word proposes the number of the window that contains the selection when the command is picked. You cannot pick the number of the window that borders the bottom and right edges of the text area.

The *to row* field lets you move the lower right corner of a window up or down on the screen. To do this, type in the number of the desired row, or press the Up or Down direction key to move a special rectangular marker along the window border to the position you desire.

The *to column* field permits you to move the lower right corner of a window left or right. Type in a column number, or press the Right or Left direction key to move the marker to the desired horizontal position.

Some early versions of Word use the term *line* instead of *row*, and *position* instead of *column*. The Window Move command works identically either way.

Resizing a window with a mouse is simple. Position the mouse pointer over the lower right corner of the window, press and hold either mouse button, move the pointer to the new location, and release the button. When Word is being run on a computer with graphics capabilities, the mouse pointer assumes the appearance of four arrows pointing in different directions while this sequence occurs.

WINDOW OPTIONS

Use the Window Options command to control whether a text window displays a style bar or ruler, to choose the background color that appears in a window of a computer running Word in color, to decide whether or not hidden text will appear in the window, and to control whether the window shows document view or outline view. When a new text window is created with the Window Split Horizontal or the Window Split Vertical command, it initially has the same options settings as the window from which it was split.

Word remembers Window Options settings for Window 1 between editing sessions by storing information in a file on disk called MW.INI. If you're using only one window, nothing will be forgotten. However, Word remembers options for the second through eighth windows only as long as they are on the screen.

Fields of the Window Options command

window number. Specify the number of the window for which you want to adjust options. The proposed window is the one that contains the selection when the Window Options command is picked. If only one window is open on the screen, the number in the *window number* field is *1*.

outline: Yes No. Beginning with version 3.0, Word provides two different kinds of views in a text window—document view and outline view. Holding down the Shift key and pressing the F2 key moves you back and forth between these views. Alternatively, the *outline* field lets you control the same thing. Pick *Yes* to specify an outline view in a window, and *No* to specify a document view.

Document view is the conventional way of looking at and working with a document. When you are in document view, all parts of a document can be seen on the screen (although you may have to scroll if the document is more than a few lines long). In document view, the lower left corner of the screen shows the word *Page* followed by the current page number, or, in the case of documents with more than one division, it shows the letters *P* and *D*, with the *P* followed by the current page number and the *D* followed by the division number.

Outline view shows a document in hierarchical form, with different levels of headings indented to reflect subsidiary ideas. In outline view, subheadings and text can be "collapsed"—removed from view on the screen—so that you can look at and modify the underlying structure of a document. When you are in outline view, the lower left corner of the screen shows the word *text* or the word *Level*. Once in outline view, you can switch into a special mode called outline edit (by pressing Shift-F5). In outline edit, the lower left corner of the screen shows the word *OUTLINE*.

Because the choice of document or outline view is a window option, you can look at a document in both views at once, using two windows.

For details on the use of outline view, see Chapter 25, "Power Tools: Outlining."

show hidden text: Yes No. Shall characters that have been formatted as "hidden" be visible in the text window? Picking *Yes* in this field causes otherwise hidden characters to appear on the screen with a dotted underline. (If your computer does not have graphics capabilities, or if you're running Word in its /c mode, the underline is solid or the hidden characters appear in color.)

When hidden text shows in a window, it also will print on a printer. If you do not want it to print, set this field to *No* before using the Print Printer or Print Repaginate commands.

Hidden text is useful for such things as annotating document with temporary or private comments, and is vital to the use of Word's Library Index and Library Table commands. Like these commands, hidden text was not introduced until version 3.0 of Word.

Recall that hidden text was introduced early in Chapter 5, "The Simple Word," and in the discussion of the Format Character command in Chapter 12, "The Family of Format Commands." For additional information, see Chapter 26, "Power Tools: Hidden Text and Indexing."

background color. Control the background color of the screen if you are running Word in color. To do this, type in a number from 0 to 14 (or 0 to 15, depending on the version of Word and your hardware). Or see a list of color samples by pressing a direction key or clicking the right mouse button with the pointer in the *background color* field. If multiple windows are in use, you can assign each a different color. In computers with a monochrome display card, including high-resolution monochrome cards such as the Hercules card, generally the only color available is 0 (black). You can choose from among 64 colors if you are using an IBM Enhanced Graphics Adapter with at least 128K of video memory and the IBM Enhanced Color Display (or a compatible high-resolution color monitor). Press the PgUp or PgDn key to move through a cycle of 64 colors. (NOTE: If you have the EGA card and the Enhanced Color Display, you'll want 128K, rather than the 64K that comes standard on the card. With 128K, the on-screen color resolution is dramatically improved.)

style bar: Yes No. Turn the style bar on and off with this field. The style bar is a two-space-wide gutter that, when turned on, runs from the top to the bottom of the text window immediately to the right of the border of the left window. A fringe benefit of the style bar is that it can be used as part of the selection bar to its immediate right. But the style bar is primarily of value when a style sheet is attached to a document. The bar shows you the one- and two-character key codes of the paragraph styles you've assigned.

There is another benefit of using the style bar, even when a document doesn't have a style sheet. The style bar indicates where paragraphs that you've formatted to be running heads will print: *t* means at the top of the page; *b* means at the bottom of the page; *o* means only on odd pages; *e* means only on even pages; and *f* means only on the first page. (Don't confuse this *t* with the *t* signifying "text" that may appear when you are in outline view.)

ruler: Yes No. Word displays a ruler at the top of a text window that shows tab stops and indents whenever the Format Paragraph, Format Tabs Set, or Format Tabs Clear command is used. Whether a ruler is displayed at other times is up to you. It is turned on and off with the *ruler* field.

The ruler shows a number for every inch of pica-sized characters. A left bracket ([) shows the position of the left indent of the paragraph that contains the selection; a vertical bar (|) indicates the special indentation (if any) of the first line of the paragraph that contains the selection; and a right bracket (]) marks the right indent of the selected paragraph.

If the selected paragraph(s) contain tab stops you've created with the Format Tabs Set command, they'll show in the ruler, too. If more than one paragraph is selected, the tab stops will show only if they are the same in each paragraph.

An *L* marks a left-aligned tab stop; *C* marks a center-aligned stop; *R* marks a right-aligned stop; and *D* marks a decimal-aligned stop. A period, hyphen, or underline immediately preceding a tab-stop letter indicates that the tab stop is formatted with that particular punctuation mark as a leader character. (Tab stops are explained in detail in Chapter 12, "The Family of Format Commands.")

If you find the ruler distracting, you can turn it off with the Window Options command. You can also turn it on and off by clicking either button when the mouse pointer is in the upper right corner of a text window. Even when turned off, the ruler reappears briefly when you use the Format Paragraph, Format Tabs Set, or Format Tabs Clear command.

NOTE: If the ruler is on in a window, the upper border of an associated footnote window will contain numerals, too.

III

Mastering

Tips, strategies, advanced features
and techniques ... when you're ready to
master Word, these chapters will start
you on your way.

Speed

An accomplished writer I know organizes her manuscripts and magazine articles on toilet paper. White is her favorite color, and inexpensive brands are best because they're not too soft.

When she's finished her research and is ready to put her thoughts and notes in order, she opens a fresh roll of paper and feeds the loose end into her typewriter. Bang, bang, bang, the ideas are pounded out, one to a square. She tears them apart and deals them like cards into piles around the floor. Observations or quotations of similar suit are stacked together, possibly off to her left. An intriguing sequence of events may be laid down, like a triumphant poker hand, to her right. Over and over, she shuffles and reshuffles the tissue squares until she's stacked a winning deck. Only then, when her resources and ideas are lined up from beginning to end, does she begin to write.

More commonly, writers use index cards. Another time-honored tactic is "cut-and-paste," in which the elements of a document are written in sections, cut apart, rearranged in some new and pleasing order, and pasted or taped back together to form a draft. Other writers, other methods. Whatever the technique, the goals are the same: to work quickly and efficiently.

Paper outlines, index cards, and other conventional tools for writing efficiently aren't made obsolete by computers, any more than pencils were made obsolete by typewriters. But, like the typewriter, the computer has supplemented the writer's tools in powerful ways. Either Word's glossary feature or its outlining feature, for instance, can be used as fast, modern adaptations of the cut-and-paste technique: Dozens of elements in an article or a manuscript can be shuffled around electronically without scissors, paste, or glue.

This chapter is the first of eleven on mastering Microsoft Word. In them, you'll learn finer control of the Microsoft Mouse. You'll discover how to use Word's glossary, windows, search, and replace features in powerful ways—often, ways the creators of Word didn't dream of. You'll learn how to use Word's new outlining feature to organize documents, and how to compile indexes and tables of contents automatically.

You'll be introduced to the subtleties of using Word's style sheets and Print Merge capabilities—including step-by-step instructions on using five popular database and filing programs to create mailing lists that Word can use automatically for personalized form letters and other documents. Finally, you'll learn how to get top performance using Word with a hard disk.

From here on, it's presumed you understand the fundamentals of Word and are ready for hints, tips, and strategies.

To use an automobile analogy: By now you know how to operate a car and are prepared for suggestions on ways and places to drive. We begin at the racetrack, with tips on speed.

Tip #1: Keys that move the selection

The F7, F8, F9, and F10 keys, used with and without the Shift and F6 keys, give you rapid and flexible ways to move and extend the selection. Experiment with these keys, and try combining them with the direction keys. Their usefulness exceeds most people's first impressions. Here are some lesser-known tactics:

♦ Press the F10 key once to select a paragraph. Press it a second time to select the next paragraph. This technique, which works beginning with Word version 3.0, is a fast way to move through a document.

♦ Move rapidly through one sentence or several by alternately pressing Shift-F7 and F7 (to move the selection backward in a document) or Shift-F8 and F8 (to move the selection forward). The Shift-F8/F8 combination positions the selection at the beginning of the next sentence, and the Shift-F7/F7 combination positions the selection at the end of the preceding sentence. This technique not only moves you rapidly, it also positions the selection at the proper location to add content to the beginning or end of any sentence.

♦ Extend the selection from the middle to the end of a word by pressing F6 followed by F8. Extend the selection from the middle to the beginning of a word by pressing F6 followed by F7.

♦ Extend the selection from the middle to the end of a sentence by pressing F6 followed by Shift-F8. Extend the selection from the middle to the beginning of a sentence by pressing F6 followed by Shift-F7.

♦ Extend the selection from the middle to the end of a paragraph by pressing F6 followed by alternating use of Shift-F8 and F8. Extend the selection from the middle to the beginning of a paragraph by pressing F6 followed by alternate presses of Shift-F7 and F7.

♦ When the selection has been extended with the F7 through F10 keys, add text at the *beginning* of the selection simply by typing. Add text *following* the extended selection by pressing F6 if the extended mode is on, then pressing the Right direction key or F8 before typing. Add text *to the end* of the extended selection by pressing F6 if the extended mode is on, then pressing the Right direction key or F8, followed by the Left direction key or the Backspace key.

Tip #2: F9, F10, and the paragraph mark

The F9 key selects a sentence; the F10 key selects a paragraph. The distinction is unmistakable—until you select a single-sentence paragraph. At first glance, either key appears to highlight the sentence/paragraph. But F10 also selects the paragraph mark at the end. If the paragraph mark has not been made visible, the difference in the two selections isn't obvious. But the effects are. Two examples:

♦ Suppose you delete the selection. The whole paragraph disappears if F10 was used, but the paragraph mark remains if F9 was used. Consequently, with F9 the space occupied by the paragraph mark and formatting of the paragraph remain, even though the paragraph mark itself may not be visible.

♦ Suppose you apply character formatting to the selection. If F9 was used, the formatting is limited to the visible characters. But if F10 was used, the paragraph mark is formatted, too. This means any new writing at the location of the mark—or in a new paragraph formed by pressing the Enter key at the end of the existing paragraph— will have the same character formatting. This can, for example, cause underlining in places you don't expect or want it.

Tip #3: Changing an initial letter

When capitalizing or otherwise changing the first letter of a selected word or sentence, first type the new letter and then press the Del key. Do not reverse the order of these steps, or the selection will vanish.

Tip #4: Transposing letters

To transpose two characters rapidly, select one of the characters to be transposed and press the Del key. Then press the direction key corresponding to the direction in which you want to move the letter, and press the Insert key.

Tip #5: Moving two passages simultaneously

To move two unconnected passages at the same time:

1. Delete one of the passages into the glossary, giving it a name.
2. Delete the other passage into the scrap.
3. Scroll to the destination for the passage in the scrap and insert it by pressing the Ins *key*.
4. Scroll to the destination for the passage in the glossary and insert it with the F3 key or the Insert *command* (using the glossary name you gave it).

An alternate method uses the mouse:

1. Delete the first passage into the scrap; select the second passage.
2. Place the mouse pointer in the scroll bar so that the selection doesn't change, and scroll to the destination for the selected passage.

3. Position the mouse pointer where you want to insert the selected passage; hold down the Ctrl key and click either mouse button to complete the move.

4. Move the selection to the new location for the text in the scrap and insert it.

Tip #6: Three ways to combine often-used text

If you frequently use the same passages in different documents, don't overlook any of three tools Word provides to make your job easier:

♦ The glossary lets you store passages in memory for insertion in the active document. If you wish, you can save these passages on disk, as a glossary file, for use in subsequent editing sessions.

♦ The Transfer Merge command inserts the entire contents of a document stored on disk into the current document, at the location of the selection. A document on disk need not be long; it can be as short as a word or two. The Transfer Merge command is particularly useful when you have boilerplate paragraphs you want listed on your disk directories as separate, easily identified elements.

♦ If you know how to use Word's Merge feature, bear in mind that the instruction «*INCLUDE filename.doc*» merges any document from disk directly into the document containing the selection. This instruction is similar to the Transfer Merge command, except that «INCLUDE» does not display the inserted text on the screen; the text is merged into the document at the time of printing. The «INCLUDE» instruction requires use of the Print Merge instead of the Print Printer command. (If you are not familiar with Merge—Word's ability to produce personalized form letters and other documents—see Chapter 23, "Power Tools: Merge.")

Tip #7: Returning to the last editing location

Sometimes it is desirable to return to the place in a document where you were last adding text or editing. For example, you jump or scroll away and want to return to the spot where you were typing . . . or you accidentally select a paragraph and want to return the selection to where it was before . . . or you change your mind while quitting Word and want the selection to resume its previous size and location.

To return to the last place you changed content: Use the Undo command twice in a row, then press the Right direction key. This will shrink the selection to a single character, positioned immediately after your last insertion or edit of text.

Tip #8: Returning to the beginning of an insertion

When you insert a passage with the Insert command, the Ins key, or the Transfer Merge command, the action finishes with the selection positioned on the first character following the insertion. To return the selection to the beginning of the insertion, use the Undo command twice in a row, then (optionally) press the Left direction key.

If you conclude by pressing the Left direction key, any new typing will be at the location of the character preceding the selection. If you don't press the Left direction key, any new typing will be at the location of the first character of the selection.

Tip #9: Selecting paragraphs

Sometimes, as when you're updating a mailing list, you may have a large number of paragraphs you want to move around or delete. One way to do this is to use the F10 key to select whole paragraphs. As noted in Tip #1, pressing the F10 key twice moves you to the next paragraph and selects it. An even faster way, if you also are moving upward in the document on occasion, is to switch into outline edit temporarily. This is accomplished by holding down the Shift key and pressing F2, and then holding down Shift and pressing F5. Once in this mode, whole paragraphs are always selected, and can be easily deleted or moved. Pressing the Up or Left direction key moves you to a preceding paragraph, and pressing the Down or Right key moves you to the following paragraph.

Tip #10: Formatting a new paragraph

To create a new paragraph that matches the formatting of an adjacent, existing paragraph, create the new paragraph from the old one:

♦ Place the selection on the first character of the existing paragraph, press the Enter key, and then press the Up direction key. This creates a new, similarly formatted paragraph that precedes the existing one. Or:

♦ Place the selection on the paragraph mark at the end of the existing paragraph and press the Enter key. This creates a new, similarly formatted paragraph that follows the existing one.

Keep these techniques in mind when you add a paragraph between two existing paragraphs that have different formatting. Choose which paragraph you want the new one to match, and press the Enter key inside that paragraph either on its first character or on its paragraph mark.

Tip #11: Adding Characters to a formatted zone

When adding new characters to the very end of a string of characters that are underlined or otherwise formatted, decide whether you want the new characters to have the same formatting as the existing ones. If you do, position the selection on the last formatted character, retype it, and then continue typing. Conclude by deleting the character you retyped. If you don't want new characters to be formatted like the others, begin typing at the first space following the formatted characters.

Tip #12: Copying formatting with the keyboard

You can use the keyboard to copy character, paragraph, or division formatting from one location to another, without copying content. You can even copy formatting from one document to another, using several windows. These are the steps:

1. Select some text that is formatted in the desired way. This text can be a single character with the character formatting you want, or it can be part of a paragraph or division that is formatted the way you want.

2. Pick the appropriate Format command, and, without making any changes in its command fields, press the Enter key to carry it out. For example, if you want to copy character formatting, pick the Format Character command and press Enter.

3. Before doing any other editing, select the character(s), paragraph(s), or division(s) you want to format to match the sample. If the text to be formatted is a paragraph or a division, remember that you needn't select it all.

4. Press the F4 key, which repeats the last editing act. The formatting from the sample will be applied to the selected text.

Tip #13: Calling for a list

The usual means of calling for a list of choices in a command field is to press a direction key or to click the right mouse button. With many versions of Word, you can also press the F1 key to call up lists. Some people find this method more convenient.

Tip #14: Speedier scrolling

Word version 3.0 scrolls faster than earlier versions, and starting Word with the /c option speeds up the scrolling of any version of Word.

Turning off the style bar can significantly increase the speed at which the screen's contents are updated when you scroll or move window borders. In all these cases the savings aren't as noticeable on the new generation of high-powered computers, such as the IBM PC AT.

If you're scrolling more than a few screens down toward the end of a document, clicking the right mouse button when the mouse pointer is near the bottom of the left window border is faster than pressing the PgDn key. And if you're scrolling several screens up toward the beginning of a document, clicking the left button with the mouse pointer at the bottom of the left border is much faster than the PgUp key. When you click the left button several times, Word jumps right up in the document, rather than scrolling through the intermediate screens.

Tip #15: Queued printing

Don't overlook queued printing, which lets you print one document while continuing to write or edit another. The Print Options command permits you to put a document on disk in a queue for printing, and four Print Queue commands give you control once printing has begun. Queued printing is a mixed blessing, however, because it slows the performance of Word. Although it's more trouble, you'll get better performance by printing files to disk with the Print File command (discussed in Chapter 15, "The Family of Print Commands") and then printing the files with the DOS Print command.

Tip #16: Two copies of Word

Since Word is not copy protected (beginning with version 3.0), you can make two or more versions and customize the options differently for each. For instance, one version might show invisible characters on the screen and have a style bar and ruler in the first window, while a second version might not. Different versions can be set up for different colors, if you have a color monitor.

Although you can put different versions on different floppy disks, this tip is most useful if you have a hard disk. Set up two directories and copy Word into each. Put both directories in the path. Rename WORD.COM in one of the directories to WORD2.COM. Depending on whether you type *word* or *word 2*, you'll use different customized versions. For information on directories and paths, see Chapter 28, "Using a Hard Disk."

Tip #17: Virtues of superior hardware

As with many other activities, the quality of your tools can affect the quality and speed of your work. A high-speed printer not only saves time, it encourages you to make frequent printouts of your work in progress. Reading your words on paper probably gives you a better sense of the flow and organization of your writing, and so a fast printer may contribute indirectly to better writing.

Sharp screen resolution helps many people work more quickly, and stick with it longer. Good monochrome monitors offer higher resolution than color monitors, even the IBM Enhanced Color Display. Television sets are terrible for word processing. Glare shields, if they are good ones, can help you work more comfortably, too.

Among video circuit boards for IBM computers, the best choices for resolution include the monochrome card, the Enhanced Graphics Adapter (which offers both high-resolution and graphics in either monochrome or color), the Hercules Graphics Card and Hercules Graphics Card Plus, and cards by other manufacturers that are compatible with these.

The IBM color/graphics board produces markedly lower resolution than the IBM monochrome board, and the loss of resolution is a substantial price to pay for graphics (in which italics appear as italics and the mouse pointer takes on different shapes).

If you use the color/graphics board, using the color option (starting Word with the command *word /c*) increases resolution substantially, although the clarity still doesn't compare with that of the other choices. The /c option also speeds up the performance of the Hercules Graphics Card (but, unless you're using the Hercules Graphics Card Plus, you lose the graphics, and thus make it perform as just an expensive monochrome card). The /m option increases resolution if you're using an Enhanced Color Display with an Enhanced Graphics Adapter, and the adapter has only 64K of dedicated video memory.

Finally, the computer itself makes a difference. Unlike less sophisticated word processors, Word takes full advantage of the computing speed of the new generation of faster personal computers based on such chips as the Intel 80286. If you have an 8088-based computer, such as the original IBM PC, Word works fine; but you can squeeze extra performance by installing an add-on board with a faster processor. And a hard disk not only increases storage, it significantly speeds up the operation of Word and increases the utility of Word's ability to use multiple windows.

Tip #18: Monitoring progress with a spreadsheet

To track the total number of pages in a manuscript or report, consider using a spreadsheet program. You can run it through Word (see Tip 20), devoting one spreadsheet row to each chapter or section. Cells can show the chapter's number of words or illustrations, or the projected number of pages (by dividing the number of words by the estimated number of words per page). It can calculate, on an ongoing basis, your total number of words or pages, and how close you are to completion.

Incidentally, you can incorporate the output of a spreadsheet into a Word document. This is useful if you want to show a table of numbers, or if you want to include data from your spreadsheet without retyping it. Spreadsheet programs generally can print an ASCII file to disk. Multiplan does this with its Print File command, and Lotus 1-2-3 has a Print File Options Other command that lets you direct "unformatted" output to a file. Word loads these like any other unformatted files, and you can merge or copy them into documents.

Tip #19: Renaming programs as Library Run commands

You can add your own commands to Word, in a sense, by renaming outside programs so that they have single-character names. Take, for example, the Spell utility program called LOOKUP.COM, which comes with Word. You can make a copy of it called L.COM and put it on your Word program disk or somewhere in the path of your hard disk. Then, to look up a spelling, you can use the program as if there were a Word command called Library Run Lookup: Press Esc, L, R, L; press the Spacebar; type the word the spelling of which you want to check; and press Enter.

Tip #20: Batch files

Taking Tip 19 a little further, you can create a batch file with a single-letter name. For instance, you can run Multiplan and load a particular Multiplan file (or do any number of other things in sequence) just by typing Library Run and a single letter.

A batch file is a simple DOS program you can write using Word. The "program" is nothing more than a series of DOS-level commands (instructions such as the ones you type at the DOS prompt A> or C>). For instance, the first line of a batch file might be *c:* (to change to drive C), the next line might be *cd\spread* (to change directories to one called SPREAD), and the third line might be *mpcount* (to start Multiplan and load the Multiplan file called COUNT). Press the Enter key at the end of each line when writing a batch file. Save the file with Word's Transfer Save command, giving it a name ending with the extension *.BAT,* and choosing *No* in the *formatted* field.

Batch files can be run from DOS or through Word's Library Run command. If you want the ease of a single-letter command, name the batch file C.BAT or something similar. If you use the make-believe Library Run Count command (Esc, L, R, C, Enter), the lines in the batch file will be executed just as if you had typed them at DOS: The computer will change to the C drive, change to the SPREAD directory, start Multiplan, and load the file named COUNT. When you quit Multiplan, the computer returns you to where you left off in your Word document. (There is a lot more that is useful to know about batch files. See your DOS manual.)

Tip #21: Dedicating your computer to Word

You can set up your Word disk or hard disk so that whenever you start or reboot your computer, Word automatically starts, too. This is done with a special kind of batch file, called AUTOEXEC.BAT, that runs automatically whenever your computer is started. For general details on AUTOEXEC.BAT, see Chapter 28, "Using a Hard Disk."

If you make *word* the last line in the AUTOEXEC.BAT file, Word will start automatically. If you make the line *word /l*, instead, Word will load the document you were working on when you last quit Word.

Tip #22: Using macros

A *macro* is a sequence of keystrokes that you give a name or assign to an otherwise-unused combination of keys. Then, when you use the name or the key combination, the sequence of keystrokes is executed extremely quickly. This can speed up many tasks.

For example, a macro can define Ctrl-F8 to mean F10 followed by the Right direction key followed by the Left direction key. With this macro in place, when you press Ctrl-F8, the selection jumps immediately to the paragraph mark at the end of whichever paragraph contains the selection (or cursor). Of course, you can accomplish the same thing by pressing the F10, Right direction, and then Left direction key. A macro might be created that executes a sequence of commands, or adjusts Word's various options in one way or another. Chapter 26 includes examples of macros useful when coding a document for automatic indexing.

Word's glossary is a macro feature of sorts, in that you can name a series of letters or words to be typed into a document, and then simply type the name and press F3. Style sheets are kind of a macro for formatting, although they can be used in more powerful ways than a conventional macro.

But if Word's macro features aren't sufficient for you, or you want to use the same macros for various programs, several separate "keyboard-enhancer" programs allow you significant macro powers. Perhaps the best known of these is ProKey. (ProKey 4.0, Release 10, is compatible with Word 3.0 and 3.1. Earlier releases of ProKey may interfere with your ability to collapse and expand headings in outline view.)

You load ProKey by typing *pkload* at the DOS prompt, or putting the instruction *pkload* in the AUTOEXEC.BAT file. Then, to use Word, you execute a three-line batch file that: (1) loads into ProKey the macros you've previously defined for Word, (2) starts Word, and (3) removes the macros for Word and installs other macros for DOS when you return to DOS. Assuming that the macros for Word are stored in a file called WORD.PRO on the root directory of hard disk C, and the macros for DOS are stored in a file called DOS.PRO at the same location, this is what the batch file might contain:

```
prokey c:word.pro /f0
word %1 %2
prokey c:dos.pro/r f1 t0
```

If this batch file were named PROWORD.BAT, to run Word with ProKey you would type *proword* and press Enter. If you wanted to start Word in character mode (*word/c*), or if you wanted to load a document, you would type *proword/c* or *proword* followed by the name of the document (this capability is possible because of the *%1* and *%2* in the batch file).

You may want to make the second line of the batch file *word/c %1 %2*, if you have graphics capabilities and always want to start Word in character mode. Word runs faster in character mode, and the chances of incompatibility between Word and ProKey are reduced.

Two last things: ProKey seems to slow the performance of some aspects of Word slightly, and if you use the Library Run command to run other programs, the ProKey macros for Word will remain in effect during their use.

Tip #23: Word graphics with Sidekick, ProKey, and other resident programs

Depending on your computer equipment and the software versions you're using, it may at first seem impossible to run certain resident programs when Word is in graphics mode.

(A "resident" program is one that remains in your computer's random-access memory— RAM—even when you run another program, such as Word. Resident programs must *always* be loaded into memory from DOS before you start Word. The command that loads Sidekick is *sk,* and the command that loads ProKey is *pkload.* Often, these commands are placed in the AUTOEXEC.BAT file. If you make the mistake of loading a resident program through Word's Library Run command, you'll be forced to quit Word and you'll lose any unsaved editing changes to documents.)

People who use Sidekick and ProKey have traditionally started Word in character mode rather than graphics mode, to avoid problems. (If you have a monochrome display adapter without graphics capabilities, this isn't an issue.)

But a simple technique allows you to run Word in graphics mode and use resident programs that "pop" onto your screen.

When using Word, press Esc-L-R (for Library Run) and press the Enter key. If you're using Word from a floppy disk, press the letter Y when it asks you to. Then, when the message *Press any key to resume Word* appears, use your resident program (by pressing both Shift keys for Sidekick or Alt and the / key for ProKey). When you've quit the resident program, pressing any key will take you right back into Word, where you left off in your document.

Tip #24: Making and modifying .PRD files

Printer description (.PRD) files tell Word which printer you are using, what fonts and font sizes the printer handles, and what coded instructions the printer expects to be given to perform various tasks (such as underlining).

More than 100 .PRD files come with Word, but you can create your own by modifying any of the 100 with a program that comes with Word. The program is called MAKEPRD. (Prior to Word 3.0, it was called CONVPRD.)

MAKEPRD will translate the computer code in a .PRD file into English-language descriptions, which you can modify like any other Word document. Then, MAKEPRD will translate the modified document into a modified .PRD file. This is useful, for example, when you want to enhance the capability of a .PRD file for use with a new printer.

Word's .PRD files changed beginning with version 3.0, although they may have the same names they had before. If you want to use an old .PRD file with a new version of Word, you can transform it to proper format by running the .PRD file through MAKEPRD twice— once to change it into English, and once to change it back to computer code.

Most people will have no need to use MAKEPRD, and so the rather substantial details of its use are outside the scope of this book. However, the knowledgeable or unintimidated can puzzle out the use of the program with the Word manual.

Tip #25: The extended character set

You can access any of up to 255 characters, including mathematical symbols, foreign letters, and graphics symbols, by pressing the Alt key and typing the number of the ASCII character you desire on the calculator-style numeric keypad. (When certain resident programs such as ProKey are in use, you access this "extended character set" by holding down both Shift and Alt, and then typing the number on the keypad.)

You'll find a list of ASCII characters in your DOS or Word manuals, or—prior to Word 3.0—in the Keyboard section of Word's on-screen Help command. Here, however, are a few of the more interesting characters and their numbers:

LETTER CODES

Code	Character	Code	Character	Code	Character
0	(null)	15	☼	30	▲
1	☺	16	►	31	▼
2	☻	17	◄	32	(space)
3	♥	18	↕	33	!
4	♦	19	‼	34	"
5	♣	20	¶	35	#
6	♠	21	§	36	$
7	•	22	▬	37	%
8	◘	23	↨	38	&
9	(tab)	24	↑	39	'
10	◙	25	↓	40	(
11	♂	26	→	41	)
12	♀	27	←	42	*
13	♪	28	∟	43	+
14	♫	29	↔	44	,

LETTER CODES

Code	Character	Code	Character	Code	Character
128	Ç	144	É	160	á
129	ü	145	æ	161	í
130	é	146	Æ	162	ó
131	â	147	ô	163	ú
132	ä	148	ö	164	ñ
133	à	149	ò	165	Ñ
134	å	150	û	166	ª
135	ç	151	ù	167	º
136	ê	152	ÿ	168	¿
137	ë	153	Ö	169	⌐
138	è	154	Ü	170	¬
139	ï	155	¢	171	½
140	î	156	£	172	¼
141	ì	157	¥	173	¡
142	Ä	158	₧	174	«
143	Å	159	ƒ	175	»

GRAPHICS

Code	Character	Code	Character	Code	Character
176	░	192	└	208	╨
177	▒	193	┴	209	╤
178	▓	194	┬	210	╥
179	│	195	├	211	╙
180	┤	196	─	212	╘
181	╡	197	┼	213	╒
182	╢	198	╞	214	╓
183	╖	199	╟	215	╫
184	╕	200	╚	216	╪
185	╣	201	╔	217	┘
186	║	202	╩	218	┌
187	╗	203	╦	219	█
188	╝	204	╠	220	▄
189	╜	205	═	221	▌
190	╛	206	╬	222	▐
191	┐	207	╧	223	▀

Tip #26: Don't ignore your brain

Writing with Word and a computer permits you to dash off ideas, store them in computer memory or on disk, shuffle them around in new combinations, and print them in various forms. It's a wonderful augmentation of human creativity and capacity. But it can breed lazy mental habits, because it's easy to write before you think and then use the computer to manipulate and revise endlessly. The final product may be good, even very good, but it can take longer to try out myriad ideas on the screen than it would to think through what you want to say ahead of time. A partial analogy can be found in the pocket calculator, which has reduced the abilities of some people to manipulate numbers mentally. Do you reach for a calculator to add 213 and 127?

If you find that your written product bears little resemblance to your first draft, and that it takes a long time for your ideas to evolve on the screen, you may be relying too heavily on the computer as a writing crutch. Take full advantage of your computer's speed and Word's flexibility, but don't ignore the power of your mind.

Power Tools:
The Mouse

Okay, trivia fans. When used with Word, the Microsoft Mouse:

♦ Moves in units called "mickeys." A mickey is approximately a hundredth of an inch.

♦ Runs at either of two speeds. Rolling the mouse quickly moves the pointer twice as far on the screen as does rolling the mouse slowly the same distance. "If you're moving the mouse fast, chances are you want to go somewhere far away, so we get you there a little faster," explained one of Word's designers.

♦ Comes in serial and bus versions, which behave identically, although their means of connection to a computer differ. The serial version plugs into a serial port. The bus version connects via a printed circuit card. IBM refers to the bus mouse as a "parallel" mouse in the instructions for its windowing program, TopView.

♦ Needs little rolling space on a desktop. The original model of the mouse (with green buttons and a metal ball underneath) needs only 3.2 inches by 2 inches when rolled quickly, and 6.4 inches by 4 inches when rolled slowly. A newer model, which has a smoother plastic ball and a more rounded shape, needs even less desk space.

♦ In the plural is often called "mouses," not "mice."

♦ Works with a growing range of programs other than Word. Both TopView and Microsoft Windows are windowing packages that take advantage of the capabilities of the mouse.

♦ Is used in the most unusual ways by unguided newcomers who may pick it up and roll it around the face of the computer screen . . . or use grand sweeps of their arms, instead of slow motions of an inch or two . . . or, not realizing they can lift the mouse and set it down elsewhere to continue a motion, roll the mouse to the edge of the desk and wonder what to do . . . or lift the keyboard with one hand and roll the mouse under it with the other . . . .

AN ADVANCED TOOL

Much hoopla is made over the simplicity a mouse brings to learning and using computers. The truth is, with a little practice, the keyboard is faster than the mouse as a means of accomplishing many relatively simple things, such as selecting a word or picking a command. With experience, people often find themselves moving away from the mouse to perform certain editing functions, while continuing to use the mouse for other tasks. This is as it should be. Every tool has it own uses.

Most uses of the mouse involve describing something to the computer by pointing. The mouse proves its worth when the same instruction would require considerably more effort to describe in keystrokes. It comes into its own when you select large passages of text; move the selection a considerable distance on the screen; use multiple windows; copy content, formatting, or both from one place to another; manipulate tabular material; or scroll without moving the selection.

Highest productivity often comes when the keyboard and mouse are used together. For example, you might choose a command with the keyboard, but jump to a particular field in the command with the mouse. With time, you'll develop your own favorite ways to use the mouse. Meanwhile, here are some tips.

Tip #1: A mouse in the hand

The mouse needn't be on a desk when you scroll through a long document. You can hold it in your hand. Position the mouse pointer on the left border (the scroll bar) of the text window, preferably near the bottom if you want to scroll a whole screen at a time. Pick up the mouse and hold it in any position, even upside down. Put your feet up on the desk and lean back in your chair, if you prefer. Click the left button to scroll toward the beginning of the document and the right button to scroll toward the end.

Tip #2: Look around with the scroll bar

You can roam around a document on a long tether, if you use the mouse in the scroll bar but leave the selection unmoved. (Unlike scrolling with the PgUp or PgDn keys, or with the Jump Page command, using the mouse with the scroll bar doesn't move the selection.) To return to the selection, just press any direction key.

Tip #3: An unconventional use for the manual

Since it's possible to do so much editing with the mouse, try using the Word manual or another small, hard, smooth surface as a portable desktop. Lean back, put the manual in your lap, and run the mouse over its surface.

Tip #4: Command shortcuts

Clicking the left mouse button moves you one step at a time when you're executing a command; it's the same as if you were executing the command with the keyboard. Clicking the right mouse button takes you two steps instead of one when you're executing most commands; it's a shortcut. Here's a summary of what happens when you click on certain names in the Edit menu:

Command	Clicking Left	Clicking Right
Copy	Shows *COPY to:* {}	Copies to the scrap
Delete	Shows *DELETE to:* {}	Deletes to the scrap
Format	Shows Format submenu	Shows Format Character fields
Gallery	Shows Gallery menu	Shows Gallery menu
Insert	Shows *INSERT from:* {}	Inserts from the scrap
Jump	Shows Jump submenu	Shows Jump Page field
Library	Shows Library submenu	Shows Library Autosort fields (in version 3.0)
Print	Shows Print submenu	Executes Print Printer command
Quit	Asks confirmation before quitting Word	Saves without confirmation, then quits Word
Transfer	Shows Transfer submenu	Shows Transfer Load fields
Window	Shows Window submenu	Shows Window Split Horizontal fields

Tip #5: Copy formatting without copying content

Don't overlook the power of the mouse to copy character and paragraph formatting from one location to another, without copying text. Both techniques work in the Gallery as well as in document or outline modes.

To copy character formatting:

1. Select the passage to be formatted.
2. Move the mouse pointer outside the selection, to a single character that is formatted the way you desire.
3. Hold down the Alt key and click the *left* mouse button. (If you're a user of style sheets, note that this method copies either direct character formatting or a character style; it doesn't copy the character formatting that is part of a paragraph style.)

To copy paragraph formatting:

1. Select the paragraph(s) to be formatted.
2. Move the mouse pointer to the selection bar, to the left of a paragraph that is formatted as you desire. This paragraph cannot be inside the selection.
3. Hold down the Alt key and click the *right* mouse button. (If you're a user of style sheets, note that this method copies either direct paragraph formatting or a paragraph style.).

Tip #6: A menu of formatting choices

When creating a document with complicated or repeatedly changing formats, set up an on-screen menu of format choices to take advantage of the mouse's ability to copy formatting.

Open a vertical window at one side of the screen and place samples of character and paragraph formatting in it, using as many lines as you need. Describe the formatting of each sample. For example, if you use underlined characters in the document, one sample line could say *Underlining* and be underlined. When editing, use the mouse to copy the formatting of the sample to selected text in the document.

Alternatively, you can set up a series of small windows in a horizontal strip across either the top or bottom of the text area. Display a different part of the main document in each window. Scroll the text in the small windows so that one sample of formatting shows in each, then use the mouse to copy the formatting to other locations as needed.

As a variation, you can use a single horizontal window with various samples of character formatting displayed across the screen. This technique is less efficient, however, because you need to scroll samples of paragraph formats into the window before copying them.

Tip #7: One-step text copying

People often overlook the mouse as a means of copying or moving text from one place to another, particularly from one window to another. The mouse is faster than using the scrap or the glossary. This technique also has the advantage of being a single-step editing process, so the Undo command can operate on an entire text movement. Follow these steps:

1. Select the text to be moved or copied.
2. Scroll to the location at which you want the text to appear. Use the scroll bar, so that the selection remains in the location specified in step 1.
3. Move the mouse pointer to the exact destination for the selected text.
4. Hold down either the Ctrl key or the Shift key and press the left mouse button. If you hold down the Ctrl key, the selection will be moved. If you hold down the Shift key, the selected text will be copied.

If you accidentally move the selection to a different window before completing the copy or move, press the F1 key one or more times. This restores the selection to the previous window.

Tip #8: Write without typing

Try composing a simple document without typing. First, split off a small horizontal window at the bottom of the screen and type into it all the letters of the alphabet in both upper- and lowercase. Enter a paragraph mark, too. Optionally, you can type in a few common words or letter combinations, and maybe even some specially formatted characters or formatted paragraph marks.

Then, create words and sentences in the upper window by using the letters, words, and symbols in the lower window as building blocks.

1. Select the element (letter, letter combination, word, or symbol) in the lower window that you want to use in the upper window.
2. Copy the element into the scrap by picking the Copy command with the mouse, then click the right mouse button.
3. Select the place in the upper window where you want the element to appear.
4. Insert the scrap contents by picking the Insert command with the mouse. Click the right mouse button.

This is slow going, but it's an interesting exercise. Speed it up by placing a list of commonly used words in a vertical window at the side of the screen. (You can generate such a list easily by running the WORDFREQ program that comes as a utility with Microsoft Spell.) Select a whole word at a time from the list by clicking the right mouse button; copy it to the scrap; select the place for it in the document you are creating, and insert it.

Such a system might seem tedious at first, but with practice, it could work well for people physically unable to use a keyboard comfortably.

Tip #9: Homemade mouse games

The Microsoft Mouse comes with several games on disk, including Doodle, Life, and Piano. Of these, only Piano can be used if you don't have graphics capabilities. You can easily create additional, though more primitive, games on your own, to give yourself experience with Word and the mouse. Two sample games:

♦ Spot a letter somewhere on the screen. Close your eyes. Roll the mouse, stop when you think the mouse pointer is on the letter you picked, then click the left mouse button. Open your eyes and see how close you came.

♦ Draw pictures using the mouse and the ASCII graphics characters built into IBM personal computers and compatibles. To view the available characters, use Word's Help command and pick *Keyboard*. Press N (for *Next*) a number of times. Note the ASCII number of any character you want to use. Return to Word and open a horizontal window at the bottom of the screen. In the window, place each of the ASCII graphics characters you want to use. Enter an ASCII character by holding down the Alt key, while typing on the numeric keypad the number corresponding to the ASCII character. Once you've completed your menu of graphics characters, create your artwork with the mouse, copying characters from the menu to desired positions in your artwork document by using the Shift-key/left mouse button combination described in tip #7. If you wish to avoid using the keyboard entirely, copy each desired character to the scrap with the Copy command, select the location for the character, and use the Insert command.

You can print your creations if you have an IBM Graphics Printer.

Tip #10: Installing the bus mouse

This tip applies if you have difficulty making your computer perform properly—especially reboot properly—after installing the circuit board of the *bus* version of the Microsoft Mouse.

You may have to change a simple *jumper* setting on the mouse circuit board. Hold the board so that the gold connectors are facing downward and the side with writing and electronic components on it is facing you. Near the bottom, labeled J4, is a set of four pairs of metal pins marked 2, 3, 4, and 5. The jumper slides over one pair to make an electrical connection. You can move the jumper to any pair, and you may need to experiment with different settings if you have a hard disk, special add-on boards, or other equipment in your computer. You'll know you've used a wrong setting if your hard disk doesn't reboot properly or if some other piece of equipment stops functioning when the mouse is installed.

Generally, follow these guidelines:

♦ Do not use pair 2 if you have an IBM PC AT (or compatible 80286-based computer), or an IBM 3270 PC (with or without a hard disk).

♦ Do not use pair 3 if you have either an asynchronous communications adapter (including built-in modem) or a binary synchronous communications adapter connected to your second serial port (COM2).

♦ Do not use pair 4 if you have either an asynchronous communications adapter (including built-in modem) or a binary synchronous communications adapter connected to your first serial port (COM1).

♦ Do not use pair 5 if you have an IBM PC XT, an IBM PC with a hard disk, an IBM 3270 PC with a hard disk, or a computer compatible with any of these computers.

If these guidelines seem confusing, a rough rule of thumb is that you should use jumper pair 2 unless you have an IBM PC AT (or compatible), in which case use jumper pair 5.

NOTE: These rules also apply if you have an *Inport* version of the bus mouse, although the jumpers may be in a different location than they are on the circuit board of the original bus mouse.

Power Tools: The Glossary

You've already seen that the glossary can be used to insert any word, phrase, or longer passage into a document as often as you wish. As you become adept with Word, you may find yourself using the Transfer Glossary commands to set up separate glossary files for different word-processing tasks. You might keep one set of glossary entries as a glossary file called COVER.GLY for use when writing cover letters, for example, and another set in a file called PTA.GLY for use when editing a PTA newsletter. When writing, you could use the Transfer Glossary Merge command to bring either or both files (and their specialized entries) into the glossary as needed.

These are practical uses of the glossary, but conventional ones, too. This chapter goes a step further and explores three "power tool" uses of the glossary:

♦ A means of organizing and outlining.

♦ A system of alternate scraps.

♦ A speedy way to format documents.

AN ORGANIZING AND OUTLINING TOOL

Passages, quotations, and other elements of a document can be stored on disk under individual glossary names. Instead of selecting and moving long passages or scrolling through the pages of a lengthy document to find what you seek, simply insert appropriate glossary entries back into your document when and where they are needed. Or you type the glossary names, shuffle them around into the order you want, and then transform the glossary names into the corresponding text by placing the selection after each name and pressing the F3 key. You can even use the glossary names as the elements of a formal outline, and then transform the series of names into a document with the F3 key.

Organizing the document

Imagine that you're writing about pasta. You could be writing a magazine article, a cookbook chapter, or a long letter to a relative. Regardless, pasta is the topic. You've already written passages on a variety of pastas—cannelloni, tortellini, tagliolini, cappelletti, ravioli—and you've typed two or three recipes for each into your computer. You've also written a passage about sauces, and a few paragraphs about stuffed pastas. In short, most of the elements have been gathered into a single Word document, which you call PASTA. Now you must organize the elements and add an introduction, a conclusion, and some transitions. This is where the power of the glossary makes it a useful editing tool.

Each element of the document can be deleted into the glossary and assigned its own descriptive glossary name. Once all the pieces are stored, you can start your document fresh, or nearly fresh, and call forth material from the glossary as it is needed. You can insert passages into the document more than once, to try them out in various locations. If you change your mind about some editing, you can delete it and start again from scratch by calling forth the needed elements from the glossary. You're not forced to search through the document to find particular subjects, because each desired passage is represented by a glossary name and is instantly accessible to you. And if editing takes longer than a single session, you can save the glossary entries as a glossary file and pick up later where you left off.

Preparing the glossary entries

Let's assume you've assembled your material for the document PASTA, and are ready to store the passages in the glossary. Here is a step-by-step example of how you might proceed:

1. Select a passage of text. Make it small enough or complete enough that you aren't likely to want to break it up later into independent pieces. Depending on your vision of the finished document, you might select the whole section on cannelloni, a smaller section on cannelloni with butter sauces, or a single cannelloni recipe. By segmenting your material and labeling each part descriptively, you allow yourself the later luxury of being able to extract tightly focused sections.

2. Pick the Delete command. Word proposes the scrap.

3. You want to delete to the glossary, not the scrap, so think up an appropriate glossary name for the selected text. If it is about cannelloni in general, you might pick an easily remembered name, such as *Cannelloni*. Or you might shorten it to *Can*. Or, for convenience, just *C*. If the selected text is about cannelloni with butter sauce, you might call it *Cannelloni—Butter* or *CanBut*. For that matter, you could call it *Beethoven* or any other string of up to 31 letters, numbers, and acceptable symbols. But a meaningful name helps you later, when you want to retrieve text from the glossary.

4. Type the name and press the Enter key. The selected text vanishes from the document PASTA, and is placed in the glossary under its name.

5. Repeat the process for the other passages. A section on tortellini might be named *Tort*. Sections on tagliolini, cappelletti, and ravioli could be filed away, too.

You're finished when each segment of the document either has been deleted outright or has been deleted to the glossary, under an appropriate name. If you wish to quit Word at this point and leave the reorganizing for another time, you can store all the glossary entries in a file with the Transfer Glossary Save command. Such a file might be called PASTA.GLY. If you do this, when you resume work, use the Transfer Glossary Merge command to restore the entries in PASTA.GLY to the glossary in memory.

Using the glossary entries

Now, you're ready to organize. Perhaps you begin your document with a general introduction telling how different areas in Italy have developed regional variations in cuisine. That done, you move on to the main part of your text. Time to mention the different sauces? Call the sauce section from the glossary. The first pasta you want to write about is cannelloni? Call the cannelloni passage back from the glossary.

Recall that there are two ways to retrieve text from the glossary. You can type the glossary name at the place in the document where you wish the entry to appear and press the F3 key. Or you can pick the Insert command and, if need be, request a list of available glossary names for insertion. If you want a printed list of the glossary entries, call up the list, hold down the Shift key, and press the PrtSc key if this method works with your printer.

Putting the pieces of a document together can be as easy as catalog shopping. If glossary entries have names that suggest their content, you can pick and choose from the list.

Outlining the document

Perhaps you want to outline your document before working with the text itself. Type each glossary name on a separate line of what can be either a formal or informal outline. Shuffle the order of the lines as you will, moving them either with the mouse or to and from the scrap. Once the names are in the desired order, position the selection after each one and, in turn, press the F3 key to insert the text it represents.

Once you've inserted all the passages from the glossary back into your text, your document might be just about complete, though you'd probably smooth out the transitions between passages, write a conclusion, and give it a final editing.

Clever use of the glossary lets you redirect the organization of a document with little trouble. In PASTA, for example, you might at first group recipes according to which pasta noodle they use. Perhaps you'd insert the glossary entries named *Cannelloni_Butter*, *Cannelloni_Tomato*, and *Cannelloni_Olive_Oil* in succession. But after reading the resulting document, maybe you decide you really want all the tomato-sauce pasta recipes in one place, all the butter-sauce ones in another, and all the olive-oil-based ones in yet another. Using the glossary, it's easy. Delete what you've written or open a new document and start over again. To group the tomato-sauce recipes together this time around, you could use the glossary to insert *Cannelloni_Tomato*, followed by *Ravioli_Tomato*, *Manicotti_Tomato*, and so on.

Word's outlining capabilities can be used to accomplish much the same thing as this technique's adaptation of the glossary. You can type a descriptive line for each paragraph or group of related paragraphs, and turn the line into a heading. Then, by collapsing the text, you can re-order the elements of a document easily in outline edit mode. See Chapter 25, "Power Tools: Outlining."

A variation: Numbers as names

As often as not, I use numbers as glossary names when I'm massively reorganizing a document. Unlike other techniques, with this one you make decisions with pencil and paper.

On a printout of the unrevised document, circle or bracket complete passages you wish to keep. Number the passages in the order in which you ultimately wish them to appear. Mark any passages you want to eliminate altogether.

Once all passages are marked in some fashion, put Word to the task. Working from the beginning of the on-screen version of the document, dispose of every paragraph or passage by deleting it either to the scrap (to eliminate it) or to the glossary (to save it). When deleting to the glossary, use the number you gave the passage on paper as the glossary name. When you reach the end of the document, nothing will be left of it. Every passage will have been eliminated or assigned to a number in the glossary.

Now comes the snappy part. Type *1* and press the F3 key. Instantly, the passage you want to be first in your revised document appears on the screen. Type *2* and press F3. The second passage appears in the document, following the first. Continue until every numbered passage has been inserted. The document will be organized as you want. With some practice, you should be able to break a 10-page document into 25 parts and juggle the pieces into an entirely new sequence—all in less than 10 minutes.

NOTE: Much the same effect can be obtained using the Library Autosort command (beginning with version 3.0 of Word). Instead of deleting paragraphs to the glossary with numbers as names, number the paragraphs in the order you want them to appear, and execute the Library Autosort command. The advantage of using the glossary, instead, is that you can assign a number to a passage that extends for several paragraphs—or pages.

Pulling information together

The glossary can also be used to collect material from many different parts of one document or several documents. For instance, suppose you're an attorney who has hundreds of pages of transcripts in one or more Word documents. Move through the text, copying to the glossary any passages pertaining to a particular subject. (If you want to preserve the original documents, use the Copy command rather than the Delete command.) The glossary entries can be named distinctively, or they can be given abbreviated names or just numbers. Afterward, you can form documents on specific subjects in a matter of minutes.

Use the same technique to gather information on a number of topics simultaneously. A student who has amassed a jumble of notes on several subjects can read through them just once, copying or deleting passages to the glossary. Entries on fish might be named *Fish1*, *Fish2*, and *Fish3*, while entries on birds might be named *Ducks* and *Geese*. Later, the collected entries in the glossary can be inserted into new, separate documents on each subject. All of the entries with *Fish* in their names could be one document. *Ducks* and *Geese* could flock together in another.

AN ALTERNATE SCRAP OR SCRAPS

Ever wish there were more than just one scrap? With the glossary, there can be. The scrap, after all, is similar to the glossary—it is a storage place for text. In fact, you can think of the scrap as a glossary entry with some special characteristics. Unlike conventional glossary entries, the scrap always has the name { }; its contents are indicated continuously on the bottom line of the screen; the Ins and Del keys are dedicated to it; and it can't be stored in a glossary file.

Just as the scrap is a form of glossary entry, any glossary entry can be used as a form of scrap. Imagine that there are several additional scraps. You can call them *Scrap1, Scrap2*, or whatever you please. Rather than deleting a passage to the real scrap, consider deleting it to a "glossary scrap" with one of the special names. That way the deleted passage is available later on the off chance you want to resurrect some or all of it.

And keep in mind that, beginning with version 3.0 of Word, you can see a printout of your glossary entries at any time with the Print Glossary command.

A SPEEDY WAY TO FORMAT AS YOU WRITE

Character, paragraph, and division formats exist in as little as one character of text. You can copy or delete a formatted character to the glossary, giving it a distinctive name or handy abbreviation, and later insert one of these formatted characters into a document as you would any other glossary entry. Once a formatted character has been inserted from the glossary, it is like any other formatted character. You can, for instance, continue writing from that point with the benefit of the formatting.

Characters

Character formatting can be stored in a single, blank, space character. Perhaps you use capitalized, boldfaced characters frequently in preparing contracts. Apply that combination of formatting to a single space in the document and store it in the glossary with a suitable name. Perhaps you call it *CapsBold*. To insert this formatted space into a document, type *CapsBold* and press the F3 key. Then press the Left direction key once to move the selection into the formatted space, so that when you resume typing, the new text will have the character formatting of "CapsBold."

The same technique can be used for hidden-text character formatting.

Paragraphs

Recall that paragraph formatting is stored in paragraph marks. Inserting a formatted paragraph mark (from the glossary) formats the text preceding the mark (back to the previous mark). You can place several paragraph marks in the glossary, each with a different name and formatting. A paragraph mark that centers text might be given the name *Center*; a mark that double-spaces lines might be called *Double*; and so forth. In addition, both paragraph and character formatting can be stored together in the same paragraph mark. You accomplish this by formatting the mark with both Format Character and Format Paragraph commands.

Use these formatted marks instead of the Enter key to create new paragraphs that have desired formats already in place. In some cases, this technique rivals style sheets for speedy formatting. Note, however, that in version 3.0 of Word, paragraph formatting (but not character or division formatting) is forgotten by Word when the glossary entry containing the formatting is saved as a glossary file. This is not true in later versions, including 3.1, nor was it true in 2.0.

Divisions

Division formatting is stored in a division mark, which you create by holding down the Ctrl key and pressing the Enter key, and which appears as a double row of dots across the text window.

If you have a particular page layout you use for certain documents, consider formatting a division mark appropriately and storing it in the glossary. You might call the glossary entry *2col* if it contains a division mark that creates two columns on a page. To format a single-division document with this mark, you select the last character of the document, type *2col*, and press the F3 key. The division mark is inserted and causes the division formatting of the document to change. To format one division of a multiple-division document, replace the mark at the end of the division with an appropriately formatted mark from the glossary. If you often use the same formatting characters from the glossary, you can store them as a glossary file with the Transfer Glossary Save command.

An example of glossary-based formatting

To practice applying formatting with glossary entries, use the following descriptions as a tutorial. Let's assume you want to use the glossary to make each heading in a report capitalized, underlined, and centered, with two blank spaces preceding it and one following it. This is a combination of character and paragraph formatting. First you place the formatting in the glossary:

1. Select a paragraph mark at the end of a paragraph and press the Enter key to create a new paragraph mark, alone on a line. (You can see the paragraph marks if you've made normally invisible characters visible with the Options command.)

2. Pick the Format Paragraph command and choose *Centered* in the *alignment* field. Type *0* (zero) in each of the three *indent* fields, *2* in the *space before* field, and *1* in the *space after* field. Execute the command.

3. Without moving the selection, pick the Format Character command and choose *Yes* in both the *underline* and *uppercase* fields. Carry out the command to complete the formatting.

4. Still without moving the selection, pick the Delete command and type *Heading* as the glossary name. Execute the command.

A paragraph mark laden with paragraph and character formatting is now stored in the glossary under the name *Heading*. To use it to format a paragraph as a heading, type *Heading* and press the F3 key.

There are a couple of different specific ways to use the glossary entry.

If you are at the end of a paragraph and want the next paragraph to be the heading:

1. Press the Enter key at the end of the current paragraph.
2. Type *Heading* (or whatever name you've given the glossary entry).
3. Press the F3 key. This places the formatted paragraph mark in the text but also moves you to the next paragraph.
4. Press the Up direction key to return to the paragraph mark of the heading paragraph.
5. Type the text of the heading.
6. Presumably you want only one heading paragraph at a time, so don't press the Enter key. Instead, press the Down direction key to complete the heading and move to the next paragraph.

To insert a heading paragraph in the midst of other paragraphs:

1. Select the first character of the paragraph that will follow the heading.
2. Type the name of the glossary entry: *Heading*. Do not put a space after the name of the entry.
3. Press the F3 key. This inserts the new paragraph above the one you selected.
4. Press the Up direction key. This moves the selection to the new heading paragraph.
5. Type the text of the heading.

In general, glossary-based formatting is less practical than a style sheet as a means of fast formatting, unless you are skilled at using the glossary and are not too familiar with style sheets. A key difference between style sheets and glossary-based formatting is that style sheets control only the formatting of text already in the document, while glossary-based formatting also inserts content—even though it may only be a blank space, a paragraph mark, or a division mark.

Using Search and the glossary

A variation of glossary-based formatting uses the Search command to accomplish a kind of replacement that is impossible with the Replace command. You can search for text with the Search command, and once it is highlighted, replace it with text from the glossary by pressing the F3 key.

This assumes, of course, that you have copied or deleted the replacement text into the glossary, and given it the same name as the name for which you are searching.

The advantage of this method is that replacement text can have special formats (including underlining or being "hidden text") when it comes from the glossary. It can be paragraph or division formatting, as well as character formatting. A replacement made with the Replace command cannot be formatted.

(Recall that the F3 key works when a multi-character glossary name is selected or when the selection is a single character that immediately follows the glossary name. Also recall that you can speed up the searching process by pressing Shift-F4 to repeat the last search.)

Power Tools: Multiple Windows

Multiple windows aren't of much practical use until you learn to manage them. Screen room is limited enough as it is, and you can ill afford to chop what's there into awkward little spaces. But once you've become comfortable with a few management techniques, using multiple windows seems close to essential.

I use three basic techniques, each a different approach to the problem of how to apportion screen space among windows. They are:

♦ Resizing windows freely, so that whichever one you are working in is of ample size to suit your needs.

♦ Reformatting documents temporarily, to fit gracefully in smaller windows.

♦ Opening a temporary window to meet a specific need, and closing it promptly when it's unneeded.

A widely known fourth technique, scrolling horizontally, lets you read lines that are longer than a window is wide. An easy way to scroll horizontally is with the Home and End keys. Horizontal scrolling is generally a lot of work and is confusing compared to any of the three preceding approaches, because it forces you to shift the window's display back and forth, to the right and left, for each line in a document that's wider than the window.

With any of the techniques, including horizontal scrolling, you may get more satisfactory results by experimenting with the setting of the *printer display* field of the Options command.

Windows can be used effectively without a mouse, but not as easily. By way of analogy, a mouse makes the difference between using a pencil to draw a line or shape right where you want it, and having to describe, through a set of instructions (commands), where you want the line to be.

Actually, some interesting parallels exist between using multiple windows and using a mouse. Both are misunderstood by newcomers. Both at first may seem to be frilly, unnecessary, gimmicky. Both are most valuable to skilled users of Word.

RESIZING WINDOWS

Among people who haven't often used Word's windows, there is an understandable inclination to divide the screen evenly into two vertical windows, neither as wide as the document it displays. This is relatively ineffective, because you must constantly scroll horizontally in each window to read full lines.

```
1=[····¦····1·········2·········3·····2=[·········1·········2·········3·····
                     The First Docum                    The Second Docum
          This is the FIRST document. Thi          This is the SECOND document. Th
This is the FIRST document. This is      document. This is the SECOND documen
is the FIRST document. This is the F     document. This is the SECOND documen
the FIRST document. This is the FIRS     document. This is the SECOND documen
                                         document.
```

Instead, make the split at the far left or far right edge of the screen, beyond the edge of your text, and move the border freely from side to side, as your attention shifts from one document:

```
1=[····¦····1·········2·········3·········4·········5·········]·········2=0··
                        The First Document

          This is the FIRST document. This is the FIRST document.
This is the FIRST document. This is the FIRST document. This is                     doc
is the FIRST document. This is the FIRST document. This is                          doc
the FIRST document. This is the FIRST document.                                     doc
```

to the other:

```
1=0··2=[····¦····1·········2·········3·········4·········5·········]·········
                          The Second Document

              This is the SECOND document. This is the SECOND
Thi     document. This is the SECOND document. This is the SECOND
is      document. This is the SECOND document. This is the SECOND
the     document. This is the SECOND document. This is the SECOND
        document.
```

Keeping a second window open at the side of the screen, always ready to be pulled into place, is handy for notes, a cover letter, or any other companion document. For fast reference, you can display another part of the same document in the second window. Passages can be moved or copied freely between the windows.

Documents usually don't take up the full width of the screen, so you don't sacrifice anything by having a few columns at one edge devoted to another window. Neither the selection nor the scrap is affected when you move the window border.

Recall that moving a vertical window border back and forth horizontally on the screen is accomplished by moving the lower right corner of the left window. It's easy with the mouse. Just grab the corner, by holding either button, and pull the corner across the screen. In the illustration above, the window border was pulled across the screen as far to the left as possible.

There's a little more to doing it with the keyboard and the three fields of the Window Move command:

```
WINDOW MOVE lower right corner of window #:      to row:      column:
```

When you're dealing with two vertical windows, the left window is always Window 1. Pick the Window Move command, type *1* in the first field if it isn't already shown. Press the Tab key twice to move to the *column* field, and then type either *0* to move the border to the far left, or *100* to move the border to the far right.

Word can't really move the border to either 0 or 100, but these instructions cause the border to move as far as possible. Zero and 100 are easy to remember. If necessary after moving a border, use the F1 key to move the selection to a different window and use the Home key to bring the beginnings of lines into view in a window.

Cornering

Sacrifice three lines of your screen to additional window borders, and you can use four windows almost as readily as you can use two. After splitting the screen vertically, split each of the vertical windows horizontally. Again, don't put the borders in the middle of the screen, where they divide your workspace evenly. Instead, put the new horizontal splits near the tops or bottoms of the existing two windows, and move the borders up or down as need dictates. In the following example, the splits are at the bottom of the screen, but as easily could be at the top.

```
1=[····|····1·········2·········3·········4·········5·········]·········2=|··
                     The First Document                              Thi
     This is the FIRST document. This is the FIRST document.         ent
This is the FIRST document. This is the FIRST document. This         ent
is the FIRST document. This is the FIRST document. This is           ent
the FIRST document. This is the FIRST document.                      ent

     This is the FIRST document. This is the FIRST document.         Thi
This is the FIRST document. This is the FIRST document. This         ent
is the FIRST document. This is the FIRST document. This is           ent
the FIRST document. This is the FIRST document.                      ent
                                                                     ent
     This is the FIRST document. This is the FIRST document.         ent
This is the FIRST document. This is the FIRST document. This
is the FIRST document. This is the FIRST document. This is           Thi
3=[·········1·········2·········3·········4·········5·········]·········4=|··

COMMAND: Alpha Copy Delete Format Gallery Help Insert Jump Library
        Options Print Quit Replace Search Transfer Undo Window
Edit document or press Esc to use menu
Page 1   {}                        ?        Microsoft Word: FOURTH.DOC
```

I call this method "cornering," because each of the four windows is rooted to a corner. The idea is to push the three windows you're not working in at a particular moment to the corners of the screen, leaving one window dominant. The underlying philosophy is that a window should take up significant space only when it is in use. For the same reason, consider keeping footnote windows small and expanding them only to read or enter footnote text.

Cornering, then, as you see in the following illustrations, lets you shift the borders of windows quickly . . .

```
║═[ ╥2═[ · · · · · · · · ·1· · · · · · · · ·2· · · · · · · · ·3· · · · · · · · ·4· · · · · · · ·5· · · · · · · · · ·]· · · · · · · · ║
║         │                      The Second Document                                                              ║
║         │        This is the SECOND document. This is the SECOND                                                ║
║   Thi   ║║  document. This is the SECOND document. This is the SECOND                                          ║
║   is    ║║  document. This is the SECOND document. This is the SECOND                                          ║
║   the   ║║  document. This is the SECOND document. This is the SECOND                                          ║
║         ║║  document.                                                                                          ║
║   Thi   ║║        This is the SECOND document. This is the SECOND                                              ║
║   is    ║║  document. This is the SECOND document. This is the SECOND                                          ║
║   the   ║║  document. This is the SECOND document. This is the SECOND                                          ║
║         ║║  document. This is the SECOND document. This is the SECOND                                          ║
║         ║║  document.                                                                                          ║
║   Thi   ║                                                                                                       ║
║   is    ║        This is the SECOND document. This is the SECOND                                                ║
3═[ ╥4═[ · · · · · · · · ·1· · · · · · · · ·2· · · · · · · · ·3· · · · · · · · ·4· · · · · · · ·5· · · · · · · · · ·]· · · · · · ·7 ║
COMMAND: Alpha Copy Delete Format Gallery Help Insert Jump Library
         Options Print Quit Replace Search Transfer Undo Window
Edit document or press Esc to use menu
Page 1   {}                                ?              Microsoft Word: FIRST.DOC
```

so that most of the usable screen space . . .

```
1═[ · · · · │ · · · ·1· · · · · · · · ·2· · · · · · · · ·3· · · · · · · · ·4· · · · · · · ·5· · · · · · ·]· · · · · · · · ║2═[ · ·
3═[ · · · · │ · · · ·1· · · · · · · · ·2· · · · · · · · ·3· · · · · · · · ·4· · · · · · · ·5· · · · · · ·]· · · · · · · ║4═· · ·
                            The Third Document
              This is the THIRD document. This is the THIRD document.
        This is the THIRD document. This is the THIRD document. This
        is the THIRD document. This is the THIRD document. This is
        the THIRD document. This is the THIRD document. This is the
        THIRD document.

              This is the THIRD document. This is the THIRD document.
        This is the THIRD document. This is the THIRD document. This
        is the THIRD document. This is the THIRD document. This is
        the THIRD document. This is the THIRD document. This is the
        THIRD document.

              This is the THIRD document. This is the THIRD document.
COMMAND: Alpha Copy Delete Format Gallery Help Insert Jump Library
         Options Print Quit Replace Search Transfer Undo Window
Edit document or press Esc to use menu
Page 1   {}                                ?              Microsoft Word: SECOND.DOC
```

is devoted to the window in which you are working.

```
1═0··2═0·············1·········2·········3·········4·········5·········6······
3═[··'4═[····'····1·········2·········3·········4·········5·········]·······
                        The Fourth Document
                    And finally we have the FOURTH document. And finally we
     Thi     have the FOURTH document.
     is
     the         And finally we have the FOURTH document. And finally we
     THI     have the FOURTH document.

     Thi         And finally we have the FOURTH document. And finally we
     is      have the FOURTH document.
     the
     THI         And finally we have the FOURTH document. And finally we
             have the FOURTH document.

                 And finally we have the FOURTH document. And finally we
COMMAND: Alpha Copy Delete Format Gallery Help Insert Jump Library
         Options Print Quit Replace Search Transfer Undo Window
Edit document or press Esc to use menu
Page 1    {}                          ?          Microsoft Word: FOURTH.DOC
```

Each window can contain a separate document, different views of the same document, or a combination. For example, the availability of four windows lets you refer to and work on a table of contents, a chapter, a bibliography, and a file of notes all at once—or, a sales letter, a proposal, a schedule of delivery dates, and reference materials—or, three parts of a term paper and an outline. As you have ideas, you can shift to a different window temporarily, just as you might jot different ideas on different notepads. By the same token, you can put three views of the same document in different windows—a normal view in one, a view with hidden text showing in another, and an outline view in yet another.

Again, the mouse is the fastest way to corner. But using 0 and 100 in the fields of the Window Move command makes the technique using the keyboard easy to remember and fairly fast, too. Decide which window you want dominant, then choose the appropriate instruction or instructions from among the following.

NOTE: These instructions assume that in setting up the four windows you have made the vertical window split before the horizontal window splits—that is, that Windows #1 and #2 are at the top of the screen.

♦ To make the window (#1) in the upper left corner dominant:

```
WINDOW MOVE lower right corner of window #: 1     to row: 100  column: 100
```

♦ To make the window in the lower left corner dominant:

```
WINDOW MOVE lower right corner of window #: 1     to row: 0    column: 100
```

♦ To make the window (#2) in the upper right corner dominant, first try this instruction:

```
WINDOW MOVE lower right corner of window #: 1     to row: 100  column: 0
```

If that doesn't fully succeed, repeat the Window Move command with the same row and column values (100 and 0), but with the window number set to 2:

```
WINDOW MOVE lower right corner of window #: 2     to row: 100  column: 0
```

♦ To make the window in the lower right corner dominant, first try this instruction:

```
WINDOW MOVE lower right corner of window #: 1     to row: 0    column: 0
```

If that doesn't fully succeed, repeat the Window Move command with the same row and column values (both 0), but with the window number set to 2:

```
WINDOW MOVE lower right corner of window #: 2     to row: 0    column: 0
```

If you corner frequently and don't have a mouse, keeping the following diagram handy will remind you of the values to use in the *row* and *column* fields of the Window Move command to make any corner dominant, as long as windows #1 and #2 are at the top left and right of the screen.

```
┌1═══════════════════════════════┐┌2═══════════════════════════════┐
│                                 ││                                 │
│   Upper Left Window Dominant    ││   Upper Right Window Dominant   │
│                                 ││                                 │
│   Window #     Row    Column    ││   Window #     Row    Column    │
│      1         100     100      ││      1         100      0       │
│                                 ││                                 │
│                                 ││       Then, if necessary,       │
│                                 ││                                 │
│                                 ││      2         100      0       │
├3════════════════════════════════├4════════════════════════════════
│   Lower Left Window Dominant    ││   Lower Right Window Dominant   │
│                                 ││                                 │
│   Window #     Row    Column    ││   Window #     Row    Column    │
│      1          0      100      ││      1          0       0       │
│                                 ││                                 │
│                                 ││       Then, if necessary,       │
│                                 ││                                 │
│                                 ││      2          0       0       │
└═════════════════════════════════└═════════════════════════════════
```

Total text area can be increased three lines by turning off the Edit menu with the Options command. If you have a Hercules or EGA card, you can also increase the number of lines by starting Word in its Hercules mode (with the command *word/h*).

REFORMATTING DOCUMENTS TEMPORARILY

If you want to split your screen evenly down the middle and not move window borders, you can temporarily reformat the document or documents to have short lines that fit within the width of each window. This lets you avoid the inconvenience of horizontal scrolling.

Technically you can narrow your document by adding indentation to each paragraph, but a simpler and more easily reversible way is to reduce the page-width field of the Format Division Margins command. Word sets this field at 8½ inches, unless you tell it otherwise. You'll probably want to return to that setting before printing the document. But while working in a window half the normal width of the screen, temporarily tell Word the paper is narrower, so that the program narrows the text on the screen correspondingly.

On-the-spot experimentation will tell you what value to type into the *width* field. Try some different numbers. The proper width depends on several variables, including the widths of your margins, the font size of your document's characters, and how you've set the *measure* and *printer display* fields of the Options command.

If you're using Word's default (built in) settings for page size (8½ inches wide) and character size (12 pt), try changing the Format Division Margins page-width field to *5.8"*. This will temporarily cause the document to use only half the screen's width. If you're using the 90-column Hercules mode, set the *width* field to *6.3"*, instead.

(Changing a page width also lets you temporarily lengthen the lines of a document to use the screen's full width and show more of a document's contents at once. But this isn't effective if you have side-by-side windows. As a point of departure for your experimentation, try changing the *width* field from *8.5" to 9.8"*. If you're using Hercules mode, try setting the width to *10.8".*)

If you use a particular page-width setting frequently, consider storing an appropriately formatted division mark in the glossary for quick use, or, best yet, set up a style-sheet division style that can be invoked temporarily while the screen is split. Whatever technique you use, don't forget to change the setting back to the appropriate page width before you print.

OPENING WINDOWS TEMPORARILY

Perhaps the best use of Word's windows is hit-and-run editing—neither limiting yourself to one window nor keeping several perpetually on the screen at once. Rather, while working on one document, you briefly open another window to perform a specific task—look at something, record an idea, search for text in the same or a different document—and close the window before resuming work on the document.

Pausing work in one window to open another window temporarily is a little like using a multiple-line telephone: You put an important call on hold to take care of some quick business on another line.

Opening a window temporarily to meet a specific need is particularly attractive on a hard-disk computer system or one with a high-capacity floppy disk, because so many documents are available at any time. Indeed, if all your documents are on a hard disk, you can add a thought or two to any of them at a moment's notice, diverting your attention from the main document only briefly. Temporary windows can be used successfully even on floppy disks of limited capacity, either by grouping relevant documents on a disk or by swapping document disks in the midst of an editing session. If you swap disks, you'll encounter an *Enter Y to retry access . . .* message every time Word needs access to a file on a different floppy. Swap disks and then press Y.

Oversize tables

Working on a table too tall or too wide to see all at once on the screen can cause confusion and delay. Which heading goes with a particular cell of the table? Which stub (left-hand column) goes with the cell?

A temporary window can speed your work. Split off a small horizontal window at the top of the screen and display the table's headings in it. Or split off a narrow vertical window at the left side of the screen to display the stubs. Now you can scroll freely through the document, referring to the stationary information in the temporary window.

Quarter	Region I	Region II	Region III
4/82	2.7	3.3	1.1
1/83	3.7	1.9	5.3
3/86	8.2	5.4	1.8
4/86	4.1	9.9	0.0
1/87	6.9	9.8	8.5
2/87	8.8	9.5	6.3
3/87	5.0	2.5	3.2
4/87	6.3	6.1	14.7█

Page 6   {}   ?   Microsoft Word: REPORT.DOC

Organizing information

Temporary windows are effective for gathering and gradually organizing large amounts of information—this book being an actual example. Create a document for each major topic (chapter, in this case). At first, a document might consist of nothing more than a title and a few lines. Over time, and even as you write on other subjects, open temporary windows and type ideas, information, and passages into the appropriate documents. This is the rough equivalent of sticking sheets of paper into filing-cabinet drawers. In the end, your thoughts and words will be waiting for you, sorted by topic.

A powerful place marker

A temporary window can hold your place in a document while you work elsewhere in it. Open a small window at the top, bottom, or side of the screen and display the text to which you want to return. Use the remainder of the screen to scroll or search through the document and edit it. To return to the place you "marked" with the small window, just close the larger window. (Of course, if you are working on different documents in the two windows, you'll want to save the contents of either window before closing it.)

Other tips for temporary windows

♦ When you want to tentatively "delete" a paragraph to see how a document would read without it, split the window horizontally at the beginning of the questioned paragraph, but don't clear the new screen (with a mouse, use the left button). At this point, some or all of the questioned paragraph will appear in the lower window. Press F1 to switch to the lower window and then press the PgDn key or the Down direction key, or scroll with the right mouse button, until none of the questioned paragraph shows. This lets you read the document as if the paragraph were not there.

♦ When you already have different documents showing in different windows, swap or shuffle which documents appear in which windows. Here's an example of how to switch the contents of two windows. Split window 2 in half, creating a temporary window 3. Select window 3, and use the Transfer Load command to load the same document that is in window 1. Then, select window 1 and load into it the same document that is in window 2. Finally, close window 2, so that window 3 expands and becomes a new window 2. Now the original window 1 has the document that was in window 2, and vice versa. The technique works with more than two windows, too. Regardless of the number of windows, all documents must be named (at some point, the Transfer Save command has to have been used) or it will be impossible to load a document from one window into another. (When a document is loaded into a second window, it is the edited version that was already on the screen that is loaded, not the unedited version from disk.)

♦ Use a temporary window as sort of a visible glossary. By clearing a new window, you can place in it paragraphs or other text that you're not sure you want to delete, or that you may later want to insert back into a document.

♦ When writing macros for Word (with a program such as ProKey 4.0, release 10 or higher), consider including instructions for splitting open a window temporarily. For example, a macro might be written so that selected numbers on the screen are added (with the F2 key), the sum placed in a temporary window and subjected to other mathematical calculations, and the result copied to the scrap and then inserted back into the document window. (To get from the document window to the temporary window, include *F1* in the macro instruction. To get from the temporary window back to the document window, merely include the Window Close command—Esc, W, C, 2, Enter.)

A SURPRISE

If you're a veteran user of Word, you may have a copy of version 1.1 somewhere. If you also have a mouse, try this for fun. Load your old version; create four horizontal windows; position the mouse pointer on the right border of window number 4; simultaneously hold down the Ctrl, Shift, and Alt keys, and, while holding them, click both mouse buttons. Superman's slogan will appear in Word's message line.

```
Truth, Justice, and the American Way,
Page 1   {}                          ? 100% Free    Microsoft Word:
```

If you click the left mouse button instead, you see some initials...

```
RRB FML del pnt rmp       ♦
Page 1   {}                          ? 100% Free    Microsoft Word:
```

...belonging to Microsoft programmers—some among many who made contributions to Word.

Power Tools:
Search and Replace

Thish shentence ish confushing.

In this tipsy sample sentence, replacing the letters *sh* with the letter *s* will restore a note of sobriety. It's easy with the Replace command.

So you suspect there are better uses for the command? There are a surprising number of applications of Replace and its cousin, the Search command. With one or both of them you can move or extend the selection, use a sophisticated place-marker system, assist in the movement of passages, count paragraphs, and check your writing. As for sobering up a sentence or a paragraph, even that has value as a skill-building exercise.

It is assumed you know the basics of the Search and Replace commands, including the use of special ^ characters, as explained in Chapter 11, "The Efficiency Commands." You may also want to reacquaint yourself with the way the Replace command is used with the Library Hyphenate command, as discussed in Chapter 14, "The Family of Library Commands."

THE SEARCH COMMAND

The obvious use of the Search command is to find a word or phrase somewhere in a document. To locate the section on diesel engines in an article about automobiles, you might search for the word *diesel*.

Here are some tips:

♦ Move the selection to the top of the document, so the entire article will be searched. Or move the selection to the end of the document, and set the *direction* field to *Up*.

♦ Consider conducting the search in a temporary window, to save your place in a document. Even though you press the F1 key to move the selection from your location in the document to the window in which you conduct the search, pressing F1 again—or closing the temporary window—takes you right back to your previous location in the first window.

♦ Hold down the Shift key and press the F4 key to re-execute the Search command if you need to find another occurrence of the same text.

If you're in the midst of editing a document and need to assign a number to a new figure or table, the Search command provides a fast way to check the last assigned number. For example, suppose you can't remember whether you've already numbered six tables or seven in a document. Set the *direction* field to *Up,* to cause Word to search backward from your current position in the document. Type *Table* in the *text* field and execute the command. Word will find and select the last instance in which you used the word, allowing you to see the number associated with it. Again, you may want to conduct the search in a separate window, to preserve your location in the document.

Extending the selection

The Search command lets you extend a selection to include all text between your current location and that of a particular word or phrase. If, in the automobile article, you wanted to delete all text between the present location of the selection and the word *diesel,* you would press the F6 key to turn on the extended selection mode, then search for the word *diesel.* Word would jump to the next occurrence of the word, at the same time selecting all text between its former and new positions. If you pressed the Del key, the selection would be removed to the scrap.

Place markers

In Chapter 21, you saw that a window can be opened to hold your place in a document while you work temporarily at a different location. The Search command provides a more versatile alternative that accomplishes much the same thing.

A *single-marker system*

In its simplest form, a place marker can be formed from any character or collection of characters unique to a document. Candidates include @ # $ % & * + = and other symbols, especially in combinations. I use three asterisks (***).

Once a place marker is set, you can scroll freely through your text. When you're ready to return to your original location, move to the top of the document by holding down the Ctrl key and pressing the PgUp key. Then pick the Search command and type *** (or whatever your place marker is) in the text field.

When you execute the Search command, Word moves to the place marker and selects it. And because it is selected, you can remove it immediately by pressing the Del key. If you don't delete it, you can return to it again later by holding down the Shift key and pressing the F4 key to execute the Search command once more.

A *multiple-marker system*

More than one marker can be placed in a document. If all the markers are identical, execute the Search command until you reach the marker you want. If the markers are different, you can return to any of them selectively. And you can have the best of both worlds by creating markers that are identical except for one character. For example, *1* could be your first marker, *2* could be your second, *3* could be your third, and so on. To find marker number 2, search for *2*. To find any or all markers, regardless of the number in them, search for *?*.

If you write fiction, *L* might refer to love scenes and *F* might refer to fight scenes. You could quickly find love scenes by searching for *L*. If you write nonfiction, *C* might be a reminder to check a fact, and *S* could remind you to verify a spelling.

Removing place markers

Before printing you'll probably want to remove all place markers. The fastest way is to use the Replace command, replacing *?* with nothing (in other words, leave the *with text* field blank). If you prefer one last look at each marked passage before removing the markers, use the Search command repeatedly (remember the Shift-F4 shortcut). Specify *?* in the *text* field, and press the Del key as each marker is highlighted.

Moving text to a marker

Another use for a place marker is moving text to a particular position. Perhaps when editing near the end of a document you think of a paragraph you wrote earlier—one that would work better at your present location. Insert a place marker in the text and then scroll or jump through the document to find the desired paragraph. Copy or delete it to the scrap and use the Search command to return to your marker. Now you can replace the marker with the contents of the scrap at one go: Hold down the Shift key and press the Ins key.

Using Search as Replace

Recall from the end of Chapter 20 that the Search command, when used in conjunction with the F3 and Shift-F4 keys, can be used as a slower, but in some cases more powerful, version of the Replace command. It is more powerful because the replacement text can have character or other formatting.

Similarly, you can search for the first instance of text with the Search command, then delete it and type in the replacement text. You can format the replacement, as long as it is done *before* you type it. That is, you can apply the underlining format and then type the text, but you can't type the text and then go back and underline it. If you follow this guideline, you can search for subsequent instances of the text by pressing the Shift-F4 key, and then carry out each replacement by pressing F4—the key that repeats the last editing act.

THE REPLACE COMMAND

You're a novelist and you want to change the name of a character throughout your book. The Replace command will do it for you. Type the old name in the *text* field, the new name in the *with text* field, and execute the command. Or you're an attorney and you've decided to ask $1 million in damages instead of $12,000. Update your documents by typing the old figure in the *text* field and the new figure in the *with text* field. But these are ordinary uses of the Replace command. Now for some exotic ones.

A counting tool

A utility that counts the words in a document comes with Microsoft Spell. It is WC.COM. But what about the times you want to count the words in only a portion of a document? Or you want to count the number of paragraphs in a document? Or you want to know how many times you've used a specific overused phrase, such as "at the present moment"?

The Replace command is the unlikely answer. It makes a fine counting tool because it displays the number of times it replaces one piece of text with another. The trick is to replace the text (or symbols) you wish to count with the *same* text or symbols, by typing identical entries in both the *text* and *with text* fields. Replacing something with itself has no effect on the document, but Word tells you how many substitutions were made.

For example, to count the number of paragraphs in a document, enter the symbol for paragraph marks, $^\wedge p$ (Shift-6, followed by P) in both the *text* and *with text* fields of the Replace command:

```
REPLACE text: ^p                          with text: ^p
```

Set the *confirm* field to *No* to save time, and execute the command. Watch the message line to see how many times the paragraph mark was replaced with itself.

To count elements in a portion of a document, select the desired area before executing the command. Replace operates solely within the selection when the selection includes more than a single character.

Replacing one paragraph mark with another can foul up the paragraph formatting of a document that uses more than one format. For this reason, after you've read the message telling you how many replacements were made, it is wise to use the Undo command immediately to restore the document to its previous condition.

The Replace command hogs computer memory, and you'll often find the *SAVE* indicator coming on (or the *% Free* indicator falling dramatically) after you make an appreciable number of replacements. Saving the document after using the Replace command is a good habit, although unnecessary when only a handful of replacements are made. If you attempt too many replacements at once, Word will flash the message *Insufficient memory* and complete the portion of the replacements that it can. Save the document and execute the Replace command again to make the remaining replacements.

Changing content for formatting purposes

Sometimes you must change the contents of a document before it will work ideally with Word or another program. Often this means changing some or all of the spacing characters in the document. For example, perhaps a document created with a different word processor (or by a less experienced user of Word) has paragraph indentations formed by manually typed spaces. Or large numbers of Spacebar spaces must be removed to condense the characters in a document—as when a table has been created with the Spacebar instead of tab stops. Sometimes, spacing characters of various kinds—including both paragraph marks and tabs—must be removed.

Eliminating extra paragraph marks

If you want to remove an extra paragraph mark from between paragraphs throughout
a document, use the Replace command to change each instance of two successive paragraph
marks ($^\wedge p\,^\wedge p$) to one ($^\wedge p$).

```
REPLACE text: ^p^p                          with text: ^p
```

Indentations

If the first lines of paragraphs have been indented manually with blank spaces (five is
common), you may use the Replace command to change every occurrence of five spacebar
spaces to no space. If there are sets of five spacebar spaces you don't want to remove, you can
replace every occurrence of a paragraph mark followed by five blank spaces to just a paragraph mark. (Replace $^\wedge p$ followed by five Spacebar spaces with $^\wedge p$.) If you wish, you then
can use the Format Paragraph command to put paragraph indentation back into the document, or otherwise correct formatting that may be fouled up by the Replace command.

Spacing characters

It's a little trickier to eliminate variable numbers of excess blank spaces throughout a
document. This need can arise when you're editing a file created with a different word processor or program, or when you're editing a file that has been printed to disk with Word's
Print File command. Such documents may be riddled with long lines of spaces you want to be
rid of. Using the Replace command with the $^\wedge w$ symbol, in combination with other characters, can often solve the problem for you. The $^\wedge w$ symbol represents all kinds of spacing
characters in a document: Spacebar spaces and nonbreaking spaces, tab characters, paragraph
marks, new-line marks, and division marks. Putting $^\wedge w$ in the *text* field lets you remove
everything but printable characters from a document or file.

- ◆ To convert every type of space to a Spacebar space, type $^\wedge w$ in the *text* field and a
  Spacebar space in the *with text* field. This technique is one way to strip out such characters as nonbreaking spaces which may confuse some typesetting and other computer
  systems; the other way is to print the document to a file with the Print File command.

- ◆ To convert every occurrence of more than two Spacebar spaces into a tab character,
  type two Spacebar spaces followed by $^\wedge w$ in the *text* field, and type $^\wedge t$ in the *with text*
  field. This is useful when you are changing a table created with Spacebar spaces to one
  created with tab characters and tab formatting.

- ◆ Some database and other programs write files that contain unwanted lines of blank
  spaces preceding a quotation mark. This happens when a field enclosed in quotation
  marks has a set length, but there isn't enough text to fill the field. To eliminate these
  spaces, type $^\wedge w$" in the *text* field and " in the *with text* field.

Multiple-step replacements

The Replace command becomes more powerful when you use it for multiple passes
over a document. Make a game of coming up with an effective combination of replacements.
For example, if you have a document from which you wish to remove nonbreaking spaces, tab

characters, new-line marks, and division marks, but in which you want to maintain paragraph marks, you can use the Replace command several times:

1. Temporarily replace existing paragraph marks ($^\wedge p$) with a special symbol not used elsewhere in the document. In this example, the symbol is @!@. (This causes paragraph formatting information to be lost, but presumably if you're doing major surgery on your document you plan to format it later anyway.)

   ```
   REPLACE text: ^p                          with text: @!@
   ```

2. Next, replace all spacing characters in the document ($^\wedge w$) with a normal Spacebar space.

   ```
   REPLACE text: ^w                          with text: ▮
   ```

3. Finally, replace the special symbol (@!@) with paragraph marks ($^\wedge p$) to complete the transformation of the document.

   ```
   REPLACE text: @!@                          with text: ^p
   ```

Because the letter *Q* is virtually always followed by the letter *U*, when *Q* is paired with a different letter, it is valuable. For instance, you could replace each paragraph mark with the letters *QP*, and later replace *QP* with paragraph marks again. If you used another pair of letters, such as *AP* or *bp*, you'd risk the possibility that the letter pairs would appear naturally in your document, and would be replaced with paragraph marks; for example, *AP*PLE, sub*p*lot . . .

For practice with multiple replacements, make a passage tipsy, as in the opening of this chapter, by changing each *s* to an *sh*. Change it back and then tackle this puzzle: In some cases an *s* shouldn't be changed to an *sh*, for instance, when it precedes a *t* or is the second of two consecutive *s*'s. You might decide that an *s* at the beginning of a word shouldn't be changed to *sh*, either. How can you avoid these special cases?

The solution

Here is a solution. Follow these steps: (1) Replace each instance of a space followed by an *s* with a special character, such as @; (2) replace each instance of *st* with a different symbol, such as #; (3) replace each instance of *ss* with *s*; (4) replace each instance of *s* with *sh*; and finally, (5) return the special characters to their previous values (@ back to space-*s* and # back to *st*). You can refine step 1 by changing the space-*s* combination to two different special characters—one for use when the letter is uppercase, and one for use when it is lowercase. If you do this, refine step 5 correspondingly.

Power Tools: Merge

A few facts before we get on with the fun:

♦ Word's Merge feature allows you to create documents with contents that vary automatically by recipient and circumstance. In other words, it lets you create individualized form letters.

♦ Merge has the ability to use "conditionals." That is, it can decide on a copy-by-copy basis whether or not to include a particular message, word, or number in a document. Use conditionals thoughtfully, and you can produce a series of letters each so well tailored to its recipient that it's unlikely anyone would suspect them of a common origin.

♦ Merge can ask you for information until it knows enough to put a letter together and print it.

But let's not get bogged down in abstractions. The way to understand and learn Merge is to see it in action.

THE SCENE

You are Sarah Torayo, a professional photographer living in Seattle, Washington. Your work frequently appears in *Photo Fiesta* magazine. Most weeks you receive several letters from people who wish to purchase a color print of one photograph or another. You used to spend an afternoon each week typing replies and quoting prices. Soon you knew most paragraphs by heart.

Then you bought a computer and an elementary word processor, and your work was cut in half. You could use the same letter over and over in different forms, changing the name and address of the recipient, and the title and purchase price of the photograph. When quoting a price of more than $150, you'd add a sentence offering a smaller, less expensive print. If the potential customer lived in Washington State, you'd include your phone number and a suggestion that he or she stop by your studio. If the person lived elsewhere, you'd include only a vague invitation. Often, but not always, you'd add a personal comment. So even with a word processor, it was still a fair amount of work.

Then you discovered Word and its Merge feature. Today, your correspondence takes a few minutes a week. You write a few letters while watching television. You knock out a few more during a brief break from writing a photography textbook.

Merge in action

One day, you answer four letters while a friend watches.

Your first reply is to Thelma Matlow, who lives in San Francisco. To begin, you load an all-purpose reply letter called LETTER.DOC. Then, you execute the Print Merge command, and a moment later Word begins to request information, which you provide item by item, by typing a response in the *VALUE* field and pressing the Enter key.

First, Word asks you to *Enter today's date.* You type *March 27, 1987.*

```
SP »     《SET DATE=? Enter today's date¶
SP       《ASK TITLE=? Mr., Mrs., Ms., Miss or Dr.?¶
SP       《ASK FIRST=? Enter recipient's first name¶
SP       《ASK LAST=? Enter recipient's last name¶
SP       《ASK STREET=? Enter recipient's street address¶
SP       《ASK CITY=? Enter recipient's city¶
SP       《ASK STATE=? Enter recipient's two-letter abbreviation¶
SP       《ASK ZIP=? Enter recipient's zip code¶
SP       《ASK PHOTO=? Which photo does 《TITLE》 《LAST》 want?¶
```

```
VALUE: March 27, 1987█

Enter today's date
Page 1   {}                              ?          Microsoft Word: LETTER.DOC
```

Word moves to the next request:

```
VALUE: █

Mr., Mrs., Ms., Miss or Dr.?
Page 1   {}                              ?          Microsoft Word: LETTER.DOC
```

After you've typed *Ms.,* Word moves to the next question listed on the screen . . . and the next. Once the basics are taken care of, your friend sees Word even begin to personalize the questions it asks:

```
VALUE: █

Which photo does Ms. Matlow want?
Page 1   {}                              ?          Microsoft Word: LETTER.DOC
```

You respond:

```
VALUE: Moonset█
```

Word continues with the next request. You answer again:

```
VALUE: 250█

Enter price of "Moonset"  (no $ please)
Page 1   {}                           ?              Microsoft Word: LETTER.DOC
```

And Word concludes with:

```
VALUE: █

Any personal message for Thelma Matlow?
Page 1   {}                           ?              Microsoft Word: LETTER.DOC
```

You glance again at Ms. Matlow's stationery, with its handpainted picture of unicorns playing frisbee. You say:

```
VALUE: Your letter was quite original!█
```

The message *Formatting page 1* appears, your printer comes to life, and this is the letter it prints:

```
                              March 27, 1987



        Ms. Thelma Matlow
        2111 Kirkham
        San Francisco, CA  94107

        Dear Ms. Matlow:

              I'm pleased you enjoyed my photograph "Moonset" enough
        to want a copy.  Unfortunately, my contract with Photo
        Fiesta doesn't permit me to sell my work in the 12 months
        after publication.  I'd be happy to provide a copy in about
        a year.  The price will be $250 for an unframed, 11-by-14
        color print from the original negative.  An 8-by-10 would be
        somewhat less.

              If this interests you, please write again in several
        months.  In the meantime, if you happen to be in the Seattle
        area, I'll gladly show you some of my other work.

              Your letter was quite original!  Thank you for your
        interest.

                              Sincerely,



                       Sarah Torayo
```

Observe that the recipient's full name, including courtesy title, is in the heading of the letter. Yet, the salutation (*Dear Ms. Matlow*) omits the first name. That's possible because, when it was quizzing you, Word asked for the courtesy title, first name, and last name separately. The name and price of the photograph are included in the body of the letter. The price is more than $150 so, according to your usual practice, the letter mentions a smaller, less expensive print.

The second paragraph contains a polite, but vague, invitation to visit your studio. Since the recipient lives several hundred miles away, the paragraph isn't written in a way that assumes the invitation is likely to be accepted.

The concluding paragraph begins with your personal message.

Now compare this letter with the following three.

The second letter

Your friend watches as you answer Word's inquiries about the next letter. He notices the questions are the same as before, but that the date isn't requested this time. "Does the computer remember the date from the first letter?" he asks. You just grin and type, providing this information:

TITLE	Mr.
FIRST name	Lonnie
LAST name	Blackmore
STREET address	2523 N. Starr, No. 2
CITY	Tacoma
STATE	WA
ZIP code	98403
PHOTO name	House of Cards
PRICE in $	220

You don't want to include a personal message to Mr. Blackmore, so you press the Enter key when Word asks:

Any personal message for Lonnie Blackmore?

Almost immediately, Word begins to print the second letter:

```
                          March 27, 1987


    Mr. Lonnie Blackmore
    2523 N. Starr, No. 2
    Tacoma, WA  98403

    Dear Mr. Blackmore:

        I'm pleased you enjoyed my photograph "House of Cards"
    enough to want a copy.  Unfortunately, my contract with
    Photo Fiesta doesn't permit me to sell my work in the 12
    months after publication.  I'd be happy to provide a copy in
    about a year.  The price will be $220 for an unframed, 11-
    by-14 color print from the original negative.  An 8-by-10
    would be somewhat less.

        Perhaps there is another photograph you'd like as well
    as "House of Cards."  We could meet sometime if you're in
    downtown Seattle.  I can be reached at 555-8374.

        Thank you for your interest.

                          Sincerely,


                          Sarah Torayo
```

    This letter begins just like the letter to Ms. Matlow, except for the name and address, and the photo's name and price. But note also that this letter is to a resident of Washington State, so the second paragraph both encourages him to visit your studio and offers your telephone number. Word did this tailoring automatically.

The third and fourth letters

    The third letter is created like the preceding two. You provide this:

TITLE	Mr.
FIRST name	Will
LAST name	Gyles
STREET address	Tamiami Trail South
CITY	Sarasota
STATE	FL
ZIP code	33581
PHOTO name	Sky Climber
PRICE in $	125
PERSONAL message	(None)

And Word prints this letter.

```
                              March 27, 1987


        Mr. Will Gyles
        Tamiami Trail South
        Sarasota, FL  33581

        Dear Mr. Gyles:

             I'm pleased you enjoyed my photograph "Sky Climber"
        enough to want a copy.  Unfortunately, my contract with
        Photo Fiesta doesn't permit me to sell my work in the 12
        months after publication.  I'd be happy to provide a copy in
        about a year.  The price will be $125 for an unframed, 11-
        by-14 color print from the original negative.

             If this interests you, please write again in several
        months.  In the meantime, if you happen to be in the Seattle
        area, I'll gladly show you some of my other work.

             Thank you for your interest.

                              Sincerely,


                         Sarah Torayo
```

    Mr. Gyles is a friend of your uncle's, so you've quoted less than your usual price for "Sky Climber." And because the photograph is less than $150, the sentence about smaller, less expensive color prints is not included. Furthermore, since Mr. Gyles is from far-off Florida, only the vague invitation to visit is included.

Your fourth and last letter is a response to Dr. Kris Terminus, who has written to request a copy of "Sky Climber" for his office waiting room. You enter the usual price for this photograph, and add a personal comment:

TITLE	Dr.
FIRST name	Kris
LAST name	Terminus
STREET address	1070 S.E. Taylor
CITY	Port Orchard
STATE	WA
ZIP code	98366
PHOTO name	Sky Climber
PRICE in $	175
PERSONAL message	I think you're right. The photo would look good in a waiting room.

This letter is produced:

```
                                        March 27, 1987



        Dr. Kris Terminus
        1070 S.E. Taylor
        Port Orchard, WA  98366

        Dear Dr. Terminus:

             I'm pleased you enjoyed my photograph "Sky Climber"
        enough to want a copy.  Unfortunately, my contract with
        Photo Fiesta doesn't permit me to sell my work in the 12
        months after publication.  I'd be happy to provide a copy in
        about a year.  The price will be $175 for an unframed, 11-
        by-14 color print from the original negative.  An 8-by-10
        would be somewhat less.

             Perhaps there is another photograph you'd like as well
        as "Sky Climber."  We could meet sometime if you're in
        downtown Seattle.  I can be reached at 555-8374.

             I think you're right.  The photo would look good in a
        waiting room.  Thank you for your interest.

                                        Sincerely,


                            Sarah Torayo
```

Because "Sky Climber" is priced at more than $150, this letter mentions the availability of a smaller, less expensive copy. The letter also contains the invitation to Washington residents, and the personal message.

When this letter is completed, you press the Esc key twice to cancel the Print Merge command. You spent only a few minutes creating the four letters, and all you did was answer some questions. Your friend has watched in silence, but now he bursts forth: "How do you make Word do that?"

THE SECRET REVEALED

It is a two-step process. First you create a master document, which includes instructions and conditionals that actually make your document a simple program. Then, to print letters, you use the Print Merge command. In this case, the master document LETTER.DOC looks like this on the screen:

«SET DATE=? Enter today's date¶[1]

«ASK TITLE=? Mr., Mrs., Ms., Miss or Dr.?¶[2]

«ASK FIRST=? Enter recipient's first name¶

«ASK LAST=? Enter recipient's last name¶

«ASK STREET=? Enter recipient's street address¶

«ASK CITY=? Enter recipient's city¶

«ASK STATE=? Enter recipient's two-letter abbreviation¶

«ASK ZIP=? Enter recipient's zip code¶

«ASK PHOTO=? Which photo does «TITLE» «LAST» want?¶[3]

«ASK PRICE=? Enter price of "«PHOTO»" (no $ please)¶[4]

«ASK PERSONAL=? Any personal message for «FIRST»
«LAST»?¶
¶

                              «DATE»¶[5]

¶
¶
«TITLE» «FIRST» «LAST»¶[6]
«STREET»¶[7]
«CITY», «STATE» «ZIP»¶[8]

Dear «TITLE» «LAST»: ¶[9]

    I'm pleased you enjoyed my photograph "«PHOTO»" enough[10]
to want a copy. Unfortunately, my contract with Photo
Fiesta doesn't permit me to sell my work in the 12 months
after publication. I'd be happy to provide a copy in about
a year. The price will be $«PRICE» for an unframed, 11-by-
14 color print from the original negative. «IF PRICE>150» An[11]
8-by-10 would be somewhat less. «ENDIF»¶

    «IF STATE="WA"»Perhaps there is another photograph[12]
you'd like as well as "«PHOTO». We could meet sometime if
you're in downtown Seattle. I can be reached at 555-
8374.«ELSE»If this interests you, please write again in
several months. In the meantime, if you happen to be in the
Seattle area, I'll gladly show you some of my other
work.«ENDIF»¶

    «IF PERSONAL»«PERSONAL» «ENDIF»Thank you for your[13]
interest.¶

                    Sincerely, ¶

                    Sarah Torayo¶

Creating the master document

The first 11 paragraphs in LETTER.DOC are SET and ASK instructions that, when you execute the Print Merge command, tell Word to request from you the information it needs in order to personalize the letter. In LETTER.DOC, as in all Merge master documents, special markers (technically known as *merge delimiter characters*) are embedded in the document. You create these markers by pressing the Control-[key combination for the left marker («) and the Control-] key combination for the right marker (»). A paragraph mark can be used instead of a right marker, but a left marker must always precede an instruction.

When the Print Merge command is executed, Word carries out the instructions inside the markers as it encounters them in the document. Often an instruction tells Word to draw on a pool of information and use it in some way during printing. In our example, the information is assembled individually for each letter when you answer the program's inquiries about such things as the name and address of the letter's recipient. But, as we'll see later, it's also possible to give Word information in advance for a whole series of letters.

Let's go through LETTER.DOC a step at a time. The first four numbered explanations refer to the SET and ASK instructions at the beginning of the master document, while references 5 through 13 are to parts of the letter that are printed.

SET and ASK instructions in LETTER.DOC

1. *«SET DATE = ? Enter today's date¶*. The SET instruction lets you enter information that applies to a series of documents. In this case, the SET command instructs Word to ask you for text, and it instructs Word to assign the name DATE to the text.

The phrase *Enter today's date* between the question mark and the right marker (in this case, the paragraph mark rather than the delimiter) causes Word to display that message when it asks for the date. (Look at the first example in this chapter.)

The instruction could be simplified to «SET DATE = ?» or «SET DATE = ?¶, but then Word's only message to you would be the less informative *Enter text*. (The reserved glossary name *dateprint*, available beginning with Word 3.0, would be an even easier way to include the correct date. However, it would teach you nothing about Merge.)

2. *«ASK TITLE = ? Mr., Mrs., Ms., Miss, or Dr.?¶*. The ASK instruction is identical to the SET command in all respects except that it causes Word to make the inquiry prior to each printing of a letter. In this case, it directs Word to ask you for the courtesy title to be used with the name of the recipient of the particular letter. The optional message here is *Mr., Mrs., Ms., Miss, or Dr.?*, but it could as easily be *Enter courtesy title,* or any other appropriate reminder. When using Print Merge to create an actual form letter, you aren't limited to the choices offered in the message. It is a helpful reminder, not a menu, so Word will accept Rev. or Lt. as readily as it accepts Mr. or Ms.

The ASK instructions requesting name, address, city, state, and zip code are identical in form to the TITLE instruction. Again, any of these instructions can end in a right marker or a paragraph mark.

3. *«ASK PHOTO = ? Which photo does «TITLE» «LAST» want?»¶*. The message of this ASK instruction differs from the preceding ones, because it refers to information you supplied in response to earlier ASK instructions. When the message appears at the bottom of the screen, the entries «TITLE» and «LAST» are replaced by your earlier responses to the respective ASK instructions. Similarly, the message in the final ASK instruction (do you want a personal message in the letter?) uses the «FIRST» and «LAST» values established by earlier ASK instructions.

4. *«ASK PRICE = ? Enter price of "«PHOTO»"» (no $ please)¶*. The message of this ASK instruction reminds you not to type a dollar sign as part of the price. The dollar sign already appears in the body of the document, so if you type it here, the price in your document will be preceded by two dollar signs, like this: $$250. Furthermore, a conditional instruction in LETTER.DOC asks Word to compare the value of «PRICE» with the number 150. If you type $250 instead of 250 when you establish the value of «PRICE», Word becomes confused because you've given it more than just a number.

Avoiding unwanted line spacing

Before we examine the printable part of LETTER.DOC, let's look again at its SET and ASK instructions. Each concludes with a paragraph mark (¶), rather than a right marker (»). This maintains the proper vertical spacing of the document. If, instead, both the right marker and the paragraph mark ended each instruction, the Print Merge command would print a blank line or lines of paragraph space for each.

If you want to use right markers in SET and ASK instructions, there are two other ways to ensure that the instructions aren't treated as printable paragraphs. The first is to leave each instruction a separate paragraph, but use the Format Paragraph command to set the *line spacing*, *space before*, and *space after* fields to 0 for each. The second method is to run all the instructions into a single paragraph, like this:

```
«SET DATE=? Enter today's date»«ASK TITLE=? Mr., Mrs., Ms.,
Miss, or Dr.?»«ASK FIRST=? Enter recipient's first name»«ASK
LAST=? Enter recipient's last name»«ASK STREET=? Enter
recipient's street address»«ASK CITY=? Enter recipient's
city»«ASK STATE=? Enter recipient's two-letter state
abbreviation»«ASK ZIP=? Enter recipient's zip code»«ASK
PHOTO=? Which photo does «TITLE» «LAST» want?»«ASK PRICE=?
Enter price of "«PHOTO»" (no $ please)»«ASK PERSONAL=? Any
personal message for «FIRST» «LAST»?¶
```

The document proper

The remainder of LETTER.DOC is the part we normally think of as the letter. It's the part that is printed.

5. *«DATE»¶*. Whatever you typed for DATE in the SET instruction will be printed at this location. DATE is called a *field*. Word replaces any field with its current value when merge printing.

In this case both a right marker and a paragraph mark are used. The right marker signifies the end of the field, and the paragraph mark, because it is formatted conventionally, tells Word to treat the preceding text as a conventional paragraph, with line spacing.

6. *«TITLE» «FIRST» «LAST»¶*. These fields follow the form of the preceding example. The space separating each of the fields provides a space between the words when they print. You want *Ms. Thelma Matlow,* not *Ms.ThelmaMatlow.*

7. *«STREET»¶*. Though part of the address, this follows the form of «DATE».

8. *«CITY», «STATE»   «ZIP»¶*. Note the comma after the right marker of CITY. Note also that there are two spaces before «ZIP» because two spaces generally separate the name or abbreviation off a state and a zip code.

9. *Dear «TITLE» «LAST»:¶*. For the first time, we see text that will not change from letter to letter. *Dear* is a permanent part of the document, but the courtesy title and last name are variable.

10. *"«PHOTO»"*. The field PHOTO will print as whatever value you gave in reply to the ASK instruction requesting the photograph name. The quotation marks are outside the markers because you want the name of the photograph to be enclosed in quotation marks: "Moonset." The item *$«PRICE»* is a similar situation.

11. *«IF PRICE>150» An 8-by-10 would be somewhat less. «ENDIF»*. This is your first encounter with a conditional statement. It causes everything between the «IF» and «ENDIF» statements to be printed if the condition expressed by the «IF» statement is true. In this case, if PRICE is greater than 150, Word prints *An 8-by-10 would be somewhat less.*

The comparison here is "greater than," expressed with this symbol: >. Word also accepts "less than," expressed with <, and "equals," expressed with = .

12. *«IF STATE = "WA"»Perhaps . . . «ELSE»If this interests you . . . «ENDIF»*. The «ELSE» statement extends the power of conditionals. If the condition expressed by the «IF» statement is true, then everything between the «IF» and «ELSE» statements is printed. If the condition isn't true, everything between the «ELSE» and «ENDIF» statements is printed instead.

In the example, if STATE is "WA", Word includes the three sentences encouraging a visit and extending a telephone number. Otherwise, it includes the statement *If this interests you . . . other work.*

The «IF» statement requires quotation marks around specific text to which a field is compared. That's why "WA" is in quotation marks. If the quotation marks are missing, Word assumes the text is supposed to be a number, and gives the error message *Not a valid number*—both on-screen and on the printout.

13. *«IF PERSONAL»«PERSONAL»«ENDIF»*. This is a third variation of the conditional statement. When an «IF» statement contains a field name, such as «IF PERSONAL», Word interprets the statement as: "If a value has been assigned to the field, then this statement is true."

In this case, Word looks to see if you typed a personal message. If you did—even if all you typed was a blank space—the «IF PERSONAL» statement is considered true. But if you pressed the Enter key without typing anything, the «IF PERSONAL» statement is considered false.

When the statement is true, Word prints everything between the «IF» and «ENDIF» statements. In this example, it types the value of «PERSONAL», plus the two blank spaces preceding «ENDIF». (The spaces separate the PERSONAL message from the final sentence.)

When the «IF PERSONAL» statement is false, Word skips to whatever text follows «ENDIF».

You could add an «ELSE» statement to the paragraph: *IF PERSONAL»«PERSONAL »«ELSE» Thank you for your interest.«ENDIF»*. In this case, the sentence *Thank you for your interest.* would print only if you hadn't typed a personal message when Word asked for one in the preliminary instructions.

You can type LETTER.DOC as a Word document and experiment with it, if you like. Once you understand it, you'll grasp all the essentials of constructing documents with conditionals. But Merge has other features and possibilities, too.

MERGING DATA FROM A LIST

The good news: One of your photographs is so popular you're getting dozens of requests for it. The bad news: You have to answer the mail. Is there an even faster way than SET and ASK instructions to give Word the information it needs to create "personal" replies?

There is.

The data file

You can set up a separate document as a data file containing the information to be merged into the master documment. You don't need SET and ASK instructions at all with this method, although they can still be used to supplement information from a data file. This is how a data file would look for the four letters created with SET and ASK statements:

```
TITLE,FIRST,LAST,STREET,CITY,STATE,ZIP,PHOTO,PRICE,PERSONAL¶

Ms.,Thelma,Matlow,2111 Kirkham,San
Francisco,CA,94107,Moonset,250,Your letter was quite
original!"¶

Mr.,Lonnie,Blackmore,"2523 N. Starr, No.
2",Tacoma,WA,98043,House of Cards,220,¶

Mr.,Will,Giles,Tamiami Trail South,Sarasota,FL,33581,Sky
Climber,125,¶

Dr.,Kris,Terminus,1070 S.E. Taylor,Port Orchard,WA,98366,Sky
Climber,175,I think you're right.  The photo would look good
in a waiting room.¶
```

We'll call this data file MAILLIST.DOC. (The spaces between the paragraphs in the example were created by paragraph formatting and exist only for ease of reading. They are *not* the result of extra paragraph marks between paragraphs.)

Each paragraph of a data file (except the first) is a record. There is one record per document. A record is made up of fields. Each field provides information much as your earlier responses to the SET and ASK inquiries did: name, address, price, personal messages, and the like. In the sample data file MAILLIST.DOC, each field is separated from the others by commas, but you can also separate fields with tab characters, so that your data entries are laid out in neat columns.

The first paragraph in the data file is a *header paragraph*. It establishes an order for information that every subsequent paragraph (record) must follow. In MAILLIST.DOC, the header paragraph tells Word that the first field in each record will be TITLE, the next FIRST, the next LAST, and so on, through PERSONAL. You can include up to 256 fields in a header paragraph, provided that the same number of fields exists within each of the subsequent records.

If Merge doesn't seem to work properly, and especially if you're getting the error messages *Unknown field name, Too many fields in data record,* or *Too few fields in data record,* double-check and make sure that the number and order of fields in every record match the number and order of the fields in the header paragraph. If there is a field for which you have no entry, put an extra comma or tab character in to mark its place. You will notice that MAILLIST.DOC includes extra commas at the ends of the records of both Lonnie Blackmore and Will Gyles. Neither person is to receive a personal message, so for each the PERSONAL field is marked by a comma.

If you don't insert these commas or tab characters, you'll have too few fields in the record and Word won't know which field is which. Merge is very powerful—and very unforgiving. You must get everything just right before it will work.

Notice, too, that the record for Lonnie Blackmore has the STREET field in quotation marks. That's because the content of the field includes a comma, and Word must be told that this comma is part of the entry rather than a dividing point between fields. Quotation marks are needed around a field whenever it contains a comma, tab character, or quotation mark. To avoid possible oversights, you can routinely enclose all fields in quotation marks. It's a conservative, but all-encompassing practice. (See the example of this in the "Database Programs" section at the end of this chapter.)

A simple database

There is one advantage to using tab characters rather than commas to mark the borders between fields in a data file. It allows the data to be viewed as a table, in which all telephone numbers, for instance, are in the same column. This permits you to use Word's Column Select mode to rearrange or delete fields from all data records at once. It also allows you to use the Library Autosort command to sort the order of the records. In a sense, Word becomes a simple database program. For this to work, however, the paragraphs containing the records all have to be formatted with the same tab stops (a style sheet works well in this regard). Make the distance between tab stops greater than the width of the contents in the respective fields. To do this, you may have to set the Format Division Margins command's *width* field to a large value (22″ is the largest possible) and scroll horizontally to see all your data. If 22 inches is not enough, try formatting the characters for a very small font size, to get more on the line.

The master document

This is how the beginning of our master document looks when modified to work with the data file MAILLIST.DOC:

```
»        «DATA MAILLIST.DOC¶
         «SET DATE=? Enter today's date¶
    ¶

                              «DATE»¶

    ¶
    ¶
«TITLE» «FIRST» «LAST»¶
«STREET»¶
«CITY», «STATE»  «ZIP»¶

Dear «TITLE» «LAST»: ¶

         I'm pleased you enjoyed my photograph "«PHOTO»" enough
to want a copy. Unfortunately, my contract with Photo
Fiesta doesn't permit me to sell my work in the 12 months
after publication. I'd be happy to provide a copy in about
a year. The price will be $«PRICE» for an unframed, 11-by-
14 color print from the original negative. «IF PRICE>150» An
```

Page 1   {¶}   ?   Microsoft Word: LETTER.DOC

Observe that the master document is largely identical to the earlier version, but the ASK instructions are gone and a DATA statement is at the beginning of the document. When you are using a data file, the DATA statement must be the first entry—not even a blank space or a blank line can precede it. If anything comes before it, you get the error message *DATA after SET or ASK*. The form of the DATA statement is:

«DATA *DATAFILE.DOC*»¶

where DATAFILE.DOC represents the name of the data file. Omit the right marker if you want the printer to omit the line spacing associated with the paragraph mark.

A header paragraph can be a document by itself, if you find that's more convenient than having it at the top of the data file. The header paragraph could be a document called MAILHEAD.DOC with this content:

TITLE,FIRST,LAST,STREET,CITY,STATE,ZIP,PHOTO,PRICE,PERSONAL

In this case, you would modify the DATA statement at the top of the document to show the name of the header document, and then the name of the data file:

«DATA MAILHEAD.DOC,MAILLIST.DOC»¶

The instruction «*SET DATE = ? Enter today's date*» was preserved in the data-file version of the document because it's convenient to type the date upon executing the Print Merge command. However, the instruction could be omitted and the date typed into the master document as regular text, or the SET instruction could be included in this self-contained form:

```
 »       «DATA MAILLIST.DOC¶
         «SET DATE=March 27, 1987¶
     ¶

                              «DATE»¶

     ¶
«TITLE» «FIRST» «LAST»¶
«STREET»¶
«CITY», «STATE»  «ZIP»¶
```

Regardless of which method is used to supply data for form letters—ASK and SET statements or a data file—the printed result is the same.

NOTE: If you've set the decimal character to a comma with the Options command, use a semicolon rather than a comma to separate entries in a data file or DATA statement.

TIPS ON USING MERGE

Some of the following tips will be more valuable than others, but as you become adept with Merge you'll probably find reason to use most of them at some time. These tips range from explanations of the lesser known, simple merge instructions «NEXT» and «INCLUDE» to suggestions on how to maximize Word's performance. The chapter concludes with notes on using Merge with several popular database programs.

Y/N inquiries

ASK statements can be used to inquire whether you want a particular passage included in a specific letter. Imagine that you're sick of a mailbox stuffed with other people's form letters. You decide to reply to the junk mail with a personalized form letter of your own. Since you're particularly incensed by sweepstakes that never manage to get *you* rich quick, you include the ASK instruction:

«ASK SWEEP = ? Do you want the sweepstakes sentence included? (Y/N)»

and, in the document, you place the conditional statement:

*«IF SWEEP = "Y"»I thought I'd already seen the worst sweepstakes offer, until
I saw yours.«ENDIF»*

The missing comparison: Does not equal

As already noted, Word allows three kinds of comparisons in conditional statements: "greater than," expressed with >, "less than," expressed with <, and "equals," expressed with = . A fourth comparison, "does not equal," is useful when you want to print a passage only on the condition that something isn't true.

Word doesn't recognize the "does not equal" comparison, but you can accomplish the same thing by using an equals comparison followed immediately by an ELSE statement. Place the conditional text after the ELSE statement and conclude it with an ENDIF statement. Returning to our example earlier in the chapter, if you want to include the sentence *I've charged other people $100 for this photo,* but you only want to include it when you're not charging $100 this time, you could include the instruction: «IF PRICE=100»«ELSE» I've charged other people $100 for this photo.«ENDIF» The technique compares numbers or letters.

Mailing labels and the «NEXT» instruction

Mailing labels can be produced easily with Merge and a mailing list. The method varies slightly depending on whether you're using single-width labels or multiple-column (often three-across) labels. Either way, use the Format Division Margins command to set the top and bottom margins to 0 and the page length to 1 inch (or whatever the length of a single label happens to be). Then:

- ♦ If the labels are single-width, create a three-, four-, or five-line document containing the field names for the labels. Put the name of the mailing-list file in a data field at the beginning of the document, on the same line as the recipient's name field. The document might look like this:

```
‖ «DATA MAILLIST.DOC»«TITLE» «FIRST» «LAST»¶                    ‖
‖ «STREET»¶                                                     ‖
‖ «CITY», «STATE»  «ZIP»¶                                       ‖
```

- ♦ If the labels are multiple-column, set the Format Division Layout command's *# of cols* field to match, and repeat the name and address fields (but not the DATA statement) an appropriate number of times. For example, if the labels come on sheets three across, your document looks like this:

```
‖ «DATA MAILLIST.DOC»«TITLE» «FIRST» «LAST»¶                    ‖
‖ «STREET»¶                                                     ‖
‖ «CITY», «STATE»  «ZIP»¶                                       ‖
‖ «NEXT»¶                                                       ‖
‖ «TITLE» «FIRST» «LAST»¶                                       ‖
‖ «STREET»¶                                                     ‖
‖ «CITY» «STATE»  «ZIP»¶                                        ‖
‖ «NEXT»¶                                                       ‖
‖ «TITLE» «FIRST» «LAST»¶                                       ‖
‖ «STREET»¶                                                     ‖
‖ «CITY» «STATE»  «ZIP»¶                                        ‖
```

The «NEXT» statements after the first and second addresses tell Word to continue printing the same document (in this case, a three-column, 1-inch label) but to skip to the next record in the data file (mailing list). Without the «NEXT» statement, Word would not know what to print after the first of the three labels.

You may have to experiment somewhat with the right and left division margins until you get the placement you want. With labels that are several columns to a sheet, you may have to adjust the *space between* columns field, too, to make sure the addresses are not printed too far to the left or right on the labels. Once you've found the settings you want, save them on disk.

Paths and data instructions

If a data file is on a different drive or in a different subdirectory, include the drive letter path name in the data instruction that begins the main document. For instance: *«DATA B:MAILLIST.DOC»* or *«DATA PHOTOS\MAILLIST.DOC»*.

Powerful and easy: The «INCLUDE» instruction

The «INCLUDE» instruction causes an entire document on disk to be inserted at the location of the statement. You can store often-used paragraphs as individual documents and insert them into any document with «INCLUDE». You can also combine «INCLUDE» instructions with «IF»-«ELSE»-«ENDIF» statements, causing passages to be printed only under certain conditions. You can even print the chapters of a book or report in proper order by creating a short document that is nothing more than a series of «INCLUDE» instructions and chapter titles:

```
«INCLUDE INTRO.DOC¶
«INCLUDE CHAPTER1.DOC¶
«INCLUDE CHAPTER2.DOC¶
«INCLUDE CHAPTER3.DOC¶
```

The Print Merge command would cause the chapters to be printed in order, repaginating as it went. (Whether the numbering would restart with each chapter would depend on how you set the Format Division Page-numbers command's *numbering* and *at* fields.)

Character formatting

Text inserted from a data file or established with a SET or ASK statement has the same character formatting as the first character of the field name. If, using this chapter's earlier example, we always want the price of the photograph to be underlined, we would underline the first character of the field name «PRICE» in the document. You can format the characters of the whole field name if you prefer, but the only letter that matters is the first one.

Don't, however, confuse character formatting with upper- and lowercase, unless it is the uppercase created with the Format Character command's *uppercase* field. Field names and merge statements enclosed in left and right markers can be any combination of uppercase and lowercase. I've used uppercase throughout this chapter for clarity.

Paragraph marks and formatting

If a paragraph mark that is enclosed in quotation marks in a data-file field is merged into a document, the paragraph mark's formatting is, too. This can be a rude surprise when you print. Possible solutions:

♦ Format your data file and document identically. Or,

♦ Use the same style sheet and styles for both the document and the data file during the execution of the Print Merge command, but use other style sheets (if desired) during the writing and editing of your document and data file.

♦ Avoid merging paragraph marks into your document by deleting them from your data file when they are within fields (in other words, inside quotation marks). Place appropriately formatted paragraph marks in your master document, instead.

Merging quotation marks

When you want to merge quotation marks from a data file into a document, double them: *"He was ""honorably"" discharged."* Whenever the quoted word or phrase is the first or last in a field, it must have a triple quotation mark: *"The discharge was ""honorable."""*

Optional address lines

Some of the people to whom you address letters have business titles; others don't. Some use a company name in their address; others do not. Some have one-line street addresses; others have two. How can you vary the number of lines in an inside address without leaving unintended blank lines?

One solution is to make the name and address a single field. The drawback is that individual elements, such as first name or city, aren't available as discrete elements for other uses in the Merge document.

The elegant solution is to include conditional statements that allow additional lines only if they are needed. Study the following example. It handles everything automatically by using «IF» statements and fields named *BUSINESS TITLE, COMPANY, ADDR1* and *ADDR2* in addition to the fields used in this chapter's main example. (*ADDR1* replaces the earlier example's *STREET* field). When a particular letter is being merged and no value has been assigned to *BUSINESS TITLE, COMPANY,* or *ADDR2*, the line on which that element would appear is omitted:

```
«TITLE» «FIRST» «LAST»¶
«IF BUSINESS TITLE»«BUSINESS TITLE»¶
«ENDIF»«IF COMPANY»«COMPANY»¶
«ENDIF»«ADDR1»¶
«IF ADDR2»«ADDR2»¶
«ENDIF»«CITY», «STATE»  «ZIP»¶
```

You don't need to understand the example in order to use it as a model, but here's an explanation of why it works. Take the *BUSINESS TITLE* field as an example. If there is a business title, Word prints it, followed by a paragraph mark, just as if the title had been typed there. But if, for a particular letter, no information has been provided for the *BUSINESS TITLE* field, everything up to the «ENDIF» on the next line is omitted—including the paragraph mark, which means the line doesn't print at all, not even as a blank.

Printing records selectively

If you only want to print form letters corresponding to certain records in a data document, include an «IF» statement as the second paragraph in your main document (the paragraph immediately after the DATA instruction). The statement *«IF TITLE = "Mr."»«NEXT»«ENDIF¶* causes Word to print a letter only if the person isn't a "Mr." Note that there is no » after the ENDIF.

Using Merge with windows

Consider opening one window for your master document and another for your data file. This is useful when you're trying to find the cause of error messages, or if you want to see the data while you write the master document.

An entirely different use of two windows with the Merge command is to keep an often-used master document in a small window on a more or less continuous basis. You can work on other projects in other windows, and whenever you want to print out a few form letters, use the F1 key to select the window containing the master document, and then execute the Print Merge command. This works best if you use SET and ASK instructions exclusively, rather than a data file. If you use a data file, revise either the «DATA» statement or the contents of the file before you use Print Merge. Otherwise, you'll create the same form letters over and over, because Merge starts at the top of the data file each time you execute Print Merge.

Unless you want to see it, the data file needn't be displayed on the screen at all. It does, of course, have to be on the disk.

Preventing unacceptable line and page breaks

When you merge information into a document, it is often impossible to tell in advance where a line or a page will break for a particular printed document. Before a normal document is printed you have an opportunity to preview the layout and pagination. Not so with merged printing, because even the number of pages can change in different printings of a master document. This needn't present a problem, however, if you take preventive measures.

Use the Format Paragraph command's *keep together* and *keep follow* fields to ensure that paragraphs never break across pages at places you find unacceptable. Also, you can use the Library Hyphenate command generously on the document and the data file, if there is a data file. By hyphenating a document at various margin settings (to allow for different line breaks in different printings) you'll force numerous optional hyphens into it. These hyphens won't print unless they're needed to balance the number of characters in a line.

Keeping a file copy

Unlike a document printed with the Print Printer command, a document printed with Print Merge cannot exist on disk except in its component parts, the master document and the data file. By setting the Print Options command's *copies* field to 2, you can print an extra copy of your letters to keep on file.

Nesting conditionals

Various conditional statements can be nested inside each other. Imagine the variety you can give your documents by nesting one IF statement within another—and maybe even tossing in an «INCLUDE» statement or two.

Let's say you award bonus points to your customers and want to write them letters listing the prizes for which they're already eligible. They get different prizes depending on whether they've accumulated 10 points, 25 points, 50 points, or 100 points. Assume the number of points is called «POINTS» in your master document, and the lists of prizes are kept on disk in separate documents called 10PTS.DOC, 25PTS.DOC, 50PTS.DOC, and 100PTS.DOC. This set of nested conditionals in the master document causes each letter to print with a list of prizes appropriate to the recipient:

```
«IF POINTS>49»«IF POINTS>99»«INCLUDE
100PTS.DOC»«ELSE»«INCLUDE 50PTS.DOC»«ENDIF»«ELSE»«IF
POINTS>24»«INCLUDE 25PTS.DOC»«ELSE»«IF POINTS>9»«INCLUDE
10PTS.DOC»«ELSE»You begin to qualify for prizes when you
reach 10 points. So far, you have «POINTS»
points.«ENDIF»«ENDIF»«ENDIF»¶
```

It looks confusing, and it is. But it could save you a phenomenal amount of typing. The logic of it may be clearer to you in this form:

IF points are greater than 49, do this:
    IF points are greater than 99, do this:
       Include 100PTS.DOC
    ELSE (points are not greater than 99), do this:
       Include 50PTS.DOC
    ENDIF
ELSE (points are not greater than 49), do this:
    IF points are greater than 24, do this:
       Include 25PTS.DOC
    ELSE (points are not greater than 24), do this:
       IF points are greater than 9), do this:
          Include 10.PTS.DOC
       ELSE (points are not greater than 9, do this:
          Print the sentence: "You begin to qualify for prizes when
          you reach 10 points. So far, you have __ points."
       ENDIF
    ENDIF
ENDIF

If you want to derive the maximum power and flexibility from Merge, experiment with complex nested statements. A letter can be made to take entirely different directions depending on the recipient's gender (measured by courtesy title), place of residence, income, or other information in a data file or supplied through SET and ASK instructions.

Creating a data file manually

If you type in a data file by hand rather than by using a database program, here's a tip that can save time and trouble. Type the header paragraph, and then copy it into the scrap. Insert it into the document as many times (or more) as you will have records in the data file. Then use the F8 key to move forward a word at time through the copies of the paragraph. Each time a word is highlighted, press the Del key and replace the generic name for the field with the actual information you want in that field of the particular record. If you enter no information into a field, this technique (properly) leaves the needed extra comma.

Also, as noted previously, using tab characters instead of commas will let you sort a data file in various ways using the Library Autosort command in conjunction with Word's column-selection capabilities.

DATABASE PROGRAMS

Word's Merge facility can use mailing lists or other ASCII files from many database and filing programs. Word's Merge feature and WordStar's MailMerge use the same format for records (although the heading paragraph in MailMerge is different). So if a program says it creates mailing lists for use with WordStar, it works with Word, too.

Preparing mailing lists for merging

Most database programs can be instructed—or tricked—into creating a data file perfect for use with Merge. The goal is to produce a series of records separated by paragraph marks, in which all fields within a record are separated by commas. Database programs typically "export" data files with quotation marks around the fields, but with the commas outside the marks, like this:

```
"Ms.","Thelma","Matlow","2111 Kirkham","San
Francisco","CA","94107","Moonset","250","Your letter was
quite original!"¶

"Mr.","Lonnie","Blackmore","2523 N. Starr, No.
2","Tacoma","WA","98403","House of Cards","220",¶
```

And as you saw in the section "The data file," these quotation marks are correct—and are needed by Word whenever a data field contains a comma, tab character, or quotation mark.

Although merged printing is usually associated with form letters, you can use it as a powerful way to present information from a database program. Rather than printing out data records in raw form and then formatting them for a second printing, you can store the information in an ASCII data file, and use Merge to print it with Word's sophisticated formatting.

Following are tips on how to use five popular database and filing programs to create a data file for use with Merge. In each instance, the example assumes you want to create a mailing list limited to people who live in Washington State. In the examples, the mailing list is called MAILLIST.DOC, and is generated from a database named ADDRESS.

R:base 5000 and R:BASE System V
It is a simple matter to create a mailing list with R:base 5000 or R:BASE System V. At the R prompt (R>), type *open address* to open the database (called *address* in our example). R:base responds: *Database exists.* This database will contain one or more tables, and you must pick one that you want to export to ASCII. (To see a list of tables, type *list tables* at the R prompt.) In our example, the table to be used is called *names*.

At the R prompt, type *output*, followed by the name of the mailing list document you are creating. In our example, the name is MAILLIST.DOC. This command causes the output of R:base to be sent to the file named MAILLIST.DOC rather than to the screen.

At the R prompt, type *unload data for names as ascii sorted by last where state* = *WA* (if you're using System V, leave out the clause "*as ascii*"). At this point, your screen will look like this (assuming you're using 5000):

```
R)open address
 Database exists
R)output maillist.doc
R)unload data for names as ascii sorted by last where state = WA
```

When you press the Enter key, R:base will print on the disk a file named MAILLIST.DOC, which contains data from the records in the table called *names*. The only records included will be those in which the state is listed as *WA*. The data from the records will be alphabetized by last name.

To continue using R:base, type *output screen* or *output terminal* to cause the program to resume sending its output to the screen. If you want to use the mailing list immediately, you needn't redirect the output to the screen. Just quit R:base (type *exit* at the R prompt) and start Word.

When you load the document MAILLIST.DOC into Word, you may find spaces in places you don't want them. The Replace command can remove unwanted spaces. First, use the Options command to make invisible characters visible on the screen. Then devise an appropriate rendition of the Replace command.

For instance, you may find that each record ends with two unwanted spaces, followed by the necessary paragraph mark, and then seven more unneeded spaces. To solve this problem, select the first character in the document and use Word's Replace command. In the *text* field, press the Spacebar twice, type ^p, and then press the Spacebar seven more times. Press the Tab key to move to the *with text* field, where you type ^p. Change the *confirm* field to *No*, to save time, and press the Enter key.

If you're using System V, your file will start with some R:base commands. Delete them. Also, lines will be limited to 79 characters.

dBASE II and dBASE III

Creating a data file called MAILLIST.DOC that Word can use is easy with dBASE II and dBASE III. Type:

```
use address
copy for state = "WA" to maillist.doc delimited
quit
```

To speed up the LOCATE command, you can use the appropriate INDEX file as part of the USE command. For example: *USE ADDRESS INDEX STATE*.

If you want to limit MAILLIST.DOC to certain fields, specify them this way in the *copy to* line:

```
copy fields title,first,last,street,city,state,zip for state = "WA";
  to maillist.doc delimited
```

PC-FILE III

Creating a mailing list of Washington state residents is a two-part process with PC-FILE III. First, a new database containing the names and addresses of only Washington residents must be "cloned" from the master database ADDRESS. You could name the new database WASHFOLK. Once it is created and sorted in alphabetic or some other order, generating a matching mailing list for Word from it takes only a minute.

From the main menu, press the F8 key, followed by the number 4 key, to indicate you wish to *Export a database*. The program responds:

```
Export to which format?
  M) MailMerge or WORD
  V) VisiCalc
  C) PC-Calc
  D) DIF
  T) Text editor
```

Press M, and the program asks which drive you want the file to be created on. Type the drive letter and wait until the program tells you the mailing list has been created. Quit PC-FILE III and load the list into Word. If the database from which it was created is called WASHFOLK, the mailing list will be named WASHFOLK.WS.

pfs:File

It takes several steps, but pfs:File can produce a mailing list for use with Merge. Select the PRINT function and fill in the *retrieve specifications* to indicate you want only records in which the state is *WA*. Then:

1. In the *PRINT TO:* field specify a disk drive, a colon, and the name of a file. For example, you could type *B:MAILLIST.DOC*. In the *LINES PER PAGE* field, type *1*.

    PRINT TO: B:MAILLIST.DOC

    LINES PER PAGE: 1

2. Press F10 and then move from field to field, typing a + in every one you want printed, except the final one. In the last field to be printed, type *X*. In addition to the + or *X*, type *S* in the one field, if any, by which you want the database sorted in alphabetic or numeric order.

3. Press F10. The output will be printed to a file—in our example, the file MAILLIST.DOC.

4. Quit pfs:File and start Word. Load MAILLIST.DOC (or whatever name you gave the file). Pick the Replace command, and put two Spacebar spaces in the *text* field; type "," in the *with text* field; and pick *No* in the *confirm* field. Press the Enter key to carry out the replacements. Pick the Replace command again and change all paragraph marks (^p) to two quotation marks with a paragraph mark between them (" ^p"), again setting *confirm* to *No*.

5. If necessary, add a quotation mark to the beginning and the end of the mailing list. It is ready for use with Word.

Power Tools:
Style Sheets

Style Sheets are the secret, the key to unlocking the full potential of Microsoft Word. In this chapter you'll learn the fundamentals, and in the next three chapters you'll create and use style sheets.

Imagine you have a second keyboard—a special keyboard with 123 keys. The keys are dedicated to formatting: Each applies one format or *set* of formats to whatever text is selected. You can change the formatting associated with any key at will. Or you can change the formatting of all the keys at once, so that the special keyboard takes on different personalities for different word-processing applications. And to remind yourself of what they do, you can put your own labels on the keys. Imagine what a powerful tool such a keyboard would be. It would let you customize the look of any document or set of documents—and it would let you do it quickly.

Of course, there isn't a special keyboard devoted to formatting. But if you can imagine one, you already understand the concept underlying Word's style sheets.

STYLES: THE BUILDING BLOCKS

Word lets you use your regular keyboard as if it were dedicated to formatting. Word remembers up to 123 different formatting instructions at a time, and lets you give each instruction a one- or two-character name called a *key code*. Instead of pressing any of up to 123 formatting keys to use a formatting instruction, you hold down the Alt key and type one of up to 123 key codes on the regular keyboard. Each of the formatting instructions is called a *style*.

- Twenty-eight of the styles control character formatting. You use them instead of, or in addition to, built-in character formats and the Format Character command.

- Seventy-three of the styles control paragraph formatting. They replace or supplement the built-in paragraph formats and the Format Paragraph command. For instance, if you have a paragraph style intended for titles, you can define its formatting so that paragraphs controlled by the style will be centered. As a bonus, a paragraph style also lets you specify the character formatting that is considered "normal" in the paragraphs controlled by the style. The paragraph style intended for titles could specify that the characters in title paragraphs will be boldfaced and underlined. Whenever the style was applied to selected text, that text would be not only centered, but boldfaced and under-lined, too. (You can override the normal character formatting in a paragraph by using a character style, a built-in character format, or by selecting the Format Character command.)

♦ Twenty-two of the styles control division formatting. The formatting of a division style guides the page design of the document, or division of a document, in which it is executed.

To make style sheets easy to use, you often don't have to use a key code to apply certain styles to appropriate parts of a document. Certain styles are *dedicated* to particular tasks, and Word will use them automatically unless otherwise instructed. For example, if you create a "standard" paragraph style in a style sheet, Word will format most paragraphs with it, unless you deliberately apply other formatting. Word lets you create a special footnote paragraph style for footnote text, and will automatically assign appropriate styles to headings used in out-lines and to the various elements in an index or table of contents generated with Word version 3.0 or higher. In addition, Word automatically gives page numbers and footnote reference marks whatever character formatting you specify in appropriate character styles. Of course, you don't have to create any of these dedicated "standard" or default styles, and even when you do create them, you can override them by making other formatting choices.

You can look at pertinent information about the styles contained in a style sheet. Choose the Gallery command to cause Word to display a gallery of the individual styles that comprise the active style sheet, and choose the Gallery's Exit command to return to the regular Edit menu. (Note that the Gallery normally will only show styles if a style sheet has been attached to the active document with the Format Style Sheet command.)

In this chapter, we'll look first at styles, which are the building blocks of style sheets. You'll learn that every *style* has two parts, a *name* and a *format*. Then we'll look at the use of full style sheets in the formatting of a document. Finally, we'll examine how you can modify styles in a style sheet, and create styles and style sheets of your own, using the commands in the Gallery menu. In the next chapter, "Power Tools: Outlining," a step-by-step tutorial will help you create a useful style sheet.

Style names

You can call a style into effect in one of two ways. You can address it by using a change-able key code (such as SP), or you can call it by its permanent name (such as Paragraph Standard). The key code can be almost any one or two letters, numbers, or symbols of your choice, and is comparable to a two-letter label you might stick onto a keyboard key.

A style's name is composed of a *usage* and a *variant*. The usage tells what kind of format-ting a style does—character, paragraph, or division. A variant distinguishes one style from another within each of the three usage groups. In the style name Paragraph 1, for example, *Paragraph* is the usage, *1* is the variant. In the style name Paragraph Standard, *Paragraph* is the usage and *Standard* is the variant.

- Character styles are named Character 1, Character 2, and so on up to Character 26. There are also two dedicated styles named Character Page number and Character Footnote reference. There isn't any standard, or "normal," character style, because in Word a normal character can vary from one paragraph to the next, depending on — and corresponding to — the formatting specified in the character-formatting section of the paragraph style. If you alter character formatting in a paragraph, you can change it back at any time to the normal character formatting specified in the paragraph style, by selecting the characters and pressing Alt-Spacebar. In short, you can have 26 numbered character styles, plus one dedicated to page numbers and one dedicated to footnote references. You can assign to each style, as part of its name, a key code of one or two letters or symbols.

- Paragraph styles are named Paragraph 1, Paragraph 2, and so on, up to Paragraph 56. Additionally, a dedicated paragraph style is named Paragraph Standard, another is named Paragraph Footnote, and (beginning with version 3.0 of Word) another fifteen paragraph styles are dedicated to formatting indexes, tables of contents, and the various levels of heading you might use in a document. (In version 2.0 of Word, there are 71 numbered paragraph styles and none are dedicated to indexes, tables of contents, and levels of heading.) When a paragraph has no other paragraph formatting, Word automatically gives it the Paragraph Standard style. When a footnote has no other paragraph formatting, it is automatically assigned the Paragraph Footnote style. Assign paragraph and character formatting of your choice to the Paragraph Standard and Paragraph Footnote styles, and your document's standard paragraphs and footnotes can automatically assume the look you want.

- Division styles are named Division 1, Division 2, on up to Division 21. An additional, dedicated division style, named Division Standard, is the style Word uses automatically, unless you change the document's division formatting.

A particular character in a document can be controlled by only one character style, one paragraph style, and one division style at a time. For example, when you attach a paragraph style to a paragraph, the style dislodges whatever paragraph style was previously attached. This is a major feature of style sheets, because it enables you to wholly change the formatting of any element in a document simply by replacing one style with another.

Name differences in earlier versions

There are differences in style names among the various versions of Word, although there are the same overall number of paragraph, character, and division styles, and you use them in generally similar ways to format a document.

As we've seen, in recent versions of Word, styles are given a *usage* of Character, Paragraph, or Division, and a *variant*, which usually is a number. Prior to version 2.0, Word used two-part style names, such as *Title b* or *Emphasis d*. In these examples, *Title* is a paragraph usage and *Emphasis* is a character usage, and the letters are variants. These earlier names attempted to break down the types of styles on an advisory basis into many common uses, with a number of further variations of each. The system was abandoned because many people became confused when they didn't realize that the names were only suggestions.

There is a large degree of compatibility between the old and new systems, so style sheets created with one version of Word usually work with another. But you are far, far better off switching to a recent version of Word (such as 3.0), particularly if you're using version 1.0, 1.1, or 1.15. To avoid making this chapter needlessly confusing, we'll assume you are using version 3.0 or higher, and note some exceptions relevant to earlier versions.

Style formatting

Although the 123 styles are fixed in terms of what they are named, you can change more than just the key code of each. You can freely alter the formatting of any style. That is, you can change the effect it has on the text to which it is applied. This flexibility means, for example, you can change formatting of the Character 7 style from underlining to boldfaced italics at any time.

Why might you do that? If you include a lot of underlined passages in a long document or a collection of documents, changing them to boldfaced italics would normally be a major chore. But if you use a style, such as Character 7, to specify the underlining in the first place, all you need do is redefine the style's formatting from underlining to boldfaced italics. It takes only a few seconds to make the change in the Gallery, and your entire document (or any other document controlled by the same style sheet) is changed instantly, from beginning to end. All those passages still have their characters formatted with the Character 7 style, but the style no longer means underlining; now it means boldfaced italics. (In this example, the key code for Character 7 might have been UC, to help you remember "Underlined Character." When you changed the formatting you could also change the key code to BI or some other code indicative of "Bold Italic." But you wouldn't have to; you could leave it UC. Word wouldn't get confused, although you might.)

Formatting text with a style is sometimes referred to as *indirect formatting,* because the formatting instructions are applied to the style and the style, in turn, is applied to the text. The decided advantage of indirect formatting is that a document's appearance can be dramatically revised just by changing the definition of a style or styles or by switching from one set of styles (a "style sheet") to another. In contrast, when you use a built-in format or a format command, such as Format Character, you apply formatting instructions directly to the text. A firm link is established between the text and its formatting. Hence, this is called *direct formatting.*

To look at the descriptions of the formatting associated with styles, use the Gallery, described in Chapters 6 and 11, and later in this chapter.

Applying a style to text

You apply a style to text much as you apply any other formatting instruction. First you select the text to be formatted, then you apply the formatting. Recall that *direct formatting* is applied either with a built-in format that is called into effect by holding down an Alt-letter key combination (centering is Alt-C, boldface is Alt-B), or it is applied with a Format command, such as Format Character. With a style (*indirect formatting*) you can use a variation of either method:

♦ Select the text to be formatted and then hold down the Alt key and type the style's key code.

♦ Or, use the Format Style Paragraph, Format Style Character, or Format Style Division command. The use of these commands is explained at the end of Chapter 12, "The Family of Format Commands." They represent an alternative to memorizing key codes and let you apply styles with a mouse, if you wish.

Styles versus built-in formats

There is a strong resemblance between formatting a document with styles and with built-in formats. Both control appearance and can be put into effect by holding down the Alt key and pressing a key code. There are some differences, however:

♦ Built-in formats have unchangeable key codes, such as F for first-line indent, U for underline, and C for center. Styles can have virtually whatever one- or two-letter key codes you choose to give them. If you use a particular style frequently and want to code it with your initials, so be it.

♦ Built-in formats literally are built into Word. They are almost always available. (The only time built-in formats aren't available is when your style sheet contains a style with a key code that begins with X.) Styles, on the other hand, are available only when a style sheet containing them is attached to the document on which you are working.

♦ Built-in formats cannot be changed. Style sheets can be changed at will.

♦ Built-in formats can only be attached to documents through the use of key codes, but styles can also be attached with the Format Style commands.

♦ Because they cannot be created or modified, there is only a single step to using built-in formats: You simply apply them by key code to a selection in a document. Applying a style from an existing style sheet is just as easy; but creating styles and organizing them into usable style sheets can be a comparatively complex task.

NOTE: I strongly recommend that you use two-letter key codes rather than single-letter key codes for styles. Two letters allow for many more combinations of letters, providing you with more flexibility. The only exception is that it is convenient, and recommended, to assign the single-digit key codes Alt-1 through Alt-7 to the seven paragraph styles dedicated to heading levels, beginning with Word 3.0. More about this in the next chapter.

STYLE SHEETS: SETS OF STYLES

A *style sheet* is a collection of styles, all of which are accessible to you at the same time. By switching from one style sheet to another, you can instantly bring into Word an entirely different group of formatting styles for a document. You switch style sheets with the Edit menu's Format Style Sheet command.

Think again about our imaginary keyboard. We can change the formatting effects of all its keys at once. Changing the style sheet with the Format Style Sheet command is analogous to telling Word *BIZLETTR* when you want all the "keys" (styles) customized for formatting business letters, or telling it *REPORT* when you want the "keys" (styles) to assist you in formatting reports. (BIZLETTR and REPORT are hypothetical names for style sheets. You can use any name you want of up to eight letters for a style sheet.)

Once a different style sheet is put into place with the Format Style Sheet command, the styles that are displayed in the Gallery change, and your document takes on the appearance specified by the formatting of the new styles. This means, for example, that any text in the document with a "Paragraph 26" style assumes the formatting specified for "Paragraph 26" in the new style sheet. However, any direct formatting remains unchanged, because it was applied directly to the text with a built-in format or the Format command. For example, if you underline some characters with the built-in format Alt-x-u, these characters will remain underlined and in the same font even though you may attach a different style or style sheet. (To eliminate direct character formatting, select the characters and press Alt-Spacebar.)

Using style sheets

At this point, you've been exposed to the fundamentals of style sheets; now you can begin to put the pieces together with a little practice. When learning to use style sheets, it's best to start with a style sheet someone else has created. This is easier than trying to learn how to use, create, and modify style sheets all at the same time.

To use a style sheet to format a document:

1. Load the style sheet from disk with the Format Style Sheet command.
2. Look in the Gallery to spot a style you want to use. You can evaluate a style by examining its name, remark, and formatting description. Note its key code.

Here is a sample paragraph style as it appears in the Gallery. The first line describes the elements of the style's name; the remaining lines describe the elements of its formatting. Elements marked with superscripted, lowercase letters are explained in the following list.

```
‖ 5ᵃ SJᵇ Paragraphᶜ 4ᵈ                              STANDARD ¶, JUSTIFIEDᵉ ‖
‖      Courier (Modern a) 12/24. Justified (first line indent 0.5"), space ‖
‖      before 1 liᶠ                                                         ‖
```

a. This happens to be the fifth style in the style sheet.
b. Its key code is SJ (for *Standard Justified*), but you can use any letters you like.
c. Paragraph is the usage part of the style name.
d. This number, 4, is the variant part of the style name.
e. This is the descriptive remark, which is optional.
f. The character formatting of the paragraph style ends at the period. 12/24 means the type is a 12-point font placed in 24 points of vertical space—in other words, any paragraph to which this style is applied will be double-spaced.
g. This is paragraph formatting. Any paragraph to which this style is applied will be justified, with a first-line indent of ½ inch and one blank line preceding it.

3. Return to the Edit menu from the Gallery menu by choosing the command named Exit (or Edit, in early versions of Word).

4. Select the text you want to format.

5. Apply the style to the selected text in one of two ways: Hold down the Alt key and type the key code, or choose the appropriate Format Style command and either type in the style name or pick it from a list.

That's all there is to it.

Multiple style sheets

A document can be written with one style sheet attached to it, and printed later when a different style sheet is attached to it. For example, you might write a report draft with a style sheet that double-spaces all the lines, but print the final version with a style sheet that formats text to be single-spaced and justified—in keeping with your requirements for a polished document. It's also possible to use a whole system of style sheets that are largely interchangeable. Having an integrated set of style sheets lets you change the look of a document as fast—and as many times—as you switch its style sheet.

MODIFYING AND CREATING STYLE SHEETS

Once you've had some experience using existing style sheets, you're ready to modify or create one. Modifying an existing style sheet is easier, so we'll start there.

A style sheet is a collection of styles you can save on disk with a file name and the extension .STY (for example, REPORT.STY). The name of a style sheet can be altered with the Gallery menu's Transfer Rename command. Whole blocks of styles can be moved from one style sheet to another by selecting them and passing them through the scrap with the Gallery menu's Copy, Delete, and Insert commands.

Most often we change a style sheet a style at a time. This is accomplished by changing a style's name with the Gallery's Name command, and its formatting with the Gallery's family of Format commands.

Modifying a style's name

When you choose the Name command, you can enter any remark, key code, or variant you like. Versions of Word prior to 2.0 allow you to change the usage, too, but in later versions this is not necessary, because usages have been reduced to just three classes, corresponding to the three basic types of formatting: character, paragraph, and division.

Choose the variant from the pool of variants not already assigned to other styles of the same usage (Character, Paragraph, or Division). Word proposes the variant (number or word) the selected style had before you used the Name command. To pick a different variant, press a direction key or click the right mouse button to see a list. The possibilities fill the upper part of the screen and, beginning with version 2.0, parentheses ( ) are displayed next to the name of each variant that already has been used. Inside the parentheses are displayed the corresponding key codes, if any.

For example, the list of variant choices for the Paragraph usage might look like this in version 3.0, assuming that several variants have already been assigned styles and key codes:

```
Standard (SP)        Footnote          Heading level 1    Heading level 2
Heading level 3      Heading level 4   Heading level 5    Heading level 6
Heading level 7      Index level 1     Index level 2      Index level 3
Index level 4        Table level 1     Table level 2      Table level 3
Table level 4        1                 2                  3
4                    5                 6                  7   (DA)
8   (NA)             9   (TI)          10 (LH)            11 (IA)
12                   13  (SA)          14 (RA)            15
16                   17  (RI)          18                 19
20                   21  (CL)          22                 23
24                   25                26                 27
28                   29                30                 31
32                   33                34                 35
36                   37                38                 39
40                   41                42                 43
44                   45                46                 47
48                   49                50                 51
52                   53                54                 55
56

INSERT key code: {}                    usage: Character(Paragraph)Division
        variant: Standard              remark:
Enter variant or select from list
GALLERY {}                             ?          Microsoft Word: SEMI.STY
```

When you're editing a document and the style bar is turned on with the Window Options command, the key codes of paragraph styles are displayed in it. Paragraph styles are used far more than character or division styles, and hence justify the broadest range of key codes.

Any letters or numbers can be used for key codes, but I suggest using:

♦ A letter, followed by C, for character styles.

♦ A letter, followed by / (a division sign), for division styles.

♦ Any other two letters for paragraph styles. (Except that, as already noted, it makes sense to give *Heading level* styles the single-digit key codes Alt-1 through Alt-7.)

Try to make key codes suggestive of their uses: SP for Standard Paragraph and UC for Underlined Character, for instance. Also, avoid using X as the first character of a key code. (If you use X, you can no longer use built-in formats—such as Alt-x-u for underlining.)

Modifying a style's formatting

A style is formatted in the Gallery, with the Gallery menu. The Gallery menu was discussed briefly in Chapter 6, "Using Command Menus," and you were introduced to the Gallery as a means of viewing styles in Chapter 11, "The Efficiency Commands." Recall that the Gallery describes the formatting of a style in plain English. To change the formatting:

1. Select the style (or styles) whose formatting you want to alter. When a style is selected, its name and formatting description are highlighted. An easy way to change which style is selected is with the Up and Down direction keys. To extend the selection instead of moving it, press F6 first.

2. Use the Format commands in the *Gallery menu* to give character, paragraph (including tab), and division formatting to the selected style(s). The Gallery's Format commands

operate similarly to the Edit menu's Format commands, except that you needn't press the Esc key to initiate them.

3. Save the changes with the Gallery's Transfer Save command, if you wish to keep them.

Creating a style sheet

A style sheet is formed whenever you create a collection of styles in the Gallery. You store a style sheet with the Gallery menu's Transfer Save command.

You add a style to a style sheet with the Gallery menu's Insert command. When you choose the command, Word proposes the scrap brackets as the source of the style(s), if any, to be inserted. If you press the Enter key, any styles in the scrap are inserted into the Gallery at the selected location. That's how you move styles from one location to another — within one style sheet or between two — by copying or deleting styles to the scrap and then using the Gallery menu's Insert command.

To create a brand new style, use the Insert command, but type a key code of your choice rather than accepting the scrap brackets. Then:

1. Press the Tab key to move to the *usage* field. Beginning with Word version 2.0, this field has three choices: *Character, Paragraph,* and *Division*. Assuming you're creating a paragraph style, press the Spacebar to highlight *Paragraph*.

```
INSERT key code: H2               usage: Character Paragraph Division
         variant: 1               remark:
Select option
GALLERY  {}                       ?           Microsoft Word:
```

2. Press the Tab key to move to the *variant* field. Pick a variant from the list, or press the Enter key to accept the proposed variant, which is the lowest unused number.

Beginning with Word version 3.0, the list of paragraph variants looks like this:

```
Standard         Footnote          Heading level 1    Heading level 2
Heading level 3  Heading level 4   Heading level 5    Heading level 6
Heading level 7  Index level 1     Index level 2      Index level 3
Index level 4    Table level 1     Table level 2      Table level 3
Table level 4    1                 2                   3
4                5                 6                   7
8                9                 10                  11
12               13                14                  15
16               17                18                  19
20               21                22                  23
24               25                26                  27
28               29                30                  31
32               33                34                  35
36               37                38                  39
40               41                42                  43
44               45                46                  47
48               49                50                  51
52               53                54                  55
56
```

```
INSERT key code: {}               usage: Character(Paragraph)Division
         variant: Standard         remark:
Enter variant or select from list
GALLERY  {}                       ?           Microsoft Word:
```

Note that this is the same type of list you see when you choose the Gallery menu's Name command. In version 2.0, the list is similar, except that Standard and Footnote are the only two dedicated paragraph styles, and the numbered styles extend from 1 through 71 instead of just from 1 through 56. In versions earlier than 2.0, you pick a usage from a larger number of choices, some associated with Characters, others with Paragraphs, and others with Divisions. In this example, *Heading* has been highlighted by pressing the direction keys.

```
Emphasis            Index term       Figure reference    Footnote reference
Sequence number     Folio            Superscript         Subscript
Other character

Normal paragraph    Nested           Footnote            Quotation
Table               Heading          List                Title
Author              Affiliation      Copyright           Running head
Other paragraph

Normal division     Front matter     Appendix            Index
Contents            Other division



INSERT key code: {}  usage: Heading              variant:
                  remark:
Enter usage or select from list
GALLERY  {}                           ? 97% Free     Microsoft Word:
```

In these earlier versions, the variant list differs for each usage. For example, in versions 1.0, 1.1, and 1.15, the variant list for the Heading usage looks like this:

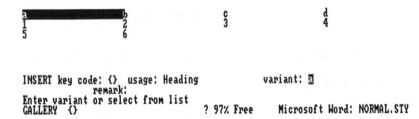

```
a                   b             c             d
1                   2             3             4
5                   6



INSERT key code: {}  usage: Heading              variant: a
                  remark:
Enter variant or select from list
GALLERY  {}                           ? 97% Free     Microsoft Word: NORMAL.STY
```

3. Press the Tab key again and type a remark. Consider typing the remark in all capitals so it will stand out among the other notations in the Gallery:

```
INSERT key code: H2              usage: Character(Paragraph)Division
           variant: Heading level 2   remark: SECOND-LEVEL HEADING
Enter text
GALLERY  {}               ?              Microsoft Word:
```

4. Press the Enter key to complete creation of the style's name.

Now you can use the Gallery menu's Format commands (which are highly similar to those in the Edit menu) to define the style's formatting. When you're done, save the style sheet with the Gallery's Transfer Save command.

REFERENCE TO THE GALLERY COMMANDS

The Gallery menu's commands are much like those of the Edit menu, and for the most part comments on commands in Chapters 9 through 17 are relevant to the Gallery versions of those commands, too. The following exceptions, however, are important:

- ♦ The Copy command copies the selected style or styles to the scrap. This is a different scrap from that of the Edit menu. In some versions of Word, the scrap is cleared whenever you use a Transfer Save command, but it may appear (from looking at the scrap brackets) that the scrap is not clear. Consequently, you may have to copy or delete styles to the scrap only *after* saving a style sheet, if later you'll want to insert the styles into a different style sheet with the Insert command.

- ♦ The Delete command deletes the selected style or styles to the Gallery scrap. See the notes on the Copy command, above.

- ♦ The Exit command switches you from the Gallery menu to the Edit menu. The command is called Exit beginning with version 2.0 of Word; it is called Edit in prior versions.

- ♦ The Format family has commands similar to those in the Edit menu, except that there are fewer of them in the Gallery menu and they pertain to styles rather than to text. The Format commands act on whatever style or styles are selected (highlighted). When you execute a command after changing the formatting, the Gallery's plain-English descriptions of the formatting change.

- ♦ The Insert command adds a new style to a style sheet, either by inserting a style that is already in the scrap or by letting you create a new one. To create a new one, type a key code of your choice, pick one of the three usages (Character, Paragraph, or Division), pick an appropriate variant, and, optionally, type a remark. The fields are almost identical to those of the Gallery's Name command, except that the Insert command lets you assign a usage.

- ♦ The Name command allows you to change the key code, variant, and/or remark in the name of an existing style. You cannot change the usage—that is, you can't transform a character style into a paragraph style or division style, for instance.

- ♦ The Print command prints the style sheet.

- ♦ The Gallery's Transfer commands are similar to those of the Edit menu, except that there are fewer of them and they pertain to style sheets (files ending with .STY) rather than documents (files ending with .DOC).

The Gallery is a version of a text window adapted to the unique needs of style sheets. Editing functions in the Gallery are largely similar to those in the Edit menu.

For example, you can scroll quickly through the styles in the Gallery by moving the mouse pointer to the left window border and clicking the mouse buttons, just as you can in a text window. You can select more than one style by pressing F6 (the Extend Selection key) and then using the direction keys. And you can use built-in formats to rapidly modify the formatting of a style: If you want underlining to be added to the formatting of a selected character or paragraph style, hold down the Alt key and press the letter U, as an alternative to using the Gallery's Format Character command.

The next three chapters will help you find practical uses for style sheets. Much, much more could be written about styles, of course. In fact, there could be a whole book about them—and there is: *Microsoft Word Style Sheets* (Microsoft Press, 1987), which I co-authored with JoAnne Woodcock. The volume explains style sheets from several perspectives, and contains several dozen carefully crafted style sheets, which are available on disk as an option.

Power Tools: Outlining

Some people draw up an itinerary before setting out on a journey. Others have only a vague idea of where they're heading. Either way, there's much to be said for having a map, both to trace where you've been and to see where you might be going.

Word's outlining feature provides new ways to look at, and think about, what you write. Partway through a document, you can review what you've already written, and see it as concisely or in as much detail as you desire. You can look ahead to ideas and passages that are only partly formed, and judge where and how they might fit into what you're fashioning. You can, in short, consult a map as you journey from the beginning of your document to its end.

"Outlining" is a modest, even inadequate, term to describe the organizational tools Word makes available. You can compose and print a formal outline, of course. Word will number it for you automatically, if you like. But by itself, printing an outline is almost a trivial use of the feature. Its special contribution is that it lets you see and edit, on an ongoing basis, an up-to-date model ("outline") of your document. You can collect ideas under headings and *collapse* the text so that only headings show. You can adjust not only the order of the headings and sub-headings that remain, but their relative importance, or *level*.

With a Word outline mapping your document, you don't have to scan through many screens to find an idea; instead, you find it summarized on a line in the outline model. You don't have to scroll through a long document to move a subsection; instead, you rearrange lines in the model, and the document reflects the changes automatically. Or you edit the document, and the outline updates itself.

It is the unprecedented integration of document and outline that sets Word apart from any other outlining tool. If you're counting outlining features, some dedicated outlining programs have more. The strength of Word (in addition to its general word-processing capabilities) is the intimate terms on which it puts documents and outlines. A document and its outline are one and the same. You can even look at a document in one window and its outline in another—and when you edit one, the other changes, too.

This integration provides some practical opportunities that have little to do with outlines in any conventional sense. To be fanciful for a moment, consider the concept of *hyperspace*, an idea borrowed from science fiction. Since nothing can travel faster than light, the science-fiction writer faces a nasty problem. How can a spaceship leap to the center of the Milky Way, when it takes light 30,000 years to travel that far? The answer comes through an act of imagination. The spaceship arrives almost instantly in the desired neighborhood by taking a shortcut through hyperspace, a place where normal rules don't apply.

You can use Word's *outline view* as a sort of hyperspace. Imagine you're writing and want to jump to an idea many pages away. You press Shift-F2 to enter outline view, where your document is mapped out as an outline, with points and subpoints listed as headings and subheadings, and where regular text is *collapsed* out of view. At a glance, you see the breadth of the document. The outline becomes a menu of places to which you can travel. You select a heading or subheading from a distant region, and press Shift-F2 to return almost instantly to normal *document view,* but at the selected destination. Many such uses for Word's outlining powers are possible. New ideas may suggest themselves to you.

If you've put off learning to use style sheets because you thought they'd be difficult or not worth the effort, you just lost your excuses. Outlining is more powerful, and in some respects easier, when you use a style sheet to format the appearance of documents.

Among the many styles possible in a style sheet are up to seven dedicated to various levels of headings. For each of these *Heading level* styles, you can design specific formatting. For example, you can decree that Level 1 headings all will be in uppercase letters, boldfaced, underlined, and centered on the page, while Level 2 headings all will be underlined and centered, but neither uppercase nor bold. A Level 3 heading might be flush left and underlined, and so forth.

With a style sheet in place, it doesn't matter whether you are working with a document or its outline. Either way, you control headings identically. For example, you can press the Alt-1 key combination to turn a single-line paragraph into a Level 1 heading. Immediately its characters become boldfaced, underlined, and uppercase—or whatever you decided when you designed the style. Change your mind? Press Alt-2, and the line becomes a Level 2 heading, formatted as you specified in the style sheet. When you're in outline view, headings are indented to reflect their relative levels. When you're in document view, the headings assume the layout dictated by the style sheet. Any time you change a heading's level in document view, it is reflected in outline view, and vice versa. A lesson later in this chapter shows you step by step how to create and use a style sheet that you can put to work immediately.

Like Word itself, the outlining feature can be used in simple or sophisticated ways. Fortunately, you can do much by learning relatively little. Later, as the rudiments become second nature, you can explore the subtleties of outline manipulation.

THE RULES

You employ various keys and key combinations in new ways when you use the outlining feature. This information—which key to push when—is worth noting at the beginning, because later, when you return to this chapter for reference, you'll appreciate having it handy. The first time, skim over the rules to get a sense of the kinds of instructions you can give. Later, after you've followed the chapter's tutorials, the rules will become more meaningful.

Which keys are which?

In addition to the function keys F2 and F5, which are used in conjunction with the Shift key to get you in and out of Word's outline modes, several other keys are vital for outlining. There can be some ambiguity, however, because of duplicate key markings on the keyboard.

When you see a reference to the Plus (+) key, it is the large (usually gray) key on the numeric keypad, not the small key on the upper row of the regular keyboard. Similarly, references to the Minus (−) key and asterisk (*) key pertain to keys on the keypad.

The Alt key is used with several number keys in outlining. These are *not* the number keys on the numeric keypad. Nor are they the function keys F1 through F10 or F12. They are the numbers on the top row of the regular keyboard.

Outline view and outline edit

Holding the Shift key and pressing F2 takes you out of normal document view and into outline view. The *outline* field of the Window Options command does the same thing.

Once you are in outline view, you have the option of switching to a more powerful mode called *outline edit*. This is accomplished by holding down the Shift key and pressing F5. Outline edit will be of increasing interest as you gain experience, but to keep things simple at first, stick with outline view as much as possible.

One distinction between outline view and outline edit is essential:

♦ In outline view, you can type, select, and edit text *within a single heading or other paragraph*. Although you can move from paragraph to paragraph, you cannot select or otherwise affect more than one paragraph at a time. In fact, you cannot delete a paragraph mark at all, unless it is the only thing in the paragraph.

♦ In outline edit, on the other hand, you can select *only whole paragraphs*. Use outline edit to delete or move a paragraph or a group of paragraphs.

The possible ways to shift among the three modes—document view, outline view, and outline edit—are shown in Figure 25-1. To get from document view to outline view, press Shift-F2. To get from outline view or outline edit back to document view, press Shift-F2. To get from outline view to outline edit, press Shift-F5 or Shift-F10 (this latter key combination also selects the entire outline/document). To get from outline edit to outline view, press Shift-F5 or begin typing (when you type, Word knows you want to affect less than a whole paragraph, so it switches you to outline view automatically).

When you are in normal document view, the lower left corner of the screen displays the word *Page* and lists a page number, or if the document has more than one division, a page and division number, such as *P7 D2*.

In outline view, the lower left corner displays the word *Level* and a number, depending on the outline level of the selected heading. If a paragraph of body text is selected instead of a heading, the word *Text* is displayed in the screen's lower left corner.

In outline edit, the advanced mode, the lower corner says *OUTLINE*. It cannot show a level number because multiple paragraphs of different levels may be selected at once.

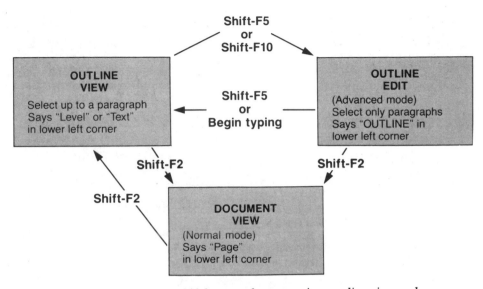

Figure 25-1: Ways to shift between document view, outline view and
outline edit.

Promoting and demoting

A Word outline is structured as a series of levels, with Level 1 headings having no left indentation, Level 2 headings having four spaces of indentation, Level 3 headings having an additional four spaces of indentation, and so forth. In a technically proper outline, everything between a Level 1 heading and the next Level 1 heading will pertain to a single broad topic, and the Level 1 heading will reflect this topic. For instance, in a book outline the first Level 1 heading might refer to the first chapter, and the next Level 1 heading to the second chapter. Major headings within a chapter would be at Level 2.

An outline may have several levels of headings, and you may want to move ideas not only from one place to another, but also from one heading level to another. Perhaps a topic you thought would make a chapter by itself seems less important now, so you incorporate it into another chapter and move it on the outline from Level 1 to Level 2.

In Word, this moving of headings from one level to another is called *promotion* (raising to a higher level) and *demotion* (lowering to a lower level). To promote or demote a heading, you must first select part or all of it. If you are in outline edit, you can select several headings, and raise or lower them at once.

Alt-9 and Alt-0

To promote a selected heading to a higher level, hold down the Alt key and type the number 9 (from the top line of the regular keyboard). To demote a selection, press Alt-0. At first glance, these keys may seem like peculiar choices for raising and lowering levels of an outline. They were picked because of the parentheses marks on the same keys. (See Figure 25-2.) With a little imagination, the (on the 9 key seems to point left, appropriate since Alt-9

Figure 25-2: Promoting and demoting headings.

moves an outline heading to the left—promotes it. Similarly, the) on the 0 key points to the right—and the key demotes a heading.

Key codes and styles

If you have a style sheet that includes *Paragraph Heading level* styles, you may use the key codes for these styles as a more powerful way to assign levels of headings in either an outline or a document.

For example, if you want to change a Level 1 heading to a Level 3 heading, hold the Alt key and type the key code for the *Level 3* style. This changes not only the heading level in the outline, but also the style of the heading in the document. If the *Level 1* style calls for a centered heading and the *Level 3* style calls for a flush-left heading, changing a heading from Level 1 to Level 3 will cause the paragraph formats of the headings to change in the document.

This book assumes that if you are using a style sheet with *Paragraph Heading level* styles, you will assign as a key code the number that corresponds to the paragraph style variant:

◆ *Alt-1* for the *Heading level 1* paragraph style;
◆ *Alt-2* for the *Heading level 2* paragraph style;
◆ *Alt-3* for the *Heading level 3* paragraph style;
◆ *Alt-4* for the *Heading level 4* paragraph style;
◆ *Alt-5* for the *Heading level 5* paragraph style;
◆ *Alt-6* for the *Heading level 6* paragraph style; and
◆ *Alt-7* for the *Heading level 7* paragraph style.

If you follow this convention, you concentrate control over heading levels in the number keys on the top line of your keyboard. Pressing Alt-1 through Alt-7 assigns the associated *Heading level* style, and pressing Alt-9 or Alt-0 promotes or demotes headings regardless of whether there is a style sheet.

Even if you use styles (key codes Alt-1 through Alt-7) to assign levels of headings, you can still use the Alt-9/Alt-0 method. There are two circumstances in which you may wish to do so.

◆ When you want to promote or demote a block of several headings and the headings are of different levels, Alt-9 will promote them all at once and Alt-0 will demote them all at once. Each heading will keep its place in the hierarchy, but the hierarchy will be promoted or demoted a level. If you select a Level 2, a Level 3, and a Level 4 heading together and promote them with Alt-9, they will become Level 1, Level 2, and Level 3 respectively. In contrast, if you select a group of headings and use a key code to apply a style, all the selected headings will assume the one heading level of the style.

♦ When you want help in keeping an outline correct in a formal sense, Alt-9 and Alt-0 help you. Technically, an outline or document should never transit directly from a Level 1 heading to a Level 3 heading. With styles, you have the freedom to make a heading any level you desire. You can follow a Level 1 heading with a Level 3, if you wish. But with the Alt-9/Alt-0 method, Word tries to protect you, and won't let you promote or demote headings in such a way that levels are skipped. If you try, Word just bleeps at you.

Body text

To promote body text into a heading, you may press Alt-9. This causes the selected body text paragraph to assume the same level as whatever heading precedes it (is above it) in the document. From there, you can adjust the level with subsequent uses of Alt-9 and Alt-0. If you are using a style sheet, merely use the key code (Alt-1 through Alt-7) for the heading style you desire.

To demote a heading into body text, use Alt-P if you are not using a style sheet, or Alt and the key code for a paragraph style if you are using a style sheet. In a style sheet you'll create later in this chapter, the key code for a standard paragraph is SP.

Expanding and collapsing

Much of the power of Word's outlining feature is the capability it gives you in outline view and outline edit to collapse subheadings and text, so that they disappear from the screen. With nonessential subheadings, and particularly with text, out of sight, you can examine the order and relationship of important headings to understand a document's underlying structure. If you need more detail on a point, you can get it by temporarily expanding a portion of the outline. When you reorganize elements in the outline, the document is automatically reorganized accordingly.

After creating an outline initially, there isn't much point in using Word's outline feature unless you keep most body text collapsed. After all, with a lot of body text showing, the document isn't condensed and you might as well be in regular document view.

If, on the other hand, you keep body text collapsed and most or all the headings expanded (visible), the outline can be highly useful. So the first thing to learn is a reliable way to achieve this situation—all headings showing, no text showing.

The five steps

To collapse all text and expand all levels of heading, press Shift-F2 to enter outline view, then follow these steps:

1. Press Shift-F10 to select the entire document (this will put you in outline edit).
2. Press the Minus key (on the keypad). This collapses the entire document so that only Level 1 headings show.
3. Press the Asterisk key (on the keypad). This expands all levels of headings, but leaves text collapsed.
4. Select the heading at which you wish to resume work in the document or outline.
5. Press Shift-F5 to return to outline view, or press Shift-F2 to return directly to document view.

The five steps are all many people will need to know at first about expanding and collapsing outlines. Using this simple method:

♦ When you want to see the body text of the document, press Shift-F2 to enter document view.

♦ When you want to see the outline, press Shift-F2 to enter outline view, then use the five steps if necessary.

The five steps, or some other method of collapsing and expanding, are usually necessary upon entering outline view from document view. This is because when you write in document view, the headings and other paragraphs you create may or may not be collapsed. Until you understand why this happens, it seems strange to return to an outline that had no body text expanded (visible) ten minutes earlier, and discover that the paragraphs you wrote since then are expanded into full view in the middle of the outline. Or that the subheading you just typed in document view, and which you expected would appear in the outline along with all the other subheadings, is nowhere to be found.

The five steps will always straighten things out, but what's going on?

What's going on?

The answer is that every paragraph in any document is either expanded or collapsed. This isn't apparent in document view, where both kinds of paragraphs show on the screen and print. But in outline view and outline edit, only expanded paragraphs appear. In an outline, the presence of collapsed paragraphs is indicated next to a visible heading by:

♦ a *t* if the collapsed text is body text, or

♦ a + if it is a collapsed heading or a combination of headings and body text.

When you're in document view and you press the Enter key to create a new paragraph, the paragraph will either be expanded or collapsed depending on what kind of paragraph the selection was in when the Enter key was pressed. If the selection (or the beginning of the selection) was in a collapsed paragraph, then any new paragraphs you create will also be collapsed. They will remain collapsed, even if you adjust the level of heading, until you expand them in outline view. On the other hand, if the selection was in an expanded paragraph when the Enter key was pressed, then any newly created paragraphs also will be expanded. Again, none of this is apparent in document view. But when you switch to outline view, the collapsed paragraphs vanish and the expanded paragraphs appear.

Though the five steps are an easy way to cope with this, there are other approaches. In document view, you can be careful when pressing the Enter key that the selection is in either a collapsed paragraph (probably body text) or an expanded paragraph (probably a heading), depending on what you want to create. Or, you can store paragraph marks in the glossary, formatted either as collapsed or expanded, and insert one of them instead of pressing Enter when you want to insert a new paragraph. Or, more practically, you can learn the rules of expanding and collapsing headings and body text, so that you can always adjust the outline to your liking upon entering outline view.

In the following descriptions of how to expand and collapse paragraphs, when sub-headings or text are said to be *below* or *under* a heading or subheading, it means they are subsidiary—in other words, they are indented to the right of the heading or subheading, and may or may not be collapsed from view. In other words, elements are below a heading if they come *after* the heading but *before* another heading of the same level.

Expanding and collapsing headings

Word provides key combinations for expanding and collapsing headings and subheadings different from the key combinations for expanding and collapsing body text.

Expanding or collapsing headings is straightforward. A heading that has subheadings collapsed below it is marked in the selection bar with a +. Also, if there are both subhead-ings and body text collapsed below it, the + appears.

Expand all. To expand all subheadings below a selected heading, press the asterisk (* on key pad).

Expand one level. To reveal just those subheadings that are one level below the selected heading, press Plus (+ on key pad).

Collapse all. To collapse all subheadings below a selected heading, press Minus (− on keypad).

Global. To expand or collapse all headings in an outline, first select the entire outline by pressing Shift-F10, then use Plus or Minus. Shift-F10 will put you automatically into outline edit. You can return to outline view by pressing Shift-F5, or to document view by pressing Shift-F2.

Expanding and collapsing body text

The rules for expanding and collapsing body text resemble those of expanding and col-lapsing subheadings, but there are important differences. A heading that has collapsed body text under it is marked in the selection bar with a *t*.

Expand text. Use Shift-Plus to expand the body text that immediately follows the se-lected heading.

Collapse text. Use Shift-Minus to collapse the body text that immediately follows the selected heading.

These actions expand and collapse only the text that directly follows the selected heading (or subheading). Unlike the case with Plus and Minus, in which all headings below the selec-tion can be affected, Shift-Plus and Shift-Minus are limited to expanding and collapsing the text that comes between two consecutive headings—regardless of the level of those headings. For example:

♦ Pressing Plus when a Level 1 heading is selected would cause all the Level 2 headings below it to be expanded into view. But,

♦ Pressing Shift-Plus when the same heading was selected would cause only the body text between the heading and the next heading (presumably a Level 2 heading) to ap-pear. It would not cause body text following any of the Level 2 headings to expand.

There is logic to the different treatment of headings and text. If you're using an outline as an ongoing tool when writing, the thing you're likely to want to know about a heading is which subheadings are associated with it and what text pertains specifically to the heading. This is the information you get by using Plus and Shift-Plus.

In contrast, when you want to read body text that falls under more than one heading, an easy method is merely to return to document view. If you prefer, however, you can enter outline edit and extend your selection across several paragraphs, so that the expand and collapse key combinations can affect the text of more than one heading at a time.

Selecting in outline edit

Selecting characters when you are in outline view is rather routine. It is much like selecting characters in document view, except that it is impossible to select more than one paragraph.

In outline edit, however, you can *only* select whole paragraphs. Consequently, several keys take on new meanings.

♦ The Up and Down direction keys select headings at the same level as that which is presently selected, while the Left and Right direction keys move up (Left key) or down (Right key) through headings regardless of level.

♦ The Home key moves you up in a document to the next higher level, while the End key moves you to the next lower level and selects the last heading in that level.

♦ The F6 key selects a heading and all the subheadings under it.

♦ To select all the subheadings without selecting the heading itself, select the first subheading under it, press F6, and press Ctrl-PgDn.

A WARNING: Be careful when you delete a heading in outline edit mode. Unlike in outline view, in outline edit, you will also delete any subheadings or text collapsed beneath it.

A mouse

A mouse has limited uses in outlining. You can use it to switch between document view and outline view, by employing it in the *outline* field of the Window Options command. If you're using a style sheet, you can promote or demote headings with the mouse by using it to pick the Format Style Paragraph command and then to choose from among a list of *Heading level* styles (and all other paragraph styles). If you're in outline edit, you can collapse a heading by pressing both mouse buttons, or expand a heading by pressing the right mouse button.

But one of the most valuable aspects of using a mouse with outlines is the ability it gives you to select any point in a document or outline. There are instances, such as when you've used the *five steps*, in which you may have selected an entire outline by pressing Shift-F10. Afterward, the whole screen remains selected, and when you press a direction key, the document/outline scrolls to its beginning or end. Word has "lost" track of the place that was selected before you pressed Shift-F10. With a mouse, however, you can point to the spot on the screen you want, and click a mouse button to select it. (If you didn't make any changes while in outline mode, you may be able to return to your previous selection in the document, even without a mouse, by using the Undo command twice in succession, followed by the Left direction key and then the Right direction key.)

A mouse also makes using multiple windows faster and easier. When you don't want to risk losing your selection spot in a document by switching to outline view, you can instead split open a new window temporarily and use the outline in the window. When you're finished, you can close the window to return to your original window—and to your original selection point.

LESSONS

In the three lessons that follow, you'll create an outline, as well as a style sheet, that can be used for outlining and other purposes. Begin the first lesson with a blank screen, either by starting Word from DOS or by using one of the Transfer Clear commands.

The subject of our outline will be the craft of the performing magician.

Lesson I: Fundamentals

From your blank screen:

Step 1. Enter outline view by holding down the Shift key and pressing the F2 key. The message *Level 1* will appear in the lower left corner of the screen, in place of the word *Page*. Press the Enter key a few times to create several blank paragraphs and to move the diamond-shaped end mark out of the way. Press the Up direction key to return to a line at or near the top of the screen, and on this line type: *Part One: The Magic of Magic*.

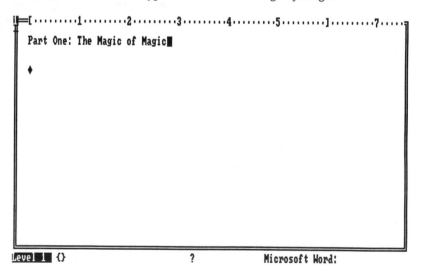

Step 2. At the end of the line, press the Enter key to end the paragraph and move to the next line. The lower corner will still say *Level 1*. The selection (cursor) will be positioned directly under the first line.

Step 3. Hold down the Alt key and press the 0 key (on the top row of the keyboard, not on the keypad). The selection moves four characters to the right, a demotion of one outline level, and the screen's lower left corner displays the words *Level 2*. Type *A Short History of Legerdemain and Illusion* and press the Enter key to move to a new line, which will be at the same level as the last line, Level 2.

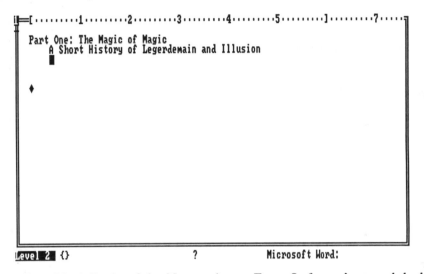

Step 4. Type *Magic By Any Other Name* and press Enter. So far you've typed the book's Part One name as a Level 1 heading, and two chapter titles as Level 2 headings.

Step 5. Press Alt-0 to move in one more level. The screen's lower left corner now displays the words *Level 3*. Type *Illusionists*.

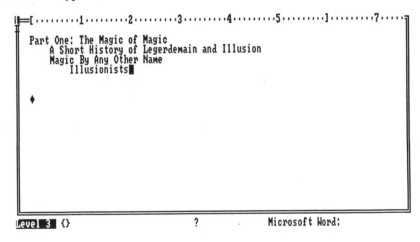

You can change a level of heading, even after the heading has been typed, with Alt-9 and Alt-0.

Step 6. Press Alt-9 twice, to promote *Illusionists* by two levels. Now it is a Level 1 heading.

You can change a heading into body text.

Step 7. Press Alt-P to turn the *Illusionists* line into body text. Observe that an uppercase *T* appears in the selection bar to the left of the line, and the lower left corner of the screen says *Text*.

```
╪═[········1·········2·········3·········4·········5·········]·········7·····╕
Part One: The Magic of Magic
        A Short History of Legerdemain and Illusion
        Magic By Any Other Name
T Illusionists█



   ◆




 Text     {}                        ?                Microsoft Word:
```

You can change body text into a heading by pressing Alt-9. Body text turned into a heading always starts at the same heading level as the most recent previous heading. Once the line is a heading, you can change its level by using Alt-9 or Alt-0.

Step 8. Press Alt-9 to turn the *Illusionists* line into a heading. It becomes Level 2, because the heading above it is Level 2.

Step 9. Press Alt-0 (zero, not the letter *O*) to demote the line to Level 3. Word won't allow you to move to Level 4 by pressing Alt-0 again, because it isn't correct for an outline to skip a level—in this case, a Level 2 heading can't be followed by a Level 4 heading.

Step 10. Press Enter and type *Manipulators*. Press Enter and type *Mind Readers*. These are both *Level 3* headings. Press Enter again, to move to a new line.

Step 11. Press Alt-0 to change the new line to Level 4. (It is possible to move to Level 4 now, because there is a Level 3 heading preceding it.) Type *Mentalism* and press Enter. On the new line, type *Clairvoyance and telepathy*.

```
║     Part One: The Magic of Magic                                          ║
║             A Short History of Legerdemain and Illusion                   ║
║             Magic By Any Other Name                                       ║
║                 Illusionists                                              ║
║                 Manipulators                                              ║
║                 Mind Readers                                              ║
║                     Mentalism                                             ║
║                     Clairvoyance and telepathy█                           ║
```

You could go back and insert a new heading after the heading *Illusionists*.

Step 12. Press the Up direction key three times and select the beginning of *Manipulators*. Type *Escape Artists*.

```
    Illusionists
    Escape Artists Manipulators
    Mind Readers
```

Step 13. Press Enter, and the new Level 3 heading will be inserted.

Step 14. Move the selection back to the end of the Level 4 line, *Clairvoyance and telepathy*, and press the Enter key. The new heading line thus formed will also be at Level 4.

Step 15. Press Alt-9 three times to change the line to Level 1. Type *Part Two: Old Standards* and press Enter. Type Alt-0 to demote the line one level, and type *Hat Tricks*. Continue typing, and adjusting levels, until you've filled your screen like this:

```
=[·········1·········2·········3·········4·········5·········]·········7·····]
Part One: The Magic of Magic
    A Short History of Legerdemain and Illusion
    Magic By Any Other Name
        Illusionists
        Escape Artists
        Manipulators
        Mind Readers
            Mentalism
            Clairvoyance and telepathy
Part Two: Old Standards
    Hat Tricks
        The illusions of Joseph Hartz
        The secrets of Joseph Hartz
            Large bandannas
            Silver-plated goblets
            Cigar boxes
            A caged canary
            Play cards and ribbon
            Glass lanterns with lighted candles
            Goldfish
            A human skull
```
```
Level 4  {}                          ?              Microsoft Word:
```

You spot a typographical error. *Play cards and ribbon* should be *Playing cards and ribbon*. Editing changes are made in outline view the same way they are in normal document view.

Step 16. Move the selection up three lines and add the needed *ing*.

Step 17. Use the Transfer Save command to save the document with the name *MAGIC1*.

So far we've only used outline view, which can be identified by the word *Level* or *Text* in the lower left corner. The other outline mode, outline edit, is more powerful. It is identified in the lower left corner by the word *OUTLINE*. Let's get a little taste of it.

Step 18. Select the first character of the line *Goldfish*, and then switch to the outline edit mode by holding down the Shift key and pressing F5. The entire line becomes highlighted, because in outline edit the smallest unit that can be selected is a paragraph.

Step 19. Press F6 to turn on the extended selection mode, and then press the Up direction key twice to extend the selection to include the two previous headings. Because we're in outline edit, whole headings are selected.

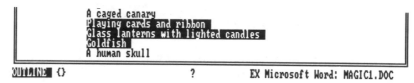

```
                 A caged canary
                 Playing cards and ribbon
                 Glass lanterns with lighted candles
                 Goldfish
                 A human skull

 OUTLINE {}                          ?          EX Microsoft Word: MAGIC1.DOC
```

Step 20. Press Shift-F5 to return from outline edit to outline view.

So far all work has been done in outlining modes. It's time to see what it looks like in document view.

Step 21. Press Shift-F2 to switch to normal document view.

All the indentation disappears, because we've been working in a document that has no paragraph formatting. The indentation has been a result of being in outline view.

```
 Mentalism
 Clairvoyance and telepathy
 Part Two: Old Standards
 Hat Tricks
 The illusions of Joseph Hartz
```

Step 22. Press Shift-F2 again, to return to outline view, where the indentation shows. Press Shift-F2 once again, and you're back in document view.

We could format the headings of the document using built-in formats or the Format Paragraph command, but let's use a more elegant, useful solution. Let's make a Word style sheet.

Lesson II: Creating a style sheet

From the Edit menu, with the document MAGIC1 still on the screen:

Step 1. Press the Esc key and the letter G to enter the Gallery. The Gallery will be blank, and the special Gallery menu will appear at the bottom. (For information on the Gallery, see Chapter 11, "The Efficiency Commands," and Chapter 24, "Power Tools: Style Sheets.")

Step 2. Press the letter I, which is the Gallery's Insert command. You use it to insert a new style, in this case the first style, into a style sheet. Initially, we'll create a standard paragraph style, which, once defined, Word will use to format any paragraph in the document that is not deliberately formatted differently.

Step 3. In the Insert command's *key code* field, type *SP*. This abbreviation stands for "standard paragraph."

Step 4. Press the Tab key to move to the next field, which is *usage*.

Step 5. Press the Spacebar once to pick *Paragraph*, then press the Tab key again to move to the next field, which is *variant*.

Step 6. In the *variant* field, type *standard.* You could also press a direction key or click the right mouse button to bring to the screen a list of all possible paragraph styles. The list begins with the choice *Standard.*

Step 7. Tab to the *remark* field and type, possibly in capital letters, *STANDARD PARAGRAPH.* (You can type anything you like, or leave the *remark* field blank.)

At this point, before you press the Enter key to carry out the Insert command, the Gallery window is still blank but the command fields at the bottom of the screen look like this.

```
INSERT key code: SP                        usage: Character(Paragraph)Division
         variant: standard                 remark: STANDARD PARAGRAPH█
Enter text
GALLERY {}                        ?              Microsoft Word: NORMAL.STY
```

Step 8. Press the Enter key to execute the Insert command. At the top of the Gallery, the style will be inserted. It is highlighted, indicating it is selected. Any formatting carried out with the Gallery's Format commands is applied to the selected style or styles.

Step 9. Pick the Format Paragraph command. Tab to the *first line* field and type *.5.* Then Tab again to the *space before* field and type *1.* This is what your screen shows:

```
├═[·····:·····1········2········3········4········5·······]·······7·····╗
║ ┃ SP Paragraph Standard                    STANDARD PARAGRAPH
║ ┃    Courier (modern a) 12. Flush left.
║ ♦




















├──────────────────────────────────────────────────────────────────────
FORMAT PARAGRAPH alignment:(Left)Centered Right Justified
       left indent: 0"          first line: .5         right indent: 0"
       line spacing: 1 li     space before: 1█        space after: 0 li
       keep together: Yes(No)  keep follow: Yes(No)  side by side: Yes(No)
Enter measurement in lines
GALLERY {}                        ?              Microsoft Word: NORMAL.STY
```

Step 10. Press the Enter key, and the formatting will be applied to the style. The highlighted description of the style will be updated to reflect the change.

```
├═[···:····1········2········3········4········5·······]·······7·····╗
║ ┃ SP Paragraph Standard                    STANDARD PARAGRAPH
║ ┃    Courier (modern a) 12. Flush left (first line indent 0.5"), space
║ ┃    before 1 li.
║ ♦
```

TECHNICAL NOTE: A paragraph style has both paragraph and character formatting. The character formatting defines what will be considered "normal" characters inside the paragraph. When you first create a style, the font that is specified is a function of the printer you are using, as expressed by a .PRD file in the *printer* field of the Print Options command. It will always be expressed as *modern a,* but the name of the font (such as Courier or Pica) will vary printer by printer. In the styles in this book, the font has been changed to *modern b,* because it is an attractive font on most printers. On dot-matrix printers, it often is a double-strike font, which creates characters that are easier to read. If your printer has no *modern b* font, Word will substitute *modern a* during printing. In the next step, you will change the paragraph style's font name from *modern a* (which may be Courier, Pica, or something else) to *modern b* (which may or may not correspond to a particular font on your printer). You may omit this step. It is included primarily to show how changes are made to the character formatting of a paragraph style.

Step 11. With the new style still selected, pick the Format Character command and tab past the other formatting choices to the *font name* field. Type *modern b* in the field.

```
FORMAT CHARACTER bold: Yes(No)      italic: Yes(No)              underline: Yes(No)
         strikethrough: Yes(No)     uppercase: Yes(No)           small caps: Yes(No)
         double underline: Yes(No)  position:(Normal)Superscript Subscript
         font name: modern b█       font size: 12                   hidden: Yes(No)
```

Step 12. Press Enter to carry out the command and apply the character formatting to the paragraph style.

Step 13. Press the Down direction key to move the selection (highlight) down away from the new style. The end mark is selected now, showing where the next style will be inserted. The first style is complete, and its formatting description shows that every standard paragraph in a document formatted with this style sheet will be in 12-point *modern b* type, with paragraphs in flush-left alignment with a first-line indent of one-half inch, preceded by a blank line.

```
╔═[·········1·········2·········3·········4·········5·········]·········7·····╗
║ 1    SP Paragraph Standard                     STANDARD PARAGRAPH           ║
║          Modern b 12. Flush left (first line indent 0.5"), space before 1   ║
║          li.                                                                ║
║  ▯                                                                          ║
╚════════════════════════════════════════════════════════════════════════════╝
```

You've seen how to create the first style in a style sheet. Figure 25-3 shows the entire style sheet. Use the same method—starting with the Insert command and ending with formatting—to create all the *Heading level* paragraph styles. Only four *Heading level* styles are shown, but you can create up to seven if you need them.

Note that the left column of numbers in the style sheet merely shows the order that the styles happen to be in. The second row of numbers, under the *SP,* contains the key codes for the associated *Heading level* styles.

Step 14. When you've finished inserting the styles and formatting them, use the Gallery's Transfer Save command. You may use the name NORMAL, if you want this style sheet to be used by default in the future by all documents on the current disk or in

```
║═[··········1·········2·········3·········4·········5·········]·········7·····┐
║ 1   SP Paragraph Standard                       STANDARD PARAGRAPH
║        Modern b 12. Flush left (first line indent 0.5"), space before 1
║        li.
║ 2   1  Paragraph Heading level 1                HEADING: UNDERLINED CENTER
║        Modern b 12 Bold Underlined Uppercase. Centered, space before 2 li
║        (keep in one column, keep with following paragraph).
║ 3   2  Paragraph Heading level 2                HEADING: CENTERED
║        Modern b 12. Centered, space before 2 li (keep in one column, keep
║        with following paragraph).
║ 4   3  Paragraph Heading level 3                HEADING: FL. LEFT UNDERLINED
║        Modern b 12 Underlined. Flush left, space before 2 li (keep in one
║        column, keep with following paragraph).
║ 5   4  Paragraph Heading level 4                HEADING: FLUSH LEFT
║        Modern b 12. Flush left, space before 2 li (keep in one column,
║        keep with following paragraph).
```

Figure 25-3. A style sheet for headings.

the current hard-disk subdirectory. If you call the style sheet NORMAL, you will have re-defined Word's built-in "normal" paragraph format, for example. This can be useful, if you want your documents to conform to a particular format, and if you want the heading styles always available. If you would rather use this particular style sheet only when you expressly ask for it, give it a name such as HEADINGS. Then, whenever you want to attach this style sheet to a document, use the Format Style Sheet command, type HEADINGS, and press Enter.

Finished creating the style sheet? Let's see what its existence means to the formatting of our outline.

Lesson III: Experimenting

If you are in the Gallery looking at the style sheet, return to the document MAGIC1 by pressing E (for Exit). If you're in document view, switch to outline view by pressing Shift-F2.

If the style bar is not turned on, use the Window Options command to turn it on. And if you're not sure whether the style sheet is attached to your document, press Esc-G to look in the Gallery, or use the Format Style Sheet command to see whether HEADINGS is listed.

In outline view, you'll see that MAGIC1 retains its familiar, indented form, but now there are numbers in the style bar. Each number is the key code for the *Heading level* style that formats it. You'll also see that certain levels of heading have assumed character formatting. Level 1 headings are uppercase, and both Level 1 and Level 3 headings are underlined. This conforms to the formatting specified in the style sheet.

```
║1  PART ONE: THE MAGIC OF MAGIC                                              ║
║2      A Short History of Legerdemain and Illusion                           ║
║2      Magic By Any Other Name                                               ║
║3          Illusionists                                                      ║
║3          Escape Artists                                                    ║
```

Step 1. To see the power of styles to assign heading levels, select lines here and there in the outline and apply different styles. For example, select the first line (Level 1) and type Alt-4. It becomes a Level 4 heading instantly, and its character formatting changes to conform to that specified in the style sheet. Select other lines and change their levels, too, by pressing the Alt key and a key code number.

This is how your outline might look after you've changed its levels.

```
4            Part One: The Magic of Magic
1    A SHORT HISTORY OF LEGERDEMAIN AND ILLUSION
3              Magic By Any Other Name
2               Illusionists
1    ESCAPE ARTISTS
```

Step 2. After you've finished experimenting with key codes and levels, return the headings to their original levels. Observe that the character formatting of heading styles is reflected when you're working in outline view, but the paragraph formatting is not.

It's time to look at the outline in document view.

Step 3. Press Shift-F2 to switch to document view. The word *Page* will appear in the lower left corner of the screen, and the headings from the outline will assume not only the character formatting, but also the paragraph formatting specified for them in the style sheet.

Step 4. Select the space (actually the paragraph mark) at the end of the Level 2 heading *A Short History of Legerdemain and Illusion*. Press Enter to create a new paragraph. This paragraph will be marked *2* in the style bar, for Level 2.

Step 5. Change the blank paragraph from Level 2 to standard by applying the style sheet's key code for a standard paragraph, *SP*. To do this, hold down the Alt key and type *SP*. Now you can type normal paragraphs—and begin to fill the outline out into a document.

Step 6. Type these paragraphs, pressing the Enter key at the end of each except the last one. Observe that the key code *SP* marks each as a standard paragraph. The style bar must be turned on in order for you to see key codes.

```
 [····|····1·········2·········3·········4·········5··········]·········7···
1           PART ONE: THE MAGIC OF MAGIC


2           A Short History of Legerdemain and Illusion

SP          Coiled in his hand, the rope looked normal enough. But
       when the East Indian magician threw one end into the air, it
       hung there, suspended.

SP          First an assistant and then the magician shinnied up
       the rope -- and disappeared at the top. From mid-air, the
       bleeding arms and legs of the assistant fell to earth. The
       magician reappeared, and after sliding back down the rope,
       reassembled his assistant.

SP          This illusion, the famed Indian Rope Trick, has become
       part of the folklore of magic and illusion. Luckily for the
       assistant, it apparently has never been performed. ▮


2           Magic By Any Other Name
```

Page 1   {}   ?   Microsoft Word: MAGIC1.DOC

***Step* 7.** Press Shift-F2 to switch back to outline view. You'll see the headings have resumed their outline-like indentations, but the body text retains its normal paragraph formatting. The paragraphs are expanded, but we want them collapsed in the outline.

```
▌═══[••••¦••••1•••••••••2•••••••••3•••••••4•••••••••5•••••••••]•••••••••7•••┐
▌1  PART ONE: THE MAGIC OF MAGIC
▌2       A Short History of Legerdemain and Illusion
▌
▌SPT      Coiled in his hand, the rope looked normal enough. But
▌    when the East Indian magician threw one end into the air, it
▌    hung there, suspended.
▌
▌SPT      First an assistant and then the magician shinnied up
▌    the rope -- and disappeared at the top. From mid-air, the
▌    bleeding arms and legs of the assistant fell to earth. The
▌    magician reappeared, and after sliding back down the rope,
▌    reassembled his assistant.
▌
▌SPT      This illusion, the famed Indian Rope Trick, has become
▌    part of the folklore of magic and illusion. Luckily for the
▌    assistant, it apparently has never been performed.█
▌2        Magic By Any Other Name
▌3            Illusionists
▌3            Escape Artists
▌3            Manipulators
▌3            Mind Readers
▌4                Mentalism
═════════════════════════════════════════════════════════════════════════
 Text▌    {}                      ?              Microsoft Word: MAGIC1.DOC
```

***Step* 8.** Select the heading above the body text, *A Short History of Legerdemain and Illusion,* and press Shift-Minus. (Use the Minus key on the numeric keypad.) The body text will collapse from view, its presence indicated only by a small *t* in the selection bar.

```
▌═══[•••••••••1•••••••••2•••••••••3•••••••••4•••••••••5•••••••••]•••••••••7•••┐
▌1  PART ONE: THE MAGIC OF MAGIC
▌2 t     A Short History of Legerdemain and Illusion█
▌2       Magic By Any Other Name
▌3           Illusionists
```

***Step* 9.** Toggle back to document view by pressing Shift-F2. You'll see that the text paragraphs that were collapsed in outline view are still apparent in document view. Select the last space (the paragraph mark) of the last paragraph you typed, and press Enter. This creates a new standard paragraph, marked with the key code *SP*, below the paragraph that ends *never been performed.* Like the paragraph above it, this new paragraph is collapsed, although that won't be evident until we return to outline view.

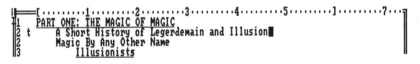
```
▌═══[••••¦••••1•••••••••2•••••••••3•••••••••4•••••••••5•••••••••]•••••••••7•••┐
▌SP       This illusion, the famed Indian Rope Trick, has become
▌    part of the folklore of magic and illusion. Luckily for the
▌    assistant, it apparently has never been performed.
▌
▌SP       █
▌
▌
▌2            Magic By Any Other Name
```

Step 10. Press Alt-2 to turn the paragraph into a Level 2 heading. Type *Harry Houdini* and press Enter. A second Level 2 paragraph forms below the *Houdini* line. Like the one from which it was created, this paragraph is collapsed. Apply the key code *SP* (Alt-SP) to turn it into a standard paragraph, and then type the paragraph shown below.

```
‖═══[····|····1·········2·········3·········4·········5·········]·········7···╕
‖SP        This illusion, the famed Indian Rope Trick, has become
‖       part of the folklore of magic and illusion. Luckily for the
‖       assistant, it apparently has never been performed.


‖2                       Harry Houdini

‖SP        If the Indian Rope Trick is the most famous illusion,
‖       Harry Houdini is arguably the most famous magician. That his
‖       name brings to mind images of spectacular escapes under
‖       seemingly impossible conditions is testimony to his skill
‖       both as a performer and as a self-promoting publicist.█

‖2                   Magic By Any Other Name
```

Step 11. Return from document view to outline view by pressing Shift-F2. You'll see that neither the Level 2 heading nor the standard paragraph appears, because they are collapsed paragraphs. Instead, a + is displayed in the selection bar beside the heading above the collapsed paragraphs.

```
‖1    PART ONE: THE MAGIC OF MAGIC                                    ‖
‖2  +    A Short History of Legerdemain and Illusion                  ‖
‖2       Magic By Any Other Name                                      ‖
‖3          Illusionists                                              ‖
```

Step 12. Press the Up direction key once to move the selection to the line that has the +. Try pressing the Plus key (on the numeric keypad) to expand the collapsed heading. Nothing happens. That's because the Plus key only expands collapsed headings that are *below* it in a hierarchical sense. The Plus sign has no effect here because the hidden heading is at Level 2, the same as the heading that has the + symbol.

Step 13. Press the Asterisk key (on the numeric keypad). The Asterisk is more powerful than the Plus, and so this time the hidden heading appears, marked in the style bar with the key code *2*, indicating it is a Level 2 heading. Both headings show a *t* in the selection bar now, because both have text collapsed under them.

```
‖1    PART ONE: THE MAGIC OF MAGIC                                    ‖
‖2  t    A Short History of Legerdemain and Illusion                  ‖
‖2  t    Harry Houdini                                                ‖
‖2       Magic By Any Other Name                                      ‖
‖3          Illusionists                                              ‖
```

Step 14. Press the Up direction key once, so that the Level 1 heading is selected. Press the Minus key. This collapses all subheadings below it, so that the next line appearing on the screen is the next Level 1 heading.

```
‖1  +  PART ONE: THE MAGIC OF MAGIC                                   ‖
‖1    PART TWO: OLD STANDARDS                                         ‖
‖2       Hat Tricks                                                   ‖
‖3          The illusions of Joseph Hartz                             ‖
```

Step 15. Press the Plus key to expand the next level, in this case Level 2. Observe that one of the Level 2 headings that appears has a + next to it, indicating there are more headings collapsed under it. These headings could be expanded either by pressing the Asterisk now, or by moving the selection to the marked line and pressing Plus.

Let's say we want to delete the heading and paragraph on Harry Houdini that we just typed into the outline/document. We could select the *Harry Houdini* line and delete it while in outline view, but that would delete only the heading and not the paragraph collapsed below it. To delete more than one paragraph at a time, we must switch to outline edit.

Step 16. Press Shift-F5 to enter outline edit. The word *OUTLINE* appears in the lower left corner of the screen. Select the *Harry Houdini* line and press the Del key. The line is deleted and, as we see inside the scrap brackets at the bottom of the screen, so is the paragraph of body text that was collapsed under the *Houdini* line. The selection remains a full paragraph, the smallest it can be in outline edit.

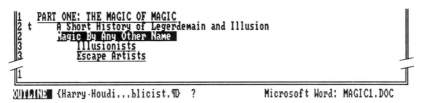

Step 17. To return to outline view, press Shift-F5. Or to return to document view, press Shift-F2.

You've had a pretty fair taste of outlining, including some of the more demanding situations into which you can get.

TIPS

A number of points may make outlining more useful.

♦ You must have a level of heading above the first text in a document if you plan to collapse that text from view.

♦ If you're using a style sheet and do not like looking at the character formatting of headings while you are in an outline mode, you can remove the character formatting by temporarily breaking the link between the style sheet and the outline/document. Pick the Format Style Sheet command and press Del, then press Enter. Or attach a different style sheet, one that has no special character formatting associated with its *Heading level* paragraph styles. When you switch back to document view, use Format Style Sheet again to reattach the style sheet that contains the character formatting.

- Outline view makes it easy to identify all headings to be coded for use by the Library Table command. (See "Finding headings in outline view" in Chapter 26, "Power Tools: Hidden Text and Indexing.")

- Sometimes you may see a + in the selection bar, and yet pressing the Plus key doesn't cause anything to happen. Pressing Shift-Plus may cause text to appear, but that doesn't explain why there was a + instead of a *t* in the selection bar. Likely as not, the heading has a lower-level heading collapsed below it (possibly one that was added by key code while you were in document view). A way to get this to show is to select the heading that has the + in the selection bar and press the *. This will reveal all collapsed levels of headings. Then, if you want body text to appear, press Shift-Plus.

- There is something to be said for making division marks first-level headings. This way, they will always appear when you're in outline view or outline edit, and you'll know when you are moving across a division boundary.

- If you are using a Tandy 1000 computer, use the F11 key to collapse a heading and the F12 key to expand a heading. Use Shift-F11 to collapse body text and Shift-F12 to expand body text.

- One of the purposes of looking at a document as an outline is to get as broad a view as possible of the structure and the flow of what you are writing. For this reason, if you are using a computer equipped with a high-resolution graphics adapter, such as an EGA or a Hercules, you may want to start word with the /h option (*word/h*). By increasing the number of lines on the screen, this option lets you see more of what you are working on at a time. Similarly, if you're using Word with the menu displayed at the bottom of the screen, you may want to turn it off with the Options command.

- When moving or copying text between windows, you could think your Ins key has stopped working—but it hasn't. If the original text is collapsed (but visible in a document window) and you insert it into an outline, it will seem not to be there. It will remain collapsed. I've pressed the Ins key two or three times, trying to make the key work, before realizing that it was working just fine. You won't see the collapsed text you've inserted until you expand it, or switch the window from outline to document view. Then, if you've pressed Ins several times, you'll find several successive copies of what was in the scrap.

Certain tricks pertain specifically to document view:

- When you are in document view and want to delete a heading and all the text that follows it, a fast technique is to select the heading, press Shift-F2, then Shift-F5, then Del, then Shift-F2 to return to document view. The deleted material will be in the scrap, and can be inserted elsewhere in the document.

- Assuming text is collapsed and you're in document view, you can jump to the next heading by pressing Shift-F2 twice in a row. However, if a heading is selected when you use this technique, that is the heading to which you will jump.

NUMBERING AND SORTING

The Library Number and Library Autosort commands give you the means to number and alphabetize elements in a document. The general use of these commands is covered thoroughly in Chapter 14, "The Family of Library Commands." But the rules change in some respects when you are in outline mode; the commands assume special characteristics and powers.

The Library Number command

When you're in normal document view, the Library Number command will update or remove existing numbers and letters that start paragraphs, but it won't assign numbers to paragraphs on its own. Because Word can only guess which elements in a document you want numbered, it doesn't try. But in an outline, matters are considerably different. Word "knows" the conventional ways of numbering an outline, and it assumes you want every element numbered (or lettered). It will number from scratch if you like.

For example, if you execute the Library Number command while you are in outline view, you'll normally get a numbering scheme like this:

```
t  I. PART ONE: THE MAGIC OF MAGIC
t        A. A Short History of Legerdemain and Illusion
t        B. Magic By Any Other Name
t           1. Illusionists
t           2. Escape Artists
t           3. Manipulators
t           4. Mind Readers
t              a) Mentalism
t              b) Clairvoyance and telepathy
t II. PART TWO: OLD STANDARDS
t        A. Hat Tricks
t           1. The illusions of Joseph Hartz
t           2. The secrets of Joseph Hartz
t              a) Large bandannas
t              b) Silver-plated goblets
t              c) Cigar boxes
```

If you type the number *1.* at the beginning of the first line of an outline that has no numbers, and then execute the Library Number command, you'll get a double-numeration (or "legal-style") scheme, often used in technical documents.

```
t 1. PART ONE: THE MAGIC OF MAGIC
t       1.1 A Short History of Legerdemain and Illusion
t       1.2 Magic By Any Other Name
t           1.2.1 Illusionists
t           1.2.2 Escape Artists
t           1.2.3 Manipulators
t           1.2.4 Mind Readers
t              1.2.4.1 Mentalism
t              1.2.4.2 Clairvoyance and telepathy
t 2. PART TWO: OLD STANDARDS
t       2.1 Hat Tricks
t           2.1.1 The illusions of Joseph Hartz
t           2.1.2 The secrets of Joseph Hartz
t              2.1.2.1 Large bandannas
t              2.1.2.2 Silver-plated goblets
```

These two numbering systems are built into Word. If you have other preferences, Word will try to oblige. It will mimic a numbering system if you give it, at the beginning of the first instance of each outline level, an example of the kind of numbering (or lettering) you want for that level. For example, if you type an *A.* at the beginning of the first Level 1 line in an outline, and *i*) at the beginning of the first instance of a Level 2 line, Word will letter your first-level headings and give lowercase Roman numerals to your second-level headings.

Regardless of which numbering system you use, the numbers not only appear in outline view, but become part of the document.

A useful facet of the Library Number command is that every group of subheadings will be numbered separately. However, if you have a group of subheadings you want to number consecutively, you can do it if you're using a style sheet with *Heading level* styles. For example, if you want to number all the Level 2 headings in a document consecutively, without regard for periodic Level 1 headings, temporarily apply a style for a lower level, such as Level 7 (Alt-7), to the Level 1 styles. This permits the Level 2 headings to be numbered consecutively.

If there are paragraphs you do not wish to have numbered, precede them with a hyphen (-), asterisk (∗), or bullet (■). (The square bullet is ASCII character 22, which may be available on your printer. Hold down the Alt key and type *22* on the numeric keypad.)

Finally, it is possible to trick Word into assigning numbers to a list that's not meant to be an outline. Just put the list in outline form temporarily: Type *1.* or *1*) at the beginning of the first line of the list, then enter outline edit (Shift-F2 followed by Shift-F5), select the elements in the list, make them Level 1 by pressing Alt-9 as many times as necessary, and then execute the Library Number command.

The Library Autosort command

Word's Library Autosort command operates differently when it alphabetizes or puts in numeric order elements in an outline.

The advantage of sorting in outline view is that you can keep groups of paragraphs together, and sort the order of a document on a group-by-group basis. The position in a document of a group of paragraphs will be based on the alphabetic or numeric value of the beginning of the group's first paragraph. You do this by making the first paragraph of each group a Level 1 heading in the outline, and making other paragraphs lower levels that follow the Level 1 heading. The Library Autosort command will put the Level 1 paragraphs in order, moving the associated lower levels with them. A good use for this capability is combining indexes. Chapter 26, "Power Tools: Hidden Text and Indexing," contains a step-by-step tutorial on using the Library Autosort command in its outline mode to accomplish this.

Power Tools: Hidden Text and Indexing

With Word, you can write with invisible ink. The question, of course, is why you would want to.

You can use hidden characters to:

♦ Annotate what you write with private comments that print or show on the screen only if you so desire.

♦ Prepare a document for automatic indexing.

♦ Code a document so that Word can automatically generate a table of contents for it.

♦ Format paragraphs in creative ways that otherwise are impossible. For instance, you can wrap text around a photograph or drawing by changing line length (indentation) several times within a long paragraph.

These techniques, available beginning with Word version 3.0, are not difficult. You can obtain pleasing results with little practice or experience. However, as with many of Word's features, if you push the possible uses of hidden text to the limit, you have much to gain but also much to learn.

THE BASICS

Except in the diversity of its purposes, hidden text is little different from italicized, boldfaced, or underlined text. "Hidden" is a character format. You apply it to selected text, or turn it on and off while typing, just as you do the character formats "italic," "bold," and "underline." But until you get used to hidden text, it can surprise you. For example, you won't be able to see what you're typing unless the *show hidden text* field of the Window Options command is set to *Yes*. And the page numbering of your document can be thrown off if hidden text is visible when you use the Print Repaginate command. You'll soon come to understand the effects of these characters that are in your document—but aren't.

Hiding existing text

Character formatting techniques were introduced in Chapter 5, "The Simple Word," and Chapter 12, "The Family of Format Commands." However, a brief review may be helpful.

Character formatting follows the Select-Do concept. First you select what you want formatted, then you do the actual formatting. If the text characters to be hidden are already in your document, you select all of them and then apply formatting in one of four ways:

1. Use the Format Character command and pick *Yes* in the *hidden* field. Or:
2. Use the built-in format (Alt-E) for hidden text. (If E seems like a peculiar choice, it's because the logical choice, Alt-H, causes Word's help feature to appear on the screen. E stands for *Erase*, by the way.) Or:
3. If a style sheet is attached to your document, use the aforementioned built-in format by typing Alt-X-E. Or:
4. If a style sheet is attached to your document and it contains a character style expressly for hidden text, use the key code for the style. For instance, the key code for a hidden-text style might be Alt-HC, for *hidden character*. This is how such a style might appear when displayed in the Gallery:

```
‖  59  HC Character 5                          HIDDEN                        ‖
           Modern b 12 Hidden.
```

Hiding new text

Sometimes you don't want to hide (or otherwise format) characters that are already in a document. Instead you want the new characters you type to be hidden. To accomplish this, select the character at which you wish to begin typing and use the built-in format (Alt-E or Alt-X-E) or a style key code (Alt-HC). The selected character won't be formatted, but any new text you type there will be.

If you use the Format Character command when a single character is selected, the actual character will receive the formatting. Sometimes this is appropriate, because you may want to hide only one character. (Recall from earlier chapters that you can also accomplish the formatting of a single character with a built-in format or style by holding down the Alt key and typing the code *twice* in a row.)

The fastest way to return hidden text to normal text is to select it and press Alt-Spacebar. This causes all character formatting (including character styles) to be discarded. If the hidden text has other character formatting you want to preserve, the Alt-Spacebar technique is too powerful. Instead, use the Format Character command and change the *hidden* field to *No*.

Notes for style sheet users: Recall that you can eliminate the effect a character style (such as HC above) has on text by applying a different character style, with different formatting, to the same text. Or by switching to a style sheet that has different formatting for the particular style. Also, recall that with a style sheet you can control which character format is considered "normal." Using Alt-Spacebar on text formatted with a style sheet causes the characters to assume whatever formatting is specified as "normal" or "standard" in the character-formatting portion of the relevant *paragraph* style.

What does hidden text look like?

What does something that is invisible look like? Like nothing you have ever seen before, of course.

Actually, "hidden" text can take several forms, depending on choices you make with the Window Options and Options commands. This chart shows the flow of decisions you might make.

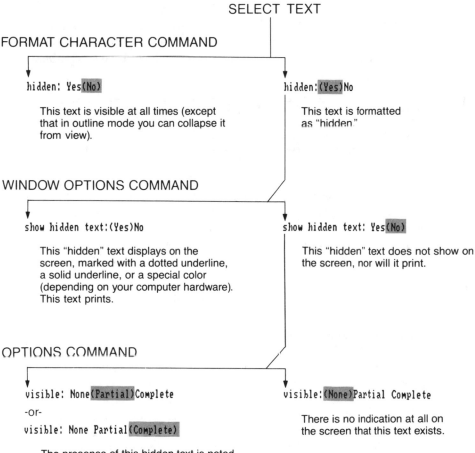

SELECT TEXT

FORMAT CHARACTER COMMAND

hidden: Yes(No)

This text is visible at all times (except that in outline mode you can collapse it from view).

hidden:(Yes)No

This text is formatted as "hidden"

WINDOW OPTIONS COMMAND

show hidden text:(Yes)No

This "hidden" text displays on the screen, marked with a dotted underline, a solid underline, or a special color (depending on your computer hardware). This text prints.

show hidden text: Yes(No)

This "hidden" text does not show on the screen, nor will it print.

OPTIONS COMMAND

visible: None(Partial)Complete
-or-
visible: None Partial(Complete)

The presence of this hidden text is noted on the screen as a double-ended arrow (↔).

visible:(None)Partial Complete

There is no indication at all on the screen that this text exists.

First, you decide whether text will be formatted as visible or hidden. All, or almost all, of the text in a document is visible, but, as already described, you can hide selected text by using the Format Character command or the Alt key methods.

Second, you decide whether text that is formatted as hidden will show on the screen or not. This choice is made in the *show hidden text* field of the Window Options command. If you pick *Yes*, and your computer has graphics capabilities, the hidden text will appear on the screen with a special underline of tiny dots. If your computer doesn't do graphics (or you've started Word in /c mode), hidden text will display with a solid underline or in a different color. "Hidden" text that appears in any readable form will print on your printer. Because *show hidden text* is a window option, the same document can be displayed simultaneously in two windows, one with hidden text showing and one with hidden text not showing.

Third, with the Options command's *visible* field, you decide whether hidden text that isn't showing should be acknowledged on the screen at all. If you pick *Partial* or *Complete*, Word will display a two-headed arrow at the spot where text is hidden. If you pick *None*, there will be no indication the hidden text exists.

```
┌─────────────────────────────────┐ ┌─────────────────────────────────┐
│ The same text is in both windows.¶│2│ The same text is in both windows.¶│
│ This sentence is hidden. ¶        │ │ ↔ ¶                              │
│ Hidden text shows in the left     │ │ Hidden text shows in the left     │
│ window, with a special underline. │ │ window, with a special underline. │
│ In the right window, hidden text  │ │ In the right window, hidden text  │
│ shows only as a special double-   │ │ shows only as a special double-   │
│ headed arrow (I'm invisible!).¶   │ │ headed arrow ↔.¶                 │
└─────────────────────────────────┘ └─────────────────────────────────┘
```

On the above screen, the same document is in both windows. Hidden text shows with a special underline in the left window, because the window is set to *show hidden text*. In the right window, where the Window Option command's *show hidden text* field is set to *No*, hidden text is indicated with a two-headed arrow. If the Options command's *visible* field were set to *None*, not even the two-headed arrow would appear in the right window.

Annotating and editing

You can use hidden text for its own sake. When writing or editing a document, you may have an idea, comment, or other annotation to add. When working on paper, you might write a note in the margin. With Word, you use hidden text.

When a comment or passage is hidden, you have freedom to look at it and print it or to make it go away temporarily. If more than one person annotates the same document with hidden comments, each might identify what they wrote by adding their initials.

When cutting a document's length, you can select passages and hide them instead of deleting them outright. Similarly, you can add passages tentatively by writing them in hidden characters. By making these hidden passages appear and disappear, you can compare the document in two forms. Any hidden text you decide to keep can be made visible. Be careful to hide paragraph marks only if you mean to, however, since the results may perplex you. More about this near the end of the chapter.

NOTE: The selection (cursor) may pause when it passes a point at which a lot of text is hidden. This is because Word "thinks" about the text, even though it's hidden. Also, there is a limit of about 65,000 consecutive hidden characters. You can get around this by putting one visible Spacebar space between two long hidden passages, but Word's performance slows when massive amounts of text are hidden.

INDEXES AND TABLES: THE THREE STAGES

There are three broad stages to indexing or creating a table of contents with Word.

The first stage is *coding,* in which you embed into the body of a document hidden instructions that indicate the words, phrases, or lines you want Word to compile into an index or table of contents. This coding must be formatted as hidden text, so to see what you're doing you'll probably want to set the *show hidden text* field of the Window Options command to *Yes.*

The second stage is *compiling,* which Word does for you when you execute the Library Index or Library Table command. Word uses the hidden coding to pull together a compilation of content and page numbers, which it can then assemble into an index or table of contents.

The optional third stage is *formatting,* in which you make the index or table look the way you want it to. As you'll recall from discussions of the Library Index and Library Table commands in Chapter 14, Word can do substantial formatting automatically when it compiles an index or table. It can even follow formatting instructions from a style sheet.

INDEXING

Indexing is no picnic, even with Word's sophisticated help. Human judgment is required to produce a high-caliber index. Index headings and subentries must be chosen with care.

Although Word can't help you decide the content of an index, it can increase your efficiency enormously. Word reduces the tedium of indexing by automatically compiling, alphabetizing, and recording page numbers. It also simplifies or eliminates the chore of formatting an index to look the way you want it to.

Coding

The first stage in indexing with Word is identifying all the places in the document at which you have words, phrases, or ideas you want referenced in the index. Each of these locations must be marked with hidden coding.

The coding follows a simple form. Immediately before the word or phrase to be indexed you type *.i.* (or *.I.*) and format it as hidden. At the end of the word or phrase, you type a semicolon (*;*)., presumably you'll also want to have hidden. These two codes, *.i.* at the beginning and the *;* at the end, identify the intervening text as an index instruction.

‖ This .i.sentence; line has its second word marked for indexing.   ‖

It doesn't matter to Word whether the text between the *.i.* and the *;* is formatted as visible or hidden. You can place the hidden coding on either side of visible text that's already in your document, as in the above example. Or you can can make the entire instruction hidden. For instance, in the following sentence the word *jetliners* has been marked as a heading for the index, even though the word isn't part of the visible text. (Note also that the visible text, *Boeing 757,* is marked as a separate index entry.)

‖ The .i.jetliners;.i.Boeing 757; symbolizes humanity's quest for   ‖

In this example, the word *jetliners* was placed before the name *Boeing 757*. Placing hidden instructions immediately before the visible text to which they refer ensures that, after repagination, both will be on the same page.

Coding subentries

The simplest indexes have entries with only one level, the heading. More commonly, books and reports have two levels, headings and subentries. This book has three levels.

Word handles multiple-level entries nicely. When coding an index subentry, you may designate a path of words or phrases leading from a heading to the relevant subentry. The method of marking, which is derived from conventional notation used by professional indexers, is to put a colon (:) between levels of a multiple-level entry instruction. For example, if page 35 of this book referred to horizontal scrolling with the mouse, you could add to the manuscript at that point a hidden instruction — *.i.Scrolling:horizontal:with mouse;* — and Word would later construct from it an index entry with three levels:

```
Scrolling
   horizontal
      with mouse  35
```

In this example, the page number appears only after the bottom-level line. To instruct Word to place the page number on all three lines, you would code three successive index instructions, all of which could be run together like this:

```
.i.Scrolling;.i.Scrolling:horizontal;.i.Scrolling:horizontal:with mouse;
```

Word allows you up to five levels in an index, and at your request will automatically format up to four of these with a style sheet. Generally, people use two or three.

Even though you may not plan to use subentries in your index, it is sound practice during the initial coding to include at least one subentry following each main-level heading in an index instruction. You can always delete some of these subentries later, if they prove unhelpful. But, as the authoritative *Chicago Manual of Style* puts it: "It is important to have them on hand at later stages in making the index, because if you do not, you may end up with nothing but unmodified headings followed by long strings of page numbers. These make an index all but useless."

Tips on coding

◆ Because semicolons (;) and colons (:) have special meanings when used as coding in an index instruction, you must enclose in quotation marks any index instruction that uses these characters as punctuation. For example, the book title *Magic: Beyond the Illusion* would mislead Word if it were marked as an index entry. Word would assume *Magic* was supposed to be a main index heading and *Beyond the Illusion* a second-level index subentry. By placing the entire title (but not the *.i.* or *;*) inside quotation marks, you signal that the colon inside the quotation marks is to be treated as punctuation, not index coding. Format the quotation marks as hidden text.

♦ You can place *see* and *see also* cross-references in your document by placing a hidden colon just before the semicolon that ends the coded instruction. The colon suppresses the page number that otherwise will be added when the index is compiled. For example, in the passage on the Boeing 757 you might insert *.i.757. See Boeing 757:;* all formatted as hidden. Word would include *757. See Boeing 757* in the index, alphabetized under *757*. No page number would follow it. (A *see* entry is used when the information can be found under a different heading: *Leona Helmsley. See Helmsley, Leona.* A *see also* entry is used to direct the reader to additional information. Generally, the words *See* and *See also* are italicized.)

♦ The *.i.* must be in hidden format. Anything else, including the final semicolon, can be visible. But unless you want the semicolon to print, hide it.

♦ Instead of using a semicolon to end an index instruction, you can use a paragraph mark. This is a handy option if you're coding a document heading that ends in a paragraph mark anyway. (Technically, a division mark can end an index instruction, too.)

♦ If your Word document has been typeset, you can still index it. Enlarge the division margin formatting so that at least as many characters appear on a Word "page" as on any typeset page. Scroll through the document and place new-page characters (Shift-Ctrl-Enter) at exactly the places they occur in the typeset version. Repaginate your Word document, and its page numbering will match that of the typeset version. This permits you to code the document with confidence that the page references in the resulting index will be accurate.

Faster coding

There are ways to speed up the coding of a document. One is to copy the hidden-text code *.i.* to the glossary, giving it a simple name such as *i*. To insert the code, you type i (or whatever glossary name) and press F3. Similarly, you can insert both *.i.* and a hidden text heading jointly by making both parts one glossary entry. This is handy when a particular index heading is used repeatedly with different subentries.

The glossary doesn't work as well for inserting hidden semicolons at the end of index entries, however, because a glossary name must be typed after a blank space in order to work with the F3 key, or else the name must be more than one character long and be selected. However, you can type a hidden semicolon rapidly by pressing Alt-E followed by a semicolon. Then you can press Alt-Spacebar to turn off the hidden format, or you can leave the formatting behind by moving away with a direction key or by clicking elsewhere with the mouse. (If a style sheet is attached to the document, use Alt-X-E or an appropriate key code instead of Alt-E.)

Replace. When a topic appears numerous times in a document, you can partly automate the coding of a key word or phrase that is repeated. You can replace every instance of *Boeing 757* with *.i.Boeing 757;*. Unfortunately, Word's Replace command is limited to content and does not insert formatting, so whatever text it inserts will be visible. You must manually select and hide every *.i.* and semicolon.

A couple of techniques speed up this manual formatting. One is using a mouse, which gets you around the screen quickly. The other is using the Search command and the F4/Shift-F4 key combination.

Search and F4. Recall that F4 repeats the last editing act and Shift-F4 repeats the last execution of the Search command. Use the Search command to find and highlight the first instance of *.i.*. Format it as hidden. Press F8 as many times as are necessary to highlight the semicolon at the end of the word or phrase. In the case of *Boeing 757,* press F8 three times— once to highlight *Boeing,* once to highlight *757,* and once to highlight the semicolon. Press the F4 key to repeat the last editing act, which in this case turns the selection into hidden text. Press Shift-F4 to search for the next occurrence of *.i.*, and press F4 to hide it (repeating the last editing act). Press F8 again, until the semicolon is highlighted, then press F4, and so on. Don't worry that the blank space after the semicolon is highlighted when you press F4. Word won't hide the space, even though it's highlighted. However, when punctuation such as a period or comma follows the semicolon, use the Left and Right direction keys to make sure only the semicolon, and not the period or comma, is highlighted. Then press F4.

Another variation: Replace *757* with *.i.Boeing 757;757* throughout a document, and then use the Search command to find the first instance of *.i.Boeing 757;*. When it is high-lighted, apply the hidden text format (Alt-E or Alt-X-E). This will leave in visible text only the original word *757*. Press Shift-F4 to search for the next instance of *.i.Boeing 757;*, and press F4 to apply the hidden format. This method reduces the amount of typing you have to do, and it causes all text references to either *Boeing 757* or *757* to be indexed as *Boeing 757*.

Macros. If you index much, you're in for a treat if you own keyboard-enhancer software that is compatible with Word. One such program is ProKey 4.0, Release 10 or later. Such soft-ware lets you define a complicated series of keystrokes as a "macro." For example, you can de-fine Ctrl-S as a series of keystrokes that code whatever is selected for indexing. Just use F7, F8, or the right mouse button to select a word or phrase, then hold down the Ctrl key and type S. Instantly, a proper, complete, hidden index instruction will be added.

But you must teach the keyboard enhancer what you want Ctrl-S to represent. This is the sequence of keystrokes: Alt-x-e (make selection hidden); Esc-c-Enter (copy the selection to the scrap); Alt-Spacebar (remove the hidden-text formatting); Left direction followed by Right direction (reduce the selection to the first character of the word or phrase); Alt-x-e (turn on hidden text); the characters *.i.i;* (coding for the beginning and end of an index in-struction); Left direction followed by Ins (insert the hidden text from the scrap between the *.i.* and the semicolon); Left and then Del (to remove an unwanted space).

If you're using ProKey, you can teach the keystrokes to the program by adding the fol-lowing instruction to a ProKey file:

      <begdef><ctrls><altx>e<esc>c<enter><altspac><lft><rgt><altx>e.i.;
      <lft><ins><lft><del><enddef>.

This keystroke sequence assumes that the word or phrase you select will include a trail-ing blank space to the right, because that's the way Word selects words when you use F7, F8, or the right mouse button. However, sometimes you'll select a word or phrase that ends in punctuation—such as a word that ends a sentence or comes before a comma or a hyphen. For these situations, a second macro should be defined, identical to the first except for the omission of the final two keystrokes, the Left direction key followed by Del. You can define this modified version as Ctrl-A, and use it when the selection does not include a right-side space.

If you're using ProKey, the instructions for the Ctrl-A macro are:

> <begdef><ctrla><altx>e<esc>c<enter><altspac><lft><rgt><altx>e.i.;
> <lft><ins><enddef>.

NOTE: If you use a version of ProKey 4.0 that has a release number lower than 10, you'll find subtle incompatibilities with Word. For instance, Word's ability to expand and collapse text in outline view will be compromised.

Compiling the index

By now, your work's almost done. Compiling the indexing instructions into an index is as easy as running the Library Index command. For details, see Chapter 14, "The Family of Library Commands." Set the *show hidden text* field of the Window Options command to *No* before executing the command, so that page numbering won't be thrown off.

Long documents may take a while to index. Have patience. Word is doing a lot: reading the document for index entries, figuring out up to five levels of heading, alphabetizing the entries by level, adding appropriate page numbers, and formatting the results.

In addition to the index per se, the Library Index command adds a couple of things to the document's content: some hidden markers and a division mark.

Hidden markers. The first line of the compiled index will say .*Begin Index.* and the final line will say .*End Index.*. Both lines are in hidden text. If you want to keep the existing version of the index and yet be able to run the Library Index command again to compile an updated version, you must first delete the existing version's .*Begin Index.* line.

The division mark. Word places a new division at the end of the document, before the index. The division mark appears on the screen as a series of colons stretching across the text window (:::::::::::::::). Word inserts this boundary between body text and index because it's trying to be helpful. It assumes you'll want to format the overall look of index pages differently from earlier pages. The division mark lets you format the regions on either side individually, using Format Division commands or division styles from a style sheet. You can make different choices for each division about the number of columns on a page, the format of page numbers, the widths of page margins, and the content and format of running heads.

If the division mark Word inserts before an index confuses you, the following discussion may be useful. Otherwise, you may wish to skip it.

Recall that the division formatting of text is stored in the division mark that comes *after* the text. When an index or other text isn't followed by a division mark, it is governed by the document's "standard" division format. This "standard" format is set by:

♦ The *Division Standard* style, if you are using a style sheet that has this style defined.

♦ Or, the *built-in division format,* if you are not using a style sheet or if you are using a style sheet that doesn't include a *Division Standard* style. (The built-in division format was described at the end of Chapter 5, "The Simple Word.")

If you change the division formatting of the index, you'll cause a division mark to be added after the index.

You may find after compiling an index that *two* division marks precede it. This means one was already at the end of the document when the Library Index command added another. The second mark has no effect, since there's no text between it and the mark above it.

Style-sheet users who rely on the *Division Standard* style come to expect it will automatically apply to any division that isn't formatted in some other way. But if they want the *Division Standard* style in a document that has an index, they should explicitly apply the style after they run the Library Index command. Although later releases of Word may differ, in version 3.0 the division mark that appears before the index is *directly* formatted with Word's built-in (default) division formatting. It is not formatted with the *Division Standard* style, even though it may have been so before the Library Index command was run, and even though the index will have the standard style. To apply the *Division Standard* style, select any character(s) inside the division and type the style's key code (such as S/).

Fixing up content

Few indexes of any substantial length are perfect at first. You'll have overlooked one thing or another. For example, you may find that you have coded *jetliner* on some pages and *jetliners* on others. These will be listed separately in the index, but you probably want to consolidate them with a single list of page numbers. You can either recode instructions and execute the Library Index command again, or fix up the index by editing it.

Alphabetization. In some circumstances, you may second-guess the alphabetical order Word uses for main index headings. Dictionaries follow a system of alphabetization called *letter by letter,* in which every letter is taken into account regardless of spaces between words. *Halfback* comes before *half sister,* because *b* comes before *s.* The other major alphabetization system, called *word by word,* is used in telephone books. It follows the letter-by-letter scheme only until the end of the first word. *Half sister* comes before *halfback,* because *half* comes before *halfback.* However, the letters of the second and subsequent words are taken into account when two or more headings begin with the same word or words. Hence, *half nelson* comes before *half sister* in both systems.

Indexes can be of either type and, as a practical matter, there usually is little difference between headings alphabetized one way or the other. The following words were chosen to emphasize differences.

```
1                         2                       3
 Letter-by-letter          Word-by-word            These two lists
                                                    of alphabetized
 halfback                  half gainer             words exaggerate
 half gainer               half nelson             the differences
 halfhearted               half rest               between the
 half nelson               half sister             alphabetization
 half rest                 halfback                systems.  Word
 half sister               halfhearted             uses the word-
 halfway                   halfway                 by-word system.
```

Word uses the *word-by-word* system, as do most microcomputer programs. If you prefer the *letter-by-letter* system, you can edit the order of the headings once they are compiled in index form. Alternatively, you can omit the space between multi-word headings when you code a document with index instructions. Omitting spaces forces a strict *letter-by-letter* sequence, but you must edit the compiled index to restore the spaces between words.

Subentries. As for subentries, a certain amount of editing is often appropriate. There may be outright mistakes. Your judgment about what is important may sharpen when surveying the results of your indexing. You may wish to delete references that seem unimportant, or gather them together at the end of the entire entry under the subentry *mentioned*.

Page numbers. Changes to page numbers may be appropriate, too. If an entry lists pages 37, 38, and 39, and you know the numbers refer to a single extended discussion, you may edit the entry to read 37-39.

Consider two versions of part of the same index.

```
Heading ————»New Zealand                    New Zealand
Subentry ————and Australia  7                 Auckland  4, 5, 12, 13, 15
             Auckland  4, 5, 13               Australia and  7, 10
Sub-subentry ———climate  5                    Christchurch  4
             Harbor  15                       economics  3, 17-18
             politics in  12                  France  9
             Australia  10                      anti-French sentiment  14
             Christchurch  4                    nuclear weapons and  15       — Entry
             France  9                        livestock  2, 4
               anti-French sentiment  14      nuclear weapons in  7, 9, 15
               nuclear weapons  15            people of  2
             livestock  4                     Rainbow Warrior affair  15, 19
             nuclear weapons  7, 9            Wellington  4
             people  2
             Rainbow Warrior  15, 19
             sheep  2
             small shops  3
             Taxation  18
             trade barriers  17
             Wellington  4
```

The left example shows an index entry for the heading New Zealand, before editing. It is displayed in Word's normal format for indexes. It has fourteen subentries, of which two, Auckland and France, have sub-subentries. The right example shows the same index entry after preliminary editing. Format hasn't changed, but content has been consolidated.

Formatting the Index

By filling out the four fields of the Library Index command, you make basic decisions about how the index will look. These fields are described in detail in Chapter 14, "The Family of Library Commands."

```
LIBRARY INDEX entry/page # separated by:  ███    cap main entries:(Yes)No
                       indent each level: 0.2"         use style sheet: Yes(No)
```

If you don't change the default settings for these fields, two spaces will be inserted between the end of each heading or subentry and the page number that follows; every heading (top-level entry) will begin with a capital letter; and every sub-subentry will be indented .2 inches relative to the higher-level entry above it.

You may not want these default settings. For instance, you may prefer that a comma and space be inserted between each heading or subentry and the associated page numbers. To make this change, type a comma and a Spacebar space in the *entry/page # separated by* field of the Library Index command.

Last is not least. The fourth field is arguably the most powerful. It is called *use style sheet*.

Indexing with a style sheet

When you use the Library Index command to tell Word to *use style sheet*, the program disregards the command's *indent each level* field. Instead of *directly* formatting the paragraphs of the index, Word formats each paragraph *indirectly*—by assigning it one of four styles and giving the styles sole control over the indentation and line spacing of the paragraphs.

- ◆ Each top-level index heading (including any heading with no subentries) is linked to the style named *Paragraph Index level 1*.
- ◆ Each subentry is linked to the style named *Paragraph Index level 2*.
- ◆ Each sub-subentry is linked to the style named *Paragraph Index level 3*.
- ◆ Each sub-sub-subentry is linked to the style named *Paragraph Index level 4*. (For this style, as for each of the other three, *Paragraph* is the usage and *Index level X* is the variant.)

The four *Index level* styles are no different from other paragraph styles in the way you create or format them in the Gallery. The difference is that they are dedicated to a particular function. If you pick *Yes* in the *use style sheets* field, Word automatically applies these styles to the appropriate levels of index headings and subentries. It is as if you had selected each line of the index individually and applied styles with the Alt key and key codes. In this sense, they are similar to other dedicated styles, such as the *Paragraph Standard* style, which is automatically applied to all paragraphs that are not deliberately formatted in some other way.

Here is a sample style sheet, which contains four *Index level* paragraph styles as well as a *Paragraph Standard* style, and a character style for hidden text. Note that the key codes for the four index styles are I1 through I4, while the key code for standard paragraphs is SP, and the key code for hidden character is HC.

```
1   SP Paragraph Standard                    STANDARD PARAGRAPH
       Modern b 12. Flush left (first line indent 0.5"), space before 1
       li.
2   I1 Paragraph Index level 1               INDEX LEVEL 1 (MAIN ENTRIES)
       Modern b 12. Flush left, Left indent 0.6" (first line indent -
       0.6").
3   I2 Paragraph Index level 2               INDEX LEVEL 2
       Modern b 12. Flush left, Left indent 0.8" (first line indent -
       0.6").
4   I3 Paragraph Index level 3               INDEX LEVEL 3
       Modern b 12. Flush left, Left indent 1" (first line indent -0.6").
5   I4 Paragraph Index level 4               INDEX LEVEL 4
       Modern b 12. Flush left, Left indent 1" (first line indent -0.4").
6   HC Character 5                           HIDDEN
       Modern b 12 Hidden.
```

Using these sample Index styles, an index would look the same initially as it would if you accepted the default settings in all the Library Index command fields (including *use style sheet* set to *No*). But by changing the formatting of the styles—either before or after an index is compiled—you can change the look of the index. For instance, you could change formatting of the *Paragraph Index level 1* style (key code I1) so that main headings print in bold type and are preceded by half a line of blank space. You could change the *Paragraph Index level 2* (key code I2) style so that subentries print with a deeper left indent and in italics. And so on.

This is how the first two *Index Level* styles might appear, once their formatting had been modified:

```
2   I1 Paragraph Index level 1               INDEX LEVEL 1 (MAIN ENTRIES)
       Modern b 12 Bold. Flush left, Left indent 0.6" (first line indent -
       0.6"), space before 0.5 li.
3   I2 Paragraph Index level 2               INDEX LEVEL 2
       Modern b 12 Italic. Flush left, Left indent 1.1" (first line indent
       -0.6").
```

Word will let you pick *Yes* in the *use style sheet* field even if the style sheet doesn't have the *Paragraph Index level* styles, or if there is no style sheet attached to the document at all. It will still "format" the index with the style names, but if no formatting instructions exist for the styles, the index paragraphs will not have proper indentation—at least, not at first. But you can still attach a style sheet or create the index styles after the index has been compiled. Word will know which style to apply to which index level.

NOTE: If Word is asked to create a five-level index entry, it formats the lowest level with the style named *Paragraph Standard*. Of course, you can select the fifth-level paragraphs and apply a different style to them manually.

Indented or run-in format?

Indexes that have subentries fall into one of two typographical styles, *indented* or *run in*. In either case, all lines are set with a hanging indent, which means the first line is flush and the rest are indented. (This is also called *flush and hang*, and is obtained in Word by giving a paragraph—or a style-sheet style—both a left indent and a negative first-line indent.)

An *indented* index indents subentries, uses a new line to start each, and can have sub-subentries. (Or sub-sub-subentries, or sub-sub-sub-...). Word compiles indexes in the *indented* style, the preferred method for complicated indexes.

More common is the *run-in* index. It uses a single paragraph for each index entry. All subentries are gathered together and tacked onto the end of the heading, following a colon. A semicolon follows the page numbers for each subentry. A *run-in* style index typically uses less room than an *indented* one.

Here is the index entry you encountered earlier, shown on the left in its original *indented* style and on the right in *run-in* style. Note the original has been changed in one regard: The double space following each subentry has been replaced with a comma and a space. This was accomplished by typing a comma and space in the *entry/page # separated by* field of the Library Index command. Also note that in the *run-in* entry, the subentry *France* is repeated several times to accommodate the sub-subentries under it. This is awkward, but it makes three levels possible in a *run-in* index.

Indented	Run-in

```
        Indented                          Run-in

New Zealand                      New Zealand: Auckland, 4, 5, 12,
  Auckland, 4, 5, 12, 13, 15       13, 15; Australia and, 7,
  Australia and, 7, 10             10; Christchurch, 4; eco-
  Christchurch, 4                  nomics, 3, 17-18; France, 9;
  economics, 3, 17-18             France, anti-French senti-
  France, 9                        ment, 14; France, nuclear
    anti-French sentiment, 14      weapons and, 15; livestock,
    nuclear weapons and, 15        2, 4; nuclear weapons in, 7,
  livestock, 2, 4                  9, 15; people of, 2; Rainbow
  nuclear weapons in, 7, 9, 15     Warrior affair, 15, 19;
  people of, 2                     Wellington, 4
  Rainbow Warrior affair, 15, 19
  Wellington, 4
```

It is possible to convert an *indented* index, as compiled by Word, into a *run-in* index. Each entry must be converted individually. Follow these steps.

1. Make sure the *indented* index you are transforming has a comma and single space before page numbers. You can achieve this by typing a comma and a space in the *entry/page # separated by* field before running the Library Index command.

2. Type a colon followed by a space (:) immediately after the last character on the heading line. In the example, you would type the colon and space after the *d* that ends *New Zealand*. If the heading is followed directly by page numbers, type the colon and space after the last page number.

3. Press the Right direction key to select the last character on the heading line. This character is the paragraph mark, which may be invisible, depending on the setting of the Options command. You can select the paragraph mark even if it is invisible: Press the Right direction key until the selection moves to the next line, then press the Left direction key once to select the paragraph mark.

4. Press the Del key to delete the paragraph mark and place it in the scrap. The heading will become indented like the subentries below it, and will join the next paragraph.

5. Move the selection to the paragraph mark that ends the line of the last subentry. Again, you can find the paragraph mark even if it isn't visible on the screen, as described in step 3.

6. Hold down the Shift key and press the Ins key. This causes the paragraph mark at the end of the entry to be replaced with the paragraph mark in the scrap. The last line of the entry will move left, as it assumes the formatting that used to belong to the entry's first paragraph.

7. Press the Left direction key twice, to move the selection to the left of the paragraph mark you just placed at the end of the entry.

8. Press F6 to turn on the extended-selection mode, and press the Up direction key until the entire entry is highlighted. It doesn't matter whether all of the first line (the line that says *New Zealand,* in our example) is highlighted, but some of it must be.

9. Choose the Replace command. In the *text* field, type ^*p* (Shift-6 followed by p). This is the symbol for a paragraph mark. In the *with text* field, type a semicolon followed by a space (;). In the confirm field, pick *No,* and press the Enter key to execute the command.

That does it. The entry will become a single *run-in* paragraph, governed by the formatting of the final paragraph mark—the paragraph mark that you moved down from the end of the first line.

NOTE: The sample *run-in* paragraph has been narrowed by giving it a 2.8-inch right indent. To achieve narrow columns, you might want to print your index in multiple columns using the Format Division Layout command. Also, the sample was hyphenated with the Library Hyphenate command.

Multiple columns

If your index is part of a manuscript, you'll probably want a single wide column, possibly in the *run-in* style. But if you are publishing a finished product, you may well want the index in two or three columns. To accomplish this, set the *number of columns* field in the Format Division Layout command. Presumably, you'll want to make sure that the index is in a separate division (or has been copied to be a separate document altogether) before you switch to a multi-column layout. If you want the word *Index* centered at the top of the multi-column page, make it part of a deep running head that is formatted (with the Format Running-head command) to print only on the first page of the division.

The other approach to multiple-column text is using side-by-side paragraphs, a technique described in Chapter 27, "Power Tools: Creating Tables." This doesn't work well for normal Word indexes, however, because the side-by-side feature can handle only up to 31 paragraphs on a page. If you're an advanced or adventuresome user, you may wish to experiment with combining lines from your index in such a way that there are fewer than 31 actual paragraphs on a page. The easiest way to do this is to use long *run-in* index paragraphs. If you must use an *indented* style index, make all the subentries under a heading a single paragraph. A technique that may accomplish this, depending on circumstances, is to format *Index level* styles with tab stops at appropriate indentation points, and then use the Replace command to change each paragraph mark ($^\wedge p$) into a new-line character followed by a tab character ($^\wedge n\, ^\wedge t$).

Combining indexes

Sometimes an indexing job seems too big for Word, or you have several separate documents (such as chapters) for which you want a single index. In either situation, the solution is to create two or more smaller indexes and combine them into one. This can be done relatively quickly through creative use of Word's outlining powers.

But first...

The Word manual suggests making a single index for several documents by merging the documents before running the Library Index command. This is ideal, if it works.

But when Word tries to compile too many index instructions at once, it gives the message *Insufficient memory.* The actual number of entries Word can accommodate is highly variable, being dependent on how long the entries are and how much memory is tied up doing other things. Under some circumstances Word can handle 4,000 entries. Often, far fewer.

Removing resident programs, such as Sidekick or print spoolers, or adding more random-access memory (RAM) chips to your computer may or may not help, depending on how Word ran out of memory. (There are two different locations at which Word can run out of memory when indexing or compiling a table of contents.) You can increase usable memory by reducing the amount Word is using for other things. Save your document, and close all windows except for the one containing the document being indexed. Type *PLAIN* in the Print Option command's *printer* field. Remove any style sheet attached to your document (type Esc-F-S-S-Del-Enter). These steps will free up memory. Then, run the Library Index command and see what happens.

If you still get the *Insufficient memory* message, you'll have to combine indexes to solve your problem. Skip to the "Step by step" section that follows.

On the other hand, if Word completes the index, you've solved one problem but may have created another. The page numbers in the index won't be correct if Word is set up with *PLAIN* instead of your printer's proper .PRD file, and the style sheet (if any) is missing. Word relies on .PRD files and such formatting instructions as style sheets when it figures out which words go on which pages.

This problem can be solved, too. Restore the correct settings for printer and style sheet, and run the Print Repaginate command to let Word show you where each page *should* start. Then go through the document and put a page-break character (Shift-Ctrl-Enter) at each location. Next, use the Format Division Margins command (or a special division style) to increase the page length to something generous, say 20 inches. You want pages long to ensure that during indexing Word always encounters one of your page-break characters before it reaches what it computes to be the end of the page. As before, return your printer setting to *PLAIN* and remove the style sheet, then run Library Index. Word will break pages at the new-page characters, and will compile an accurate index. After indexing but before you print the document, remember to restore the proper page length, .PRD file, and style sheet.

If this technique doesn't solve your problem, combining indexes will.

Step by step

Let's coin a couple of terms to help keep things straight. A *constituent index* will be any of the two or more indexes that are combined to create a *master index*.

Start a new document by clearing the screen or a text window. Copy into the document the contents of the constituent indexes (but not the *.Begin Index.* and *.End Index.* markers from them). Put the indexes one after another. When that's done, you've gathered the components of what will become the master index. But you must alphabetize them somehow into a single index.

If you were to use the Library Autosort command now, every paragraph in the index document would be alphabetized—scrambling headings with subentries and sub-subentries, all arranged from A to Z. We'll sidestep this little disaster by entering Word's outline view, where the Library Autosort command alphabetizes only one level at a time and where, when a higher level is alphabetized into a new position, the levels below it automatically follow. This is perfect for sorting an index, because you want subentries to move with their headings.

Indexes can be combined whether or not you're using a style sheet for formatting. Either way, you enter Word's outline view by holding down the Shift key and pressing F2, and then you assign levels of heading to the elements of the index. General information on Word's outline view is contained in Chapter 25, "Power Tools: Outlining."

In this step-by-step tutorial, we'll combine two short constituent indexes, each of which has two levels—headings and subentries. We'll use a style sheet in our example, because it affords the most possibilities. But first, a quick look at the other way of doing it.

Without a style sheet. If you're not using a style sheet, you assign levels of heading in outline view by holding the Alt key and pressing either the 9 or the 0 on the top row of the keyboard (*not* the numbers on the keypad to the right). A paragraph (index line) will be normal text at first, marked in the selection bar with a capital *T.* But after you select it and press Alt-9, it will assume a heading-level number, noted in the lower corner of the screen. If the heading level isn't the one you want, press Alt-9 and Alt-0 as needed.

You want to adjust main index headings to Level 1, subentries to Level 2, sub-subentries to Level 3, and so forth. Don't forget the F4 key: When you get one line adjusted to the heading level you want, you can repeat the same adjustment on another line with F4.

The balance of this discussion assumes you're using a style sheet, but if you're not, the same basic steps still work.

With a style sheet. To use a style sheet, you must attach it to the new document with the Format Style Sheet command. The style sheet must include *Paragraph Heading level* styles, as described in the previous chapter. This being an index, chances are the style sheet will have *Paragraph Index level* styles, too. However, it isn't strictly necessary, since the first thing you'll do is switch the index paragraphs to various *heading* styles so that Word's outline mode can manipulate them. Nor does it matter how the *heading* styles are formatted. Paragraph formatting isn't relevant when you're in outline view.

Recall from Chapter 25 that when you use *heading* styles there's no need to use Alt-9 and Alt-0 for assigning heading levels in outline view. Instead, hold down the Alt key and type the key code of the *heading* style desired. In this book, we assume the key code for a *heading* style is the number of the level—so if you want a line to become *Heading level 1*, type Alt-1, and if you want it to become *Heading level 2*, type Alt-2, and so forth.

Step 1. If necessary, switch from document view to outline view by holding down the Shift key and pressing F2.

Step 2. Once in outline view, change index headings to outline *Level 1*. (If you're using a style sheet, type Alt-1.) Change all subentries (second-level index lines) to outline *Level 2* (Alt-2). Change sub-subentries (third-level index lines, if any) to outline *Level 3* (Alt-3). If the indexes have fourth and fifth index levels, assign appropriate outline levels to them, too.

This illustration portrays three windows in outline view. The narrow window on the left, window 1, shows how a sample index document appears before lines are changed to headings (only the beginning of each line is shown). Observe that the style bar shows *I1* or *I2* for each line. These are key codes for *Index level 1* and *Index level 2* styles. The *T* in the selection bar next to the style bar shows that each paragraph is text, a conventional paragraph rather than an outline heading.

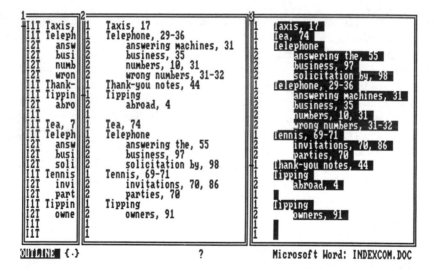

The middle window, window 2, shows the same index lines after *heading* styles have been applied. Now the key codes show 1 or 2, reflecting heading level. The *T*'s are gone, because the paragraphs no longer are conventional text.

Window 2 shows two separate portions of index, both covering parts of the letter T in a book on etiquette. The upper constituent covers pages 1-50. The lower constituent, beginning with *Tea*, covers pages 51-100. We'll combine them.

Step 3. Press Shift-F10. This simultaneously switches Word from outline view to outline edit and selects all of both indexes. Make sure the first line is selected as a level 1.

Step 4. Execute the Library Autosort command. You can accept the default settings in its fields. Double-check before you execute the command to make sure the selection begins at the top level and stretches for the full length of what you want sorted.

Word alphabetizes the selected text by first-level heading, and keeps lower-level headings with the headings to which they are related.

The right window on the previous page, window 3, shows how the document looks when the combined indexes are alphabetized by first-level heading. The headings for *Telephone* and respective subheadings have been made consecutive, for instance. The whole group remains selected until you do something else.

Step 5. Switch back from outline edit to outline view, by pressing Shift-F5.

Step 6. Eliminate duplicate main-level lines by selecting them and pressing Del twice — once to delete the text, and once to delete the paragraph mark. If you delete page numbers, add them to the remaining identical main-level heading. For instance, the left window in the next illustration shows that the second *Telephone* heading has been deleted, and the page numbers from the line have been moved up to the first *Telephone* heading. Also, the second *Tipping* line has been eliminated, and the blank line (below *Tipping-abroad*) that once separated the two constituent indexes has been deleted.

```
1   Taxis, 17                        1   Taxis, 17
1   Tea, 74                          1   Tea, 74
1   Telephone, 29-36                 1   Telephone, 29-36
2       answering the, 55            2       answering machines, 31
2       business, 97                 2       answering the, 55
2       solicitation by, 98         2       business, 35, 97
2       answering machines, 31      2       numbers, 10, 31
2       business, 35                 2       solicitation by, 98
2       numbers, 10, 31             2       wrong numbers, 31-32
2       wrong numbers, 31-32        1   Tennis, 69-71
1   Tennis, 69-71                    2       invitations, 70, 86
2       invitations, 70, 86         2       parties, 70
2       parties, 70                 1   Thank-you notes, 44
1   Thank-you notes, 44             1   Tipping
1   Tipping                          2       abroad, 4
2       abroad, 4                    2       owners, 91
2       owners, 91
```

Now that the main headings are alphabetized and consolidated, we'll do the same for the subentries.

Step 7. Switch to outline edit view by pressing Shift-F5 (*OUTLINE* will appear in the lower left corner).

Step 8. Select a line that begins a series of consecutive index subheadings — in this case, the first indented line after the main heading *Telephone*.

Step 9. Press F6 to turn on the extended selection mode. Then, hold down the Ctrl key and press PgDn to extend the selection to the end of the group of subheadings.

Step 10. Execute the Library Autosort command, using the default settings. The selected headings will be placed in alphabetical order as in the right window of the above illustration. If there are sub-subentries (there are not in the example), they will be not be alphabetized. Instead, they will move as a group with the higher-level lines with which they are associated. This is as you want it, because you can select and sort the lines later.

Step 11. If subentries need consolidation because of duplication, make the changes after switching back to outline view (Shift-F5, so that the word *Level* appears in the lower left corner). In the highlighted example, two *business* subentries are combined into one.

Press Shift-F2 to return the index to document view. If you didn't use a style sheet when combining your indexes, the lines have retained their original formatting and your index is finished. On the other hand, if you used a style sheet, there's one more step: final formatting.

Final formatting with a style sheet

When you first see the new master index in document view, you may be in for a shock. If you used a style sheet to combine the constituent indexes in outline view, your index levels are now formatted with *heading* styles—and may be centered or spaced far apart or in other forms quite unbecoming to an index.

There's a fast way to correct the situation. Enter the Gallery and format your *heading* styles so that they fashion paragraphs to look like levels of an index instead of levels of a heading. Presuming you already have index styles, you can format the *Paragraph Heading level 1* style to match the *Paragraph Index level 1* style, *Paragraph Heading level 2* to match *Paragraph Index level 2,* and so forth. With a mouse, it's particularly easy. Select a *heading* style that you want to format like an *index* style, position the mouse pointer to the left of the appropriate *index* style, and click first the left and then the right mouse buttons. The character and paragraph formatting (but not the remark or other parts of the style name) will be copied from the style near the mouse pointer to the selected style. In literally only seconds, you can revise your *heading* styles to produce a proper index.

Once you've modified the formatting of the *heading* styles, use the Gallery's Transfer Save command to give the style sheet a different name. This will create a new style sheet while retaining the old one in its unmodified form. The next time you combine indexes this way, you'll have the style sheet already available—a style sheet with *heading* styles formatted for printing an index.

You don't have to redefine formatting in your style sheet. Instead, you can reverse the process you used in the first place to convert the index lines into heading lines. Select index lines and apply index styles (Alt-I1, Alt-I2, and so forth). You can, of course, select paragraphs and manually format them with the Format Paragraph command. But that's rather inefficient compared with your other choices.

GENERATING TABLES OF CONTENTS

When you execute the Library Table command, Word automatically compiles a table of contents, or other table based on page numbers, such as a list of illustrations.

These tables can be simple or sophisticated. They can have a single level with a few entries, or as many as four levels and dozens of entries. They can follow a straightforward built-in format, or they can be formatted elaborately, and quite automatically, with a style sheet. Leaf forward a few pages, and you'll see some samples.

Numerous similarities exist between creating a table of contents and creating an index. Both tasks involve three stages—coding the document with hidden instructions, compiling the instructions into a table or index, and formatting the results for best appearance. It is assumed here that you've read about hidden text and indexing earlier in the chapter, and will refer back as necessary to Chapter 14, "The Family of Library Commands," where specifics of the Library Table command are explained.

Coding

By the time you begin coding a document with hidden table-of-contents instructions, you've already done most of the real work. This is because the toughest part about making a good table of contents is organizing the document itself. If your report, book, or other document is well ordered and you understand the kind of table of contents that you want, the remaining steps are more or less trivial.

A table of contents lets a reader find information quickly and see what subjects are covered and how they are organized. The comprehensiveness of a table is governed partly by the author's preferences, but largely by the type of document. While some books list only chapters, and others (such as this one) parts and chapters, long reports, papers, and technical textbooks are among documents that generally have tables of contents that includes headings and even subheadings from within chapters. One caution: Just don't get so carried away with subheadings and sub-subheadings that the overall flow of the book becomes difficult to discern from looking at the table of contents.

Two rules are paramount. First, the wording of a title or heading in a table of contents must exactly match its wording in the document. If the chapter is titled "Space Travel and Human Destiny," you can't call it "Space Travel and Destiny" or "Human Destiny and Space Travel" in the table of contents. Word makes it easy to follow this rule, because the table is compiled from the actual words in the document.

Second, be consistent. If you include a subheading from one chapter, you must include every subheading of identical level from every chapter.

How to code

The mechanics of coding a document are straightforward and can be automated to a large extent by using Word's glossary feature. You code a document for the Library Table command in the same general way you code it for the Library Index command. There are some important differences, however.

- Begin a table instruction with the hidden characters *.c.* or *.C.* instead of the *.i.* used for indexing.
- Actually, you can use any letter in a table instruction. The Library Table command expects you to use *.C.*, unless you tell it otherwise in executing the command. However, you can employ *.f.* for *Figures*, or you can use any other letter. You can even use *.i.*, if you want a table of your index entries. By coding different elements in a document with different letters, you can compile various tables with successive passes of the Library Table command.

♦ Although a hidden semicolon will end a table instruction, it usually isn't necessary to include semicolons. Most table instructions code heading lines that end with a paragraph mark anyway. The semicolon isn't needed if the paragraph mark is there. Similarly, you can type all of the text of an index instruction in hidden characters—but as a practical matter you'll probably want to use the existing wording.

♦ To indicate that marked text is to be moved to a lower level in the table, place hidden colons immediately after .c. (or whatever letter you use instead of c). That is, adding one colon after the code (.c.:) marks the passage for inclusion at the second level in a table. Adding two colons (.c.::) marks it for the third level, and adding three colons (.c.:::) marks it for the fourth. These colons generally don't have any text between them, unlike index instructions.

♦ You can type a hidden colon at the end of any instruction for which you do not wish to have a page number printed. For example, in the table of contents for this book, the major parts do not have page numbers listed, although the individual chapters do. Here is a sample instruction that would mark a heading as a first-level table entry for which there is to be no page number printed.

```
‖1              .c."PART ONE: THE MAGIC OF MAGIC":                    ‖
```

♦ When text contains a colon or semicolon, the text must be enclosed in quotation marks. (Observe in the example that hidden quotation marks surround the text. This is because the text contains a colon.)

♦ When the text contains printable quotation marks, you must enclose them within a second set of hidden quotation marks. This means that if a passage contains both printable quotation marks *and* a colon, you must put one set of hidden quotation marks around the printable quotation marks, and another set around the entire passage.

Coding with the glossary

Coding instructions for tables of contents can be stored in the glossary. I suggest storing a set of glossary entries permanently on disk, so that whenever you want a first-level table entry you can select the beginning of the heading, and then type 1 followed by F3 to insert the appropriate format from the glossary. Similarly, you can type 2, 3, or 4 followed by F3 to insert the hidden instructions for second-, third-, and fourth-level table entries.

To build such a set of glossary entries for use with the Library Table command, follow this sequence of keystrokes exactly.

1. Set the *show hidden text* field of the Window Options command to *Yes*.
2. Hold down the Alt key and type XE. Type .c.:::—that is, period, letter c (or other letter of your choice), period, and three colons.
3. Press Esc and U (for Undo) *twice*. This causes the hidden characters you've just typed to be selected.
4. Press Esc, C, 4, and Enter to copy the selected characters to the glossary name *4*.
5. Press the F6 key to turn on extended-selection mode. Press the Left direction key once, to reduce the selection by one character. Now .c.:: should be selected.

6. Press Esc, C, 3, and Enter to copy the selected characters to the glossary name *3*.

7. Press the F6 key to turn extended-selection mode on again. Press the Left direction key again, so the selection is reduced by one more character. Now only *.c.:* should be selected.

8. Press Esc, C, 2, and Enter to copy the selected characters to the glossary name *2*.

9. Press the F6 key one last time to turn extended-selection mode on. Press the Left direction key to reduce the selection by one more character, to *.c.* — with no colon.

10. Press Esc, C, 1, and Enter to copy the selected characters to the glossary name *1*.

You've finished defining the four glossary names. You may delete the hidden coding characters that have been selected. When you use the feature, be sure that the *show hidden text* field of the Window Options command is set to *Yes*.

To save your new glossary entries to a glossary file on disk so that you may use them anytime later, pick the Transfer Glossary Save command. If you want the entries to be among those that load into the glossary automatically whenever you start Word from the current directory, use the glossary name NORMAL.GLY. Otherwise, type a different name — but remember that to retrieve the glossary file from disk at some future date you'll have to use the Transfer Glossary Merge command and the correct name, if the name isn't NORMAL.GLY.

Finding headings in outline view

Regardless of whether you type coding in manually or use the glossary to enter it for you, you'll find it easy to locate the headings to be coded if you're using a style sheet and are familiar with Word's outline view. Press Shift-F2 to move from document view to outline view. If necessary, expand all headings and collapse all body text by pressing Shift-F10 followed by the Minus (−) key and the Asterisk (∗) key on the numeric key pad on the right side of the keyboard. (Refer to Chapter 25, "Power Tools: Outlining," if you're not sure what "collapsed" text is.) Press Shift-F5, and you'll be at the beginning of the document in outline view, with all the headings displayed (presuming you previously formatted the headings with *Paragraph Heading Level* styles).

To apply the correct table instructions, select the first character of each heading line and check the lower left corner (or the key code name) to see what heading level it is. Type that number and press F3 to insert the coding from the glossary.

The following illustration shows how the beginning of a book, when displayed in outline view, might be coded with table of contents instructions.

```
1 t  .c."PART ONE: THE MAGIC OF MAGIC":
2 t     .c.:1. A Short History of Legerdemain and Illusion
2 t     .c.:2. Magic By Any Other Name
3 t        .c.::Illusionists
3 t        .c.::Escape Artists
3 t        .c.::Manipulators
3 t        .c.::Mind Readers
4 t           .c.:::Mentalism
4 t           .c.:::Clairvoyance and telepathy
1 t  .c."PART TWO: OLD STANDARDS":
2 t     .c.:3. Hat Tricks
3 t        .c.::The illusions of Joseph Hartz
```

The numbers in the vertical style bar on the far left are key codes for the heading styles used. The document could have been coded without the assistance of a style sheet, but one was used here. The column of *t*'s in the selection bar indicates that each of the paragraphs has text collapsed beneath it, not displayed on the screen.

Each heading is coded with *.c.* in hidden text. Second-level headings have one hidden colon following the *.c.*, to tell the Library Table command that they are second-level table entries. Third-level headings have two colons, and fourth-level headings have three colons. Word can handle more than a dozen heading levels, but it's rare to need more than four.

None of the lines ends with a hidden semicolon, because each line concludes with a paragraph mark (not visible on the screen). The top-level headings in the example, however, have a hidden colon just before the paragraph mark. This colon instructs the Library Table command not to print a page number after that line.

Once the coding is in place, you're ready to pull the table together.

Compiling the table

Compile the instructions into a table of contents with the Library Table command. For details on the command and its fields, see Chapter 14, "The Family of Library Commands." Be sure to set the *show hidden text* field of the Window Options command back to *No* before executing the Library Table command, so that page numbering will be correct.

As with indexes, Word adds a division mark and hidden markers to the end of the document when it compiles a table. The comments earlier in this chapter on the division mark and the Library Index command are equally relevant to the Library Table command and should be noted. The first line of a compiled table is marked with a line that says *.Begin Table.*, and the final line says *.End Table.*. Both lines are hidden.

To update a table, execute the Library Table again. Word will highlight the existing table and ask you to *Enter Y to replace existing table or Esc to cancel.* If you wish to keep the present version of the table, delete the hidden *.Begin Table.* line before running the command.

Multiple tables

You can compile a second or subsequent table without deleting the *.Begin Text.* line, as long as the Library Table command's *index on* field is set to a different letter for each table. This causes Word to bring together a different set of table instructions. For instance, you could compile separate tables for plates (*.p.*), figures (*.f.*), maps (*.m.*), and charts (any letter, but not *.c.* if it was used for the table of contents).

When creating more than one table for a document, compile the table of contents last because you'll want it to include correct page numbers for the other tables.

Two or more tables of contents can be combined easily, because the page numbering of one table follows that of the other.

Moving a table

As you know, Word places a table in a new division it creates at the end of a document. You probably don't really want a table of contents at the end, but inserting new pages for a table near the beginning of a document would throw off all following page numbers, rendering the table obsolete from the moment it appeared.

The neatest way around this is to compile the table a first time, format it to proper length, and then move the whole thing, including the *.Begin Table.* and *.End Table.* lines, to the position in the document at which you wish it to appear. If you wish, set it off from surrounding pages either with new-page characters (Shift-Ctrl-Enter) at top and bottom or, if you want to format it specially, with division marks (Shift-Enter). Run the Library Index command again, replacing the existing version. The newly compiled table, with correct page numbers, will be inserted in the document at the same location as the previous table, rather than at the end of the document. No division mark is added to the end of the document, either.

Alternatively, you may keep the table at the end of the document or make it a separate document altogether for purposes of printing, and insert the table into the document's sequence of pages after printing. You can keep page numbers consecutive by adjusting fields of the Format Division Page-number command, or by manually inserting the correct number of blank pages at the proper place in the document. Blanks can be forced with the new-page character (Shift-Ctrl-Enter).

Formatting the table

By filling out the four fields of the Library Table command, you make basic decisions about how the index will look. These fields are described in Chapter 14, "The Family of Library Commands."

```
LIBRARY TABLE index on: ▓     entry/page # separated by: ^t
        indent each level: 0.4"       use style sheet: Yes(No)
```

If you don't change the default settings for these fields, Word will look for table instructions coded with *.c.*, a single tab character (^{t}) will be inserted between the end of each heading or subheading and the page number that follows, every subheading will be indented .4 inches relative to the higher-level heading above it, and styles from a style sheet will not be used to format the paragraphs of the table.

This is how the beginning of a table of contents looks when it is printed with the default settings.

```
Part One: The Magic of Magic
    1. A Short History of Legerdemain and Illusion        2
    2. Magic By Any Other Name                            7
        Illusionists                                      7
        Escape Artists                                    9
        Manipulators                                     11
        Mind Readers                                     13
            Mentalism                                    13
            Clairvoyance and telepathy                   14
Part Two: Old Standards
    3. Hat Tricks                                         17
        The illusions of Joseph Hartz                    18
        The secrets of Joseph Hartz                      19
            Large bandannas                              19
            Silver-plated goblets                        20
            Cigar boxes                                  20
            A caged canary                               21
```

Not special enough for you? You can change the default settings of the Library Table command, and the formatting of the paragraphs. For example, if you want to change the *entry/page # separated by* field, you can replace the default of a single tab character (^t), with a comma and some spaces, or just some spaces. Or, more powerfully, you can fill in the field with a space followed by two tab characters (^t^t). The strategy behind twin tab characters is discussed in the next chapter, "Power Tools: Creating Tables," but, briefly, it lets you include leader characters that stop short of the page numbers to which they are leading.

Look what happens to the same table of contents when a space and two tab characters are put in the *entry/page # separated by* field and *Yes* is picked in the *use style sheet* field.

These are the styles from the style sheet that performed the formatting.

```
13  T1 Paragraph Table level 1              TABLE LEVEL 1
       Modern b 12 Uppercase. Flush left, Left indent 0.2" (first line
       indent -0.2"), space before 1 li. Tabs at: 5.6" (left flush, leader
       dots), 6" (right flush).
14  T2 Paragraph Table level 2              TABLE LEVEL 2
       Modern b 12. Flush left, Left indent 0.6" (first line indent -
       0.2"). Tabs at: 5.6" (left flush, leader dots), 6" (right flush).
15  T3 Paragraph Table level 3              TABLE LEVEL 3
       Modern b 12. Flush left, Left indent 1" (first line indent -0.2").
       Tabs at: 5.6" (left flush, leader dots), 6" (right flush).
16  T4 Paragraph Table level 4              TABLE LEVEL 4
       Modern b 12. Flush left, Left indent 1.4" (first line indent -
       0.2"). Tabs at: 5.6" (left flush, leader dots), 6" (right flush).
```

Now, by just changing the style sheet, the same table looks like this:

The styles that created that look for the table:

```
1   T1 Paragraph Table level 1          TABLE LEVEL 1
       Modern b 12 Bold Underlined Uppercase. Centered, space before 3 li,
       space after 1 li.
2   T2 Paragraph Table level 2          TABLE LEVEL 2
       Modern b 12 Bold. Flush left, Left indent 0.2" (first line indent -
       0.2"), space before 1 li. Tabs at: 5.6" (left flush, leader dots),
       6" (right flush).
3   T3 Paragraph Table level 3          TABLE LEVEL 3
       Modern b 12. Flush left, Left indent 0.6" (first line indent -
       0.2"), space before 0.5 li. Tabs at: 5.6" (left flush, leader
       dots), 6" (right flush).
4   T4 Paragraph Table level 4          TABLE LEVEL 4
       Modern b 12 Italic. Flush left, Left indent 1" (first line indent -
       0.2"). Tabs at: 5.6" (left flush, leader dots), 6" (right flush).
```

And by changing the style sheet again, without changing the content of the document or index at all, we get this:

Part One: The Magic of Magic

Part Two: Old Standards

These are the styles that did it (on a Hewlett-Packard LaserJet printer):

```
1   T1 Paragraph Table level 1                TABLE LEVEL 1
    HELV (modern i) 14/12. Centered, space before 3 li, space after 1
    li.
2   T2 Paragraph Table level 2                TABLE LEVEL 2
    TMSRMN (roman a) 10/12 Bold. Flush left, Left indent 0.2" (first
    line indent -0.2"), space before 1 li. Tabs at: 5.6" (left flush,
    leader dots), 6" (right flush).
3   T3 Paragraph Table level 3                TABLE LEVEL 3
    TMSRMN (roman a) 10/12. Flush left, Left indent 0.6" (first line
    indent -0.2"), space before 0.5 li. Tabs at: 5.6" (left flush,
    leader dots), 6" (right flush).
4   T4 Paragraph Table level 4                TABLE LEVEL 4
    TMSRMN (roman a) 10/12 Italic. Flush left, Left indent 1" (first
    line indent -0.2"), space before 1.2 pt. Tabs at: 5.6" (left flush,
    leader dots), 6" (right flush).
```

For insight into style sheets, see Chapter 24, "Power Tools: Style Sheets." You may want to review the discussion of style sheets and indexing earlier in this chapter, because the same principles pertain to style sheets and tables of contents.

Adjusting page numbering

For all but informal documents, you'll probably want your table of contents to be a separate division or even a separate document, for purposes of formatting. "Front matter" pages that contain such things as tables and lists generally are numbered in a lowercase Roman style, which requires separate division formatting from the rest of the document. A table of contents typically starts on page *v* or *vii*.

If you're producing a manuscript, your table of contents should list all page numbers as 000. Later, the publisher will insert the correct pages. There are several more or less automatic ways of getting your tables to list 000 for all page numbers.

One is to instruct Word, through the Format Division Page-numbers command, to start numbering your document at, say, 9500. The Library Table command will produce a table of contents with numbers that all begin with 95 and end with two other digits. After the table has been compiled, select it and use the Replace command to change 95?? to 000. If the document that was indexed has more than 100 pages, also replace 96?? with 000. If it has more than 200 pages, replace 97?? with 000, and so forth. Before printing your document, remember to change the page numbering back to something reasonable.

Spacing out leader characters

The leader characters Word inserts in a table of contents, or any other kind of table, fill every space. Although this is appropriate for many kinds of work, the leaders in a table of contents generally should appear only every other space. Here's a technique with which advanced users may wish to experiment. Whether or not it works depends on such variables as which printer and fonts you use. (The discussion of the Print File command in Chapter 15 may be useful to people puzzling this out.)

Select the table that contains the leader characters. In the Print Options command's *range* field, pick *Selection*. Pick the Print File command and type a filename with an extension other than .DOC. For instance, you could call the file *test.fil*. Opening another window if you like, load *test.fil* into Word. You'll see a lot of printer codes on the screen. Pick the Replace command. Type two periods (..) in the *text* field and a period followed by a space (.) in the *with text* field. Set *confirm* to *No*, and execute the command. Save the file (the *formatted* field will say *No*). Pick the Library Run command, type *copy test.fil lpt1:*, and press Enter. (If your printer is hooked up to a port other than LPT1:, substitute the correct designation. For example, if the *setup* field of the Print Options command says COM1:, then the Library Run command would be *copy test.fil com1:* <Enter>).

With good fortune, your printer will print a table of contents with leader characters spaced out. If a line has dots that are staggered relative to the line directly above, repeat the whole process after loading the original table and typing one Spacebar space at the beginning of the line of leaders you want to adjust.

Politically minded cynics will suggest none of this is necessary. They'll say we have spaced-out leaders already.

HIDDEN PARAGRAPH MARKS

This is a long chapter, so we'll end it with a treat—two tricks that will delight those who have sophisticated tastes when it comes to formatting, or who enjoy experimenting.

Changing line lengths within paragraphs

According to the Word manual, the formatting of the next paragraph is impossible. Let's let the paragraph tell its own story.

```
    Length of lines, space between lines, and space between paragraphs
all are governed by paragraph formatting in Word.  Supposedly, you can
change these characteristics only by pressing the Enter key to begin a
new paragraph. The minor exception is that the first line of a paragraph
is permitted a different left indent than the rest of the paragraph. So
what's going on here?  Why is the line
length changing in this paragraph?  The
answer is that this isn't a paragraph.
It is three paragraphs, each ending
with its own paragraph mark. But two of
the paragraph marks have been selected
and hidden with Alt-X-E. The middle
paragraph has been given a wide right
indentation. The result is peculiar and
quite useful. Now, using hidden paragraph marks to redirect formatting,
you can do such things as wrap text around photographs in newsletters,
or break from one column to two columns in the middle of a "paragraph."
```

When a paragraph mark is hidden and the *show visible text* field of the Window Options command is set to *No*, Word ignores certain aspects of the *next* paragraph's formatting. It ignores the *space before, space after,* and *first line* formatting of the next paragraph, but honors that next paragraph's left and right indentation formatting. This allows paragraphs to be run together seamlessly.

If you switch *show hidden text* to *Yes*, the hidden paragraph marks "reappear" on the screen and the individual paragraphs resume control over paragraph spacing and first-line indentation. (Although the paragraph marks may "reappear" in one sense, they're still formatted as hidden. Furthermore, because paragraph marks are normally invisible, if the Option command's *visible* field is set to *None*, they won't show up in any case. But their effect on paragraph spacing and first-line indentation will be felt if the *show hidden text* field of the Window Options command is set to *Yes*.)

If you experiment, you'll discover that you can insert and delete text relatively freely from paragraphs that are formatted with hidden paragraph marks. The break point at which line length changes may shift either up or down a few lines, if you add or delete words. If the break line changes too much, you can always move the hidden paragraph mark to fix it. (To see the mark displayed as a hidden-text symbol, adjust the Option command's *visible* field.)

The rule that governs where line length changes is this: When a hidden paragraph mark is in the middle of a "paragraph," the new formatting takes effect on the next line. However, the formatting takes effect on the same line if the hidden paragraph mark is the first character of the line.

I call hidden paragraph marks *pivots*, because they are points at which you can quickly change the direction of your formatting.

This is what the previous paragraphs look like on the screen, when *show hidden text* is set to *Yes*. In both cases, they print with the same layout that they show on the screen.

```
   Length of lines, space between lines, and space between paragraphs
all are governed by paragraph formatting in Word.  Supposedly, you can
change these characteristics only by pressing the Enter key to begin a
new paragraph. The minor exception is that the first line of a paragraph
is permitted a different left indent than the rest of the paragraph. ¶

   So what's going on here?  Why is
the line length changing in this
paragraph?  The answer is that this
isn't a paragraph.  It is three
paragraphs, each ending with its own
paragraph mark. But two of the
paragraph marks have been selected and
hidden with Alt-X-E. The middle
paragraph has been given a wide right
indentation. ¶

   The result is peculiar and quite useful. Now, using hidden
paragraph marks to redirect formatting, you can do such things as wrap
text around photographs in newsletters, or break from one column to two
columns in the middle of a "paragraph."¶
```

Page 59 {Length·of·l...agraph."¶ ?   Microsoft Word: HIDDEN.DOC

Flexible document content

By hiding not just paragraph marks, but whole paragraphs, you can create documents that change in *content* depending on which style sheet is in use.

Imagine you have two style sheets that are almost identical. Both style sheets contain the same styles, and both include a style that hides whole paragraphs by making their characters hidden.

The difference is that the paragraph style formatted as *hidden* in the first style sheet is formatted as visible in the second. And the paragraph style formatted as *hidden* in the second sheet is visible in the first. Under this arrangement, one paragraph can appear and another one disappear when a different style sheet is attached. A paragraph remains formatted with *Paragraph 23* style, but the formatting of *Paragraph 23* is visible text in one style sheet and invisible in the other.

The whole tone and substance of a letter could change dramatically depending on what style sheet is attached with the Format Style Sheet command. What appears to be a business proposal with one style sheet can become a resume or a friendly note when a different style sheet is attached. The same principle can be used with character styles.

Nor is it just narrative that can be changed wholesale, and changed back again. We'll hope you keep only one set of books. But it's true that a column of numbers in a financial report can vanish or reappear at will, depending on the setting of the *show hidden text* field of the Window Options command. If you go a step further and set up two style sheets, you can have one column of numbers replace another, depending on the style sheet in use. Similarly, one column of a table of side-by-side paragraphs can be made to appear (and print) or vanish on request. You don't want customers seeing the wholesale numbers on a price list? Make the column vanish except when you want it there.

To accomplish some of these clever (and sometimes dubious) things, you need to know about more than hidden text, and more than style sheets. You need to know about selecting columns and creating side-by-side paragraphs.

Which takes us nicely into our next chapter.

Power Tools:
Creating Tables

Some people rarely create a table when they write, type, or use a word processor. Their work is mostly narrative, perhaps. Other people do little else but make tables; they fashion such things as financial statements containing long columns of numbers, or lay out brochures that use side-by-side columns to let readers compare numbers or blurbs of text.

Word offers a collection of tools that let you create effective tables relatively easily. Whether you assemble elaborate, multi-column displays containing leader characters and exacting spacing requirements, or merely want to put two or three columns of type next to each other, Word provides the means. If you're one of those people who rarely or never creates a table or uses multiple columns, becoming acquainted with this side of Word's personality may inspire new ideas about ways you can enhance the appearance of what you write.

First, a note of caution. Some of Word's most useful features, in regard to tables, were added beginning with version 3.0. If you have an earlier version, you'll want to update your copy so that you can do such things as print paragraphs side by side and easily move or delete columns of text or numbers.

We won't repeat all the details on how to use tab stops and tab formatting. The basics of using tabs are explained in the discussion of the Format Tabs commands in Chapter 12, "The Family of Format Commands." That chapter also examines the distinction between format and content as it pertains to tabbing—a vital matter, since a tab *character* (created by pressing the Tab key) is part of a document's content, but a tab *stop* is part of a document's formatting (and can be created or modified with the Format Tabs Set command). Furthermore, the discussion of the Format Tabs Set command explains an important difference between older versions of Word and those numbered 3.0 and higher. (In the older versions, tab stops were never ignored by Word; in newer versions, tab stops to the left of the selection are ignored.)

In addition, you may want to review several other parts of the book:

♦ One or more columns of text can be selected, using Word's Column Select mode. New beginning with version 3.0, this mode allows you to perform operations on rectangular sections of a document, such as columns of numbers. The Column Select mode is activated by holding down the Shift key and pressing the F6 key. Once a column is selected, Word will add (or perform other simple math on) any numbers in the selection. See the final section of Chapter 10, "The Scrap and Glossary Commands."

♦ When no other tab stops have been set in a paragraph, Word automatically places stops evenly spaced across a page. Normally, these stops occur every half inch (0.5″), but this default spacing can be changed with the Options command. Why might you want to change 0.5″ to something else? Computer programmers often need tab stops eight characters apart so that columns in a program line up when listed with DOS. A setting of 0.8″ works. Another example of when this might be helpful: Though 0.5″ provides five spaces of pica-size type (P10), if you switch to the smaller elite-size type (P12) and want the default tab stops to remain five spaces apart, a setting of 0.42″ works. You may wish to review the discussion of the Options command in Chapter 11, "The Efficiency Commands."

♦ Paragraphs can be formatted to print side by side instead of one after another. Though this subject is discussed in detail later in this chapter, a short primer on side-by-side paragraphs is also included at the end of the discussion of the Format Paragraph command in Chapter 12, "The Family of Format Commands."

♦ Splitting your screen into two or more windows can be useful when you're working on a table that is too large to see at one time on the screen. See Chapter 21, "Power Tools: Multiple Windows."

Style sheets are of immense help to people who create tables with Word, so you may also want to review Chapter 24, "Power Tools: Style Sheets." Why style sheets? Setting up the formatting for a complex table can be an exacting task, and may include some trial and error as you make sure everything prints the way you want it to. A complicated financial statement, for example, may have different formatting requirements for different lines, and each of these lines must be formatted. When you use a style sheet, the formatting instructions for various lines are conveniently stored as separate paragraph styles.

The initial formatting of a kind of table requires no less thought when you use a style sheet than when you don't. The first time, you still must format one style in a style sheet for each kind of line you want to use in the table.

Once you have a suitable style sheet, making a table from it — now or a year from now — is *extremely* easy. Instead of using various Format commands to set up a line, you simply press the Alt key and type the key code of the particular style you want to invoke from the style sheet. Word does all the formatting automatically; you only have to type in the contents of the line. Once formatting has been defined as a style, it's yours to use whenever you like in any table just by typing its key code.

TIPS ON TABLES

Before looking in some detail at a couple of the features Word offers, let's consider some general strategies and ideas that can make tables easier to manage. Here are some tips on tables (and no jokes about waiters, please):

A single page

You will almost always want a table to print on a single page, rather than breaking across two pages. A simple way to guarantee this is to make the whole table one paragraph by inserting new-line characters (with the Shift-Enter key combination) rather than paragraph marks at the ends of lines. Then pick *Yes* in the Format Paragraph command's *keep together* (or *keep*) field. This single-paragraph method works with all versions of Word, but it has one drawback: The same tab stops must be used throughout the table, since tab stops can only be changed from one paragraph to the next.

A superior alternative lets you keep on the same page a table composed of different paragraphs (with the potential for different tab stops). You must use Word version 2.0 or higher. Pick *Yes* in the *keep follow* field of the Format Paragraph command for each successive paragraph in the table, except the last paragraph.

A third alternative is to use the Print Repaginate command to preview page breaks. If a break occurs in the middle of a table, force a new page to begin immediately before the table by holding down Shift, Ctrl, and Enter. The table will print on a single page (unless it is more than one page long).

Revising formatting

Because of the way Word separates content and format, you have some freedom to change the design of existing tables without affecting the content. If you're not using a style sheet, you can select the paragraph or paragraphs in question and change the locations of tab stops by using the Format Tabs Set command. If you are using a style sheet, matters are simpler still. You can enter the Gallery and change the formatting of any style that controls part of your table. To change the formatting, select the style and use the Gallery menu's Format Tabs Set command. Whether you use a style sheet or not, you can change an existing table's spacing, alignment, and leader characters.

Spaces versus tabbing

Using Spacebar spaces to line up tabular material can cause problems when more than one font or font size is used, or when a proportionally spaced font is used. See the tip "Tabbing and spacing in tables" in Chapter 8, "Keep in Mind."

Leaders

Two tips about Word's leader characters are worth noting. One deals with creating horizontal lines in or around a table, the other with improving the look of a table that uses leaders.

Recall from the discussion of the Format Tabs Set command that a leader is a series of dots (. . . .), dashes (–––), or underline characters (____) that can be added to the formatting of a tab stop to "lead" the reader's eye across a table to corresponding information in other columns. If you pick a leader character in the *leader char* field of the Format Tabs Set command, a leader of dots, dashes, or underlines leads from left to right up to the tab stop. (Of course, this only happens at those tab stops you've actually used. You "use" a tab stop by pressing the Tab key to add a corresponding tab character to the content of the document.)

Horizontal lines

You can create horizontal lines on a page by formatting a tab stop to have the underline leader character, and then pressing the Tab key to actually create the line. The line starts at the left side of the paper (indented as far as the paragraph), and continues across the page to the right until it encounters the tab stop that is formatted with the underline leader. This is useful when, for example, you want to set a table off from the text above and below it, or you want horizontal rules inside a table.

Sometimes, as when preparing a financial statement, you may want a line to start at some point other than the left side of the page. This is easily accomplished. Format a tab where you want the line to start, but do not give this tab stop any leader character. Format the other tab stop at the point on the right where you wish the line to end, and make sure this stop has an underline leader character. Then, to actually create the line, press the Tab key once to move the selection to the left-side tab stop, then press it again to move to the second tab stop. A line will appear between the two stops.

You can set up styles in a style sheet for the express purpose of creating various kinds of predefined lines. Because the length and horizontal placement of such lines are determined by the formatting of the corresponding style, you can alter the line simply by entering the Gallery and changing the definition of the style's tab formatting.

Refining the way leaders print

You can refine the way leader characters print in tables by adding another tab stop just to the left of the tab stop you actually need, and assigning the leader character to this new tab stop instead of to the one to the right of it.

For example, consider a table of contents. Perhaps, at first, it has no leader characters.

```
⊪══════[··········1·········2·········3·········4·········5·······R·]·········7···⫞
⫢TA  Chapter 5: Poodles and Rodents                          76█                ‖
```

Observe in the above illustration that the page number is lined up with a right-aligned tab stop. (You can tell it is a right-aligned stop because of the R in the ruler. The ruler shows the formatting of whatever paragraph is selected.) In this example, the space between the end of the chapter title and the beginning of the page number was created by pressing the Tab key once, to add one tab character to the document.

Notice what happens if a leader character, in this case the dash, is added to the tab stop.

```
|⊨═[· · · · · · · · ·1· · · · · · · · ·2· · · · · · · · ·3· · · · · · · · ·4· · · · · · · · ·5· · · · · ·R·]· · · · · · · · ·7· · ·⫟
¶TB  Chapter 5: Poodles and Rodents-------------------------76█            ‖
```

The *R* in the ruler is now preceded by a dash (*–R*), indicating that the right-aligned tab stop has a dash leader character. The dashes extend from the end of the chapter title to the beginning of the page number. Professionally designed tables generally cut off leaders at least a couple of characters short of the right-hand column. You can eliminate the extra dashes by:

♦ Adding another tab stop, about four characters to the left of the tab stop meant for page numbers. Then,

♦ Setting the leader character of this new tab stop to dashes. Eliminate the leader character in the formatting of the original tab stop (the one on the far right, meant for actual page numbers). Then,

♦ Pressing the Tab key an extra time between the chapter name and the page number when typing the document, so that two tab characters are placed between the end of the chapter title and the beginning of the page number. The first of these tab characters will match up with the first tab stop (the one that has the leader character), and the second tab character will match up with the second tab stop (the one where page numbers are typed).

```
|⊨═[· · · · · · · · ·1· · · · · · · · ·2· · · · · · · · ·3· · · · · · · · ·4· · · · · · · · ·5· ··-R· · ·R·]· · · · · · · · ·7· · ·⫟
¶TC  Chapter 5: Poodles and Rodents----------------------- 76█            ‖
```

An additional, optional refinement is to type a Spacebar space at the end of the chapter title, so that the leader character starts one space to the right of the end of the title. This makes the line look like this:

```
|⊨═[· · · · · · · · ·1· · · · · · · · ·2· · · · · · · · ·3· · · · · · · · ·4· · · · · · · · ·5· ··-R· · ·R·]· · · · · · · · ·7· · ·⫟
¶TC  Chapter 5: Poodles and Rodents ---------------------- 76█            ‖
```

The above examples were created with a simple, temporary style sheet containing only three styles. Studying the style sheet and the examples may help you understand tables and style sheets, and the relationship of the two. Observe that the key codes for the three styles (TA, TB, and TC) appear in the style bar on the far left side of each example. (The style bar must be turned on with the Window Options command in order for you to see this on your computer screen.) This is the style sheet:

```
|⊨═[· · · · · · · · ·1· · · · · · · · ·2· · · · · · · · ·3· · · · · · · · ·4· · · · · · · · ·5· · · · · · · · · ·]· · · · · · · · ·7· · · · ·⫟
‖  1   TA Paragraph 1                      TABLE 1 -- DEMO STYLE        ‖
‖        Courier (modern a) 12. Flush left. Tabs at: 5.8" (right flush).‖
‖  2   TB Paragraph 2                      TABLE 2 -- DEMO STYLE        ‖
‖        Courier (modern a) 12. Flush left. Tabs at: 5.8" (right flush, ‖
‖        leader hyphens).                                               ‖
‖  3   TC Paragraph 3                      TABLE 3 -- DEMO STYLE        ‖
‖        Courier (modern a) 12. Flush left. Tabs at: 5.4" (right flush, ‖
‖        leader hyphens), 5.8" (right flush).                           ‖
```

NOTE: Recall that the discussion of tables of contents in Chapter 26 discussed how to make leader characters print every other space instead of every space.

COLUMN MANIPULATION

Word lets you select columns of text, which actually are rectangles of any size, and move them, delete them, format them, or add all the numbers contained within them. This feature is called "column manipulation," and it was added beginning with version 3.0. A simple demonstration shows its usefulness.

We'll make a three-column table showing the daily and Sunday circulations of nine major U.S. newspapers. We'll use a style sheet, and it need have only one style, to which we've assigned the arbitrary key code NC:

```
╓═[·········1·········2·········3·········4·········5·········]·········7·····╖
║ 1   NC Paragraph 1                             NEWSPAPER CIRCULATION TABLE  ║
║     Courier (modern a) 12. Flush left. Tabs at: 2.6" (left flush,          ║
║     leader dots), 4.2" (right flush), 5.9" (right flush).                  ║
```

(It is not vital that you understand style sheets to learn how to manipulate columns. The style is reproduced for those trying to learn how to create styles for tables. Note that the style could have had the paragraph field *keep follow* set to *Yes,* thereby ensuring that any table formatted with it would never split across more than one page.)

With the assistance of the style, let's type the following table:

```
╓═[·········1·········2····L··3·········4·········5·······R]·········7···╖
║NC Newspaper                          Daily        Sunday              ║
║NC                                                                     ║
║NC  Boston Globe ............       510,261       793,151              ║
║NC  Chicago Tribune ..........      762,882     1,145,387              ║
║NC  Denver Post ............:.      244,953       356,986              ║
║NC  Honolulu Star-Bulletin ...      113,608       200,462              ║
║NC  Los Angeles Times ........    1,057,536     1,321,244              ║
║NC  New York Times ...........      737,193     1,593,107              ║
║NC  S.F. Chronicle ...........      539,450       706,150              ║
║NC  Seattle Times ............      226,038       473,155              ║
║NC  Washington Post ..........:     768,288     1,042,821              ║
```

If you're following along at your computer, using this as a tutorial, be sure to press the Tab key twice after the name of each newspaper, once for the leader character stop (at 2.6″) and once for the *Daily* column stop (at 4.2″). After typing the daily circulation figure, press the Tab key once and type the Sunday circulation figure. Press Enter at the end of each line.

To avoid having leader characters on the first line of the table (after the word *Newspaper*), press the Spacebar until the selection reaches the 2.6″ mark on the ruler (it will be marked by an L, showing a left-aligned tab stop). These Spacebar spaces "use up" the space that otherwise would be filled with leader characters. (An alternate approach would be to create a second style in the style sheet, intended specifically for formatting the first line. This style would be identical to the other one, except it would not have the tab stop at 2.6″.)

With the table complete, we'll turn the Options command's *visible* field to *Complete,* so that tab characters show up on the screen (and leader characters disappear from view). It is important to see the precise location of the tab characters when we execute the next steps.

Tab characters are displayed as small right-facing arrows. Spacebar spaces are displayed as small dots, and you can see these dots between words and after the word *Newspaper* in the following example. Recall that we typed the Spacebar spaces after the word *Newspaper*, to avoid a leader appearing there.

```
┃═══[·········1·········2····,L···3·········4·R·······5········R]·········7···┓
┃NC Newspaper················→         Daily▤         Sunday¶                  ┃
┃NC ¶                                                                          ┃
┃NC Boston·Globe·→            →        510,261→        793,151¶                ┃
┃NC Chicago·Tribune·→         →        762,882→      1,145,387¶                ┃
```

Observe that the tab character immediately following the word *Daily*, on the top line, is selected. Normally when we select a tab character, the highlight extends from the location of the actual character (the arrow) to the right until it reaches any other character.

But it becomes a single-character selection as soon as we turn on the Column Selection mode by holding down the Shift key and pressing F6. When the Column Selection mode is on, the selection is reduced in size to a single character, the letters CS appear on the bottom line of the screen, and we are ready to make a rectangular selection. This is the situation illustrated above. The single selected character, in this case a tab character represented by an arrow, will be one corner of what we select.

Press the Down and Right direction keys (or move the mouse), extending the selection until it reaches the character just to the left of the last paragraph mark on the screen. As you can see below, we've selected a rectangle: a column of numbers, and the tab characters (right-facing arrows) that precede each number.

```
┃═══[·········1·········2····,L···3·········4·R·······5········R]·········7···┓
┃NC Newspaper················→         Daily▤         Sunday¶                  ┃
┃NC ¶                                                                          ┃
┃NC Boston·Globe·→            →        510,261▌       793,151¶                 ┃
┃NC Chicago·Tribune·→         →        762,882▌     1,145,387¶                 ┃
┃NC Denver·Post·→             →        244,953▌       356,986¶                 ┃
┃NC Honolulu·Star-Bulletin·→  →        113,608▌       200,462¶                 ┃
┃NC Los·Angeles·Times·→       →      1,057,536▌     1,321,244¶                 ┃
┃NC New·York·Times·→          →        737,193▌     1,593,107¶                 ┃
┃NC S.F.·Chronicle·→          →        539,450▌       706,150¶                 ┃
┃NC Seattle·Times·→           →        226,038▌       473,155¶                 ┃
┃NC Washington·Post·→         →        768,288▌     1,042,821¶                 ┃
```

As an aside, if we press the F2 key now, Word will add all the numbers that are selected and put the sum in the scrap. In this case, the sum would be 7,632,463, the combined Sunday circulations of the nine newspapers. We could insert the sum from the scrap anywhere into the document if we wished (see the end of Chapter 10).

But instead of adding the numbers in the selected column with the F2 key, let's delete the column entirely.

Press the Del key, or pick the Delete command. The selection is removed to the scrap. Observe that the scrap contains little boxes. These indicate the end of a line, and remind you at a glance that the scrap contains a column selection.

To insert the column from the scrap back into the document at a different location, we press the Ins key. This is much the same as the way we move text conventionally with the Del and Ins keys (or Delete and Insert commands).

Before inserting the selected column back into the document, we must select the point where we want it to reappear. We do this by selecting the character in the document where we want the upper left corner of the column to be positioned.

In this case, we select the tab character preceding the word *Daily*.

```
  ╓═══[·········1·········2····,L···3·········4·R········5········R]·········7···╖
  ║NC   Newspaper················→[         ]Daily¶                               ║
  ║NC   ¶                                                                         ║
  ║NC   Boston·Globe·→        →        510,261¶                                   ║
  ║NC   Chicago·Tribune·→     →        762,882¶                                   ║
  ║NC   Denver·Post·→         →        244,953¶                                   ║
  ║NC   Honolulu·Star-Bulletin·→ →     113,608¶                                   ║
  ║NC   Los·Angeles·Times·→   →      1,057,536¶                                   ║
  ║NC   New·York·Times·→      →        737,193¶                                   ║
  ║NC   S.F.·Chronicle·→      →        539,450¶                                   ║
  ║NC   Seattle·Times·→       →        226,038¶                                   ║
  ║NC   Washington·Post·→     →        768,288¶                                   ║
```

The tab character is elongated, stretching from the tab character's arrow all the way to the word *Daily*. If Column Selection mode were still on, which it isn't, only the arrow would be highlighted. (The Column Selection mode, which we turn on with Shift-F6, turns itself off automatically after certain commands are executed. This is similar to the way the normal Extend Selection mode, which we turn on with F6, turns itself off. Alternatively, you can turn either mode off manually by pressing the same key or keys that turned it on.)

The next step is to insert the column back into the document by pressing the Ins key. When that is done, we set the Option command's *visible* field back to *None,* and the document looks much as it did when we started, except that the two columns of numbers have exchanged positions.

```
  ╓═══[·········1·········2·········3·········4·········5·········]·········7···╖
  ║NC   Newspaper                    Sunday         Daily                        ║
  ║NC                                                                            ║
  ║NC   Boston Globe ............    793,151       510,261                       ║
  ║NC   Chicago Tribune ..........  1,145,387      762,882                       ║
  ║NC   Denver Post .............     356,986      244,953                       ║
  ║NC   Honolulu Star-Bulletin ...    200,462      113,608                       ║
  ║NC   Los Angeles Times ........  1,321,244    1,057,536                       ║
  ║NC   New York Times ...........  1,593,107      737,193                       ║
  ║NC   S.F. Chronicle ...........    706,150      539,450                       ║
  ║NC   Seattle Times ............    473,155      226,038                       ║
  ║NC   Washington Post ..........  1,042,821      768,288                       ║
```

Some points to keep in mind about column manipulation:

♦ When moving a column, select the rectangle in such a way that it includes a set of tab characters either on one side or the other of the column of numbers (or text) you want. If you select and delete only the numbers, you'll leave behind an extra set of tab characters that will probably spoil the appearance of the document. Furthermore, if you leave the tab characters behind, you'll miss their effect when you insert the selection back into the document somewhere else.

♦ You can generate a column of tab characters by selecting the column in which you want the characters to appear and pressing the Tab key. This technique is handy, particularly when you want to add a tab character to the end of each line of a table in preparation for moving the last column of the table to a new location.

♦ By selecting a column and using the Library Autosort command, you can rearrange the order of the lines in a table. For detailed instructions and a tutorial, refer to the Library Autosort command in Chapter 14, "The Family of Library Commands."

♦ Column selection is impossible when Word is in outline view. This safety measure protects you from the havoc you could wreak on a document if, for example, it was in outline form with subheadings or text collapsed from view and you deleted a column. You would mistakenly delete all kinds of things you couldn't even see, and you wouldn't discover the damage until you returned to document view by pressing Shift-F2.

♦ Sometimes you may want to insert a column in such a way that its upper left corner appears on the screen as if it is in the *middle* of the highlighted bar to the right of a tab character. To do this, select the first character to the right of the highlighted bar, press Shift-F6, and press the Left direction key until the spot is highlighted. Now press Ins. (This works because Word inserts at the beginning of any selection.)

♦ If all the lines in a column don't fit neatly into a rectangle, it probably means the tab stop is center-aligned or decimal-aligned. If all else fails, you can temporarily change the alignment of the tab stop, using the Format Tabs Set command or, if a style sheet is being used, by entering the Gallery and temporarily changing the tab formatting of the relevant style(s).

♦ Don't forget the Undo command. If you insert the column into a place that isn't quite right, use the Undo command right away and try inserting the column at a different location.

SIDE-BY-SIDE PARAGRAPHS

One of the most common questions posed by users of Word is: "How do I get a page that has both single-column and double-column (or triple-column) text on it at the same time?"

Another common question is: "How can I juxtapose text, so that related paragraphs appear next to each other instead of one after the other?"

Another is: "How can I have multi-line side heads in the margins of my document?"

There have been answers to these questions, but until version 3.0 of Word, they've been somewhat disappointing. Word has always been able to print "snaking columns," in which a whole page or several pages are formatted to print in multiple columns, like a newspaper article. But this capability, which is controlled through Word's division formatting, wasn't designed to let you specify exactly which paragraphs should print adjacent to each other, nor to let you combine different numbers of columns on the same page. You could coax the program into doing some of these things, but not easily. It was small consolation that Word's capabilities with side-by-side text, although somewhat awkward, exceeded those of most competing word-processing programs.

Now there are better ways to work with side-by-side text. Beginning with version 3.0, Word gives paragraphs a new characteristic: the ability to be printed next to each other on a page. A field in the Format Paragraph command is called *side by side,* and when you set this to *Yes* for a series of two or more paragraphs, you open the door to various possibilities.

```
        For instance, you can print two (or more) paragraphs
next to each other.

Versions 1.0 through 2.0        But versions beginning with
let you print a whole           3.0 also let you put any
document in a "snaking"         number of paragraphs side-
two-column format.              by-side, like these two.

        On the screen, the paragraphs are indented properly
from the left and right margins, but they don't appear side-
by-side. One follows after the other, maintaining a definite
beginning-to-end order to the paragraphs. But when the
document is printed, the paragraphs are juxtaposed.
```

On the screen, the above passage looks like this:

```
SP      For instance, you can print two (or more) paragraphs
next to each other.

LS   Versions 1.0 through 2.0
let you print a whole
document in a "snaking"
two-column format.
RS                              But versions beginning with
                                3.0 also let you put any
                                number of paragraphs side-
                                by-side, like these two.

SP      On the screen, the paragraphs are indented properly
from the left and right margins, but they don't appear side-
by-side. One follows after the other, maintaining a definite
beginning-to-end order to the paragraphs. But when the
document is printed, the paragraphs are juxtaposed.
```

In this example of side-by-side paragraphs, the first paragraph (marked in the style bar with the key code LS) is indented from the right so that it prints on the left side of the page. The second paragraph (marked in the style bar with the key code RS) is indented from the left so that it prints on the right side of the page. The key codes indicate the two paragraphs were formatted with styles from a style sheet. These are the styles:

```
17  LS Paragraph 46                          LEFT SIDE OF SIDE-BY-SIDE
       Modern b 12. Flush left, right indent 3.3", space before 1 li.
       Place side by side.
18  RS Paragraph 47                          RIGHT SIDE OF SIDE-BY-SIDE
       Modern b 12. Flush left, left indent 3.3". Place side by side.
```

These styles are meant for use in documents that use Word's default page width of 6 inches (paper 8.5 inches wide, less 1.25-inch margins on left and right sides). These two styles are parts of a comprehensive system of style sheets created for Word and described fully in the book I co-authored with JoAnne Woodcock, *Microsoft Word Style Sheets* (Microsoft Press, 1987).

You don't have to use styles to format paragraphs for side-by-side printing, but it is by far the easiest way. With one style of your style sheet dedicated to each position on the page at which you wish side-by-side paragraphs to appear, you format any paragraph for proper placement simply by selecting it and typing the corresponding key code. The style takes care of all details, including the appropriate indentations and turning on the side-by-side feature.

You will notice that the LS (left side) paragraph style has a right-side indentation of 3.3 inches. This forces the paragraph to be printed only on the left, in a column width of 2.7 inches (6 inches minus the 3.3-inch right-side indent equals 2.7 inches). Note also that the side-by-side feature is turned on, making any paragraph formatted with this style eligible to be printed beside another paragraph.

If you weren't using a style to format a left-side paragraph, you could obtain the same formatting by selecting a paragraph and filling out the fields of the Format Paragraph command this way:

```
FORMAT PARAGRAPH alignment: LEFT Centered Right Justified
     left indent: 0"            first line: 0"       right indent: 3.3"
     line spacing: 1 li     space before: 1 li       space after: 0 li
     keep together: Yes(No)  keep follow: Yes(No)  side by side:(Yes)No
```

You will notice that the RS (right side) paragraph style has a left-side indentation of 3.3 inches, which forces the paragraph to be printed in a width of 2.7 inches on the right side of the page. It also has the side-by-side feature turned on. The formatting looks like this when expressed with the Format Paragraph command:

```
FORMAT PARAGRAPH alignment: LEFT Centered Right Justified
     left indent: 3.3"          first line: 0"       right indent: 0"
     line spacing: 1 li     space before: 0 li       space after: 0 li
     keep together: Yes(No)  keep follow: Yes(No)  side by side:(Yes)No
```

You may have noticed that formatting for the left-side paragraph includes one line of blank *space before* the beginning of the paragraph, while the right-side paragraph formatting does not have this blank line. This is intentional. The left-side paragraph is the first one Word encounters in the document, and the extra blank line separates the paragraph from whatever paragraph is above it. The right-side paragraph, however, is meant to line up across from the preceding paragraph, the left-side paragraph. If we formatted the right-side paragraph to print with an extra "space before," it would print one line lower on the page than the corresponding left-side paragraph.

Although the example shows only two paragraphs side by side, Word can juxtapose any number of them, provided each has *side by side* set to *Yes* and is indented from the right and left margins in such a way that it doesn't occupy the same space as another paragraph.

As a practical matter, columns get pretty narrow when more than three are placed side by side on a letter-sized page. But five or even more columns are feasible when a small enough type font is employed, when wide paper is used, or when letter-sized paper is printed sideways (as is possible with the landscape mode of the Hewlett-Packard LaserJet printer, for instance).

To increase the average number of characters that print on a line in a narrow column, you may want to use the Library Hyphenate command. Allowing words to break from one line to another at syllabic divisions often improves the appearance of short lines by filling them out more fully.

The rules Word follows

So far you've learned enough to use side-by-side paragraphs, but perhaps not without occasional confusion. You can gain insight by understanding the rules Word follows when it prints paragraphs that are formatted to be side by side. When you grasp these rules, you can predict what Word will do. Understanding how Word "thinks" removes any mystery—and mystery, nice as it may be in other realms, is the enemy when it comes to word processing.

These are the rules Word follows.

1. When Word encounters the first paragraph marked for side-by-side printing, it considers it the beginning of a *cluster* of paragraphs that are to be printed in juxtaposition to each other.

2. Word examines the succeeding paragraphs, looking for the last one in the cluster. The cluster ends when:
    — Word encounters the last paragraph marked to be printed side by side, *or*
    — Word reaches a paragraph that has a left indent less than the side-by-side paragraph that came before it, *or*
    — It reaches the 31st successive paragraph marked to be printed side by side.

3. Word draws an imaginary line across the page, at the location of the first printable line in the first paragraph of the cluster. This line is the *ceiling* for the cluster, and Word uses it as the vertical starting point for printing any columns that are formatted to appear to the right of the first paragraph in the cluster.

4. Word checks to see if the whole cluster will fit on the remainder of the page presently being printed. If not, Word begins a new page to start printing the cluster's paragraphs.

5. Word prints the first paragraph.

6. Word looks at the second paragraph. If the paragraph is indented so that it will fit on the page to the right of the first paragraph, Word prints the paragraph there, pressed up against the ceiling. If the second paragraph won't fit to the right of the first paragraph, because it tries to occupy some of the same space as the first paragraph, Word prints it below the first paragraph.

7. Word continues in this fashion. Each paragraph is given horizontal placement according to its indentation from the left and right page margins, and each is printed as high on the page (as close to the cluster's ceiling) as possible.

8. When it reaches the end of the cluster, Word resumes printing normal paragraphs or, if the next paragraph is marked to be printed side by side, Word starts a new cluster and begins the process over again.

NOTE: If a cluster of paragraphs is too large to fit on a single page, Word isn't sure how you want the paragraphs aligned. So it gives up, basically, and prints one column to a page. Take this as a signal to break the cluster into smaller pieces before printing it again.

Now that you know the rules, or at least can refer to them, let's consider some typical uses for side-by-side paragraphs—and see how using the rules can guide us to achieve what we want.

Tables and scripts

Perhaps the most common use for side-by-side paragraphs is to create a table or script in which related paragraphs appear next to each other.

For instance, if you're a financial consultant you might produce a newsletter that compares investment opportunities point by point in two or more columns. This is easy to do, especially if you use a style sheet to handle paragraph indentation. The paragraphs in a cluster will print next to each other, lined up against the ceiling. Each time you format a paragraph to have less left-side indentation than the preceding paragraph, a new cluster is started. In this way, you control which paragraphs print in direct juxtaposition.

Imagine that you want to print three side-by-side paragraphs about each of four investment opportunities. This forms a grid of twelve paragraphs, three wide and four deep. You would mark each paragraph for side-by-side printing, and use different indentations for the paragraphs in each column. The following illustration shows the first two clusters (rows). The page margins are 6 inches apart, each of the three columns is 1.8 inches wide, and there is a 0.3-inch gutter between columns.

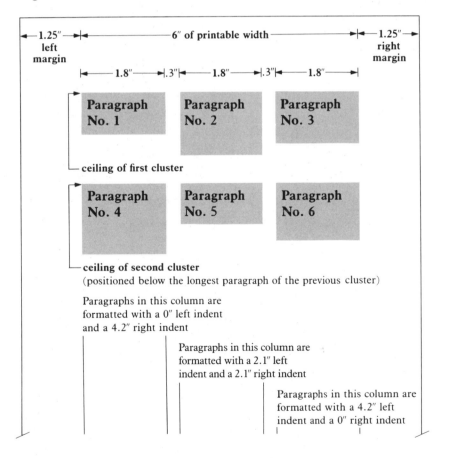

Word starts a new cluster for each row, because the first paragraph of each has a smaller left indent than the paragraph that preceded it. For example, Paragraph No. 4 has a left indent of 0″ while the paragraph preceding it, No. 3, has a left indent of 4.2″. (The possible exception is Paragraph No. 1, which might not have a smaller left indent than the paragraph before it. Presumably, the paragraph before it is not marked for side-by-side printing.)

You can also print two or more successive paragraphs in the same column by keeping indentations the same for each. In the previous illustration, for example, Paragraph No. 6 would have printed below Paragraph No. 5 if the indentations for the two were the same. The same side-by-side techniques can be used to create those kinds of scripts, including radio scripts, that require blocks of type to be beside each other.

This answers the question: "How can I juxtapose text so that related paragraphs appear next to each other instead of one after the other?"

Side heads

Word's capacity for side-by-side printing is distinguished by its flexibility. Not only can text print in any number of columns that fit, but individual columns can be of different widths. Among other things, this means that Word does a fine job with side heads.

| **This side head** **is on the left** | Side heads are effective in certain kinds of publications, including newsletters. The Microsoft Word manual uses them extensively. |
| | Word's ability to align paragraphs side by side, even when the paragraphs are of different widths, makes it easy to use side heads. |

| Side heads can appear on either side of a page. Frequently, side heads are put on the left side of even-numbered pages and on the right side of odd-numbered pages. | **This side head** **is on the right** |

The above example is composed of six paragraphs, all but one of which had *side by side* set to *Yes*. It was printed on the Hewlett-Packard LaserJet printer, using the B font cartridge (and the printer-description file HPLASPS.PRD). The division formatting was set so that the page had 6.5 inches of printable width (to achieve this, the left and right margins were both set to 1 inch).

The first paragraph in the document is the sentence *This side head is on the left.* The character formatting is HELV 14. The paragraph formatting has a 5.1-inch right indent, *line spacing* is 1.5, and *space before* is 1.

The second paragraph, which begins *Side heads are effective,* has a left indent of 1.8 inches, to make room for the side head to the left of it. *Space before* is set to 0, to keep the top of the paragraph up against the ceiling of the cluster.

The third paragraph (beginning *Word's ability...*) is identical in format to the second one, except that it has a *space before* of 1. This could be a standard paragraph format for text that is to appear to the right of a side head. This paragraph ends the first cluster, because the next paragraph has a smaller left indent.

The fourth paragraph has no printable content. It is a paragraph mark placed in the document solely to create extra blank space between examples. Significantly, it is *not* formatted to print side by side.

The fifth paragraph begins *Side heads can appear,* and starts the second cluster. It is placed in the document *before* the side head that prints to the right of it. When paragraphs are to be printed side by side, the one to the left must always come first in the document. The paragraph is formatted with a *right indent* of 1.8 inches, to make room for the side head, and a *space before* of 1 line.

The sixth paragraph is the side head that says *This side head is on the right.* The character formatting is HELV 14. The paragraph formatting has a 5.1-inch left indent, *line spacing* is 1.5, and there is no *space before* (because we want the paragraph to press up against the ceiling of the cluster).

This example answers the question: "How can I have multi-line side heads in the margins of my document?"

Multiple columns

If you want to print a document with multiple columns, and it doesn't matter which paragraphs are adjacent to each other, a simple solution may suffice. The *number of columns* field of the Format Division Layout command lets you specify any number of columns on a page: Just type in the number, and Word does the rest. (Prior to version 3.0 of Word, it was the *# of cols* field of the Format Division command.)

There is a drawback to the *number of columns* method, however. It is impossible to print single- and double-column text on the same page, except by using a running-head technique that requires considerable patience.

(What is this running-head technique? Any text you format to be a running head at the top or bottom of a page will remain one column wide, even if the division formatting for the balance of the page calls for two or more columns. You can mix single- and multiple-column text in a rudimentary way by including such things as full-width headlines or introductory paragraphs in a deep running head at the top of a page. Meanwhile, the main body of the document can print in a multiple-column division format. For this to work, the top page margin of the division must be made large enough to accommodate everything you're putting in the running head, since running heads print in the margins.)

Side-by-side columns

Word's side-by-side feature provides a far easier, much more flexible means to mix the number of columns on a page. It's not difficult, although it's not automatic, either.

Let's say you have several paragraphs you want printed in two columns, with the first half on the left side of the page and the second half on the right side.

The basic formatting technique is to give the first half a wide right indent, the second half a wide left indent, and mark all of it for side-by-side printing.

Although this can be accomplished using the Format Paragraph command, a style sheet makes it easier. When using the side-by-side feature to print text in columns, some experimenting with the layout of the paragraphs is generally needed before results are satisfactory. A style sheet lets you experiment easily, because you can switch a paragraph from right-side printing to left-side printing at the touch of a key code.

Let's look again at the styles we used earlier in the chapter, when we were formatting side-by-side *paragraphs*. This time we're interested in side-by-side *columns* of text, and so we've added a third style, one with the key code RO.

```
17  LS Paragraph 46                        LEFT SIDE OF SIDE-BY-SIDE
       Modern b 12. Flush left, right indent 3.3", space before 1 li.
       Place side by side.
18  RS Paragraph 47                       RIGHT SIDE OF SIDE-BY-SIDE
       Modern b 12. Flush left, Left indent 3.3". Place side by side.
19  RO Paragraph 48                       RIGHT SIDE OF S-B-S (w/OPEN)
       Modern b 12. Flush left, Left indent 3.3", space before 1 li. Place
       side by side.
```

The RO style is almost identical to the RS style. Both cause a paragraph to print as a column on the right side of a page (presuming the printable width of the page is 6 inches). The difference is that RO, in addition to pushing a paragraph to the right, incorporates open paragraph spacing—in other words, it puts one *space before* (blank line) above every paragraph to which it is attached, thereby matching the spacing of left-side paragraphs.

RS: In the earlier instance, we didn't want our right-side paragraphs to have open spacing, because we were placing paragraphs in juxtaposition to each other across a page. We wanted each right-side paragraph to line up with the ceiling of the paragraph to the left. The RS style had no *space before* because starting a paragraph with a blank line would cause it to print one line lower than the ceiling.

RO: But now we're doing something different. We're printing several successive paragraphs in a column on the left, followed by several successive paragraphs in an adjacent column on the right. (Whereas before the second paragraph in the cluster was directly to the right of the first one, now the second paragraph is below the first one. Perhaps the fourth or fifth paragraph *happens* to be to the right of the first one.) When we're printing text in columns this way, only the first paragraph on the right—the top one, the one that will press up against the ceiling—needs the RS style (with its lack of *space before*). Each of the other right-side paragraphs uses the new RO style, with a blank space printed above it.

Step by step through side by side

Now, step by step, let's use these three styles—LS, RS, and RO—to put paragraphs into a two-column format. We'll assume you've already completed writing and editing your document, and are formatting it for final printing. We'll also assume that none of the paragraphs in the document is marked *side by side* to begin with. This is important, to avoid confusing results.

NOTE: You don't have to use styles; you can use the Format Paragraph command, instead, to set left and right indentations and adjust the *side by side* field of paragraphs. Nor do you have to use exactly the indentation in the sample styles. If your page width is different, or if you want more or less space between columns, or if you want more than two columns on the page, adjust the indentations accordingly.

Step 1. While the whole document is still in a single column, use the Print Repaginate command to determine where page breaks would occur if you were to print now. (Page breaks are indicated by a » symbol immediately to the left of the first line of a new page.)

Step 2. Examine the page on which you want to switch from single to double columns. We'll call this Page A. Consider how much single-column text will appear at the top of Page A (between the page-break symbol and the beginning of what will become double-column text), and whether there will be sufficient room below it on the page for *all* of the two-column text. If there is room, matters are simplified and you can skip now to Step 15.

Step 3. Assuming that there isn't room for all of the two-column text at the bottom of Page A, you must decide whether it's acceptable for the bottom of the page to be blank. When a cluster of paragraphs won't fit on a single page, Word doesn't break it into pieces and print it across more than one page; instead, Word prints the cluster beginning on a new page. In other words, it leaves the bottom of Page A blank and begins printing the side-by-side material on what we'll call Page B. If the blank space is acceptable to you, skip now to Step 14.

The initial page

The way to fill out the bottom of the page with double-column text is to create left-side and right-side columns that are just the proper length.

Step 4. Select the first paragraph that will be in double-column format, and assign it the LS style. (Hold down the Alt key and type LS.) If you're not using the style sheet, you can instead pick the Format Paragraph command and specify a right indent of 3.3", a *space before* of *1 li,* and *Yes* in the *side by side* field. The paragraph will become narrow, and appear on the left side of the screen. It is the first side-by-side paragraph of the cluster.

Step 5. Use the Print Repaginate command to check the current location of page breaks. If the page-break symbol marking the top of the next page is below the bottom of the paragraph you just reformatted, continue on to Step 6. But if the page-break symbol has moved up to the first line of the paragraph, skip to Step 8.

Step 6. Select the next paragraph, and give it the same left-side formatting as the previous paragraph. Do this by using the LS style or the Format Paragraph command. (Hint: Style sheets are fastest, but if you're not using them you can still copy the formatting from one paragraph to another. See the tip "Copying formatting with the keyboard" in Chapter 18, "Speed.")

Step 7. Just as you did in Step 5, use the Print Repaginate command. If the page-break symbol marking the beginning of the next page remains below the paragraph you just formatted, repeat step 6, working your way down through the paragraphs of the document one at a time, and formatting them (with the LS style) to appear on the left side of the page.

At some point, you'll format one paragraph too many, and the page-break symbol will move back up to the beginning of the first line of the first side-by-side paragraph. This means you've asked Word to print a column too long for the current page, and Word has responded by moving the whole column to the next page. At this point, you're ready for the next step.

Step 8. The paragraph you just formatted for the left side won't fit on the page. You'll have to move some or all of it to the top of the right column. If you want the entire paragraph moved, skip to Step 10 and then Step 12 (skipping Step 11).

Step 9. Divide the paragraph into two paragraphs, by selecting the *first* (not last) character of one of its middle lines and pressing the Enter key. The Enter key adds a (normally invisible) paragraph mark at the point at which it is pressed. After you press Enter, the first character of the second paragraph will be selected.

Step 10. To make this paragraph print at the top of the right column, assign it the RS style. (Hold down the Alt key and type RS.) If you're not using the style sheet, you can instead pick the Format Paragraph command and specify a left indent of 3.3″ and *Yes* in the *side by side* field. Either way, the paragraph will become narrow, and appear on the right side of the screen.

Step 11. Use the Print Repaginate command again, and check to see where the page break falls. Experiment. You'll know the left-side column is too long if the page-break symbol moves up to the top of the cluster of side-by-side paragraphs (the left-side paragraph from Step 4). You may want to find the dividing point that makes the column as long as possible.

Step 12. One at a time, format all the paragraphs destined for the right-side column, except the first one, with the RO style. (Hold down the Alt key and type RO.) Recall that this style is identical to RS, except that it has a *space before* of *1.* If you're not using the style sheet, you can instead pick the Format Paragraph command and specify a left indent of 3.3″, a *space before* of *1*, and *Yes* in the *side by side* field.

Step 13. Basically, repeat Steps 6 through 11, adjusted for the fact that you're fitting text into a right-side column instead of a left-side column. Work your way down through the paragraphs of the right column one at a time, assigning the RO style and using the Print Repaginate command to assess what the effect is on page breaks. When you format one paragraph too many for the right side, the page-break symbol will move up to the top of the cluster (the left-side paragraph from Step 4), and you'll know it's time to switch back to the LS style, thereby causing a new cluster to begin on the next page.

The next page

Step 14. Beginning a cluster of side-by-side paragraphs on a new page is easy. Just make sure paragraph formatting is marked for side-by-side treatment. The first half of the text to be printed side by side should be formatted for printing on the left (with the LS style, for instance), and the second half should be formatted for the right (the RS and RO styles). If the text is too long for the page, use the strategy outlined in Steps 4 through 13. This allows you to make each column as long as possible, and move leftover text onto the following page.

On the other hand, if the text is too short to fill the rest of the page, you need to learn a new technique if you want the columns to be the same length.

Step 15. Assuming you are putting two columns on the page, estimate the location of the middle of the text that is to be split into columns on the page. We will call this middle point the column boundary.

Step 16. Format the paragraphs before the column boundary with the LS style, and the paragraphs after the column boundary line with the RO style (except that the first paragraph after the column boundary should have the RS style).

Step 17. Use the Print Repaginate command to make sure the text really will print on the page. This will also tell you the page number.

Step 18. Print the one page, using the Print Options command to specify the number of the single page to be printed.

Step 19. Examine the printout to see how close the two columns are to being the same length. Count the number of lines by which one column is longer than the other, divide the number in half, and move the column boundary by that many lines toward the longer column (away from the shorter column). For instance, if the right column is 10 lines longer than the left column, move the column boundary so that the "long" column becomes 5 lines shorter, and the "short" column becomes 5 lines longer. This will make the columns the same length.

NOTE: To move the column boundary by lines, use the paragraph-splitting technique explained in Step 9.

Simple? Well, not entirely. But not difficult when you get the hang of it. Convoluted as these steps may appear on paper, by working through them you'll come to understand Word's flexible power with side-by-side columns. These steps should remove unwanted mystery, and answer the question: "How do I get a page that has single-column and double-column (or triple-column) text on it at the same time?"

Pointers

Several points are worth bearing in mind when laying out multi-column documents with the side-by-side feature.

♦ Although our discussion has assumed two-column printing, the techniques can be adapted for three or more columns. Basically, every additional column is formatted like the right-side columns in the above examples. Of course, the paragraph indents must be changed to reflect three (or more) side-by-side paragraphs or columns.

♦ Use the Print Repaginate command liberally, because you can deduce a good deal about the way columns will print if you watch where Word wants to put page breaks and if you think about the rules Word follows. You'll appreciate the speed of a fast computer, such as an IBM PC AT with a hard disk, if you use the Print Repaginate command much.

♦ If Word prints out just one column of what you thought would be side-by-side columns, it means the cluster of paragraphs is too large to fit on a single page. Break the cluster into smaller pieces before printing the document again.

♦ If you're just experimenting with side-by-side paragraphs and columns, consider numbering each paragraph in advance. This will make it evident what order Word has used for printing paragraphs. The paragraphs needn't make sense in content, or differ from each another. An easy way to produce a document of numbered paragraphs is to type one short paragraph which begins with the number 1., copy it to the scrap, insert it into the document 20 or 30 times, and use the Library Number command to update the number of each. *Do not* format all of these paragraphs with *side by side* set to *Yes* copy at the outset. Word will think you are trying to make the whole document one cluster. Turn *side-by-side* on selectively in paragraphs as you experiment.

♦ Some people prefer paragraphs to have indented first lines, even in narrow columns. Although you may freely change the *first line* fields of the LS and RO styles to provide indented first lines, think twice before giving the RS style a first-line indent. When a paragraph from the bottom left of a page is divided in two, you give the portion brought to the top of the right column the RS style. If the style includes a "first line" of other than 0, there will be inappropriate indentation. (If this doesn't make sense on paper, try it.)

Using a Hard Disk

Nothing supercharges Word as much as running it on a computer with a hard disk. A close second is running it on a computer with a fast processor. A speedy printer and a mouse shouldn't be overlooked, but a hard disk not only gives superior storage capacity, it grants you extra speed and flexibility.

If ignorance is bliss and you have no hope of getting a hard disk, perhaps you should not read this chapter. But hard disks are getting cheaper, and Word was written with the new generation of computers in mind. Though it's competitive with the best of word processors when it's running on a floppy-disk system, Word excels when used with a hard disk. If you experience Word on a hard disk, it's likely you'll no longer be satisfied with floppy disks—even high-capacity floppy disks, such as IBM's 1.2 megabyte disks.

With a hard disk you quickly become accustomed to the speed with which Word and your documents are loaded. You get used to opening a text window and—in just a few seconds—being able to see your choice of anything you've written in months appear. It becomes second nature to move passages from document to document, with or without the use of multiple windows, without ever touching a floppy disk. And you never worry about how to get all the programs you need —Word, Spell, DOS, and so forth—on the same disk at the same time.

Preparing and using a hard disk in the best way possible for your overall needs sometimes requires specifics that are beyond the scope of this chapter. Here you will find guidelines on using Word well with a hard disk. For more details, see your DOS manual.

INITIAL HARD-DISK SETUP

A new hard disk must be formatted, much as floppy disks are formatted. It is possible to partition the disk into sections devoted to different operating systems, but unless you also use a form of UNIX (such as XENIX), you'll probably forgo multiple partitions and leave all the room for MS-DOS programs. The DOS command FDISK creates the DOS partitions.

To format the hard disk and copy DOS to it, put your DOS disk in drive A and (assuming drive C is your hard disk), at the A> prompt, type:

```
format c: /s
```

Copy COMMAND.COM from the DOS disk to drive C, too. Do not copy the remainder of the DOS programs (such as FORMAT.COM and CHKDSK.COM). Later, you'll copy them to a special directory that could have any name, but that is often called BIN.

DOS SUBDIRECTORIES

From the standpoint of organizing your work, the ability DOS gives to create separate directories (subdirectories) in hierarchical arrangements can be invaluable. You can create directories dedicated to particular kinds of writing, and store related documents, style sheets, and glossary files in each: BIZ might be a subdirectory for business letters, MEMO a subdirectory for notes and memoranda, both grouped under a broader directory called DOC. Another directory called 123 could hold Lotus 1-2-3, or a directory called MP could contain Multiplan and its files.

Most of the following discussion of directories and path names technically applies to floppy disks as well as to hard disks. But, except for high-capacity floppy disks, creating subdirectories on floppy disks may not be worth the effort, because of their smaller storage capacity. With a floppy-disk-based system, each document disk represents a directory of sorts, anyway.

Paths

The DOS Path command tells your computer where to search for executable programs if they can't be found on the active (logged) drive or directory. You give it at the DOS prompt, and follow this form:

```
A)path=c:\bin
```

This example tells DOS to look in a directory named BIN on drive C if it can't find a program you request in the logged directory or drive. WORD.COM is the program that gets Word running when you type *word* at the DOS prompt. Assume for the sake of example that WORD.COM is in the BIN directory and you're working on a floppy disk in drive A. If you type *word*, the computer will first look in drive A for WORD.COM, and failing to find it there, will look in BIN. The program will execute from BIN, but you'll remain logged on drive A, and Word will look on drive A for documents. If you quit Word, you'll return to drive A, not to C:\BIN.

Creating a subdirectory

The DOS command for creating a directory is MD (Make Directory), followed by a space and the name of the new directory. Here, let's make one called BIN. You could use any name other than BIN for the directory; BIN is a UNIX convention. (I once discussed this "UNIX convention" with a friend who didn't seem to understand. . . . I later discovered she thought I'd said "eunuchs' convention.")

At any rate, to create the directory BIN, at the C> prompt, type:

```
md bin
```

Now you can copy into BIN any executable programs that are designed to be compatible with path names. Such programs have the file name extension .COM or .EXE and perform a task—"execute"—when you type their names. Path-compatible programs include WORD.COM, MOUSE.COM, all DOS commands, and most other programs written by Microsoft and some other manufacturers. For instance, typing *word* executes the program WORD.COM, and starts Word. You can place WORD.COM in any subdirectory, but by placing it in a subdirectory that is in the DOS path, you'll be able to execute Word from any subdirectory or drive you are using, without touching a floppy or changing directories.

COPYING WORD TO THE HARD DISK

NOTE: If you purchased a version of Word created for a computer other than the family of IBM PCs and compatibles, check your manual for instructions on putting Word on a hard disk.

Beginning with version 2.0, running a utility program called SETUP will install Word and its various files on your hard disk. With version 2.0, you can do this only once for each of the two copies of your Program disk. Beginning with version 3.0, Word is not copy-protected, and you can technically (though not legally) install the program on any number of hard disks. SETUP is used by putting the Utilities disk in drive A, typing *setup*, and following the on-screen instructions.

With Word versions 1.0, 1.1, and 1.15, a utility called MWCOPY will place Word on your hard disk. You run the utility by typing *mwcopy* and following the on-screen instructions.

Either SETUP or MWCOPY will ask for the drive letter of the hard disk onto which you wish to copy Word—which will probably be C—and will ask what path name you want the Word files copied to. You may want to type \ *bin* if you've created a BIN directory for executable programs. However, if you have a recent version of Word (3.0 or above), you may want to type \ *word*. More about this later. Regardless of whether you're using SETUP or MWCOPY, the program will ask you to swap disks as needed. Beginning with version 3.0, SETUP copies all Word files to whichever subdirectory you specify. If you have a recent version of Word, skip to the "Versions 3.0 and higher" heading below.

Versions 1.0 to 2.0

In versions prior to 3.0, either SETUP or MWCOPY automatically creates a directory called MSTOOLS in which (again, automatically) it places almost all the files and programs necessary to make Word run. For example, printer description (.PRD) files are placed in MSTOOLS.

You needn't concern yourself with MSTOOLS, because Word gets from it whatever it needs without your assistance. The files that SETUP or MWCOPY place in the subdirectory you specify (\ bin in our example) are WORD.COM, MOUSE.COM, possibly some miscellaneous style sheets and document examples, and—if you have SETUP and Word version 2.0—the files of Microsoft Spell.

This all sounds complicated, but really it is simple if you follow the on-screen instructions. At the risk of making this seem *really* complicated, there is one additional wrinkle to consider. You can create a separate subdirectory called Spell, add \SPELL to your path (PATH=C:\BIN;C:\SPELL), and copy all the files from the Spell disk to the Spell subdirectory. This will keep \BIN uncluttered, and help organize your hard disk. You can change the name of WORD.COM to something else if you like. If you prefer typing your sweetheart's name instead of *Word*, use the DOS Rename command to change WORD.COM to MATHILDA.COM or JOHNNY.COM or whatever. The file—regardless of what you call it—can be moved freely from directory to directory. Wherever WORD.COM is, it will find the tools it needs in the MSTOOLS subdirectory. However, if BIN is in your path, there should be no reason to have WORD.COM in any subdirectory other than BIN.

Versions 3.0 and higher

Copying Word to your hard disk is a simple matter if you have a recent version of Word. You can simply run SETUP, and Word will be installed in a subdirectory of your choice—such as a subdirectory called *word*. Unlike with earlier versions of SETUP, this subdirectory will contain *all* Word files, not just WORD.COM. It will even install an appropriate PATH command in your AUTOEXEC.BAT file, so that you don't have to bother with it. (More about AUTOEXEC.BAT later.) It will also, with your permission, remove the Word files from the MSTOOLS subdirectory, which is useful if you are upgrading from an earlier version of Word. (Earlier versions used an MSTOOLS subdirectory that contained hidden files that cannot be deleted by normal means. You should remove these hidden files, since they consume disk space even though you cannot detect their presence.)

It is possible, however, that you will not want to run all of the SETUP program. You may want to create a separate subdirectory for Spell files, and copy the contents of the Spell disk to the subdirectory. If so, be sure to add \SPELL to your path, preferably by amending your AUTOEXEC.BAT file.

SETTING UP CONFIG.SYS AND AUTOEXEC.BAT

Unless SETUP (versions 3.0 and above) has done this for you and to your satisfaction, perhaps the first thing to do after copying Word to your hard disk is to create CONFIG.SYS and AUTOEXEC.BAT files. Once established, these files will execute automatically whenever you start or reboot your computer. Each line in these files contains an instruction. The correct combination of instructions customizes the operation of your computer to your needs. Both CONFIG.SYS and AUTOEXEC.BAT should be stored in the top-level directory of the hard disk, the same place that COMMAND.COM should be. Before creating the files, to make sure you're at the top-level directory, after the DOS prompt, type:

```
cd \
```

CONFIG.SYS

Start Word. If you have an existing CONFIG.SYS file, load it with the Transfer Load command. Otherwise, start with a blank text window and create CONFIG.SYS. Type:

```
device=\bin\mouse.sys
```

One to a line, add to the file any other commands you might need for other purposes or programs. When this is done, choose the Transfer Save command, type *config.sys* in the *filename* field, choose *No* in the *formatted* field, and press the Enter key. Confirm the loss of formatting when Word asks you to.

The line *device = \ bin\ mouse.sys* tells the computer to load the device driver program MOUSE.SYS, which in this case you have copied to the BIN directory. MOUSE.SYS tells the computer how to use the mouse with Word and other programs. If you have a recent version of Word or of the Microsoft Mouse, the file MOUSE.SYS will work regardless of whether you have a serial or bus version of the mouse. If you're not using a mouse, you don't need the mouse software at all—or, for that matter, the CONFIG.SYS instruction line *device = \ bin\ mouse.sys.*

If MOUSE.SYS is in the /Word subdirectory, the line in CONFIG.SYS should be *device = \ word\ mouse.*

AUTOEXEC.BAT

The extension .BAT is short for "batch." A batch file contains commands you want DOS to carry out without your having to type each one separately. AUTOEXEC.BAT is a special batch file that is executed whenever you start up or reboot your computer. If you already have an AUTOEXEC.BAT file, load it into Word. Otherwise, clear the screen (with Word's Transfer Clear command) and type the following, or your own variation:

```
path=C:\bin;c:\word;c:\spell
prompt=$P$G
mode com1:12,N,8,1,p
date
time
```

As already described, the command *path = C:\ bin;c:\ word;c:\ spell* tells DOS to look in the directory BIN, then WORD, then SPELL for executable programs. Several directories can be listed in the path name as long as they are separated by semicolons. Although you don't need more than one, having several reduces the number of programs in each. For example, in BIN I keep all DOS programs (except the DOS system) and certain other programs such as Multiplan; in a subdirectory called Word I keep Word; and in the subdirectory Spell I keep the contents of the Spell disk.

The Prompt command is a part of DOS that lets you change your prompt from the single-drive letter to any of several other choices. The line *prompt = PG* causes DOS to first display the drive letter, followed by the path name of the subdirectory and the familiar >. For instance, if you're on drive C, in the subdirectory BIZ of the directory DOC, the prompt would be:

```
C:\doc\biz>
```

Without this on-screen reminder, you can become confused about which directory you are in.

The DOS Mode command is needed if you are using a serial printer. The command as shown will work with the Diablo 620 and Diablo 630 printers, among others, when hooked to the first serial port (COM1:).

Date and Time cause DOS to ask you to type the date and time. If you have a battery-powered clock in your computer, eliminate the words *Date* and *Time* or replace them with the name of the clock software, such as CLOCK or ASTCLOCK. Some computers, such as the IBM PC AT, do not require you to load clock software.

Save your AUTOEXEC.BAT file: Choose the Transfer Save command, type the name *autoexec.bat* in the *filename* field, choose *No* in the *formatted* field, and press the Enter key. Word will ask you to confirm the loss of formatting. See your DOS manual for additional information on DOS commands suitable for use in the AUTOEXEC.BAT file.

CHANGING DIRECTORIES

One consequence of having several directories is that you must occasionally change from one to another, and know how to tell Word where to find documents, style sheets, and glossary files that are in other subdirectories.

From DOS

To change from one subdirectory to another while you're at the DOS level, type *cd* (Change Directory) followed by a space, a backslash, and the path necessary to get from the top-level (or root) directory to the desired directory. Your DOS manual has details, but if your tree of subdirectories looks like this:

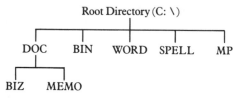

and you're on drive C, the DOS command for moving from any subdirectory to the BIZ subdirectory would be:

```
cd \doc\biz
```

From Word

The same terminology holds true when loading or saving documents with Word. If your disk is set up according to the example, you switch the active ("logged") directory to BIZ by using the Transfer Options command and typing in the *setup* field:

```
\doc\biz
```

If you wish to load a document called WINDSURF that is in the BIZ directory, but you're in a different directory and don't wish to use the Transfer Options command first, you can use the Transfer Load command to type:

```
\doc\biz\windsurf
```

Versions 1.0-2.0

In this case you might find that the document has "lost" its formatting, if you're using a version of Word prior to 3.0. This merely means the document has a style-sheet name attached to it, but there isn't a copy of the style sheet itself in the active directory. One solution is to use the Format Style Sheet command to change the name of the style sheet attached to the document. If the style sheet for WINDSURF is called MAGAZINE.STY, the Format Style Sheet's command shows this before you change it:

```
FORMAT STYLE SHEET: magazine.sty
```

Either by retyping the whole thing or else by pressing the F9 key and typing just the path name, you could change it to:

```
FORMAT STYLE SHEET: \doc\biz\magazine.sty
```

Versions 3.0 and higher

Beginning with version 3.0, style sheets (like documents) are stored with their path names as well as their names, making some of the foregoing discussion irrelevant. Because a Word document remembers both the name of its style sheet and the name of the path for the style sheet, loading a document from a different subdirectory shouldn't cause the style sheet to be unavailable.

With any version of Word, if you decide you want the style sheet to be in the active directory permanently, you can load it into the Gallery and then copy it to the current subdirectory with the Gallery menu's Transfer Save command, leaving off the path name to the original subdirectory.

```
TRANSFER SAVE style sheet name: magazine.sty
```

Or you can move the style sheet to the active directory by using the Gallery menu's Transfer Rename command and typing the style-sheet name without a path name:

```
TRANSFER RENAME style sheet name: magazine.sty
```

The last Word

A final tip for sophisticated users of Word: Place all your style sheets in a subdirectory of their own, possibly a subdirectory with the name S. Then regardless of which directory you're in when using the Format Style Sheet command, specify \s\ before the style sheet name. This makes all style sheets easily available from all directories—and augments your word-processing power.

IV

Appendices

Messages

Messages from Word are displayed on the second-to-last line of the screen. Any of more than 175 messages can appear, one at a time, depending on what you're doing at a particular moment. This appendix explains all messages other than those that are obvious or infrequently encountered, or are well explained in the Word manual.

The *x*'s in the first three messages listed refer to numbers or letters that change depending on circumstances. When the menu is turned off (with the Options command), messages appear on the bottom line of the screen.

xxxxxxx bytes free

Whenever Word looks at the document disk, this message reports how many bytes of disk space are available. Try to start each writing session with (roughly) at least three times the number of free bytes on your document disk as you expect your document will need. This leaves room for the document (.DOC), the backup copy (.BAK) Word automatically stores, and temporary files (.TMP).

xxxxx characters

The number of characters in a document or style sheet is reported after a Transfer Load or Transfer Save command is used. The number of characters is less than the number of bytes reported by the DOS command Dir, because Word's count includes only the characters that you place in a document; the Dir command measures the full size of the file, including invisible formatting characters. Typically, there are 85 to 95 percent as many characters as there are bytes in a document, and 30 to 40 percent as many characters as there are bytes in a style sheet.

xxxxxx < — Not in Dictionary; Retype? (Y/N)

This is a Spell message, telling you Word doesn't recognize the spelling of the word you've typed with the Correct command. Press Y to retype the word; otherwise, press N.

Access to this file required. Enter Y to retry or Q to quit Word

This message probably isn't good news. It means Word must have access to a particular file, and it has asked for the file with the message *Enter Y to retry access to* (filename). You have pressed the Esc key, but Word can't back down from its request for the file. If you have changed disks in the course of the editing session, the file Word needs may be on a disk that is no longer in the drive. Return the old disk to the drive, and press Y. If all fails, it may mean there is a problem with the disk or drive. Press Q to quit Word. (You'll lose any unsaved changes in your document.)

Cannot delete file

You have asked Word to delete a document or other file that it is unable to delete from the disk.

♦ Possibly a floppy disk has a write-protect tab on it. Remove the tab if you're certain you won't be deleting valuable information.

♦ Possibly you gave an incorrect or incomplete name for the file. Request a list of valid file names by pressing a direction key.

♦ Possibly you have used the file since starting the present Word editing session. If so, Word won't delete it. Start a new editing session with the Transfer Clear All command, but beware: Transfer Clear All causes Word to forget everything that hasn't been saved to disk.

Cannot find *xxxxxx* and Cannot read *xxxxxx*

These Spell messages tell you Word can't find a particular program, dictionary, or document needed to carry out the task you've requested. It may be necessary to specify a disk drive, or—if you're using subdirectories—a path.

Cannot rename file

You've asked Word to rename the active document, but something must be corrected before the program can do so.

♦ Possibly the disk has a write-protect tab on it. Remove the tab if you are sure renaming the file will not cause later problems.

♦ Possibly another document on the disk already has the name you proposed. Check the names of existing documents by picking the Transfer Load command and pressing a direction key, but once you have seen the list, press Esc.

♦ Possibly the name you proposed is too long or contains illegal characters, such as blank spaces. If so, the unacceptable characters are highlighted and can be deleted by pressing the Del key.

Cannot save file

Word is unable to save the file because the document disk is full or faulty; see *Document disk full*. (For Word version 1.0 or 1.1, see *Disk full*, instead.) If the disk is not full, see *Disk error*.

Cannot write to read-only file

You have attempted to save a document that is marked read-only by DOS. Choose the Transfer Save command again, but specify a different filename, or specify the same name but a different disk or directory. See the message *Document is read-only*.

Command field requires response

You left a command field blank. Fill in the blank and try the command again. (Many command fields do not require responses, but some do.)

DATA after SET or ASK

You've executed the Print Merge command, but the master document is incorrectly constructed. A DATA statement must be absolutely the first item in the document. Press the Esc key twice, then edit the document so that nothing, not even a space, precedes the word *DATA*.

Disk error

Word is unable to use the disk. With luck, the problem is minor: The disk is improperly inserted in the drive or the read-write notch is covered by a write-protect tab. If neither of these is the problem, try a new formatted disk, if possible. Later, check the bad disk with the DOS Check Disk command, chkdsk; you may be able to copy individual files off the faulty disk. The possibility of disk failure is an argument for keeping vital documents backed up.

Disk full

This message is displayed in versions 1.0 and 1.1 of Word. It means that all storage room has been exhausted on either the Program disk or the document disk. A disk can fill up more quickly than you expect, because Word creates temporary working files and backup files as you work.

First, determine which disk is full. If the message appears while you're using the Transfer Save command, it indicates that the document disk has filled up before the entire document could be saved. The chances of this happening increase when you have long or multiple files on the disk, especially if the active document or documents are also long. See *Document disk full* for instructions.

The Program disk is the likely culprit if the *Disk full* message suddenly appears while you are writing, editing, or using queued printing. Either all room is used on the Program disk, or the temporary "scratch" file on the disk has reached 64K, its limit. Editing commands may freeze. See *Program disk full* for instructions.

As preventive steps, try to keep as much blank space on your Program disk as possible (at least 64K) and avoid putting long documents into queued printing unless you've freed up a lot of space on the Program disk by copying unneeded Word files (such as the Help files) to another disk. If you type tens of thousands of characters during a single editing session, save your documents and use the Transfer Clear All command every few hours. These steps are not as important in versions of Word beginning with 1.15.

Document disk full

The document disk has run out of room during a Transfer Save operation. To save the document, you must either make room on the disk or use a different disk with more storage space on it. To make room on the same disk, use the Transfer Delete command to eliminate unneeded or backup copies of documents. You cannot delete any document that has been used during an editing session. If you cannot or do not want to delete files, you must use a new disk to save your document.

If you have three drives, using a different disk is easy. Leave the Program and document disks in place and insert a previously formatted blank (or sufficiently blank) disk in the third drive. Use the Transfer Save command, but save the name of the document to the disk in the third drive (for example, *c:filename*). Word will write the document to the third disk, using the disks in the other two drives for needed information.

With a two-drive floppy-disk computer system, you may have to do a significant amount of disk swapping to save the document. The number of swaps depends on the length of the document and the amount of RAM (memory) in your computer. I've traded disks more than 20 times to save a long document. Leave the drive containing the Word Program disk alone, and replace the full document disk with a new (or sufficiently blank) formatted disk. Execute the Transfer Save command. Word begins to record the document on the new disk, but can go only so far before needing information from the full document disk. To get this information, Word tells you to swap the new disk for the old one with the message *Enter Y to retry access to filename*. *Filename* in the message is the name of the needed file from the old disk. Swap disks and press Y. Word will read from the needed file and continue to issue the *Enter Y. . .* message as often as it needs you to swap disks so that it can read and write information.

Don't be puzzled when you see a file name ending in .TMP in the *Enter Y. . .* message during some of the swaps. It is a temporary file name Word gives to documents and files.

If your system has a single floppy-disk drive, swapping is still the solution to a full disk, but the swaps will probably be frequent and numerous.

Document is read-only

DOS allows certain files to be marked *read-only,* which means changes cannot be made to them. When you load such a file into Word as a document, this message notifies you that you won't be able to save to disk any changes you might make in the document. If you make changes and want to save them, you must give the document a different name or else store it on a different drive or in a different directory of a hard disk. To change the name, do not use the Transfer Rename command. Use Transfer Save, and type in a different name from the one Word proposes.

Download file not found

You're printing a document that is formatted with fonts that are in software form and must be downloaded from your computer. In other words, Word needs to send information about the fonts from a disk to the printer before the printer can handle the character formatting specified in the document. The message means Word cannot find the file that contains the font information. Downloadable fonts work only with selected printers, such as the Hewlett-Packard LaserJet Plus. They do not come with Word; they must be purchased from your printer dealer. If you are running Word from a hard disk, copy the downloadable fonts to the same directory that contains Word. If you are running Word from a floppy disk and you see this message, swap the disk containing the downloadable font file into the drive that has the Word Program disk.

Edit style sheet or choose Exit to see document

You've chosen the Gallery command. This message tells you that you can view or edit styles in the style sheet, or press the letter E (for Exit) to return to the Edit menu and your document. If the Gallery is blank and you don't know why, see Chapter 11.

End mark cannot be edited

The end mark is the small diamond that appears at the end of a document or style sheet. You cannot edit it. If you're working on a document when you see this message, you've attempted character formatting with the end mark selected (highlighted). If you are in the Gallery working on a style sheet, you're attempting to use the Gallery's Copy, Delete, Format, or Name command while the end mark is selected. Move the selection and try the command again.

End of index (*or* table) not found

You have executed the Library Index (or Library Table) command, and Word has located an existing index (or table of contents) in your document. However, Word cannot find the special line that marks the end of the index or table. Add the line (which is either *.end index.* or *.end table.*, formatted as hidden characters) and retry the Library Index (or Library Table) command. Alternatively, you can delete all of the index or table, or at least the line *.begin index.* (or *.begin table.*) before retrying the command.

Enter a printer name in Print Options

You have attempted to use the Print Printer, Print Direct, Print File, Print Merge, Print Repaginate, Library Hyphenate, Library Index, or Library Table command, but have not specified a printer description (.PRD) file. Press the Esc key and use the Print Options command and enter an appropriate .PRD filename in the *printer* field.

Enter character style or select from list

You are using the Format Style Character command to apply a character style from the style sheet to selected characters in text. Type an appropriate key code, a character-style name such as Character 2, or pick from a list by pressing a direction key.

Enter division style or select from list

You are using the Format Style Division command to apply a division style from the style sheet to selected division(s) in text. Type an appropriate key code or a division style name, or pick from a list.

Enter DOS command

You picked the Library Run command, and Word is asking what program other than Word you want to run. You can type any instruction that you normally would enter at the DOS prompt (such as A> or C>), except that Word cannot resume operation if you use a command name that causes computer memory to be made resident. For information, see Chapter 14, "The Family of Library Commands," and Chapter 18, "Speed."

Enter drive or directory

You have picked the Transfer Options command. Type in the drive and/or directory on which you wish Word to look for documents and press Enter.

Enter filename

You are using a Transfer command to save a document, style sheet, or glossary file on disk. Type a name and press Enter. If you omit a file name extension, Word automatically assigns .DOC, .STY, or .GLY, as appropriate.

Enter filename or select from list

You're using a Transfer command to load or merge a file from disk onto the screen. Word is reminding you to type the name of the document, style sheet, or glossary file or to pick from the list.

Enter font name or select from list

You are using the Format Character command and are in the *font name* command field. You can type a specific name, such as *Pica* or *Courier,* if the font is supported by your printer. Or you can see a list of fonts that are supported. The list varies, depending on the printer description (.PRD) file you have specified with the Print Options command.

Enter font size in points or select from list

You are using the Format Character command and are in the *font size* command field. Word assumes you have already made a choice in the *font name* field, and now wants to know what size, in points, to make the font.

You can specify any font size or choose one from a list. Word uses the closest size that the printer description file (.PRD) you specified can handle.

Daisy-wheel printers refer to font sizes in pitch, rather than points. Typically, 12-point type is 10-pitch (10 characters to the inch); 10-point type is 12-pitch (12 characters to the inch); and 8-point type is 15-pitch (15 characters to the inch). During printing Word converts points to pitch for you and will give the appropriate font size in pitch, as in the message *Enter Y after mounting Pica 10.*

Enter glossary name or select from list

You're using the Insert command and haven't yet specified what text you want to insert into the document. You can insert the contents of the scrap or a glossary entry.

To insert the contents of the scrap, press Enter. To insert from the glossary, type a glossary name or pick one from a list, and then press Enter.

Enter glossary names or leave blank to clear all

You have picked the Transfer Glossary Clear command, which permits you to delete from Word's memory some or all of the glossary entries that otherwise are available to you with the Insert command or F3 key. You may see a list of the glossary names that represent the glossary entries, by pressing a direction key. Type the names of the glossary entries you wish to delete, separating each with a comma. Or leave the field blank and press Enter to delete all glossary entries.

NOTE: The Transfer Glossary Clear command does not directly affect glossary files on disk, only glossary entries in memory.

Enter key code

You are in the Gallery and have picked either the Insert or the Name command. Type a one- or two-letter key code as a shorthand name for the style you are creating (with the Insert command) or modifying (with the Name command). If you leave the key-code field blank, Word creates a style without a key code (if you're using the Insert command), or retains the existing key code (if you're using the Name command). If you leave every field of the Insert command blank, the style or styles in the Gallery's scrap are inserted into the style sheet when you press Enter.

Enter measurement

You are using a Format command, and a field requires you to specify a measurement. If you omit a unit of measurement, Word assumes the number you type is in whatever unit of measurement is specified in the *measurement* field of the Options command.

Enter measurement in lines

You are in a field of the Format Paragraph command that sets vertical spacing. If you type a number without also typing a unit of measurement (", cm, P10, P12, pt), Word assumes you are specifying a distance measured in "lines." A "line" is 12 points, a sixth of an inch.

Enter measurement in lines or type Auto

You are in the *line spacing* field of the Format Paragraph command. See the comments for the preceding message. If you type *Auto* instead of typing a number, Word will automatically change line spacing to more or less suit the font size of the characters used in the paragraph.

Enter page number

You are using the Jump Page command, and Word wants to know which page you want displayed in the text window. Type a page number and press Enter. Beginning with Word version 3.0, you can jump to a particular page number in a particular division of a document in those documents that have more than one division. To do this, type the page number followed by a *d* (or *D*) and the division number.

Enter paragraph style or select from list

You are using the Format Style Paragraph command to apply a paragraph style from the style sheet to the paragraph(s) containing the selection in the text. Type an appropriate key code or a paragraph style name, or pick from a list of paragraph styles.

Enter printer name or select from list

You are using the Print Options command and are in the *printer* command field. Word wants to know what printer description file (.PRD file) to install. If a name appears in the command field, a printer description file has already been installed. If the .PRD file matches your printer, do nothing. Otherwise, type the name of an appropriate .PRD file or pick one from a list. If the list does not contain a .PRD file matching your printer, use one of the files beginning with TTY, such as TTY.PRD or TTYWHEEL.PRD.

Enter second character of key code

You pressed the Alt key and, while holding it down, pressed a letter on the keyboard that corresponds to the first letter of a two-letter key code in your style sheet. Word assumes you want to use a key code to apply a style, and with this message prompts you to type the second character. If you pressed the Alt key by accident, press Esc.

Enter usage or select from list

You are in the *usage* field of the Gallery's Insert command or (prior to version 2.0) its Name command. Word wants to know which usage you want for the style. After picking the usage, press the Tab key or use the mouse to move to the next field, *variant*.

Enter variant or select from list

You're in the Gallery menu, creating a style with the Insert command or modifying one with the Name command. Word wants to know which variant of the usage you want for the style. Type in a variant number (in some cases, a name or letter) or pick from a list. Beginning with Word version 2.0, any variant in a list that has already been used in the style sheet is followed by parentheses that enclose the key code for the style.

Enter Y after mounting *font name*

This message appears only when a daisy-wheel printer or other impact-type printer is in use. It asks you to mount a particular wheel on the printer and press Y. The message is displayed at the beginning of printing, and when the document's formatting calls for font and/or size changes. Bear in mind that font name is expressed in pitch in this message, even though font size was specified in points when you were formatting the document. Generally, characters formatted as 12-point with the Format Character command are referred to as 10-pitch, and characters formatted as 10-point are referred to as 12-pitch.

You need not mount the exact typeface specified in the message, because Word won't know the difference. But you should mount a wheel with the requested pitch number, to avoid improperly spaced characters. If the document formatting calls for a character type or size that the printer can't handle, Word requests the closest possible substitute. In this case, Word prints the document with proper formatting for the type size actually used.

Enter Y to confirm...

You've asked Word to do something with potentially significant consequences. The program wants to be sure you're not making a mistake, and gives you this chance to reconsider. If you are sure you want to complete the action, press Y or click the right mouse button. If you change your mind, press Esc or click both mouse buttons. For the mouse methods to work, the mouse pointer must be in the command area. If you're switching from one version of Word to another, pay special attention to these messages. Some differ from version to version. Here are the *Enter Y* messages you may encounter.

♦ *Enter Y to confirm loss of edits.* You've chosen the Transfer Clear All command or the Transfer Clear Window command, or you're closing a window by clicking both mouse buttons with the mouse pointer on the top or right window border. But unsaved editing changes will be lost if Word complies. Press Y or click the right mouse button to lose the editing changes. Or, press Esc or both mouse buttons to return to the Edit menu. From the menu, return to editing with the Alpha command or save the document with the Transfer Save command. When you use the Transfer Clear All command, Word highlights any document with unsaved changes. This is helpful when different windows contain different documents. (Beginning with Word 3.0, this message no longer is used. Instead, the message is *Enter Y to save glossary, N to lose edits, or Esc to cancel.* Note that this means the effect of pressing Y is reversed.)

♦ *Enter Y to confirm loss of edits to glossary.* You've chosen the Transfer Clear All command, but glossary entries will be lost if the command is executed. If you press Y, the command is executed and the glossary entries are lost. If you press Esc, the command is canceled, and you can review the glossary entries with the Insert command (press a direction key for a list). Glossary entries can be deleted with the Transfer Glossary Clear command. Remaining entries that you wish to retain as a set in a file can be saved with the Transfer Glossary Save command. (Beginning with Word version 3.0, this message no longer is used. Instead, the message is *Enter Y to save glossary, N to lose edits, or Esc to cancel.* Note that this reverses the effect of pressing Y.)

♦ *Enter Y to confirm loss of edits to style sheet.* You chose the Transfer Clear All command or the Transfer Clear Window command, or you tried to close a window with the mouse pointer on the top or right window border. Your action, if completed, will remove a document from the screen—but the document has a style sheet with unsaved editing changes that will be lost. If you have more than one window and a document is highlighted, that's the one with unsaved changes to an attached style sheet. Press Y or click the right mouse button in the command area to accept the loss of editing and complete the command. Or, press Esc or click both mouse buttons to return to the Edit menu. From the Edit menu, move to the Gallery and use its Transfer Save command to store the changes to the style sheet. (Beginning with Word version 3.0, this message no longer is used. Instead, the message is *Enter Y to save glossary, N to lose edits, or Esc to cancel.* Note that this reverses the effect of pressing Y.)

♦ *Enter Y to confirm loss of formatting.* You have instructed Word to save a formatted document onto the disk in an unformatted form. If you press Y to confirm your intention, the formatting cannot be recovered. Consider saving the document twice, formatted and unformatted, with different names. Storing a document with the *formatted* command field set to *No* will not cause formatting to disappear from the version on the screen, but unless you store the screen version as a formatted document, the formatting will be lost when the screen is cleared.

♦ *Enter Y to confirm, N to ignore, or use direction keys.* This wording appeared only in version 2.0. It has been replaced with the message *Enter Y to insert hyphen, N to skip, or use direction keys.* Refer to that message.

♦ *Enter Y to confirm or R to remove.* This is a Print Repaginate command message that appears only in versions of Word beginning with 2.0. While repaginating your document, Word has encountered a page break you inserted earlier with the Shift-Ctrl-Enter key combination or by changing a page-break location during a previous use of the Print Repaginate command. Keep the page break at the same line (press Y), or remove the page break so Word can propose a different one (press R).

♦ *Enter Y to confirm or use direction keys.* This is a Print Repaginate command message that appears only in versions of Word beginning with 2.0. Word has proposed a line on which it will end a page if you press Y. If you want the page break to occur on an earlier line, use the Up direction key to select the line and then press Y.

Enter Y to continue or Esc to cancel

Word has paused during printing. Press Y when you want printing to resume; press Esc if you don't want it to resume. Sometimes the message means the printer isn't ready. More often, it means the Print Options command's *feed* field is set to *Manual* and Word wants permission to print a new page. Press Y each time a sheet is in place for printing.

The message also appears if you press Esc during printing. It asks whether you want to abort the printing task or to continue. Press Y to resume printing or Esc to cancel it.

Enter Y to create file

You have instructed Word to load a document that doesn't exist on disk. Press Y if you mean to create a file with the name. Otherwise, press Esc.

Enter Y to create style sheet

You have asked Word to load a nonexistent style sheet. If you mean to create a new style sheet with the name you specified, press Y. Otherwise, press Esc.

Enter Y to insert hyphen, N to skip, or use direction keys

This is a Library Hyphenate command message. Word has selected a proposed hyphenation point in a word and wants you to accept it (press Y), reject the word for hyphenation (press N), or pick a different place in the word for the hyphen (press a direction key, followed by Y). Press the Left and Right direction keys to move a character at a time through the word. Press the Up and Down direction keys to jump to other acceptable hyphenation points in the word.

Enter Y to download fonts, N to skip, Esc to cancel

Beginning with version 3.0, Word supports the use of downloadable fonts in certain printers. A downloadable font is a typeface that is loaded into a printer's memory in digital form, having been transmitted to the printer from the computer. The printer description (.PRD) files for certain printers tell Word of the printer's capability to handle downloadable fonts. You see this message the first time you print with downloadable fonts during an editing session. Enter Y to give Word permission to send the downloadable font information to the printer. If you didn't mean to use a downloadable font, or haven't yet purchased a font disk, press Esc to cancel the Print Printer command.

Enter Y to overwrite file

You've used a Transfer command (or the Print File command) and picked a name for a document or file, but you've already used the name for another file on the same disk or subdirectory. If you press Y, the old file will be erased and the file on-screen will be stored on disk with the name of the old file. If you press Esc, the command will be canceled, allowing you to pick a different, unused name. If you've forgotten the content of the file that already has the desired name, consider creating a new window temporarily and loading the mystery file into it.

Enter Y to process, N to discard, or Esc for previous

This is a Spell message. You've reviewed the list of words that were unrecognized in a document. Press Y to change the spellings as you decided to do during the just-completed review. Press N to discard your review decisions, or press Esc to review your decisions.

If the message says *Esc to resume* instead of *Esc for previous,* you gave the Quit command before reviewing all unrecognized words. Press Esc to resume using Spell.

Enter Y to replace existing index (*or* table), or Esc to cancel

You have executed the Library Index command (or the Library Table command), but Word has found that the document already has an index (or table). If you press Y, Word will delete the existing index (or table) and replace it with a new one. If you press Esc, the command will be aborted. (It is possible to keep an existing index or table, by deleting the *.begin index.* or *.begin table.*)

Enter Y to replace, N to ignore, or press Esc to cancel

You're using the Replace command with the *confirm* command field set to *Yes*. Word has found the text you may want to replace with other text, and is asking for instructions. Press Y to make the replacement and search for the next potential replacement. Press N to skip this occurrence, but look for the next one. Press Esc to cancel the command, but keep the replacements already made.

Enter Y to retry access to *filename*

Word can't find the file identified in the message. Perhaps it isn't on the disk, or you misspelled its name. Perhaps the disk is improperly inserted in the drive, or a write-protect tab is covering the notch on the disk. Often, this message is Word's way of asking you to swap disks. Press Y if you're able to solve the problem without canceling the command. Press N or Esc to cancel the command.

The message probably refers to the drive containing the Program disk if the file name in the message has the extension .PRD. The message probably refers to the drive containing the document disk if the message lists the file names NORMAL.STY, NORMAL.GLY, or NEWFILE.TMP, or a file name with one of these extensions: .DOC (for document), .BAK (for backup document), .STY (for style sheet), or .GLY (for glossary). If the file name is MW, followed by several numbers and ending with the extension .TMP, it probably refers to the Program disk if your version of Word is lower than 3.0. Beginning with 3.0, MW XXXXXX.TMP messages can refer to files on either disk.

This message is a normal part of saving a document when disk-swapping is needed because a disk is full. And if you swapped disks earlier in the editing session, this message is likely to be Word's way of telling you to swap again to return the original disk to the drive. (See *Disk full* and *Document disk full* for more details.)

Enter Y to retry access to Word Program disk

This message first appeared in Word version 3.0. It is a refinement and specialization of the *Enter Y to retry access to filename* message. It tells you that the file Word needs is on the Word Program disk. If you're on a floppy-disk system, put the Word Program disk back in drive A (or whichever drive you started Word in).

Enter Y to save, N to lose edits, or Esc to cancel

You've chosen a command that threatens a document that has unsaved editing changes. The command may be Quit, or, beginning with Word version 3.0, it may be Transfer Load, Transfer Clear All, Transfer Clear Window, or Window Close. If you have several documents on the screen, the appropriate document is highlighted to help you identify it. The message will be repeated for each threatened document (in other words, those with unsaved changes). Sometimes the "changes" are as trivial as page-break marks resulting from printing the document since you last saved it.

Press Y to save the editing changes. (If the document hasn't been named with the Transfer Save command, the message *Not a valid file* will appear and the command will be canceled.) Press N to quit and lose the editing changes. Press Esc to cancel the command, then name and save the document with the Transfer Save command if necessary.

Enter Y to save glossary, N to lose edits, or Esc to cancel

You've chosen the Transfer Clear All or the Quit command, but glossary entries will be lost if the command is executed. If you press Y, the entries will be saved to the glossary file NORMAL.GLY, unless a different glossary file has been used during the editing session. If you press N, the Quit command will be executed and the glossary entries lost. If you press Esc, the command is canceled. You can then review the glossary entries with the Insert command and use the Transfer Glossary Save command, if appropriate.

Enter Y to save style sheet, N to lose edits, or Esc to cancel

You've chosen any of several commands that threaten a style sheet that contains unsaved editing changes. The document to which the style sheet is attached is highlighted, so that you can identify it if you have multiple documents and style sheets in different windows. If you press Y, the style sheet is saved with the name NORMAL.STY, unless you have given it another name. If you press N, the command is executed and the changes are lost. If you press Esc, the command is canceled. You can then review the style sheet in the Gallery and use the Gallery menu's Transfer Save command, if appropriate. Depending on the version of Word, this message may be a response to any of the following Edit-menu commands: Format Style Sheet, Quit, Transfer Clear All, Transfer Clear Window, or Window Close. Or, it may refer to any of these Gallery-menu commands: Exit, Transfer Load, or Transfer Clear.

Field name redefined

This is a Print Merge message. Some field you're using is being defined twice, once in the header file and again with a SET or an ASK instruction. Remove the duplication.

File is not available

This message occurs, under some circumstances, when you attempt to load a document with the Transfer Load command *and* you either have set the command's *read only* field to *Yes,* or you are using a network version of Word. If the *read only* field is set to *Yes,* the message means the file does not exist. Word *would* give you the *Enter Y to create file* message, except the *read only* setting doesn't permit it. If you're using a network version of Word (and *read only* is set to *No*), it means someone else on your network is using the document that you want to use.

File not found

This is a Spell message. Word can't find a file with the name you typed. Make sure the document is on the disk, and that you are spelling its full name correctly (including the extension if it isn't .DOC). Specify a drive letter if necessary.

Font download unsuccessful

Word is unable to transfer downloadable fonts from a disk to your printer. Before trying again, make sure your printer is connected properly and to the same port that is specified in the *setup* field of Word's Print Options command. For serial printers, make sure the correct baud rate setting has been specified with the DOS Mode command.

Formatting too complex

You've attempted to format a document, but to carry out your wishes Word must temporarily store more information in memory than there is memory available. Increasing the amount of RAM in your computer may not alleviate this problem. Instead, save the document and try the formatting task again. If you get the message again, save the document and then use the Transfer Clear All command. Afterwards, load the document again and retry the formatting task. (Alternatively, quit Word and restart the program using the /1 switch: word/1.)

% Free

Word versions 1.0, 1.1, and 1.15 use this instead of the *SAVE* message to indicate when files should be saved. You should save when the percentage drops to 55 or 60. See *SAVE* for more details.

Glossary name not defined

You have used the Insert command and typed the name of a glossary entry, but the name isn't in the active glossary. Try the command again, this time picking the name from the list. If the name isn't on the list, it may mean that the glossary entry wasn't made or it has been stored on disk as part of a glossary file. To retrieve a glossary file, use the Transfer Glossary Merge command after making sure the proper disk is in the document drive.

Insert the disk containing *program* and press Y when ready

You chose the Library Spell or the Library Run command and Word can't find the program identified in the message. If you have a floppy-disk system, replace the Word Program disk with the disk containing the needed program. If you have a hard disk, include the program in a directory that is in the path. This message was removed beginning in version 3.0. Now the message is: *Replace Word disk if necessary. Enter Y when ready*.

Insufficient memory

Random access memory (RAM) in your computer has been used up.

If you are editing, use the Transfer Save command immediately to store your document, and if you've made editing changes to a style sheet or your glossaries, save those files, too. If you see this message frequently, use the Transfer Save command more often, or consider adding more RAM to your computer. You get this message if you attempt too many replacements with the Replace command between uses of the Transfer Save command. You also see this message if you use the Library Run command and try to run a program that requires more free memory than you have available.

If you are using the Library Index or Library Table command, it means you have either used up the RAM that Word reserves for itself, or you don't have enough free RAM in your computer system. See Chapter 26.

Key code not defined

While writing or editing a document, you have pressed the Alt key and typed a one- or two-character key code that has no meaning to Word. You may get this message if your left hand accidentally brushes the Alt key while you are typing.

Key codes conflict

You are working on a style sheet in the Gallery. Two styles have the same key codes, or a single-character key code is the same as the first letter or number of a two-character key code. If you're using Word version 1.0, 1.1, or 1.15, this message may mean your style sheet is large and has too many similar key codes.

List is empty

You requested a list of choices, but there aren't any where you're looking. Word only lists names that meet your request exactly. For example, if you request a list of documents with the Transfer Load command, the only names displayed are those on the current disk drive that have the extension .DOC. If a list surprises you by being empty, perhaps the information is on another disk or another disk drive, or perhaps it has a different file name extension. To change the current drive, use the Transfer Options command. To see a full list of all files regardless of extension, type *.* before pressing the direction key.

NOTE: If you use a hard disk and specify a path name when requesting a list, you will get the *List is empty* message if you don't include the final backslash at the end of the path name.

Math overflow

You are using Word version 3.0 or higher, and have pressed the F2 Key. Word has performed mathematical operations on the selected text, but the answer exceeds 14 digits.

Program stayed resident. Press a key to quit Word.

This message is bad news. It means that while using the Library Run command you ran a program that stayed resident in your computer—that is, it used some RAM (memory) and didn't release it when you quit the program. DOS Mode is an example of one such resident program. The problem is that Word can't operate if memory it counts on is tied up by resident programs run through Library Run. Such resident programs can be executed only before you start Word. (Next time, quit Word, run the resident program, and start Word again.) For now, all you can do is press a key and watch Word quit, taking with it any unsaved editing changes in your documents. (It is a good practice to use the Transfer Save command before using Library Run, just in case.)

No entries found

You have executed either the Library Index or Library Table command, but Word cannot find any entries in the selected document. Entries are marked with three characters *formatted to be hidden*. The characters are a period, a letter, and a period. In the case of indexing, the letter between the periods must be *i*, as in *.i.*; in the case of tables of contents, any letter except *i* can be used, but it must match the letter specified with the Library Table command.

No such page

The page mark (») you want to jump to no longer exists. It was deleted when characters, words, or paragraphs around it were deleted during editing. Use the Jump Page command to jump to a preceding or following page number, then scroll to the location desired. Or use the Print Printer or Print Repaginate command to renumber pages.

Not a valid action for column selection

You have pressed Shift-F6 to turn on Word's mode in which it selects columns instead of regular text passages. This is fine, except that you have attempted to execute a command that does not work when the selection is a column.

Not a valid action for footnotes

Editing actions are limited when you are working with the text of a footnote. You cannot start a new division in a footnote, nor can you footnote a footnote. When deleting footnote text, you cannot delete a selection that contains the (normally invisible) paragraph mark at the end of the footnote. A footnote window can be closed, but it can't be cleared. It is impossible to write in a footnote window until a footnote reference mark has been placed in the main text with the Format Footnote command. You cannot load a document into a footnote window.

To delete the entire footnote, delete the footnote reference mark in the main text of your document.

Not a valid file

You've attempted to load a file that has an inappropriate name. Possibly the file name is too long or contains an illegal character, such as a comma. Possibly it has the wrong extension: Files ending with .DOC must be loaded with the Edit menu's Transfer Load command; files ending with .STY must be loaded with the Gallery menu's Transfer Load command; files that end with .GLY must be loaded with the Edit menu's Transfer Glossary Load command. If you're using Spell, this message may mean you tried to carry out the Dictionary or Filename command without typing a filename.

Not a valid font name

You are using the Format Character command. You've probably misspelled a font name or used a font name that isn't recognized by the currently installed .PRD.

Not a valid glossary name

You've specified a glossary name with the Copy or the Delete command, but the name contains characters that are not allowed. Change the name and try again. A glossary name may not contain spaces, but, beginning with version 1.15, an underline is allowed between words to distinguish them.

Not a valid key code

You're working on a style sheet and have tried to create a key code with the Insert or the Name command. Key codes must be one or two letters long. You tried to make the key code longer, or you included "illegal" characters. Use the Backspace key to eliminate one or both letters, or press Esc and try the command again.

Not a valid option

You are in a menu or submenu of commands or command fields, and have typed a letter that isn't the first letter of any of the available options.

Not a valid portname

You have typed the name of a printer port, using the Print Options command, but the name you typed does not exist. In MS-DOS, the only ports allowed are LPT1:, LPT2:, LPT3:, COM1:, and COM2:. The LPT ports are parallel. The COM ports are serial. Make sure you type the colon at the end of the portname. Or, you can press a direction key to pick from a list of valid portnames—but remember, your printer must be connected to the port you pick.

Not a valid style

You are editing a document and using the Format Style Character, Format Style Paragraph, or Format Style Division command. These commands apply a style from a style sheet to the selected text. Either you left the command field blank or misspelled the style or key code. To see an appropriate list of styles, press a direction key.

Not a valid variant

Either you're in the Gallery assigning a variant to a style, or you're using one of the Edit menu's Format Style commands to apply a style to the selection. You've chosen a variant that doesn't exist for the style's usage. Type another variant or pick from a list.

Not a valid window split

You've attempted to open a new window, but your request is breaking a rule. Word allows up to eight windows, but only three side-by-side windows. The other windows must be horizontal divisions. You cannot split a window that has a footnote window, nor can you split a footnote window. No split is permitted if either resulting window would display fewer than five characters of one line (seven characters if a style bar is used).

Not enough disk or directory space

This is a Spell message telling you there isn't enough blank space on your Spell disk for the revised document or for ERRWORDS.TXT, the file Word creates that contains all the unrecognized words from your document. Erase any unneeded files from the Spell disk, or copy the Spell programs and needed dictionaries to a different disk. (The only dictionaries you need are MAINDICT.CMP, HIGHFREQ.CMP, UPDICT.CMP, and any appropriate user or document dictionary.)

Pagination is required

You have attempted to use the Jump Page command, but Word hasn't yet computed page breaks or numbers. Use the Print Repaginate command or the Print Printer command, and the Jump Page command will work.

Print wheel change ignored

You are using queued printing to print a document to a file or to print it on a daisy-wheel printer. The document contains a change of character formatting that would normally cause Word to pause and request that you change the daisy wheel. This is not possible when a document has been queued, so the whole document is being printed with whatever daisy wheel is on the printer.

Printer is not ready

The printer hasn't notified Word that it is ready to print. Perhaps the printer is off, off-line, or out of paper or ribbon. Perhaps the cable has come loose. If it is a daisy-wheel printer, perhaps there is some difficulty with the daisy wheel. If none of these is a problem, check the settings in the Print Options command fields. In particular, make sure that the *set up* command field is correct for the printer you want to use. COM1: and COM2: are the setups usable with serial printers; and LPT1:, LPT2:, and LPT3: are the setups usable with parallel printers. If you have a serial printer, make sure the DOS Mode command has been used properly (if you're using a Zenith 150 or other computer that doesn't use the Mode command, check the CONFIGUR program, instead).

Generally, the *Printer is not ready* message vanishes in anything from a few moments to a minute or more, depending on the printer (and, for serial printers, how the DOS Mode command is set). If the message doesn't vanish, try the Esc key. If that fails, press the "break" key combination—on the IBM PC, Control-Scroll Lock. If the printer is off when you get the message, turn it on briefly to regain control of your system.

Program already in use

Your computer is hooked to a network that shares a hard disk with other terminals, and your version of Word does not allow more than one person to use it at a time. This message means someone else is already using Word on another computer terminal.

Program disk full

This message means either that all room is used on the Word Program disk, or else that the temporary "scratch" file on the Program disk has reached its limit of 64K. Use the Transfer Save command immediately on every document displayed in a window on the screen. Queued printing takes up space on the Program disk, so if you are using queued printing, consider either waiting for it to finish or using the Print Queue command to stop it. In any case, use the Transfer Clear All command as soon as possible.

If these steps don't solve the problem, save any other files you want to keep, then use the Transfer Clear All command to start a new editing session.

Read only: document may not be edited

You're attempting to edit a document after protecting it against changes by picking *Yes* in the Transfer Load command's *read only* field. Load the document again, this time with *read only* set to *No*.

Replace document (*or* Learning Word *or* Word program disk...)

When you are using Word on a floppy-disk-based system, several different messages prompt you to replace one disk with another. For instance, one set of messages prompts you to replace your document disk with a Learning Microsoft Word disk, and later to return the document disk to its drive. (These messages occur, beginning with Word version 3.0, when you pick *Tutorial* from the Help menu.) Another set of messages tells you to replace the Word Program disk (which usually is in drive A) with a Spell disk or other disk for the duration of your use of the Library Spell or Library Run command.

You will see the message *Replace Word disk if necessary. Enter Y when ready.* either when you use Library Run or when you use a downloadable font. If you are using a downloadable font, Word needs the .EXE file corresponding to your .PRD file. Insert the disk that has the file (probably the Word Printer or Utilities disk) and press Y to continue.

Reserved Glossary Name

You have used the Copy or Delete command and specified a glossary name, but the name you've picked is one of Word's permanent glossary names, which are reserved. These words are *page* and *footnote* in all versions of Word, and also include *date, dateprint, time,* and *timeprint,* beginning with version 3.0.

SAVE

This message appears at the center of the bottom line of the screen when you are running out of computer memory, or when the scratch file on the Word program disk is filling up. Use the Transfer Save command at the next convenient moment. If the SAVE command begins to flash, use Transfer Save promptly. Prior to Word version 2.0, there was a *% Free* message instead of *SAVE*.

If the *SAVE* sign is displayed and the Transfer Save command does not eliminate it, try each of the following steps, in order, until it goes away:

1. Delete a single character of text. Delete another single character of text.

2. Use the Transfer Save command on each document in a text window.

3. If a style sheet has been edited and you wish to keep the editing changes, use the Gallery's Transfer Save command. Return to the Edit menu by using the Exit command.

4. If you've added glossary entries you wish to save, use Transfer Glossary Save.

5. Now that everything you want has been saved, use the Transfer Clear All command.

6. To retrieve the documents you were working on, use the Transfer Load command. To retrieve the style sheet, use the Format Style Sheet command. To retrieve the glossary entries, use the Transfer Glossary Merge command.

Scratch file full

You have used up all the room in the scratch file on your Word Program disk. Follow the numbered steps given for the *SAVE* message.

Select destination for copying text

You're using the mouse to copy selected text to a different location and are pressing both the Shift key and one of the mouse buttons. Move the mouse pointer to the destination for the text before releasing the mouse button.

Select destination for moving text

You're using the mouse to move selected text to a different location and are pressing both the Ctrl key and one of the mouse buttons. Move the mouse pointer to the destination for the text before releasing the mouse button.

Select dictionary

This is a Spell message. Word is displaying a word it doesn't recognize. You've chosen the Add command. Word wants to know which dictionary to add the word to: the *Standard* dictionary, the *Document* dictionary, or the *User* dictionary.

Select text to copy formatting from

You have selected text and want to format it to match the character or paragraph formatting of other text. You're holding down the Alt key and one of the mouse buttons. Move the mouse pointer to the text to copy from, and release the mouse button. To copy character formatting, press the left mouse button, position the pointer directly on a formatted character, and release the button. To copy paragraph formatting, press the right mouse button, position the pointer in the selection bar just to the left of the sample paragraph, and release the button.

Selection must be a running head

You're using the Format Running-head command, but your selection includes text that cannot be turned into a running head (the text of a footnote, for example).

Style already defined

Beginning with Word version 2.0, this message is encountered when you try to use the Gallery menu's Insert and Name commands to assign a variant to a style, but the same variant has already been assigned to another style of the same usage. For example, if you try to create a Paragraph 7 style when a Paragraph 7 style already exists, press a direction key to see a list of available variants (those not followed by parentheses), or let Word pick a variant for you.

In versions prior to 2.0, it is possible to create more than one style with the same combination of usage and variant, but you cannot save such a style sheet, nor can you return from it to your document. Instead, you see this message and one of the duplicated style names is selected to steer you to the problem. Use the Name command to change either the usage or variant of one of the duplicate style names.

With any version of Word, it's also possible to inadvertently duplicate style names by merging one style sheet into another with the Transfer Merge command when both style sheets contain the same style name. See the discussion in the preceding paragraph.

Style and format conflict

This message tells you that you are attempting to use a Format Style command to assign a usage that is inappropriate to the particular command. The Format Style Division command can only assign division styles, the Format Style Paragraph command can only assign paragraph styles, and the Format Style Character command can only assign character styles. Press a direction key to pick from a list of appropriate styles.

With Word versions 1.0, 1.1, and 1.15, this message can also be encountered when you're in the Gallery. You're using the Gallery's Name command to change the usage of a style, but the new usage you've proposed is at odds with the formatting previously assigned to the style.

Style sheet is not available

This is a message seen when more than one person is using Word at once, on a network. You are attempting to load a style sheet—or a document that has a style sheet attached to it—and the style sheet is being edited by a different user.

Too few (*or* many) fields in data record

These are Merge messages. One of the records in your data file ("data record") contains a different number of fields than the header paragraph (or separate header file).

Unknown field name

This is a Merge message. A field is used in your main document that isn't defined in a header paragraph, header file, ASK, or SET statement.

A P P E N D I X   B

A Tour of the
Keyboard

You can realize considerable extra efficiency in your writing, editing, and formatting of documents if you master the many possibilities of the Word keyboard.

Actions possible with the keyboard fall into several categories: using commands, changing the printable content of a document, inserting spacing characters, accessing built-in formats, selecting text, scrolling in a document, changing the modes in which Word operates, and manipulating outlines.

This guide assumes you are using the original IBM PC keyboard, or the original IBM PC AT keyboard. Other keyboards tend to be similar. The new IBM keyboard, for instance, has a separate numeric (calculation-style) keypad and its function keys are in a row above the keyboard, but from Word's standpoint, it largely resembles the original keyboard.

Using Commands

TO:	USE:
Pick a command	Esc and first letter of command name
Back out of a command	Esc
Return to editing	Esc-A (for Alpha)
Move to next command field	Tab
Move to previous field	Shift-Tab
Move right in a field's menu	Spacebar
Move left in a field's menu	Backspace
Edit menu responses	F7, F8, F9, F10, Backspace, and/or Del
Execute a command	Enter

Changing Printable Content

TO:	USE:
Type a number	Numbers (not function keys) on the top row or numeric keypad on right. To use keypad, press Num Lock or hold Shift
Type a symbol such as $, %, or @	Shift and appropriate key. Caps Lock key won't work
Delete selection to scrap	Del
Kill selection (not to scrap)	Shift and Del
Rub out (back up and kill characters)	Backspace
Insert scrap into document	Ins
Replace selection with scrap's contents	Shift and Ins
Insert from glossary	F3 (after typing glossary name)
Move selected text	Del followed by Ins, or hold Ctrl and click left mouse button
Copy selected text	Copy command and Ins, or hold Shift and click left mouse button
Use ASCII characters (foreign, math, graphics)	Alt and numeric keypad. (Type ASCII number, as shown in Word or DOS manuals. The cents sign is Alt-155, for example)
Type a nonbreaking hyphen (keeps both words on same line)	Shift, Ctrl, and hyphen key on top line of keyboard. (Prior to version 3.0, use minus key on numeric keypad)
Type a dash	Two nonbreaking hyphens

Adding Spacing Characters

TO INSERT:	USE:
Normal space	Spacebar
Non-breaking space (keeps both words on same line)	Ctrl-Spacebar
Tab character	Tab
Paragraph mark	Enter
New-line character (force new line, same paragraph)	Shift-Enter
New-page character (force new page)	Shift-Ctrl-Enter
New-division character (force new division)	Ctrl-Enter
Optional hyphen (appears between syllables only when needed)	Ctrl and hyphen key on top line of keyboard

Built-in Formats

TO MAKE CHARACTERS:	USE:
Bold	Alt-b (Alt-x-b if a style sheet is attached to the document)
Underlined	Alt-u (Alt-x-u)
Italic	Alt-i (Alt-x-i)
Hidden	Alt-e (Alt-x-e)
Small caps	Alt-k (Alt-x-k)
With strikethrough	Alt-s (Alt-x-s)
Superscripted	Alt-= (Alt-x-=) (Think of this as Alt-+)
Subscripted	Alt-minus key on top row
Standard (remove special character formats)	Alt-Spacebar

NOTE: When a style sheet is in use, Alt-Spacebar gives the selected characters whatever formatting is specified in the character portion of the governing paragraph style.

TO MAKE PARAGRAPHS:	USE:
Centered	Alt-c (Alt-x-c if a style sheet is attached to the document)
Open-spaced (blank line before paragraph)	Alt-o (Alt-x-o)
Double-spaced	Alt-2 (Alt-x-2)
Half-inch indented on first line	Alt-f (Alt-x-f)
Left-aligned	Alt-l (Alt-x-l)
Right-aligned	Alt-r (Alt-x-r)
Nested (indented half an inch)	Alt-n (Alt-x-n)
Unnested (indent reduced half an inch)	Alt-m (Alt-x-m)
With hanging indents (all lines after first indented)	Alt-t (Alt-x-t)
Standard	Alt-p (Alt-x-p)

NOTE: If a style sheet is in use, any paragraph, character, or division style can be applied by holding the Alt key and typing a corresponding one- or two-key code of your choice.)

Selecting Text

TO SELECT THE:	USE:
Next character left	Left direction
Next character right	Right direction
Character above	Up direction
Character below	Down direction
Word left	F7
Word right	F8
Previous sentence	Shift-F7
Next sentence	Shift-F8
Sentence	F9
Line	Shift-F9
Paragraph	F10
Next paragraph	F10 twice
Whole document	Shift-F10
Beginning of line	Home
End of line	End
Top of window	Ctrl-Home
Bottom of window	Ctrl-End
First character of document	Ctrl-PgUp
Last character of document	Ctrl-PgDn
Document in next window	F1
Document in previous window	Shift-F1
Extended set of characters	F6
Column or other rectangle	Shift-F6

NOTE: Sometimes the mouse is a faster way to select text. Click the left mouse button to select a character, the right mouse button to select a word, and both buttons to select a sentence. Or, position the mouse pointer in the selection bar to the left of a line and click the left button to select the paragraph, or both buttons to select the entire document.

Scrolling

TO SCROLL VERTICALLY TO:	USE:
Previous screen (move up)	PgUp
Next screen (move down)	PgDn
Beginning of document	Ctrl-PgUp
End of document	Ctrl-PgDn
Next line up	Turn on Scroll Lock, press Up direction, turn off Scroll Lock
Next line down	Turn on Scroll Lock, press Down direction, turn off Scroll Lock

WHEN LINES ARE WIDER THAN THE TEXT WINDOW, TO SCROLL HORIZONTALLY TO:	USE:
Beginning of line	Home
End of line	End
Left	Turn on Scroll Lock, press Left direction, turn off Scroll Lock
Right	Turn on Scroll Lock, press Right direction, turn off Scroll Lock

Changing Word's Modes

TO TURN ON/OFF:	USE:
Extend Selection mode	F6
Column Selection mode	Shift-F6
Number Lock mode	Num Lock
Scroll Lock mode	Scroll Lock
Capital-letter mode	Caps Lock
Overtype mode	F5
Calculate (perform math on selected numbers)	F2
Outline view	Shift-F2
Outline edit (once already in Outline view)	Shift-F5

Manipulating Outlines

IN OUTLINE VIEW, TO:	USE:
Enter or exit outline view from normal document	Shift-F2
Enter or exit outline edit (only from outline view)	Shift-F5
Lower a heading one level	Alt-0 (zero, not on keypad)
Raise a heading one level	Alt-9 (not on keypad)
Collapse headings	Minus on keypad
Collapse body text	Shift-Minus on keypad
Expand next-lower headings	Plus on keypad
Expand all headings	Asterisk on keypad
Expand body text	Shift-Plus on keypad

IN OUTLINE EDIT, TO:	USE:
Select headings of same level	Up direction and Down direction
Select previous heading	Left direction
Select next heading	Right direction
Select nearest heading at next higher level	Home
Select last heading at next lower level	End
Extend selection to subheadings and body text below current heading	F6

NOTE: To select an entire outline, press Shift-F10. This will also place you in outline edit if you are in outline view. Also, a fast way to collapse all body text and expand all headings is to press Shift-F10, followed by the Minus on the keypad and then the Plus on the keypad.

Using the Thesaurus

TO:	USE:
See a list of synonyms	Ctrl-F6
See more of the list	PgDn
Insert a synonym	Enter
See synonyms of a synonym	Ctrl-F6
Return to previous list	Ctrl-PgUp
Leave the thesaurus	Esc

NOTE: The thesaurus is available beginning with version 3.1.

INDEX

Peter Rinearson

Journalist Peter Rinearson has been using word processors since 1976. He has received several national writing awards, including the 1984 Pulitzer Prize for feature writing—awarded for "Making It Fly," an account of the creation of the Boeing 757 jetliner published in the *Seattle Times*. In addition, Peter won the 1984 American Society of Newspaper Editors Distinguished Writing Award for business writing. He is working on a book about the creation of the Boeing 757 jetliner, and in mid-1986 was named one of forty finalists in the United States in NASA's Journalist-in-Space Project. A native of the Pacific Northwest, Peter currently lives in Seattle, Washington.

The manuscript for this book was prepared on an IBM PC AT and submitted to Microsoft Press in electronic form. Text files were processed and formatted using Microsoft Word.

Cover design by Ted Mader and Associates.
Interior text adapted by Darcie Furlan
from John Berry's original design.

The screen displays were created on the IBM PC with Microsoft Press custom software and printed on the Hewlett-Packard LaserJet printer.

Text composition by Microsoft Press in Plantin using the CCI composition system and the Mergenthaler Linotron 202 digital phototypesetter.

Other Titles From Microsoft Press

Running MS-DOS, 2nd Edition
The Microsoft guide to getting the most out of its standard operating system
Van Wolverton $21.95

The Peter Norton Programmer's Guide to the IBM PC
The ultimate reference guide to the entire family of IBM personal computers
Peter Norton $19.95

Command Performance: dBASE III
The Microsoft desktop dictionary and cross-reference guide
Douglas Hergert $22.95

Variations in C
Programming techniques for developing efficient professional applications
Steve Schustack $19.95

Presentation Graphics on the IBM PC
How to use Microsoft Chart to create dazzling graphics for corporate and
professional applications
Steve Lambert $19.95

Xenix at Work
Edited by JoAnne Woodcock
and Michael Halvorson $21.95

MS-DOS Technical Reference Encyclopedia (Versions 1.0–3.2) $134.95

Advanced MS-DOS
The Microsoft guide for assembly language and C programmers
Ray Duncan $21.95

Programmers at Work
Interviews with 19 of today's most brilliant programmers
Edited by Susan Lammers $16.95

Available Wherever Fine Books Are Sold